Other books by Woody Allen

GETTING EVEN

WITHOUT FEATHERS

SIDE EFFECTS

Four Films of Woody Allen

FOUR FILMS

of

WOODY ALLEN

Annie Hall
Interiors
Manhattan
Stardust Memories

Random House New York

Screenplay Copyright © 1977, 1978, 1979, 1980 by United Artists Corporation
Compilation and stage directions Copyright © 1982 by Random House, Inc.
All rights reserved under International and Pan-American Copyright Conventions.
Published in the United States by Random House, Inc., New York, and
simultaneously in Canada by Random House of Canada Limited, Toronto.
Photographs by courtesy of United Artists Corporation

Library of Congress Cataloging in Publication Data
Allen, Woody.
Four films of Woody Allen.
Contents: Annie Hall — Interiors —
Manhattan — [etc.]
I. Title.
PS3551.L44A6   1982   791.43'75   81–48315
ISBN 0–394–52443–8
ISBN 0–394–71229–3 (pbk.)

Manufactured in the United States of America
24689753
First Edition

THE ITALICIZED PASSAGES THAT DESCRIBE THE ACTION
HAVE BEEN PROVIDED BY THE PUBLISHER.

Contents

Annie Hall

Screenplay by Woody Allen
and Marshall Brickman

United Artists

United Artists Company
A Transamerica Company

ANNIE HALL

A JACK ROLLINS–CHARLES H. JOFFE PRODUCTION

EDITED BY
RALPH ROSENBLUM, A.C.E.

ART DIRECTOR
MEL BOURNE

COSTUME DESIGNER
RUTH MORLEY

DIRECTOR OF PHOTOGRAPHY
GORDON WILLIS, A.S.C.

WRITTEN BY
WOODY ALLEN AND MARSHALL BRICKMAN

PRODUCED BY
CHARLES H. JOFFE

DIRECTED BY
WOODY ALLEN

(Sound and Woody Allen monologue begin)

FADE IN:

White credits dissolve in and out on black screen. No sound.

FADE OUT credits

FADE IN:

Abrupt medium close-up of Alvy Singer doing a comedy monologue. He's wearing a crumbled sports jacket and tieless shirt; the background is stark.

ALVY   There's an old joke. Uh, two elderly women are at a Catskills mountain resort, and one of 'em says: "Boy, the food at this place is really terrible." The other one says, "Yeah, I know, and such . . . small portions." Well, that's essentially how I feel about life. Full of loneliness and misery and suffering and unhappiness, and it's all over much too quickly. The—the other important joke for me is one that's, uh, usually attributed to Groucho Marx, but I think it appears originally in Freud's wit and its relation to the unconscious. And it goes like this—I'm paraphrasing: Uh . . . "I would never wanna belong to any club that would have someone like me for a member." That's the key joke of my adult life in terms of my relationships with women. Tsch, you know, lately the strangest things have been going through my mind, 'cause I turned forty, tsch, and I guess I'm going through a life crisis or something, I don't know. I, uh . . . and I'm not worried about aging. I'm not one o' those characters, you know. Although I'm balding slightly on top, that's about the worst you can say about me. I, uh, I think I'm gonna get better as I get older, you know? I think I'm gonna be the—the balding virile type, you know, as opposed to say the, uh, distinguished gray, for instance, you know? 'Less I'm neither o' those two. Unless I'm one o' those guys with saliva dribbling out of his mouth who wanders into a cafeteria with a shopping bag screaming about socialism. *(Sighing)* Annie and I broke up and I—I still can't get my mind around that. You know, I—I keep sifting the pieces o' the relationship through my mind and —and examining my life and tryin' to figure out where did the screw-up come, you know, and a year ago we were . . . tsch, in love. You know, and-and-and . . . And it's funny, I'm not—I'm not a morose type. I'm not a depressive character. I-I-I, uh, *(Laughing)* you know, I was a reasonably happy kid, I guess. I was brought up in Brooklyn during World War II.

CUT TO:
INTERIOR. DOCTOR'S OFFICE—DAY.

Alvy as young boy sits on a sofa with his mother in an old-fashioned, cluttered doctor's office. The doctor stands near the sofa, holding a cigarette and listening.

MOTHER *(To the doctor)*   He's been depressed. All off a sudden, he can't do anything.

DOCTOR *(Nodding)*   Why are you depressed, Alvy?

MOTHER *(Nudging Alvy)* Tell Dr. Flicker. *(Young Alvy sits, his head down. His mother answers for him)* It's something he read.

DOCTOR *(Puffing on his cigarette and nodding)* Something he read, huh?

ALVY *(His head still down)* The universe is expanding.

DOCTOR The universe is expanding?

ALVY *(Looking up at the doctor)* Well, the universe is everything, and if it's expanding, someday it will break apart and that would be the end of everything!
Disgusted, his mother looks at him.

MOTHER *(Shouting)* What is that your business? *(She turns back to the doctor)* He stopped doing his homework.

ALVY What's the point?

MOTHER *(Excited, gesturing with her hands)* What has the universe got to do with it? You're here in Brooklyn! Brooklyn is not expanding!

DOCTOR *(Heartily, looking down at Alvy)* It won't be expanding for billions of years yet, Alvy. And we've gotta try to enjoy ourselves while we're here. Uh?
He laughs.

CUT TO:

Full shot of house with an amusement-park roller-coaster ride built over it. A line of cars move up and then slides with great speed while out the window of the house a hand shakes a dust mop.

ALVY'S VOICE   My analyst says I exaggerate my childhood memories, but I swear I was brought up underneath the roller—

CUT TO:
INTERIOR. HOUSE.

Alvy as a child sits at the table eating soup and reading a comic book while his father sits on the sofa reading the paper. The house shakes with every move of the roller coaster.

ALVY'S VOICE   —coaster in the Coney Island section of Brooklyn. Maybe that accounts for my personality, which is a little nervous, I think.

CUT TO:

Young Alvy at the food-stand concession watching three military men representing the Army, the Navy and the Marines arm in arm with a blond woman in a skirted bathing suit. They all turn and run toward the foreground. The girl stops before the camera to lean over and throw a kiss. The sign over the concession reads "Steve's Famous Clam Bar. Ice Cold Beer," and the roller coaster is moving in full gear in the background.

ALVY'S VOICE   You know, I have a hyperactive imagination. My mind tends to jump around a little, and I-I-I-I have some trouble between fantasy and reality.

CUT TO:

Full shot of people in bumper cars thoroughly enjoying bumping into each other as Alvy's father stands in the center of the track directing traffic.

ALVY'S VOICE   My father ran the bumper-car concession. *(Alvy as a child moves into the frame driving a bumper car. He stops as other cars bombard him. His father continues to direct the traffic)* There-there he is and there I am. But I-I-I-I used to get my aggression out through those cars all the time.
Alvy backs up his car offscreen.

INTERIOR. SCHOOLROOM—DAY.

The camera pans over three austere-looking teachers standing in front of the blackboard. The chalk writing on the board changes as each teacher lectures. While Alvy speaks, one of the male teachers puts an equation on the blackboard: "2 × 10 = 20" and other arithmetic formulas.

ALVY'S VOICE   I remember the staff at our public school. You know, we had a saying, uh, that "Those who can't do, teach, and those who can't teach, teach gym." And . . . uh, h'h, of course, those who couldn't do anything, I think, were assigned to our school. I must say—

CUT TO:

A female teacher standing in front of an old-fashioned schoolroom. The blackboard behind her reads "Transportation Administration."
The camera pans her point of view: a group of young students sitting behind their desks. Alvy as a child sits in a center desk while all around him there is student activity; there is note-passing, ruler-tapping, nose-picking, gum-chewing.

ALVY'S VOICE   —I always felt my schoolmates were idiots. Melvyn Greenglass, you know, fat little face, and Henrietta Farrell, just Miss Perfect all the time. And-and Ivan Ackerman, always the wrong answer. Always.
Ivan stands up behind his desk.

IVAN   Seven and three is nine.
Alvy hits his forehead with his hand. Another student glances over at him, reacting.

ALVY'S VOICE   Even then I knew they were just jerks. *(The camera moves back to the teacher, who is glaring out at her students)* In nineteen forty-two I had already dis—
As Alvy talks, the camera shows him move from his seat and kiss a young girl. She jumps from her seat in disgust, rubbing her cheek, as Alvy moves back to his seat.

IST GIRL *(Making noises)*   Ugh, he kissed me, he kissed me.

TEACHER *(Offscreen)*   That's the second time this month! Step up here!
As the teacher, really glaring now, speaks, Alvy rises from his seat and moves over to her. Angry, she points with her hand while the students turn their heads to watch what will happen next.

ALVY   What'd I do?

TEACHER   Step up here!

ALVY   What'd I do?

TEACHER   You should be ashamed of yourself!
The students, their heads still turned, look back at Alvy, now an adult, sitting in the last seat of the second row.

ALVY (AS ADULT) *(First offscreen, then onscreen as camera moves over to the back of the classroom)*   Why, I was just expressing a healthy sexual curiosity.

TEACHER *(The younger Alvy standing next to her)*   Six-year-old boys don't have girls on their minds.

ALVY (AS ADULT) *(Still sitting in the back of the classroom)*   I did.
The girl the young Alvy kissed turns to the older Alvy; she gestures and speaks.

1ST GIRL   For God's sakes, Alvy, even Freud speaks of a latency period.

ALVY (AS ADULT) *(Gesturing)*   Well, I never had a latency period. I can't help it.

TEACHER *(With young Alvy still at her side)*   Why couldn't you have been more like Donald? *(The camera pans over to Donald, sitting up tall in his seat, then back to the teacher)* Now, there was a model boy!

ALVY (AS CHILD) *(Still standing next to the teacher)*   Tell the folks where you are today, Donald.

DONALD   I run a profitable dress company.

ALVY'S VOICE   Right. Sometimes I wonder where my classmates are today.
The camera shows the full classroom, the students sitting behind their desks, the teacher standing in the front of the room. One at a time, the young students rise up from their desks and speak.

1ST BOY   I'm president of the Pinkus Plumbing Company.

2ND BOY   I sell tallises.

3RD BOY   I used to be a heroin addict. Now I'm a methadone addict.

2ND GIRL   I'm into leather.

INTERIOR ROOM.

Close-up of a TV screen showing Alvy as an adult on a talk show. He sits next to the show's host, Dick Cavett, a Navy man sits on his right. Static is heard throughout the dialogue.

ALVY   I lost track of most of my old schoolmates, but I wound up a comedian. They did not take me in the Army. I was, uh . . . Interestingly enough, I was—I was four-P.
Sounds of TV audience laughter and applause are heard.

DICK CAVETT   Four-P?

ALVY   Yes. In-in-in-in the event of war, I'm a hostage.
More audience laughter joined by Dick Cavett and the naval officer.

INTERIOR. THE HOUSE WHERE ALVY GREW UP.

Alvy's mother sits at the old-fashioned dining-room table peeling carrots and talking as she looks offscreen.

MOTHER   You always only saw the worst in people. You never could get along with anyone at school. You were always outta step with the world. Even when you got famous, you still distrusted the world.

EXTERIOR. MANHATTAN. STREET—DAY.

A pretty Manhattan street with sidewalk trees, brownstones, a school; people mill about, some strolling and carrying bundles, others hurried. The screen shows the whole length of the sidewalk, a street, and part of the sidewalk beyond. As the following scene ensues, two pedestrians, indistinguishable in the distance, come closer and closer toward the camera, recognizable, finally, as Alvy and his best friend, Rob, deep in conversation. They eventually move past the camera and offscreen. `Traffic noise is heard in the background.

ALVY   I distinctly heard it. He muttered under his breath, "Jew."

ROB   You're crazy!

ALVY   No, I'm not. We were walking off the tennis court, and you know, he was there and me and his wife, and he looked at her and then they both looked at me, and under his breath he said, "Jew."

ROB   Alvy, you're a total paranoid.

ALVY   Wh— How am I a paran—? Well, I pick up on those kind o' things. You know, I was having lunch with some guys from NBC, so I said . . . uh, "Did you eat yet or what?" and Tom Christie said,

"No, didchoo?" Not, did you, didchoo eat? Jew? No, not did you eat, but jew eat? Jew. You get it? Jew eat?

ROB   Ah, Max, you, uh . . .

ALVY   Stop calling me Max.

ROB   Why, Max? It's a good name for you. Max, you see conspiracies in everything.

ALVY   No, I don't! You know, I was in a record store. Listen to this —so I know there's this big tall blond crew-cutted guy and he's lookin' at me in a funny way and smiling and he's saying, "Yes, we have a sale this week on Wagner." Wagner, Max, Wagner—so I know what he's really tryin' to tell me very significantly Wagner.

ROB   Right, Max. California, Max.

ALVY   Ah.

ROB   Let's get the hell outta this crazy city—

ALVY   Forget it, Max.

ROB   —we move to sunny L.A. All of show business is out there, Max.

ALVY   No, I cannot. You keep bringing it up, but I don't wanna live in a city where the only cultural advantage is that you can make a right turn on a red light.

ROB   (Checking his watch)   Right, Max, forget it. Aren't you gonna be late for meeting Annie?

ALVY   I'm gonna meet her in front of the Beekman. I think I have a few minutes left. Right?

EXTERIOR. BEEKMAN THEATER—DAY.

Alvy stands in front of glass doors of theater, the ticket taker behind him just inside the glass doors. The sounds of city traffic, car horns honking, can be heard while he looks around waiting for Annie. A man in a black leather jacket, walking past the theater, stops in front of Alvy. He looks at him, then moves away. He stops a few steps farther and turns around to look at Alvy again. Alvy looks away, then back at the man. The man continues to stare. Alvy scratches his head, looking for Annie and trying not to notice the man. The man, still staring, walks back to Alvy.

IST MAN   Hey, you on television?

ALVY *(Nodding his head)*   No. Yeah, once in a while. You know, like occasionally.

IST MAN   What's your name?

ALVY *(Clearing his throat)*   You wouldn't know it. It doesn't matter. What's the difference?

IST MAN   You were on . . . uh, the . . . uh, the Johnny Carson, right?

ALVY   Once in a while, you know. I mean, you know, every now—

IST MAN   What's your name?
Alvy is getting more and more uneasy as the man talks; more and more people move through the doors of the theater.

ALVY *(Nervously)*   I'm . . . I'm, uh, I'm Robert Redford.

IST MAN *(Laughing)*   Come on.

ALVY   Alvy Singer. It was nice—nice . . . Thanks very much . . . for everything.
They shake hands and Alvy pats the man's arm. The man in turn looks over his shoulder and motions to another man. All excited now, he points to Alvy and calls out. Alvy looks impatient.

IST MAN   Hey!

2ND MAN *(Offscreen)*   What?

IST MAN   This is Alvy Singer!

ALVY   Fellas . . . you know—Jesus! Come on!

IST MAN *(Overlapping, ignoring Alvy)*   This guy's on television! Alvy Singer, right? Am I right?

ALVY *(Overlapping ist man)*   Gimme a break, will yuh, gimme a break. Jesus Christ!

IST MAN *(Still ignoring Alvy's protestations)*   This guy's on television.

ALVY   I need a large polo mallet!

2ND MAN *(Moving into the screen)*   Who's on television?

IST MAN   This guy, on the Johnny Carson show.

ALVY *(Annoyed)*   Fellas, what is this—a meeting o' the teamsters? You know . . .

2ND MAN *(Also ignoring Alvy)*   What program?

1ST MAN *(Holding out a matchbook)*   Can I have your autograph?

ALVY   You don't want my autograph.

1ST MAN *(Overlapping Alvy's speech)*   Yeah, I do. It's for my girl friend. Make it out to Ralph.

ALVY *(Taking the matchbook and pen and writing)*   Your girl friend's name is Ralph?

1ST MAN   It's for my brudder. *(To passers-by)* Alvy Singer! Hey! This is Alvy—

2ND MAN *(To Alvy, overlapping 1st man's speech)*   You really Alvy Singer, the . . . the TV star?
Nodding his head yes, Alvy shoves 2nd man aside and moves to the curb of the sidewalk. The two men follow, still talking over the traffic noise.

1ST MAN   —Singer!

2ND MAN   Alvy Singer over here!
A cab moves into the frame and stops by the curb. Alvy moves over to it about to get in.

ALVY *(Overlapping the two men and stuttering)*   I-i-i-it's all right, fella. *(As Alvy opens the cab door, the two men still behind him, Annie gets out)* Jesus, what'd you do, come by way of the Panama Canal?

ANNIE *(Overlapping Alvy)*   All right, all right, I'm in a bad mood, okay? *Annie closes the cab door and she and Alvy move over to the ticket booth of the theater as they continue to talk.*

ALVY   Bad mood? I'm standing with the cast of *The Godfather.*

ANNIE   You're gonna hafta learn to deal with it.

ALVY   Deal! I'm dealing with two guys named Cheech!

ANNIE   Okay. *(They move into the ticket line, still talking. A billboard next to them reads "INGMAR BERGMAN'S 'FACE TO FACE,' LIV ULL-MANN")* Please, I have a headache, all right?

ALVY   Hey, you are in a bad mood. You-you-you must be getting your period.

ANNIE   I'm not getting my period. Jesus, every time anything out of the ordinary happens, you think that I'm getting my period!
They move over to the ticket counter, people in front of them buying tickets and walking offscreen.

ALVY *(Gesturing)*   A li-little louder. I think one of them may have missed it! *(To the ticket clerk)* H'm, has the picture started yet?

TICKET CLERK   It started two minutes ago.

ALVY *(Hitting his hand on the counter)*   That's it! Forget it! I—I can't go in.

ANNIE   Two minutes, Alvy.

ALVY *(Overlapping Annie)*   No, I'm sorry, I can't do it. We-we've blown it already. I—you know, uh, I-I can't go in in the middle.

ANNIE   In the middle? *(Alvy nods his head yes and let's out an exasperated sigh)* We'll only miss the titles. They're in Swedish.

ALVY   You wanna get coffee for two hours or something? We'll go next—

ANNIE   Two hours? No, u-uh, I'm going in. I'm going in.
She moves past the ticket clerk.

ALVY *(Waving to Annie)*   Go ahead. Good-bye.
Annie moves back to Alvy and takes his arm.

ANNIE   Look, while we're talking we could be inside, you know that?

ALVY *(Watching people with tickets move past them)*   Hey, can we not stand here and argue in front of everybody, 'cause I get embarrassed.

ANNIE   All right. All right, all right, so whatta you wanna do?

ALVY   I don't know now. You—you wanna go to another movie? *(Annie nods her head and shrugs her shoulders disgustedly as Alvy, gesturing with his hand, looks at her)* So let's go see *The Sorrow and the Pity*.

ANNIE   Oh, come on, we've seen it. I'm not in the mood to see a four-hour documentary on Nazis.

ALVY   Well, I'm sorry, I-I can't . . . I-I-I've gotta see a picture exactly from the start to the finish, 'cause—'cause I'm anal.

ANNIE *(Laughing now)*   H'h, that's a polite word for what you are.

INTERIOR. THEATER LOBBY.

A lined-up crowd of ticket holders waiting to get into the theater, Alvy and Annie among them. A hum of indistinct chatter can be heard through the ensuing scene.

MAN IN LINE *(Loudly to his companion right behind Alvy and Annie)* We saw the Fellini film last Tuesday. It is not one of his best. It lacks a cohesive structure. You know, you get the feeling that he's not absolutely sure what it is he wants to say. 'Course, I've always felt he was essentially a—a technical film maker. Granted, *La Strada* was a great film. Great in its use of negative energy more than anything else. But that simple cohesive core . . .
Alvy, reacting to the man's loud monologue, starts to get annoyed while Annie begins to read her newspaper.

ALVY *(Overlapping the man's speech)* I'm-I'm-I'm gonna have a stroke.

ANNIE *(Reading)* Well, stop listening to him.

MAN IN LINE *(Overlapping Alvy and Annie)* You know, it must need to have had its leading from one thought to another. You know what I'm talking about?

ALVY *(Sighing)* He's screaming his opinions in my ear.

MAN IN LINE Like all that *Juliet of the Spirits* or *Satyricon*, I found it incredibly . . . indulgent. You know, he really is. He's one of the most indulgent film makers. He really is—

ALVY *(Overlapping)* Key word here is "indulgent."

MAN IN LINE *(Overlapping)* —without getting . . . well, let's put it this way . . .

ALVY *(To Annie, who is still reading, overlapping the man in line who is still talking)* What are you depressed about?

ANNIE I missed my therapy. I overslept.

ALVY How can you possibly oversleep?

ANNIE The alarm clock.

ALVY *(Gasping)* You know what a hostile gesture that is to me?

ANNIE I know—because of our sexual problem, right?

ALVY Hey, you . . . everybody on line at the New Yorker has to know our rate of intercourse?

MAN IN LINE It's like Samuel Beckett, you know—I admire the technique but he doesn't . . . he doesn't hit me on a gut level.

ALVY *(To Annie)* I'd like to hit this guy on a gut level.
The man in line continues his speech all the while Alvy and Annie talk.

ANNIE Stop it, Alvy!

ALVY *(Wringing his hands)* Well, he's spitting on my neck! You know, he's spitting on my neck when he talks.

MAN IN LINE And then, the most important thing of all is a comedian's vision.

ANNIE And you know something else? You know, you're so egocentric that if I miss my therapy you can think of it in terms of how it affects you!

MAN IN LINE *(Lighting a cigarette while he talks)* Gal gun-shy is what it is.

ALVY *(Reacting again to the man in line)* Probably on their first date, right?

MAN IN LINE *(Still going on)* It's a narrow view.

ALVY Probably met by answering an ad in the *New York Review of Books.* "Thirtyish academic wishes to meet woman who's interested in Mozart, James Joyce and sodomy." *(He sighs; then to Annie)* Whatta you mean, *our* sexual problem?

ANNIE Oh!

ALVY I-I-I mean, I'm comparatively normal for a guy raised in Brooklyn.

ANNIE Okay, I'm very sorry. *My* sexual problem! Okay, *my* sexual problem! Huh?
The man in front of them turns to look at them, then looks away.

ALVY I never read that. That was—that was Henry James, right? Novel, uh, the sequel to *Turn of the Screw? My Sexual* . . .

MAN IN LINE *(Even louder now)* It's the influence of television. Yeah, now Marshall McLuhan deals with it in terms of it being a—a high, uh, high intensity, you understand? A hot medium . . . as opposed to a . . .

ALVY *(More and more aggravated)* What I wouldn't give for a large sock o' horse manure.

MAN IN LINE   . . . as opposed to a print . . .
Alvy steps forward, waving his hands in frustration, and stands facing the camera.

ALVY *(Sighing and addressing the audience)*   What do you do when you get stuck in a movie line with a guy like this behind you? I mean, it's just maddening!
The man in line moves toward Alvy. Both address the audience now.

MAN IN LINE   Wait a minute, why can't I give my opinion? It's a free country!

ALVY   I mean, d— He can give you— Do you hafta give it so loud? I mean, aren't you ashamed to pontificate like that? And-and the funny part of it is, M-Marshall McLuhan, you don't know anything about Marshall McLuhan's . . . work!

MAN IN LINE *(Overlapping)*   Wait a minute! Really? Really? I happen to teach a class at Columbia called "TV Media and Culture"! So I think that my insights into Mr. McLuhan—well, have a great deal of validity.

ALVY   Oh, do yuh?

MAN IN LINE   Yes.

ALVY   Well, that's funny, because I happen to have Mr. McLuhan right here. So . . . so, here, just let me—I mean, all right. Come over here . . . a second.
Alvy gestures to the camera, which follows him and the man in line to the back of the crowded lobby. He moves over to a large stand-up movie poster and pulls Marshall McLuhan from behind the poster.

MAN IN LINE   Oh.

ALVY *(To McLuhan)*   Tell him.

MCLUHAN *(To the man in line)*   I hear—I heard what you were saying. You—you know nothing of my work. You mean, my whole fallacy is wrong. How you ever got to teach a course in anything is totally amazing.

ALVY *(To the camera)*   Boy, if life were only like this!

INTERIOR. THEATER. A CLOSE-UP OF THE SCREEN SHOWING FACES OF GERMAN SOLDIERS.

ANNIE HALL

Credits appear over the faces of the soldiers:

THE SORROW
AND
THE PITY
© CINEMA 5 LTD., 1972
© MARCEL OPHULS, ANDRE HARRIS, 1969
Chronicle of a French town during
the Occupation

NARRATOR'S VOICE *(Over credits and soldiers)* June fourteenth, nineteen forty, the German army occupies Paris. All over the country, people are desperate for every available scrap of news.

CUT TO:
INTERIOR. BEDROOM—NIGHT.

Annie is sitting up in bed reading.

ALVY *(Offscreen)* Boy, those guys in the French Resistance were really brave, you know? Got to listen to Maurice Chevalier sing so much.

ANNIE M'm, I don't know, sometimes I ask myself how I'd stand up under torture.

ALVY *(Offscreen)* You? You kiddin'? *(He moves into the frame, lying across the bed to touch Annie, who makes a face)* If the Gestapo would take away your Bloomingdale's charge card, you'd tell 'em everything.

ANNIE That movie makes me feel guilty.

ALVY Yeah, 'cause it's supposed to.
He starts kissing Annie's arm. She gets annoyed and continues to read.

ANNIE Alvy, I . . .

ALVY What-what-what-what's the matter?

ANNIE I—you know, I don't wanna.

ALVY *(Overlapping Annie, reacting)* What-what—I don't . . . It's not natural! We're sleeping in a bed together. You know, it's been a long time.

ANNIE I know, well, it's just that—you know, I mean, I-I-I-I gotta sing tomorrow night, so I have to rest my voice.

ALVY (*Overlapping Annie again*)   It's always some kind of an excuse. It's— You know, you used to think that I was very sexy. What . . .   When we first started going out, we had sex constantly . . . We're-we're probably listed in the *Guinness Book of World Records*.

ANNIE (*Patting Alvy's hand solicitously*)   I know. Well, Alvy, it'll pass, it'll pass, it's just that I'm going through a phase, that's all.

ALVY   M'm.

ANNIE   I mean, you've been married before, you know how things can get. You were very hot for Allison at first.

CUT TO:
INTERIOR. BACKSTAGE OF AUDITORIUM—NIGHT.

Allison, clipboard in hand, walks about the wings, stopping to talk to various people. Musicians, performers and technicians mill about, busy with activity. Allison wears a large "ADLAI" button, as do the people around her. The sounds of a comedian on the stage of the auditorium can be heard, occasionally, interrupted by chatter and applause from the offscreen audience. Allison stops to talk to two women; they, too, wear "ADLAI" buttons.

ALLISON (*Looking down at the clipboard*)   Ma'am, you're on right after this man . . . about twenty minutes, something like that.

WOMAN   Oh, thank you.
Alvy moves into the frame behind Allison. He taps her on the shoulder; she turns to face him.

ALVY (*Coughing*)   Excuse . . . excuse me, when do I go on?

ALLISON (*Looking down at the clipboard*)   Who are you?

ALVY   Alvy . . . Alvy Singer. I'm a comedian.

ALLISON   Oh, comedian. Yes. Oh, uh . . . you're on next.

ALVY (*Rubbing his hands together nervously*)   What do you mean, next?

ALLISON (*Laughing*)   Uh . . . I mean you're on right after this act.

ALVY (*Gesturing*)   No, it can't be, because he's a comic.

ALLISON   Yes.

ALVY   So what are you telling me, you're putting on two comics in a row?

ALLISON   Why not?

ALVY   No, I'm sorry, I'm not goin'—   I can't . . . I don't wanna go on
after that comedian.

ALLISON   It's okay.

ALVY   No, because they're—they're laughing, so *(He starts laughing
nervously)* I-I-I'd rather not. If you don't mind, I prefer—

ALLISON *(Overlapping)*   Will you relax, please? They're gonna love you,
I know.

ALVY *(Overlapping)*   —I prefer not to, because . . . look, they're laughing at him. See, so what are yuh telling me—
They move closer to the stage, looking out from the wings.

ALLISON *(Overlapping)*   Yes.

ALVY *(Overlapping)*   —that I've got to . . . ah . . . ah . . . They're gonna
laugh at him for a couple minutes, then I gotta go out there, I gotta
. . . get laughs, too. How much can they laugh? *(Offscreen)* They-they-
they're laughed out.

ALLISON *(Offscreen)*   Do you feel all right?
*As Allison and Alvy look out at the stage, the camera cuts to their point of
view: a comedian standing at a podium in front of huge waving pictures of
Adlai Stevenson. The audience, laughing and clapping, sits at round tables
in clusters around the room.*
*The camera moves back to Allison and Alvy watching the stage. Alvy is
wringing his hands nervously.*

COMEDIAN *(Offscreen, onstage)*   You know . . .
*Alvy starts looking Allison up and down; people in the background mill
about.*

ALVY *(Above the chatter around him)*   Look, what's your—what's your
name?

COMEDIAN *(Offscreen)*   . . . General Eisenhower is not . . .

ALLISON *(Looking out at the stage)*   Allison.

ALVY   Yeah? Allison what?

ALLISON *(Still looking offscreen)*   Portchnik.

COMEDIAN   . . . a group from the . . .

ALVY *(Over the comedian's voice)*   Portchnik . . . that's nice.
He nods his head.

ALLISON   Thank you.

ALVY *(In disbelief, almost to himself)*   Allison Portchnik . . . ! *(He whistles and sticks out his tongue offscreen, reacting)* So, uh . . . whatta yuh telling me, yuh work for the Stevenson all the time, or what?

ALLISON *(Still looking offscreen)*   No, no, no, I'm, uh, I'm in the midst of doing my thesis.

ALVY   On what?

ALLISON   "On Political Commitment in Twentieth-Century Literature."

ALVY   Y-y-you like New York Jewish Left-Wing Liberal Intellectual Central Park West Brandeis University . . . uh, the Socialist Summer Camps and the . . . the father with the Ben Shahn drawings, right? And you really, you know, strike-oriented kind of—uh, stop me before I make a complete imbecile of myself.

ALLISON   No, that was wonderful. I love being reduced to a cultural stereotype.

ALVY   Right, I'm a bigot, you know, but for the left. *(He stands, hands in pockets, looking out at the stage. The comedian is finished and the audience is applauding. Allison looks at him as people bustle around them)* Oh, I have to go out there.
He puts his hands on Allison's shoulders.

ALLISON *(Looking at Alvy)*   Yes.
Alvy straightens his tie nervously.

ALVY   Say something encouraging quickly.

ALLISON   I think you're cute.

ALVY   Thank you.

ALLISON *(Laughing)*   M'mmm, h'h. Go ahead.
The crowd applauds. Alvy moves onto the stage as the previous comedian walks off. The audience continues to applaud as he moves to the podium. Allison stands in the wings watching, toying with the pencil from her clipboard.

ALVY *(Coughing)*   Thank you. I-I don't know why they would have me at this kind of rally 'cause . . . *(He clears his throat)* Excuse me, I'm not essentially a political comedian at all.
The audience starts to laugh.

ALVY   I . . . interestingly had, uh, dated . . . a woman in the Eisenhower Administration . . . briefly . . . and, uh, it was ironic to me 'cause, uh . . . tsch . . . 'cause I was trying to, u-u-uh, do to her what Eisenhower has been doing to the country for the last eight years. *The audience is with him, laughing, as Allison continues to watch offstage.*

INTERIOR. APARTMENT BEDROOM.

Allison and Alvy are on the bed, kissing. There are books all over the room; a fireplace, unlit, along one of the walls. Alvy suddenly breaks away and sits on the edge of the bed. Allison looks at him.

ALVY   H'm, I'm sorry, I can't go through with this, because it—I can't get it off my mind, Allison . . . it's obsessing me!

ALLISON   Well, I'm getting tired of it. I need your attention.
Alvy gets up from the bed and starts walking restlessly around the room, gesturing with his hands.

ALVY   It—but it-it . . . doesn't make any sense. He drove past the book depository and the police said conclusively that it was an exit wound. So—how is it possible for Oswald to have fired from two angles at once? It doesn't make sense.

ALLISON   Alvy.
Alvy, stopping for a moment at the fireplace mantel, sighs. He then snaps his fingers and starts walking again.

ALVY   I'll tell you this! He was not marksman enough to hit a moving target at that range. But . . . *(Clears his throat)* if there was a second assassin . . . it— That's it!
Alvy stops at the music stand with open sheet music on it as Allison gets up from the bed and retrieves a pack of cigarettes from a bookshelf.

ALLISON   We've been through this.

ALVY   If they-they recovered the shells from that rifle.

ALLISON   *(Moving back to the bed and lighting a cigarette)*   Okay. All right, so whatta yuh saying, now? That e-e-everybody o-o-on the Warren Commission is in on this conspiracy, right?

ALVY   Well, why not?

ALLISON   Yeah, Earl Warren?

ALVY   *(Moving toward the bed)*   Hey . . . honey, I don't know Earl Warren.

ALLISON   Lyndon Johnson?

ALVY   *(Propping one knee on the bed and gesturing)*   L-L-Lyndon Johns— Lyndon Johnson is a politician. You know the ethics those guys have. It's like—uh, a notch underneath child molester.

ALLISON   Then everybody's in on the conspiracy?

ALVY   *(Nodding his head)*   Tsch.

ALLISON   The FBI, and the CIA, and J. Edgar Hoover and oil companies and the Pentagon and the men's-room attendant at the White House?
Alvy touches Allison's shoulder, then gets up from the bed and starts walking again.

ALVY   I-I-I-I would leave out the men's-room attendant.

ALLISON   You're using this conspiracy theory as an excuse to avoid sex with me.

ALVY   Oh, my God! *(Then, to the camera)* She's right! Why did I turn off Allison Portchnik? She was—she was beautiful. She was willing. She was real . . . intelligent. *(Sighing)* Is it the old Groucho Marx joke? That—that I-I just don't wanna belong to any club that would have someone like me for a member?

EXTERIOR. BEACH HOUSE—DAY.

Alvy's and Annie's voices are heard over the wind-browned exterior of a beach house in the Hamptons. As they continue to talk, the camera moves inside the house. Alvy is picking up chairs, trying to get at the group of lobsters crawling on the floor. Dishes are stacked up in a drying rack, and bags of groceries sit on the counter. There's a table and chairs near the refrigerator.

ANNIE   Alvy, now don't panic. Please.

ALVY   Look, I told you it was a . . . mistake to ever bring a live thing in the house.

ANNIE   Stop it! Don't . . . don't do that! There.
The lobsters continue to crawl on the floor. Annie, holding out a wooden paddle, tries to shove them onto it.

ALVY   Well, maybe we should just call the police. Dial nine-one-one, it's the lobster squad.

ANNIE   Come on, Alvy, they're only baby ones, for God's sake.

ALVY   If they're only babies, then you pick 'em up.

ANNIE   Oh, all right. All right! It's all right. Here.
She drops the paddle and picks up one of the lobsters by the tail. Laughing, she shoves it at Alvy who jerks backward, squeamishly.

ALVY   Don't give it to me. Don't!

ANNIE *(Hysterically)*   Oooh! Here! Here!

ALVY *(Pointing)*   Look! Look, one crawled behind the refrigerator. It'll turn up in our bed at night. *(They move over to the refrigerator; Alvy moves as close to the wall as possible as Annie, covering her mouth and laughing hysterically, teasingly dangles a lobster in front of him)* Will you get outta here with that thing? Jesus!

ANNIE *(Laughing, to the lobster)*   Get him!

ALVY *(Laughing)*   Talk to him. You speak shellfish! *(He moves over to the stove and takes the lid off a large steamer filled with boiling water)* Hey, look . . . put it in the pot.

ANNIE *(Laughing)*   I can't! I can't put him in the pot. I can't put a live thing in hot water.

ALVY *(Overlapping)*   Gimme! Gimmee! Let me do it! What—what's he think we're gonna do, take him to the movies?
Annie hands the lobster to Alvy as he takes it very carefully and drops it gingerly into the pot and puts the cover back on.

ANNIE *(Overlapping Alvy and making sounds)*   Oh, God! Here yuh go! Oh, good, now he'll think— *(She screams)* Aaaah! Okay.

ALVY *(Overlapping Annie)*   Okay, it's in. It's definitely in the pot!

ANNIE   All right. All right. All right.
She moves hurriedly across the kitchen and picks up another lobster. Smiling, she places it on the counter as Alvy stands beside the refrigerator trying to push it from the wall.

ALVY   Annie, there's a big lobster behind the refrigerator. I can't get it out. This thing's heavy. Maybe if I put a little dish of butter sauce here with a nutcracker, it will run out the other side, you know what I mean?

ANNIE *(Overlapping)*   Yeah. I'm gonna get my . . . I'm gonna get my camera.

ALVY   You know, I—I think . . . if I could pry this door off . . . We shoulda gotten steaks 'cause they don't have legs. They don't run around.
Annie rushes out of the room to get her camera as Alvy picks up the paddle. Trying to get at the lobsters, he ends up knocking over dishes and hitting the chandelier. Holding the paddle, he finally leans back against the sink. Annie, standing in the doorway, starts taking pictures of him.

ANNIE   Great! Great! *(Screaming)* Goddammit! *(Screaming)* Ooooh! These are . . . p-p-p-pick this lobster up. Hold it, please!

ALVY   All right! All right! All right! All right! Whatta yuh mean? Are yuh gonna take pictures now?

ANNIE   It'll make great— Alvy, be— Alvy, it'll be wonderful . . . Ooooh, lovely!

ALVY *(Picking up the lobster Annie placed on the counter earlier)*   All right, here! Oh, God, it's disgusting!
Alvy drops the lobster back down on the counter, sticking out his tongue and making a face.

ANNIE   Don't be a jerk. One more, Alvy, please, one more picture. *(Reluctantly Alvy picks up the lobster again as Annie takes another picture)* Oh, oh, good, good!

EXTERIOR. OCEAN FRONT—DUSK.

The camera pans Annie and Alvy as they walk along the shore.

ALVY   So, so—well, here's what I wanna know. W-what . . . *(He clears his throat)* Am I your first big romance?

ANNIE   Oh . . . no, no, no, no, uh, uh. No.

ALVY   Well, then, w-who was?

ANNIE   Oh, well, let's see, there was Dennis, from Chippewa Falls High School.

CUT TO:
FLASHBACK OF DENNIS LEANING AGAINST A CAR.

It's night. Behind him is a movie theater with "MARILYN MONROE, 'MISFITS' " on the marquee. He looks at his watch as the younger Annie, in a beehive hairdo, moves into the frame. They kiss quickly and look at each other, smiling.

ALVY'S VOICE *(Offscreen)*   Dennis—right, uh, uh . . . local kid probably, would meetcha in front of the movie house on Saturday night.

ANNIE'S VOICE   Oh, God, you should've seen what I looked like then.

ALVY'S VOICE *(Offscreen, laughing)*   Oh, I can imagine. P-p-probably the wife of an astronaut.

ANNIE'S VOICE   Then there was Jerry, the actor.

CUT TO:
FLASHBACK OF BRICK-WALLED APARTMENT—NIGHT.

The younger Annie and Jerry lean against the wall; Jerry is running his hand down Annie's bare arm. Annie and Alvy walk into the room, observing the younger Annie, in jeans and T-shirt, with Jerry.

ALVY'S VOICE *(Laughing)*   Look at you, you-you're such a clown.

ANNIE'S VOICE   I look pretty.

ALVY'S VOICE   Well, yeah, you always look pretty, but that guy with you . . .

JERRY   Acting is like an exploration of the soul. I-it's very religious. Uh, like, uh, a kind of liberating consciousness. It's like a visual poem.

ALVY *(Laughing)*   Is he kidding with that crap?

YOUNGER ANNIE *(Laughing)*   Oh, right. Right, yeah, I think I know exactly what you mean, when you say "religious."

ALVY *(Incredulous, to Annie)*   You do?

ANNIE *(Still watching)*   Oh, come on—I mean, I was still younger.

ALVY   Hey, that was last year.

JERRY   It's like when I think of dying. You know how I would like to die?

YOUNGER ANNIE No, how?

JERRY I'd like to get torn apart by wild animals.

ALVY'S VOICE Heavy! Eaten by some squirrels.

ANNIE'S VOICE Hey, listen—I mean, he was a terrific actor, and look at him, he's neat-looking and he was emotional . . . Y—hey, I don't think you like emotion too much.
Jerry stops rubbing the younger Annie's arm and slides down to the floor as she raises her foot toward his chest.

JERRY Touch my heart . . . with your foot.

ALVY'S VOICE I-I may throw up!

CUT BACK TO:
EXTERIOR. BEACH—DUSK.

It's now sunset, the water reflecting the last light. The camera moves over the scene. The offscreen voices of Alvy and Annie are heard as they walk, the camera always one step ahead of them.

ANNIE He was creepy.

ALVY Yeah, I-I think you're pretty lucky I came along.

ANNIE *(Laughing)* Oh, really? Well, la-de-da!

ALVY La-de-da. If I—if anyone had ever told me that I would be taking out a girl who used expressions like "la-de-da" . . .

ANNIE Oh, that's right. That you really like those New York girls.

ALVY Well, no . . . not just, not only.

ANNIE Oh, I'd say so. You married—

CUT TO:
INTERIOR. NEW YORK CITY APARTMENT—NIGHT.

A cocktail party is in progress, the rooms crowded with guests as Alvy and Robin make their way through the people. A waiter, carrying a tray, walks past them. Alvy reaches out to pick up a glass; Robin reaches over and picks it off the tray first. There is much low-key chatter in the background.

ANNIE *(Offscreen)* —two of them.

ROBIN   There's Henry Drucker. He has a chair in history at Princeton. Oh, the short man is Hershel Kaminsky. He has a chair in philosophy at Cornell.

ALVY   Yeah, two more chairs and they got a dining-room set.

ROBIN   Why are you so hostile?

ALVY *(Sighing)*   'Cause I wanna watch the Knicks on television.

ROBIN *(Squinting)*   Is that Paul Goodman? No. And be nice to the host because he's publishing my book. Hi, Doug! Douglas Wyatt. "A Foul-Rag-and-Bone Shop-of-the-Heart."
They move through the rooms, Robin holding a drink in one hand, her arm draped in Alvy's; the crowd mills around them.

ALVY *(Taking Robin's hand)*   I'm so tired of spending evenings making fake insights with people who work for *Dysentery.*

ROBIN   *Commentary.*

ALVY   Oh, really, I heard that *Commentary* and *Dissent* had merged and formed *Dysentery.*

ROBIN   No jokes—these are friends, okay?

INTERIOR. BEDROOM.

Alvy sits on the foot of the bed watching the Knicks game on television.

TV ANNOUNCER *(Offscreen)* Cleveland Cavaliers losing to the New York Knicks.
Robin enters the room, slamming the door.

ROBIN Here you are. There's people out there.

ALVY Hey, you wouldn't believe this. Two minutes ago, the Knicks are ahead fourteen points, and now . . . *(Clears his throat)* they're ahead two points.

ROBIN Alvy, what is so fascinating about a group of pituitary cases trying to stuff the ball through a hoop?

ALVY *(Looking at Robin)* What's fascinating is that it's physical. You know, it's one thing about intellectuals, they prove that you can be absolutely brilliant and have no idea what's going on. But on the other hand . . . *(Clears his throat)* the body doesn't lie, as-as we now know.
Alvy reaches over, pulls Robin down onto the bed. He kisses her and moves farther up on the bed.

ROBIN Stop acting out.
She sits on the edge of the bed, looking down at the sprawled-out Alvy.

ALVY No, it'll be great! It'll be great, be-because all those Ph.D.s are in there, you know, like . . . discussing models of alienation and we'll be in here quietly humping.
He pulls Robin toward him, caressing her as she pulls herself away.

ROBIN Alvy, don't! You're using sex to express hostility.

ALVY " 'Why—why do you always r-reduce my animal urges to psychoanalytic categories?' *(Clears his throat)* he said as he removed her brassiere . . ."

ROBIN *(Pulling away again)* There are people out there from *The New Yorker* magazine. My God! What would they think?
She gets up and fixes the zipper on her dress. She turns and moves toward the door.

INTERIOR. APARTMENT—NIGHT.

Robin and Alvy are in bed. The room is in darkness. Outside, a siren starts blaring.

ROBIN Oh, I'm sorry!

ALVY Don't get upset!

ROBIN Dammit! I was so close.
She flips on the overhead lamp and turns on her side. Alvy turns to her.

ALVY *(Gesturing)* Jesus, last night it was some guy honking his car horn. I mean, the city can't close down. You know, what-whatta yuh gonna do, h-have 'em shut down the airport, too? No more flights so we can have sex?

ROBIN *(Reaching over for her eyeglasses on the night table)* I'm too tense. I need a Valium. My analyst says I should live in the country and not in New York.

ALVY Well, I can't li— We can't have this discussion all the time. The country makes me nervous. There's . . . You got crickets and it-it's quiet . . . there's no place to walk after dinner, and . . . uh, there's the screens with the dead moths behind them, and . . . uh, yuh got the-the Manson family possibly, yuh got Dick and Terry—

ROBIN *(Interrupting)* Okay, okay, my analyst just thinks I'm too tense. Where's the goddamn Valium?
She fumbles about the floor for the Valium, then back on the bed.

ALVY Hey, come on, it's quiet now. We can—we can start again.

ROBIN I can't.

ALVY What—

ROBIN My head is throbbing.

ALVY Oh, you got a headache!

ROBIN I have a headache.

ALVY Bad?

ROBIN Oswald and ghosts.

ALVY Jesus!
He begins to get out of bed.

ROBIN Where are you going?

ALVY Well, I'm-I'm gonna take another in a series of cold showers.

EXTERIOR. MEN'S LOCKER ROOM OF THE TENNIS CLUB.

Rob and Alvy, carrying tennis rackets, come through the door of the locker room to the lobby. They are dressed in tennis whites. They walk toward the indoor court.

ROB   Max, my serve is gonna send yuh to the showers—

ALVY   Right, right, so g-get back to what we were discussing, the failure of the country to get behind New York City is-is anti-Semitism.

ROB   Max, the city is terribly worried.

ALVY   But the— I'm not discussing politics or economics. This is foreskin.

ROB   No, no, no, Max, that's a very convenient out. Every time some group disagrees with you it's because of anti-Semitism.

ALVY   Don't you see? The rest of the country looks upon New York like we're-we're left-wing Communist, Jewish, homosexual, pornographers. I think of us that way, sometimes, and I-I live here.

ROB   Max, if we lived in California, we could play outdoors every day, in the sun.

ALVY   Sun is bad for yuh. Everything our parents said was good is bad. Sun, milk, red meat, college . . .

INTERIOR. TENNIS COURT.

Annie and Janet, in tennis whites, stand on the court holding tennis rackets and balls. They are chattering and giggling.

ANNIE   *(Laughing)*   I know, but ooh— Egads, here he comes. Okay. *Rob and Alvy enter the court and walk over to the two women. Rob kisses Janet and makes introduction.*

ROB   You know Alvy?

JANET   Oh, hi, Alvy.

ANNIE   *(To Rob)*   How are yuh?

ROB   *(To Alvy)*   You know Annie?

JANET   I'm sorry. This is Annie Hall.

ALVY Hi.

ANNIE Hi.
Annie and Alvy shake hands.

JANET *(Laughing)* Alvy.

ROB *(Eager to begin)* Who's playing who here?

ALVY Well, uh . . . you and me against them?

ANNIE *(Overlapping Alvy)* Well . . . so . . . I can't play too good, you know.

JANET *(Laughing)* I've had four lessons!
The group, laughing and chatting, divide up—Rob and Annie moving to the other side of the net, Alvy and Janet standing where they are. They start to play mixed doubles, each taking turns and playing well. At one point in the game Annie starts to talk to Rob, then turns and sees a ball heading toward her.

ANNIE *(Hitting the ball back)* Holy gods!

INTERIOR. LOBBY.

Alvy, dressed, puts things into a gym bag. One knee is on the bench and his back is turned from the entrance. Annie walks toward the entrance door dressed in street clothes and carrying her tennis bag over her shoulder. Seeing Alvy, she stops and turns.

ANNIE Hi. Hi, hi.

ALVY *(Looking over his shoulder)* Hi. Oh, hi. Hi.

ANNIE *(Hands clasped in front of her, smiling)* Well . . . bye.
She laughs and backs up slowly toward the door.

ALVY *(Clearing his throat)* You-you play . . . very well.

ANNIE Oh, yeah? So do you. Oh, God, whatta—*(Making sounds and laughing)* whatta dumb thing to say, right? I mean, you say it, "You play well," and right away . . . I have to say well. Oh, oh . . . God, Annie. *(She gestures with her hand)* Well . . . oh, well . . . la-de-da, la-de-da, la-la.
She turns around and moves toward the door.

ALVY *(Still looking over his shoulder)* Uh . . . you-you wanna lift?

ANNIE *(Turning and aiming her thumb over her shoulder)* Oh, why—uh
. . . y-y-you gotta car?

ALVY No, um . . . I was gonna take a cab.

ANNIE *(Laughing)* Oh, no, I have a car.

ALVY You have a car? *(Annie smiles, hands folded in front of her)* So
. . . *(Clears his throat)* I don't understand why . . . if you have a car,
so then—then wh-why did you say "Do you have a car?" . . . like you
wanted a lift?

ANNIE I don't . . . *(Laughing)* I don't . . . Geez, I don't know, I've
. . . I wa— This . . . yeah, I got this VW out there . . . *(Laughing
and gesturing toward the door)* What a jerk, yeah. Would you like a lift?

ALVY *(Zipping up his bag)* Sure. W-w-w-which way yuh goin'?

ANNIE Me? Oh, downtown!

ALVY Down— I'm-I'm goin' uptown.

ANNIE *(Laughing)* Oh, well, I'm goin' uptown, too.

ALVY Uh, well, you just said you were going downtown.

ANNIE Yeah, well, I'm, but I . . .
   *Alvy picks up his bag and moves toward the door. As he turns his bag around,
   the handle of the tennis racket hits Annie between the legs.*

ALVY *(Laughing)* So sorry.

ANNIE *(Laughing)* I mean, I can go uptown, too. I live uptown, but
. . . uh, what the hell, I mean, it'd be nice having company, you know
—I mean, I hate driving alone.

ALVY *(Making sounds)* Yeah.
   They walk out the door.

EXTERIOR. NEW YORK STREET—DAY.

*Alvy and Annie in the VW as Annie speeds down a city street near the East
River.*

ALVY So, how long do you know Janet? Where do you know her from?

ANNIE *(Laughing)* Oh, I'm in her acting class.

ALVY Oh, you're an actress.

ANNIE Well, I do commercials, sort of . . .
She zooms down the wrong lane, cars swerving out of her way. A horn blows.

ALVY I, uh . . . well, you're not from New York, right?

ANNIE No, Chippewa Falls.

ALVY Right! *(A pause)* Where?

ANNIE Wisconsin.

ALVY *(Finally reacting)* Uh, you're driving a . . . bit rapidly.

ANNIE Uh, don't worry, I'm a very—*(A car moves closer to the VW, almost on top of it in the wrong direction. Annie swerves away at the very last minute)*—a very good driver. *(Alvy rubs his head nervously, staring out the window as Annie speeds along)* So, listen—hey, you want some gum, anyway?
Annie looks down beside her, searching for the gum.

ALVY No, no thanks. Hey, don't—

ANNIE Well, where is it? I—

ALVY No, no, no, no, you just . . . just watch the road. I'll get it—

ANNIE Okay.
They both fumble around in her pocketbook. Alvy looks up to see the entire front of a truck in Annie's windshield. She swerves just in time.

ALVY —for yuh.

ANNIE Okay, that's good.
Alvy continues to look for the gum while Annie zooms down the city streets.

ANNIE All right.

ALVY I'll getcha a piece.

ANNIE Yeah . . . so, listen—you drive?

ALVY Do I drive? Uh, no, I gotta—I gotta problem with driving.

ANNIE Oh, you do?

ALVY Yeah. I got, uh, I got a license but I have too much hostility.

ANNIE Oh, right . . .

ALVY Nice car.

ANNIE   Huh?

ALVY   You keep it nice. *(He pulls a half-eaten sandwich out of her bag)* Can I ask you, is this—is this a sandwich?

ANNIE   Huh? Oh, yeah.

EXTERIOR. STREET—DAY.

Cars are parked on both sides of the street as the VW rounds the corner.

ANNIE   I live over here. Oh, my God! Look! There's a parking space! *With brakes squealing, Annie turns the VW sharply into the parking spot. Annie and Alvy get out, Alvy looking over his shoulder as he leaves the car.*

ALVY   That's okay, you . . . we-we can walk to the curb from here.

ANNIE   Don't be funny.

ALVY   You want your tennis stuff?

ANNIE   Huh? Oh . . . yeah.

ALVY   You want your gear? Here you go.
Alvy reaches into the back of the car and takes out tennis equipment. He hands her her things. People pass by on the street.

ANNIE   *(Laughing)*   Yeah, thanks. Thanks a lot. Well . . .

ALVY   *(Sighing)*   Well, thanks, thank you. You-you're . . . you're a wonderful tennis player.

ANNIE   *(Laughing)*   Oh.
Alvy shakes hands with Annie.

ALVY   You're the worst driver I've ever seen in my life . . . that's including any place . . . the worst . . . Europe, United . . . any place . . . Asia.

ANNIE   *(Laughing)*   Yeah.

ALVY   And I love what you're wearin'.
Alvy touches the tie Annie is wearing around her neck.

ANNIE   Oh, you do? Yeah? Oh, well, it's uh . . . this is, uh . . . this tie is a present, from Grammy Hall.
Annie flips the bottom of the tie.

ALVY Who? Grammy? Grammy Hall?

ANNIE *(Laughing and nodding her head)* Yeah, my grammy.

ALVY You're jo— Whatta yuh kid— What did you do, grow up in a Norman Rockwell painting?

ANNIE *(Laughing)* Yeah, I know.

ALVY Your grammy!

ANNIE I know, it's pretty silly, isn't it?

ALVY   Jesus, my-my grammy . . . n-never gave gifts, you know. She-she was too busy getting raped by Cossacks.

ANNIE *(Laughing)*   Well . . .

ALVY   Well . . . thank you again.

ANNIE   Oh, yeah, yeah.

ALVY   I'll see yuh.

ANNIE *(Overlapping, gesturing)*   Hey, well, listen . . . hey, you wanna come upstairs and, uh . . . and have a glass of wine and something? Aw, no, I mean . . . I mean, you don't have to, you're probably late and everything else . . .

ALVY   No, no, that'll be fine. I don't mind. Sure.

ANNIE   You sure?

ALVY *(Overlapping)*   No, I got time.

ANNIE   Okay.

ALVY   Sure, I got . . . I got nothing, uh, nothing till my analyst's appointment.
They move toward Annie's apartment building.

ANNIE   Oh, you see an analyst?

ALVY   Y-y-yeah, just for fifteen years.

ANNIE   Fifteen years?

ALVY   Yeah, uh, I'm gonna give him one more year and then I'm goin' to Lourdes.

ANNIE   Fifteen—aw, come on, you're . . . yeah, really?

INTERIOR. ANNIE'S APARTMENT.

Alvy, standing, looks around the apartment. There are lots of books, framed photographs on the white wall. A terrace can be seen from the window. He picks up a copy of Ariel, by Sylvia Plath, as Annie comes out of the kitchen carrying two glasses. She hands them to Alvy.

ALVY   Sylvia Plath.

ANNIE   M'hm.

ALVY   Interesting poetess whose tragic suicide was misinterpreted as romantic, by the college-girl mentality.

ANNIE   Oh, yeah.

ALVY   Oh, sorry.

ANNIE   Right. Well, I don't know, I mean, uh, some of her poems seem neat, you know.

ALVY   Neat?

ANNIE   Neat, yeah.

ALVY   Uh, I hate to tell yuh, this is nineteen seventy-five, you know that "neat" went out, I would say, at the turn of the century. *(Annie laughs)* Who-who are—who are those photos on the wall?

ANNIE   *(Moving over to the photographs)*   Oh . . . oh, well, you see now . . . now, uh, that's my dad, that's Father—and that's my . . . brother, Duane.

ALVY   Duane?

ANNIE   *(Pointing)*   Yeah, right, Duane—and over there is Grammy Hall, and that's Sadie.

ALVY   Well, who's Sadie?

ANNIE   Sadie? Oh, well, Sadie . . . *(Laughing)* Sadie met Grammy through, uh, through Grammy's brother George. Uh, George was real sweet, you know, he had that thing. What is that thing where you, uh, where you, uh, fall asleep in the middle of a sentence, you know—what is it? Uh . . .

ALVY   Uh, narcolepsy.

ANNIE   Narcolepsy, right, right. Right. So, anyway, so . . . *(Laughing)* George, uh, went to the union, see, to get his free turkey, be-because, uh, the union always gave George this big turkey at Christmastime because he was . . . *(Annie points her fingers to each side of her head, indicating George was a little crazy)* shell-shocked, you know what I mean, in the First World War. *(Laughing hysterically, she opens a cabinet door and takes out a bottle of wine)* Anyway, so, so . . . *(Laughing through the speech)* George is standing in line, oh, just a sec . . . uh, getting his free turkey, but the thing is, he falls asleep and he never wakes up. So, so . . . *(Laughing)* so, he's dead . . . *(Laughing)* he's dead. Yeah.

Oh, dear. Well, terrible, huh, wouldn't you say? I mean, that's pretty unfortunate.
Annie unscrews the bottle of wine, silent now after her speech.

ALVY   Yeah, it's a great story, though, I mean, I . . . I . . . it really made my day. Hey, I think I should get outta here, you know, 'cause I think I'm imposing, you know . . .

ANNIE   *(Laughing)*   Oh, really? Oh, well . . . uh, uh, maybe, uh, maybe, we, uh . . .

ALVY   . . . and . . . uh, yeah, uh . . . uh, you know, I-I-I . . .
They move outside to the terrace, Alvy still holding the glasses, Annie the wine. They stand in front of the railing, Annie pouring the wine into the held-out glasses.

ANNIE   Well, I mean, you don't have to, you know.

ALVY   No, I know, but . . . but, you know, I'm all perspired and everything.

ANNIE   Well, didn't you take, uh . . . uh, a shower at the club?

ALVY   Me? No, no, no, 'cause I ne—   I never shower in a public place.

ANNIE   *(Laughing)*   Why not?

ALVY   'Cause I don't like to get naked in front of another man, you know—it's, uh . . .

ANNIE   *(Laughing)*   Oh, I see, I see.

ALVY   You know, I don't like to show my body to a man of my gender—

ANNIE   Yeah. Oh, yeah. Yeah, I see. I guess—

ALVY   —'cause, uh, you never know what's gonna happen.

ANNIE   *(Sipping her wine and laughing)*   Fifteen years, huh?

ALVY   Fifteen years, yeah.

ANNIE   Yeah. Oh, God bless!
They put their glasses together in a toast.

ALVY   God bless.

ANNIE   *(Laughing)*   Well, uh . . . *(Pausing)* You're what Grammy Hall would call a real Jew.

ALVY *(Clearing his throat)*   Oh, thank you.

ANNIE *(Smiling)*   Yeah, well . . . you—She hates Jews. She thinks that they just make money, but let me tell yuh, I mean, she's the one—yeah, is she ever. I'm tellin' yuh.

ALVY *(Pointing toward the apartment after a short pause)*   So, did you do those photographs in there or what?

ANNIE *(Nodding, her hand on her hip)*   Yeah, yeah, I sorta dabble around, you know.
(Annie's thoughts pop on the screen as she talks: I dabble? Listen to me—what a jerk)

ALVY   They're . . . they're . . . they're wonderful, you know. They have . . . they have, uh . . . a . . . a quality.
(As do Alvy's: You are a great-looking girl)

ANNIE   Well, I-I-I would—I would like to take a serious photography course soon.
(Again, Annie's thoughts pop on: He probably thinks I'm a yo-yo)

ALVY   Photography's interesting, 'cause, you know, it's—it's a new art form, and a, uh, a set of aesthetic criteria have not emerged yet.
(And Alvy's: I wonder what she looks like naked?)

ANNIE   Aesthetic criteria? You mean, whether it's, uh, good photo or not?
   (*I'm not smart enough for him. Hang in there*)

ALVY   The-the medium enters in as a condition of the art form itself. That's—
   (*I don't know what I'm saying—she senses I'm shallow*)

ANNIE   Well, well, I . . . to me—I . . . I mean, it's-it's-it's all instinctive, you know. I mean, I just try to uh, feel it, you know? I try to get a sense of it and not think about it so much.
   (*God, I hope he doesn't turn out to be a* shmuck *like the others*)

ALVY   Still, still we—   You need a set of aesthetic guide lines to put it in social perspective, I think.
   (*Christ, I sound like FM radio. Relax*)

They're quiet for a moment, holding wine glasses and sipping. The sounds of distant traffic from the street can be heard on the terrace. Annie, laughing, speaks first.

ANNIE   Well, I don't know. I mean, I guess—I guess you must be sorta late, huh?

ALVY   You know, I gotta get there and begin whining soon . . . otherwise I—   Hey . . . well, are you busy Friday night?

ANNIE   Me? Oh, uh . . . (*Laughing*) no.

ALVY (*Putting his hand on his forehead*)   Oh, I'm sorry, wait a minute, I have something. Well, what about Saturday night?

ANNIE (*Nodding*)   Oh . . . nothing. Not—no, no!

ALVY   Oh, you . . . you're very popular, I can see.

ANNIE (*Laughing*)   I know.

ALVY   Gee, boy, what do you have? You have plague?

ANNIE   Well, I mean, I meet a lot of . . . jerks, you know—

ALVY   Yeah, I meet a lotta jerks, too.

ANNIE (*Overlapping*)   —what I mean?

ALVY   I think that's, uh—

ANNIE *(Interrupting)* But I'm thinking about getting some cats, you know, and then they . . . Oh, wait a second—oh, no, no, I mean . . . *(Laughing)* oh, shoot! No, Saturday night I'm gonna—*(Laughing)* I'm gonna sing. Yeah.

ALVY You're gonna sing? Do you sing?

ANNIE Well, no, it isn't—

ALVY *(Overlapping)* No kidding?

ANNIE *(Overlapping)* —this is my first time.

ALVY Oh, really? Where? I'd like to come.

ANNIE *(Laughing)* Oh, no, no, no, no, no!

ALVY No, I'm interested!

ANNIE *(Laughing)* Oh, no—I mean, I'm just a-auditioning sort of at this club. I don't—

ALVY *(Overlapping)* No, so help me—

ANNIE *(Overlapping)* —it's my first time.

ALVY That's okay, 'cause I know exactly what that's like. Listen—

ANNIE *(Interrupting)* Yeah.

ALVY *(Overlapping)* —you're gonna like night clubs, they're really a lotta fun.

INTERIOR. NIGHT CLUB—NIGHT.

Annie stands on center stage with a microphone, a pianist behind her. A bright light is focused on her; the rest of the club is in darkness. There are the typical sounds and movements of a night-club audience: low conversation, curling smoke, breaking glass, microphone hum, moving chairs, waiters clattering trays, a ringing phone as Annie sings "It Had to Be You."

EXTERIOR. CITY STREET—NIGHT.

Alvy and Annie walk quickly down the sidewalk.

ANNIE I was awful. I'm so ashamed! I can't sing.

ALVY Oh, listen, so the audience was a tad restless.

ANNIE   Whatta you mean, a tad restless? Oh, my God, I mean, they hated me.

ALVY   No, they didn't. You have a wonderful voice.

ANNIE   No, I'm gonna quit!

ALVY   No, I'm not gonna letcha. You have a great voice.

ANNIE   Really, do you think so, really?

ALVY   Yeah!

ANNIE   Yeah?

ALVY   It's terrific.

ANNIE   *(Overlapping)*   Yeah, you know something? I never even took a lesson, either.
They stop in the middle of the sidewalk. Alvy turns Annie around to face him.

ALVY   Hey, listen, listen.

ANNIE   What?

ALVY   Gimme a kiss.

ANNIE   Really?

ALVY Yeah, why not, because we're just gonna go home later, right?

ANNIE Yeah.

ALVY And-and . . . uh, there's gonna be all that tension. You know, we never kissed before and I'll never know when to make the right move or anything. So we'll kiss now we'll get it over with and then we'll go eat. Okay?

ANNIE Oh, all right.

ALVY And we'll digest our food better.

ANNIE Okay.

ALVY Okay?

ANNIE Yeah.
They kiss.

ALVY So now we can digest our food.
They turn and start walking again.

ANNIE We can digest our—

ALVY Okay? Yeah.

INTERIOR. DELI—NIGHT.

Annie and Alvy sit down in a booth. The deli is fairly well lit and crowded. Conversation, plates clattering, can be heard over the dialogue. The waiter comes over to them to take their order.

ALVY *(To the waiter)* I'm gonna have a corned beef.

ANNIE *(To the waiter)* Yeah . . . oh, uh, and I'm gonna have a pastrami on white bread with, uh, mayonnaise and tomatoes and lettuce. *(Alvy involuntarily makes a face as the waiter leaves)* Tsch, so, uh, your second wife left you and, uh, were you depressed about that?

ALVY Nothing that a few mega-vitamins couldn't cure.

ANNIE Oh. And your first wife was Allison?

ALVY My first . . . Yes, she was nice, but you know, uh, it was my fault. I was just . . . I was too crazy.

ANNIE Oh.

INTERIOR. DARKENED BEDROOM—NIGHT.

Alvy and Annie in bed together.

ANNIE   M'm, that was so nice. That was nice.

ALVY   As Balzac said . . .

ANNIE   H'm?

ALVY   . . . "There goes another novel." *(They laugh)* Jesus, you were great.

ANNIE   Oh, yeah?

ALVY   Yeah.

ANNIE   Yeah?

ALVY   Yeah, I'm-I'm-I'm a wreck.

ANNIE   No. *(She turns and looks at Alvy, then laughs)* You're a wreck.

ALVY   Really. I mean it. I-I'll never play the piano again.

ANNIE   *(Lighting a joint and laughing)*   You're really nuts. I don't know, you really thought it was good? Tell me.

ALVY   Good? I was—

ANNIE   *(Overlapping)*   No.

ALVY   No, that was the most fun I've ever had without laughing.

ANNIE   *(Laughing)*   Here, you want some?

ALVY   No, no, I-I-I, uh, I don't use any major hallucinogenics because I took a puff like five years ago at a party and I—

ANNIE   Yeah?

ALVY   —tried to take my pants off over my head . . . *(Annie laughs)* . . . my ear.

ANNIE   Oh, I don't know, I don't really. I don't do it very often, you know, just sort of, er . . . relaxes me at first.

ALVY   M'hm. *(He pushes himself up from the bed and looks down at Annie)* You're not gonna believe this, but—

ANNIE   What? What?

CUT TO:
INTERIOR. BOOKSTORE—DAY.

Annie and Alvy browsing in crowded bookstore. Alvy, carrying two books, Death and Western Thought *and* The Denial of Death, *moves over to where Annie is looking.*

ALVY Hey?

ANNIE H'm?

ALVY I-I-I'm gonna buy you these books, I think, because I-I think you should read them. You know, instead of that cat book.

ANNIE *(Looking at the books Alvy is holding)* That's, uh . . . *(Laughing)* that's pretty serious stuff there.

ALVY Yeah, 'cause I-I'm, you know, I'm, I'm obsessed with-with, uh, with death, I think. Big—

ANNIE *(Overlapping)* Yeah?

ALVY —big subject with me, yeah.

ANNIE Yeah?
They move over to the cashier line.

ALVY *(Gesturing)* I've a very pessimistic view of life. You should know this about me if we're gonna go out, you know. I-I-I feel that life is-is divided up into the horrible and the miserable.

ANNIE M'hm.

ALVY Those are the two categories . . .

ANNIE M'hm.

ALVY . . . you know, they're— The-the horrible would be like, uh, I don't know, terminal cases, you know?

ANNIE M'hm.

ALVY And blind people, crippled . . .

ANNIE Yeah.

ALVY I don't—don't know how they get through life. It's amazing to me.

ANNIE M'hm.

ALVY You know, and the miserable is everyone else. That's—that's all. So-so when you go through life you should be thankful that you're miserable, because that's— You're very lucky . . . to be . . . *(Overlapping Annie's laughter)* . . . to be miserable.

ANNIE U-huh.

EXTERIOR. PARK—DAY.

It's a beautiful sunny day in Central Park. People are sitting on benches, others strolling, some walking dogs. One woman stands feeding cooing pigeons. Alvy's and Annie's voices are heard offscreen as they observe the scene before them. An older man and woman walk into view.

ALVY Look, look at that guy.

ANNIE M'hm.

ALVY There's-there's-there's-there's Mr. When-in-the-Pink, Mr. Miami Beach, there, you know? *(Over Annie's laughter)* He's the latest! Just came back from the gin-rummy farm last night . . . He placed third.

ANNIE *(Laughing)* M'hm. Yeah. Yeah.
The camera shows them sitting side by side relaxed on a bench.

ALVY *(Watching two men approach, one lighting a cigar)* Look at these guys.

ANNIE Yeah.

ALVY Oh, that's hilarious. They're back from Fire Island. They're . . . they're sort of giving it a chance—you know what I mean?

ANNIE Oh! Italian, right?

ALVY Yeah, he's the Mafia. Linen Supply Business or Cement and Contract, you know what I mean?

ANNIE *(Laughing)* Oh, yeah.

ALVY No, I'm serious. *(Over Annie's laughter)* I just got my mustache wet.

ANNIE Oh, yeah?

ALVY *(As another man walks by)* And there's the winner of the Truman Capote look-alike contest.

EXTERIOR. STREET—NIGHT.

Alvy and Annie walk almost in silhouette along the dock, the New York City skyline in the background. Alvy has his arm around Annie and they walk slowly. No one else is around.

ANNIE   You see, like you and I . . .

ALVY   You are extremely sexy.

ANNIE   No, I'm not.

ALVY   Unbelievably sexy. Yes, you are. Because . . . you know what you are? You're-you're polymorphously perverse.

ANNIE   Well, what does—what does that mean? I don't know what that is.

ALVY   Uh . . . uh, you're—you're exceptional in bed because you got —you get pleasure in every part of your body when I touch you.

ANNIE   Ooooh!
They stop walking. Holding Annie's arms, Alvy turns her to face him. The 59th Street Bridge, lit up for the night, is in the background.

ALVY   You know what I mean? Like the tip o' your nose, and if I stroke your teeth or your kneecaps . . . you get excited.

ANNIE   Come on. *(Laughing)* Yeah. You know what? You know, I like you, I really mean it. I really do like you.

ALVY   You— Do you love me?

ANNIE   Do I love you?

ALVY   That's the key question.

ANNIE   Yeah.

ALVY   I know you've only known me a short while.

ANNIE   Well, I certainly . . . I think that's very— Yeah, yeah . . . *(Laughing)* yeah. Do you love me?

ALVY   I—uh, love is, uh, is too weak a word for what—

ANNIE   Yeah.

ALVY   —I . . . I lerve you. *(Over Annie's laughter)* You know I lo-ove you, I-I loff you. *(Over Annie's laughter)* There are two *f*s. I-I have to in-vent— Of course I love you.

ANNIE Yeah.

ALVY *(Putting his arms around her neck)* Don't you think I do?

ANNIE I dunno.
They kiss as a foghorn sounds in the distance.

INTERIOR. ALVY'S APARTMENT.

Alvy, somewhat distraught, is following Annie around his apartment, which is filled with boxes and suitcases, clothes and framed pictures. They both carry cartons.

ALVY Whatta you mean? You're not gonna give up your own apartment, are you?

ANNIE *(Putting down the carton)* Of course.

ALVY Yeah, bu-bu-but why?

ANNIE Well, I mean, I'm moving in with you, that's why.

ALVY Yeah, but you-you got a nice apartment.

ANNIE I have a tiny apartment.

ALVY Yeah, I know it's small.

ANNIE *(Picking up the suitcases and walking into the bedroom)* That's right, and it's got bad plumbing and bugs.

ALVY *(Picking up some pictures and following Annie into the bedroom)* All right, granted, it has bad plumbing and bugs, but you-you say that like it's a negative thing. You know, bugs are-are—uh, entomology is a . . . *(Annie, reacting, tosses the suitcases and some loose clothing onto the bed. She sits down on the edge, looking away. Alvy walks in, pictures and carton in hand, still talking)* . . . rapidly growing field.

ANNIE You don't want me to live with you?

ALVY How— I don't want you to live with me? How— Whose idea was it?

ANNIE Mine.

ALVY Ye-ah. Was it . . . It was yours actually, but, uh, I approved it immediately.

ANNIE I guess you think that I talked you into something, huh?

ALVY *(Putting pictures on the mantel)* No—what, what . . . ? I . . . we live together, we sleep together, we eat together. Jesus, you don't want it to be like we're married, do yuh?
He moves over to the carton of books on the window seat and reaches in. He starts tossing books offscreen.

ANNIE *(Looking up at Alvy)* How is it any different?

ALVY *(Gesturing)* It's different 'cause you keep your own apartment. *(Holding a book, he starts walking around the room)* Because you know it's there, we don't have to go to it, we don't have to deal with it, but it's like a-a-a free-floating life raft . . . that we know that we're not married.
He tosses the book on the bed and walks back to the window seat.

ANNIE *(Still sitting on the bed)* That little apartment is four hundred dollars a month, Alvy.

ALVY *(Looking at Annie)* That place is four hundred dollars a month?

ANNIE Yes, it is.

ALVY *(Whistling)* It's—it's got bad plumbing and bugs. Jesus, I'll— My accountant will write it off as a tax deduction, I'll pay for it.

ANNIE *(Shaking her head)* You don't think I'm smart enough to be serious about.

ALVY Hey, don't be ridiculous.
Alvy moves over to the bed and sits down next to Annie.

ANNIE Then why are you always pushing me to take those college courses like I was dumb or something?

ALVY *(Putting his hand to his forehead)* 'Cause adult education's a wonderful thing. You meet a lotta interesting professors. You know, it's stimulating.

EXTERIOR. COUNTRY HIGHWAY—DAY.

Annie and Alvy, in Annie's VW, driving to their summerhouse. The camera moves with them as they pass a house with a lighted window, blooming foliage. There is no dialogue, but it is a comfortable quiet. Classical music plays in the background.

CUT TO:
INTERIOR. COUNTRY HOUSE—NIGHT.

Annie, sitting cross-legged on a wooden chest in the bedroom, is browsing through a school catalogue. Alvy lies in bed reading.

ANNIE *(Reading)*   Does this sound like a good course? Uh, "Modern American Poetry"? Uh, or, uh—let's see now . . . maybe I should, uh, take "Introduction to the Novel."

ALVY   Just don't take any course where they make you read *Beowulf.*

ANNIE   What? *(Laughing)* Hey, listen, what-what do you think? Do you think we should, uh, go to that-that party in Southampton tonight? *Alvy leans over and kisses her shoulder.*

ALVY   No, don't be silly. What-what do we need other people for? *(He puts his arms around her neck, kissing her, Annie making muffled sounds)* You know, we should—we should just turn out the lights, you know, and play hide and salam or something.

ANNIE *(Laughing)*   Well, okay. Well, listen, I'm gonna get a cigarette, okay?

ALVY *(Yelling out to her as she leaves the room)*   Yeah, grass, right? The illusion that it will make a white woman more like Billie Holiday.

ANNIE *(Offscreen)*   Well, have you ever made love high?

ALVY   Me, no. You . . . I-I—you know, if I have grass or alcohol or anything I get unbearably wonderful. I get too, too wonderful for words. You know, I don't—I don't know why you have to, uh, get high every time we make love.

ANNIE *(Moving back into the room and lighting a joint)*   It relaxes me.

ALVY   Oh, you-you have to be artifically relaxed before we can go to bed?

ANNIE *(Closing the door)*   Well, what's the difference, anyway?

ALVY   Well, I'll give you a shot of sodium pentothal. You can sleep through it.

ANNIE   Oh, come on, look who's talking. You've been seeing a psychiatrist for fifteen years. *(She gets into bed and takes a puff of marijuana)* You should smoke some o' this. You'd be off the couch in no time.

ALVY   Oh, come, you don't need that.
Alvy, sitting down on the bed, moves over to Annie and takes the weed from her.

ANNIE   What are you doing?

ALVY *(Kissing her)*   No, no, no, what . . .   You can once, you can live without it once. Come on.

ANNIE   Oh, no, Alvy, please. Alvy, please. *(Laughing and making sounds)* M'mmm.

ALVY   M'm, wait, I got a great idea. *(He gets up and goes over to the closet, taking out a light bulb. He goes back to the bed and turns out the lamp on the night table)* Hang in there for a second. I got a little-little artifact. A little erotic artifact, that-that I brought up from the city, which I think, uh, is gonna be perfect. *(He turns the lamp back on, having replaced the bulb with the red one from the closet)* I just . . . there . . . There's a little Old New Orleans . . . essence. Now-now we can go about our business here and we can even develop photographs if we want to. There, now there. *(He undresses and crawls into bed, taking Annie in his arms)* M'mmm. M'mmm. Hey, is something wrong?

ANNIE   Uh-uh—why?

ALVY   I don't know. You—   It's like you're—you're removed.

ANNIE   No, I'm fine.
As Annie speaks, her inner self, ghostlike, moves up from the bed and sits down on a chair, watching.

ALVY   Really?

ANNIE   U-huh.

ALVY   I don't know, but you seem sort of distant.

ANNIE   Let's just do it, all right?

ALVY *(Kissing and caressing Annie)*   Is it my imagination or are you just going through the motions?

ANNIE'S SPIRIT   Alvy, do you remember where I put my drawing pad? Because while you two are doing that, I think I'm gonna do some drawing.

ALVY *(Reacting)*   You see, that's what I call removed.

ANNIE Oh, you have my body.

ALVY Yeah, but that's not—that's no good. I want the whole thing.

ANNIE *(Sighing)* Well, I need grass and so do you.

ALVY Well, it ruins it for me if you have grass *(Clearing his throat)* because, you know, I'm, like, a comedian—

ANNIE *(Overlapping)* M'hm.

ALVY *(Overlapping)* —so if I get a laugh from a person who's high, it doesn't count. You know—'cause they're always laughin'.

ANNIE Were you always funny?

ALVY Hey, what is this—an interview? We're supposed to be making love.

CUT TO:
INTERIOR. OFFICE.

A typical old-fashioned theatrical agency in a Broadway office building. Autographed 8 1/2 × 11's plaster the sloppy room. The agent, chewing a cigar, sits behind his desk talking to one of his clients, a comedian, who stands with his hands in his pockets. A young Alvy sits stiffly in a chair nearby watching.

AGENT This guy is naturally funny. I think he can write for you.

COMIC *(Buttoning his jacket)* Yeah, yeah. Hey, kid, he tells me you're really good. Well, lemme explain a little bit o' how I work. You know, you can tell right off the bat that I don't look like a funny guy when I come—you know, like some o' the guys that come out. You know, right away *(Gesturing)* they're gonna tell yuh their stories, you're gonna fall down, but I gotta be really talented. Material's gotta be sensational for me 'cause I work, you know, with very, very . . . Come on, I'm kinda classy, you know what I mean? Uh . . . uh . . . lemme explain. For instance, I open with an opening song. A musical start like *(Ad-lib singing)* and I walk out *(Ad-lib singing)*. "Place looks wonderful from here and you folks look wonderful from here! *(Singing):*
> "And seein' you there
> With a smile on your face
> Makes me shout
> This must be the place."

Then I stop right in the middle and then I open with some jokes. Now, that's where I need you, right there. For instance, like I say,

"Hey, I just got back from Canada, you know, they speak a lotta French up there. The only way to remember Jeanne d'Arc means the light's out in the bathroom!" *(He laughs. Seated Alvy looks up smiling)* "Oh, I met a big lumberjack . . ."

ALVY'S VOICE *(To himself)*   Jesus, this guy's pathetic.

COMIC *(Overlapping above speech)*   ". . . big lumberjack . . ."

ALVY'S VOICE *(To himself while the comic continues his routine)*   Look at him mincing around, like he thinks he's real cute. You wanna throw up. If only I had the nerve to do my own jokes. I don't know how much longer I can keep this smile frozen on my face. I'm in the wrong business, I know it.

COMIC *(Overlapping above speech)*   " 'Cherie, come back. I love you. *(Shaking his lips and mimicking)* But, uh, Cheri, what will I do with this, uh?' He says, 'Aw, Marie, sometime you make me so mad.' " *(Laughing)* Oh, they scream at that. Now, write me somethin' like that, will yuh? Kinda French number, can yuh do it? Huh, kid?

INTERIOR. THEATER—NIGHT.

The darkened auditorium is filled with college students applauding and cheering, excited, as Alvy stands on spotlighted stage holding the microphone.

ALVY *(Gesturing)*   W-where am I? I-I keep . . . I have to reorient myself. This is the University of Wisconsin, right? So I'm always . . . I'm tense and . . . uh, when I'm playin' a col— I've a very bad history with colleges. You know, I went to New York University and, uh, tsch, I was thrown out of NYU my freshman year . . . for cheating on my metaphysics final. You know, I looked within the soul of the boy sitting next to me— *(The audience laughs; they're with him)* —and when I was thrown out, my mother, who's an emotionally high-strung woman, locked herself in the bathroom and took an overdose of mah-jongg tiles. *(More applause and laughter)* And, uh, tsch, I was depressed. I was . . . in analysis, I-I, uh, was suicidal; as a matter of fact, uh, I would have killed myself but I was in analysis with a strict Freudian and if you kill yourself . . . they make you pay for the sessions you miss.

INTERIOR. BACKSTAGE OF THEATER.
Students mill around Alvy handing him pens and paper for autographs. Annie is next to him, talking over the chattering fans.

ANNIE   Alvy, you were . . .   Alvy, you were just great. I'm not kidding. It was—   You were so neat.

ALVY   C-c-coll—   College audiences are so wonderful.

ANNIE   Yeah. Yeah. And you know something? I think that I'm starting to get more of your references, too.

ALVY   Are yuh?

ANNIE   Yeah.

ALVY   Well, the twelve o'clock show is completely different than the
nine.

YOUNG WOMAN *(Interrupting)*   May I have your autograph?

ANNIE *(Overlapping above speech)*   Oh.

ALVY *(To Annie, while autographing)*   You're so sure about it.

ANNIE   Oh, I'm really, uh, looking forward to tomorrow. I mean, you
know, I think that it'll be really nice to meet Mother and Father.
*They start moving toward the exit, a girl snapping a picture of Alvy with
a flash camera as they walk through the crowd.*

ALVY   Yeah, I know, they'll hate me immediately. *(To one of his fans)*
Thank you.

ANNIE   No, I don't think so. No, I don't think they're gonna hate you
at all. On the contrary, I think—

ALVY   Yeah.

ANNIE   It's Easter. You know, we'll have a nice dinner, we'll sit down
and eat. I think they're gonna really like you.

EXTERIOR. ANNIE'S PARENTS' HOME—DAY.

*The camera shows a neat two-story house surrounded by a well-manicured
green lawn, then cuts to:*

INTERIOR. DINING ROOM.

*Alvy and the Halls are eating Easter dinner. The sun is pouring through a
big picture window, shining on a large, elegantly laid out table. Alvy sits,
at one end, rubbing his nose and chewing, the Halls flanking him on either
side: Mr. and Mrs. Hall, Grammy, and Annie's brother, Duane.*

MOM HALL *(Holding her wine glass)* It's a nice ham this year, Mom.
Grammy Hall takes a sip of her wine and nods.

ANNIE *(Smiling at Duane)* Oh, yeah. Grammy always does such a good
job.

DAD HALL *(Chewing)* A great sauce.

ALVY It is. *(Smacking his lips)* It's dynamite ham.
*Grammy Hall stares down the table at Alvy; a look of utter dislike. Alvy
tries not to notice.*

MOM HALL *(To Dad Hall, smoothing her hair)* We went over to the swap
meet. Annie, Gram and I. Got some nice picture frames.

ANNIE We really had a good time.
*Grammy continues to stare at Alvy; he is now dressed in the long black coat
and hat of the Orthodox Jew, complete with mustache and beard.*

MOM HALL *(Lighting a cigarette and turning to Alvy)* Ann tells us that
you've been seeing a psychiatrist for fifteen years.

ALVY *(Setting down his glass and coughing)* Yes. I'm making excellent
progress. Pretty soon when I lie down on his couch, I won't have
to wear the lobster bib.
*Mom Hall reacts by sipping from her glass and frowning. Grammy continues
to stare.*

DAD HALL   Duane and I went out to the boat basin.

DUANE   We were caulkin' holes all day.

DAD HALL   Yeah. *(Laughing)* Randolph Hunt was drunk, as usual.

MOM HALL   Oh, that Randolph Hunt. You remember Randy Hunt, Annie. He was in the choir with you.

ANNIE   Oh, yes, yes.
Alvy, leaning his elbow on the table, looks out toward the camera.

ALVY *(To the audience)*   I can't believe this family. *(Making chewing sounds)* Annie's mother. She really's beautiful. And they're talkin' swap meets and boat basins, and the old lady at the end of the table *(Pointing to Grammy)* is a classic Jew hater. And, uh, they, they really look American, you know, very healthy and . . . like they never get sick or anything. Nothing like my family. You know, the two are like oil and water.
The screen splits in half: on the right is Alvy's family—his mother, father, aunt and uncle—busily eating at the crowded kitchen table. They eat quickly and interrupt one another loudly. On the left the Halls in their dining room. Both dialogues overlap, juxtaposed.

ALVY'S FATHER   Aw, let 'im drop dead! Who needs his business?!

ALVY'S MOTHER   His wife has diabetes!

ALVY'S FATHER   Di-diabetes? Is that any excuse? Diabetes?

ALVY'S UNCLE   The man is fifty years old and doesn't have a substantial job.

ALVY'S AUNT *(Putting more meat on her husband's plate)*   Is that a reason to steal from his father?

ALVY'S UNCLE   Whatta you talkin' about? You don't know what you're talking about.

ALVY'S AUNT   Yes, I know what I'm talking about.

ALVY'S MOTHER *(Interrupting)*   George, defend him!

ALVY'S UNCLE *(Over Alvy's father's muttering)*   No Moskowitz he had a coronary.

ALVY'S AUNT   You don't say.

ALVY'S MOTHER   We fast.

MOM HALL   Stupid Thelma Poindexter . . . to the Veterans Hospital.

DAD HALL   My God, he's the new president of the El Regis. Let me tell you, the man is somethin' else.

MOM HALL   That's Jack's wife. We used to make that outta raisins—

ANNIE   Oh, yes, that's right. Did you see the new play?

MOM HALL   Oh, you remember her, Annie.

ANNIE   Yes, I do.
The two families start talking back and forth to one another. The screen is still split.

MOM HALL   How do you plan to spend the holidays, Mrs. Singer?

DAD HALL   Fast?

ALVY'S FATHER   Yeah, no food. You know, we have to atone for our sins.

MOM HALL   What sins? I don't understand.

ALVY'S FATHER   Tell you the truth, neither do we.

CUT TO:
INTERIOR. DUANE'S BEDROOM—NIGHT.

Duane, sitting on his bed, sees Alvy walking past the open door.

DUANE   Alvy.

ALVY *(Walking in)*   Oh, hi, Duane, how's it goin'?

DUANE   This is my room.

ALVY *(Looking around)*   Oh, yeah? *(He clears his throat)* Terrific.

DUANE   Can I confess something?
Alvy sighs and sits down, leaning his arm on Duane's dresser. Duane's face is highlighted by a single lamp.

DUANE   I tell you this because, as an artist, I think you'll understand. Sometimes when I'm driving . . . on the road at night . . . I see two headlights coming toward me. Fast. I have this sudden impulse to turn the wheel quickly, head-on into the oncoming car. I can anticipate the explosion. The sound of shattering glass. The . . . flames rising out of the flowing gasoline.

ALVY *(Reacting and clearing his throat)* Right. Tsch, well, I have to—I have to go now, Duane, because I-I'm due back on the planet earth. *He slowly gets up and moves toward the door.*

INTERIOR. THE HALLS' LIVING ROOM.

Mom and Dad Hall walk into the living room; Annie is with them.

MOM HALL Now, don't let it be so long, now.

ANNIE No.

DAD HALL And look up Uncle Bill, you promise.

ANNIE Okay. Okay.

MOM HALL Oh, he's adorable, Annie.

ANNIE You think so? Do you really?

MOM HALL We're going to take them to the airport.

DAD HALL Oh, no—Duane can. I haven't finished my drink.

ANNIE Yes, Duane is. I'll be right—

MOM HALL M'mmm.

ANNIE I just have time to get the, uh—
She walks out of the room as Mom and Dad Hall kiss.

EXTERIOR. ROAD—NIGHT.

Duane, behind the wheel, stares straight ahead. It is raining very hard, the windshield wipers are moving quickly. The headlights of another car brightens the interior of Duane's car as the camera shows first Duane, then Annie, then Alvy tensely staring straight ahead.

EXTERIOR. STREET—DAY.

The camera holds on a quiet New York City street; the buildings, brownstones. It's a warm day—people sit on front stoops, window boxes are planted. Annie walks into the frame first, then Alvy, who is walking to her right. They walk quickly, side by side, their voices heard before they move into the frame.

ANNIE *(Offscreen)* You followed me. I can't believe it!

ALVY *(Offscreen)* I didn't follow you!

ANNIE   You followed me!

ALVY   Why? 'Cause I . . . was walkin' along a block behind you staring at you? That's not following!

ANNIE   Well, what is your definition of following?

ALVY   *(Gasping)*   Following is different. I was spying.

ANNIE   Do you realize how paranoid you are?

ALVY   Paranoid? I'm looking at you. You got your arms around another guy.

ANNIE   That is the worst kind of paranoia.

ALVY   Yeah—well, I didn't start out spying. I-I thought I'd surprise yuh. Pick you up after school.

ANNIE   Yeah—well, you wanted to keep the relationship flexible, remember? It's your phrase.

ALVY   Oh, stop it. But you were having an affair with your college professor. That jerk that teaches that incredible crap course "Contemporary Crisis in Western Man"!

ANNIE   'S—"Existential Motifs in Russian Literature"! You're really close.

ALVY   What's the difference? It's all mental masturbation.

ANNIE   *(Stopping for a moment)*   Oh, well, now we're finally getting to a subject you know something about!
She walks away.

ALVY   *(Catching up to her)*   Hey, don't knock masturbation! It's sex with someone I love.

ANNIE   *(Continuing to walk quickly)*   We're not having an affair. He's married. He just happens to think I'm neat.

ALVY   *(Still walking next to her)*   "Neat"! There's that— What are you —twelve years old? That's one o' your Chippewa Falls expressions! "He thinks I'm neat."

ANNIE   Who cares? Who cares?

ALVY   Next thing you know he'll find you keen and peachy, you know? Next thing you know he's got his hand on your ass!
They both stop in the middle of the street.

ANNIE   You've always had hostility toward David ever since I mentioned him!

ALVY   David? You call your teacher David?

ANNIE   It's his name.

ALVY   Well, listen, that's, a nice bi—it's a biblical name. Right? W-What does he call you? Bathsheba?
He walks away.

ANNIE   *(Calling after him)*   Alvy! Alvy! You're the one who never wanted to make a real commitment. You don't think I'm smart enough! We had that argument just last month, or don't you remember that day?

CUT TO:
INTERIOR. KITCHEN.

Alvy is at the sink washing dishes as the screen cuts to the scene of last month's argument. Annie's voice is heard.

ANNIE   *(Offscreen)*   I'm home!

ALVY *(Turning)* Oh, yeah? How'd it go?

ANNIE *(Comes into the kitchen and puts down a bag of groceries on the kitchen table)* Oh, it was . . . *(Laughing)* really weird. But she's a very nice woman.

ALVY Yeah?

ANNIE And I didn't have to lie down on the couch, Alvy, she had me sitting up. So I told her about—about the-the family and about my feelings toward men and about my relationship with my brother.

ALVY M'm.

ANNIE And then she mentioned penis envy . . . Did you know about that?

ALVY Me? I'm—I'm one of the few males who suffers from that, so, so . . . you know.

ANNIE M'hm.

ALVY G-go on, I'm interested.

ANNIE Well, she said that I was very guilty about my impulses toward marriage, and-and children.

ALVY M'hm.

ANNIE And then I remembered when I was a kid how I accidentally saw my parents making love.

ALVY Tsch. Rea— All this happened in the first hour?

ANNIE M'hm.

ALVY That's amazing. I-I-I . . . I've been goin' for fifteen years, I—you know, I don't got . . . nothing like that in—

ANNIE Oh, I told her my dream and then I cried.

ALVY You cried? I've never once cried. Fantastic . . .

ANNIE *(Taking groceries from the bag)* Yeah.

ALVY I whine. I-I-I sit and I whine.

ANNIE In-in . . . Alvy, in my dream Frank Sinatra is holding his pillow across my face and I can't breathe.

ALVY Sinatra?

ANNIE   Yeah, and he's strangling me . . .

ALVY   Yeah?

ANNIE   . . . and I keep, you know, it's—

ALVY   *(Taking a bottle of juice and some celery from the bag)*   Well, well, sure . . . because he's a singer and you're a singer, you know, so it's perfect. So you're trying to suffocate yourself. It-it makes perfect sense. Uh, uh, that's a perfect analytic . . . kind of insight.

ANNIE   *(Pointing her finger at Alvy)*   She said, your name was Alvy Singer.

ALVY   *(Turning to Annie)*   Whatta you mean? Me?

ANNIE   Yeah, yeah, yeah, you. Because in the dream . . . I break Sinatra's glasses.

ALVY   *(Putting his hand to his mouth)*   Sinatra had gl—   You never said Sinatra had glasses. So whatta you saying that I-I'm suffocating you?

ANNIE   *(Turning, a jar in her hand)*   Oh, and God, Alvy, I did . . . this really terrible thing to him. Because then when he sang it was in this real high-pitched voice.

ALVY   *(Thinking)*   Tsch, what'd the doctor say?

ANNIE   *(Putting away some groceries)*   Well, she said that I should probably come five times a week. And you know something? I don't think I mind analysis at all. The only question is, Will it change my wife?

ALVY   Will it change your wife?

ANNIE   Will it change my life?

ALVY   Yeah, but you said, "Will it change my wife"!

ANNIE   No, I didn't. *(Laughing)* I said, "Will it change my life," Alvy.

ALVY   You said, "Will it change . . ." Wife. Will it change . . .

ANNIE   *(Yelling out, angry)*   Life. I said, "life."
Alvy turns toward the camera.

ALVY   *(To the audience)*   She said, "Will it change my wife." You heard that because you were there so I'm not crazy.

ANNIE   And, Alvy . . . and then I told her about how I didn't think you'd ever really take me seriously, because you don't think that I'm smart enough.
She walks out of the room.

ALVY *(To Annie's back, gesturing)*   Why do you always bring that up? Because I encourage you to take adult-education courses? I think it's a wonderful thing. You meet wonderful, interesting professors.

CUT TO:
EXTERIOR. STREET.

Annie stands at the open door of a cab, Alvy next to her gesturing as people and cars move by.

ALVY   Adult education is such junk! The professors are so phony. How can you do it?

ANNIE   I don't care what you say about David, he's a perfectly fine teacher!

ALVY *(Interrupting)*   David! David! I can't believe this!

ANNIE   And what are you doing following me around for, anyway?

ALVY   I'm following you and David, if you—

ANNIE *(Interrupting)*   I just think we oughta call this relationship quits!
Annie gets into the cab; Alvy leans over and closes the door.

ALVY   That's fine. That's fine. That's great! *(He turns toward the camera as the cab drives away)* Well, I don't know what I did wrong. *(Gesturing)* I mean, I can't believe this. Somewhere she cooled off to me! *(He walks up to an older woman walking down the street carrying groceries)* Is it—is it something that I did?

WOMAN ON THE STREET   Never something you do. That's how people are. Love fades.
She moves on down the street.

ALVY *(Scratching his head)*   Love fades. God, that's a depressing thought. I-I-I-I have to ask you a question. *(He stops another passer-by, a man)* Don't go any further. Now, with your wife in bed, d-d-does she need some kind o' artificial stimulation like-like marijuana?

MAN ON THE STREET   We use a large vibrating egg.
He walks on.

ALVY *(Continuing to walk)*   Large vibrating egg. Well, I ask a psychopath, I get that kind of an answer. Jesus, I-I, uh, here . . . *(He moves up the sidewalk to a young trendy-looking couple, arms wrapped around each other)* You-you look like a really happy couple. Uh, uh . . . are you?

YOUNG WOMAN   Yeah.

ALVY   Yeah! So . . . so h-h-how do you account for it?

YOUNG WOMAN   Uh, I'm very shallow and empty and I have no ideas and nothing interesting to say.

YOUNG MAN   And I'm exactly the same way.

ALVY   I see. Well, that's very interesting. So you've managed to work out something, huh?

YOUNG MAN   Right.

YOUNG WOMAN   Yeah.

ALVY   Oh, well, thanks very much for talking to me.
He continues to walk past some other passers-by and moves into the street. A mounted policeman comes by and stops near him. Alvy looks at the horse, as if to speak.

ALVY'S VOICE-OVER   You know, even as a kid I always went for the wrong women. I think that's my problem. When my mother took me to see *Snow White*, everyone fell in love with Snow White. I immediately fell for the Wicked Queen.
The scene dissolves into a sequence from the animated Snow White and the Seven Dwarfs. *The Wicked Queen, resembling Annie, sits in the palace before her mirror. Alvy, as a cartoon figure, sits beside her, arms crossed in front of him.*

WICKED QUEEN   We never have any fun anymore.

CARTOON FIGURE ALVY   How can you say that?

WICKED QUEEN   Why not? You're always leaning on me to improve myself.

CARTOON FIGURE ALVY   You're just upset. You must be getting your period.

WICKED QUEEN   I don't get a period! I'm a cartoon character. Can't I be upset once in a while?
Rob, as a cartoon figure, enters and sits down on the other side of the Wicked Queen.

CARTOON FIGURE ROB Max, will you forget about Annie? I know lots of women you can date.

CARTOON FIGURE ALVY I don't wanna go out with any other women.

CARTOON FIGURE ROB Max, have I got a girl for you. You are going to love her. She's a reporter—
The cartoon figures of Alvy and Rob walk past the Wicked Queen; the screen dissolves into the interior of a concert hall. Rob's voice carries over from the cartoon scene as the screen shows Alvy with the female reporter. It's very crowded, noisy; policeman and reporters are everywhere. Alvy stands with his hands in his pockets, watching the commotion.

CARTOON FIGURE ROB'S VOICE-OVER —for *Rolling Stone.*

FEMALE REPORTER I think there are more people here to see the Maharishi than there were to see the Dylan concert. I covered the Dylan concert . . . which gave me chills. Especially when he sang "She takes just like a woman And she makes love just like a woman Yes, she does And she aches just like a woman But she breaks just like a little girl." *(They move toward the aisles as a guard holds up his hands to stop them)* Up to that I guess the most charismatic event I covered was Mick's Birthday when the Stones played Madison Square Garden.

ALVY *(Laughing)* Man, that's great. That's just great.

REPORTER You catch Dylan?

ALVY *(Coughing)* Me? No, no. I-I couldn't make it that ni— My-my raccoon had hepatitis.

REPORTER You have a raccoon?

ALVY *(Gesturing)* Tsch, a few.

REPORTER The only word for this is trans-plendid. It's trans-plendid.

ALVY I can think of another word.

REPORTER He's God! I mean, this man is God! He's got millions of followers who would crawl all the way across the world just to touch the hem of his garment.

ALVY Really? It must be a tremendous hem.

REPORTER I'm a Rosicrucian myself.

ALVY   Are you?

REPORTER   Yeah.

ALVY   I can't get with any religion that advertises in *Popular Mechanics.*
Look— *(The Maharishi, a small, chunky man, walks out of the men's room,*
huge bodyguards flanking him while policemen hold back the crowds)—
there's God coming outta the men's room.

REPORTER   It's unbelievably trans-plendid! I was at the Stones concert
in Altamount when they killed that guy, remember?

ALVY   Yeah, were yuh? I was—I was at an Alice Cooper thing where
six people were rushed to the hospital with bad vibes.

INTERIOR. ALVY'S BEDROOM—NIGHT.

The reporter is sitting up in bed, lighted cigarette in her hand. Alvy, lying
next to her, rubs his eyes and puts on his eyeglasses.

REPORTER   *(Looking down at herself)*   I hope you don't mind that I took
so long to finish.

ALVY   *(Sighing)*   Oh, no, no, don't be . . . tsch . . . don't be silly. You
know, *(Yawning)* I'm startin' t'—I'm startin' to get some feeling back
in my jaw now.

REPORTER   Oh, sex with you is really a Kafkaesque experience.

ALVY   Oh, tsch, thank you. H'm.

REPORTER   I mean that as a compliment.

ALVY   *(Making sounds)*   I think—I think there's too much burden placed
on the orgasm, you know, to make up for empty areas in life.

REPORTER   Who said that?

ALVY   *(Rubbing his chin and shoulder)*   Uh, oh, I don't know. It might
have been Leopold and Loeb. *(The telephone rings. Alvy picks it up,*
rising up slightly from the bed, concerned, as he talks) Hello . . . Oh, hi
. . . Uh, no, what—what's the matter? What-what-what . . . You
sound terrible . . . No, what— Sure I— Whatta yuh—what kind
of an emergency? . . . No, well, stay there. Stay there, I'll come over
right now. I'll come over right now. Just stay there, I'll come right
over.
He hangs up. The reporter sits in bed still, taking in the situation.

INTERIOR. ANNIE'S APARTMENT. HALLWAY.

Annie, looking slightly distraught, goes to open the door to Alvy's knock.

ALVY   What's— It's me, open up.

ANNIE *(Opening the door)*   Oh.

ALVY   Are you okay? What's the matter? *(They look at each other, Annie sighing)* Are you all right? What—

ANNIE   There's a spider in the bathroom.

ALVY *(Reacting)*   What?

ANNIE   There's a big black spider in the bathroom.

ALVY   That's what you got me here for at three o'clock in the morning, 'cause there's a spider in the bathroom?

ANNIE   My God, I mean, you know how I am about insects—

ALVY *(Interrupting, sighing)*   Oooh.

ANNIE   —I can't sleep with a live thing crawling around in the bathroom.

ALVY   Kill it! For Go— What's wrong with you? Don't you have a can of Raid in the house?

ANNIE *(Shaking her head)*   No.
Alvy, disgusted, starts waving his hands and starts to move into the living room.

ALVY *(Sighing)*   I told you a thousand times you should always keep, uh, a lotta insect spray. You never know who's gonna crawl over.

ANNIE *(Following him)*   I know, I know, and a first-aid kit and a fire extinguisher.

ALVY   Jesus. All right, gimme a magazine. I— 'cause I'm a little tired. *(While Annie goes off to find him a magazine, Alvy, still talking, glances around the apartment. He notices a small book on a cabinet and picks it up.)* You know, you, you joke with—about me, you make fun of me, but I'm prepared for anything. An emergency, a tidal wave, an earthquake. Hey, what is this? What? Did you go to a rock concert?

ANNIE   Yeah.

ALVY   Oh, yeah, really? Really? How-how'd you like it? Was it—was it, I mean, did it . . . was it heavy? Did it achieve total heavy-ocity? Or was it, uh . . .

ANNIE   It was just great!

ALVY   *(Thumbing through the book)*   Oh, humdinger. When— Well, I got a wonderful idea. Why don'tcha get the guy who took you to the rock concert, we'll call him and he can come over and kill the spider. You know, it's a—
He tosses the book down on the cabinet.

ANNIE   I called you; you wanna help me . . . or not? H'h? Here.
She hands him a magazine.

ALVY   *(Looking down at the magazine)*   What is this? What are you— Since when do you read the *National Review?* What are you turning into?

ANNIE   *(Turning to a nearby chair for some gum in her pocketbook)*   Well, I like to try to get all points of view.

ALVY   It's wonderful. Then why don'tcha get William F. Buckley to kill the spider?

ANNIE *(Spinning around to face him)* Alvy, you're a little hostile, you know that? Not only that, you look thin and tired.
She puts a piece of gum in her mouth.

ALVY Well, I was in be— It's three o'clock in the morning. You, uh, you got me outta bed, I ran over here, I couldn't get a taxi cab. You said it was an emergency, and I didn't ge— I ran up the stairs. Bel — I was a lot more attractive when the evening began. Look, uh, tell— Whatta you— Are you going with a right-wing rock-and-roll star? Is that possible?

ANNIE *(Sitting down on a chair arm and looking up at Alvy)* Would you like a glass of chocolate milk?

ALVY Hey, what am I—your son? Whatta you mean? I-I came over t'—

ANNIE *(Touching his chest with her hand)* I got the good chocolate, Alvy.

ALVY Yeah, where is the spider?

ANNIE It really is lovely. It's in the bathroom.

ALVY Is he in the bathroom?

ANNIE *(Rising from chair)* Hey, don't squish it, and after it's dead, flush it down the toilet, okay? And flush it a couple o' times.

ALVY *(Moving down the hallway to the bathroom)* Darling, darling, I've been killing spiders since I was thirty, okay?

ANNIE *(Upset, hands on her neck)* Oh. What?

ALVY *(Coming back into the living room)* Very big spider.

ANNIE Yeah?

ALVY Two . . . Yeah. Lotta, lotta trouble. There's two of 'em.
Alvy starts walking down the hall again, Annie following.

ANNIE Two?

ALVY *(Opening a closet door)* Yep. I didn't think it was that big, but it's a major spider. You got a broom or something with a—

ANNIE Oh, I-I left it at your house.

ALVY *(Overlapping)* —snow shovel or anything or something.

ANNIE *(Overlapping)*   I think I left it there, I'm sorry.
Reaching up into the closet, Alvy takes out a covered tennis racquet.

ALVY *(Holding the racquet)*   Okay, let me have this.

ANNIE   Well, what are you doing . . . what are you doing with—

ALVY   Honey, there's a spider in your bathroom the size of a Buick.
He walks into the bathroom, Annie looking after him.

ANNIE   Well, okay. Oooh.
*Alvy stands in the middle of the bathroom, tennis racquet in one hand, rolled
magazine in the other. He looks over at the shelf above the sink and picks up
a small container. He holds it out, shouting offscreen to Annie.*

ALVY   Hey, what is this? You got black soap?

ANNIE *(Offscreen)*   It's for my complexion.

ALVY   Whatta—whatta yuh joining a minstrel show? Geez. *(Alvy turns
and starts swapping the racquet over the shelf, knocking down articles and
breaking glass)* Don't worry! *(He continues to swat the racquet all over the
bathroom. He finally moves out of the room, hands close to his body. He walks
into the other room, where Annie is sitting in a corner of her bed leaning
against the wall)* I did it! I killed them both. What-what's the matter?
Whatta you— *(Annie is sobbing, her hand over her face)*—whatta you sad
about? You—   What'd you want me to do? Capture 'em and rehabil-
itate 'em?

ANNIE *(Sobbing and taking Alvy's arm)*   Oh, don't go, okay? Please.

ALVY *(Sitting down next to her)*   Whatta you mean, don't go? Whatta-
whatta-what's the matter? Whatta you expecting—termites? What's
the matter?

ANNIE *(Sobbing)*   Oh, uh, I don't know. I miss you. Tsch.
*She beats her fist on the bed. Reacting, Alvy puts his arm around her shoulder
and leans back against the wall.*

ALVY   Oh, Jesus, really?

ANNIE *(Leaning on his shoulder)*   Oh, yeah. Oh. *(They kiss)* Oh! Alvy?

ALVY   What?
He touches her face gently as she wipes tears from her face.

ANNIE   Was there somebody in your room when I called you?

ALVY   W-w-whatta you mean?

ANNIE   I mean was there another—   I thought I heard a voice.

ALVY   Oh, I had the radio on.

ANNIE   Yeah?

ALVY   I'm sorry. I had the television set . . . I had the television—

ANNIE   Yeah.
Alvy pulls her to him and they kiss again.

CUT TO:
INTERIOR—ALVY'S BED.

Alvy is lying in bed next to Annie, who is leaning on her elbow looking down at him. He rubs her arms and she smiles.

ANNIE   Alvy, let's never break up again. I don't wanna be apart.

ALVY   Oh, no, no, I think we're both much too mature for something like that.

ANNIE   Living together hasn't been so bad, has it?

ALVY   It's all right for me, it's been terrific, you know? Better than either one of my marriages. See, 'cause . . . 'cause there's just something different about you. I don't know what it is, but it's great.

ANNIE *(Snickering)*   You know I think that if you let me, maybe I could help you have more fun, you know? I mean, I know it's hard and . . .   Yeah.

ALVY   I don't know.

ANNIE   Alvy, what about . . . what if we go away this weekend, and we could—

ALVY   Tsch, why don't we get . . . why don't we get Rob, and the three of us'll drive into Brooklyn, you know, and we show you the old neighborhood.

ANNIE   Okay, okay. Okay.

ALVY   That'd be fun for yuh. Don't you think—

ANNIE   Yeah.
Alvy raises up his head and they kiss.

EXTERIOR. HIGHWAY.

Annie is behind the wheel in her VW, Rob is beside her, Alvy in the back seat leaning forward so that his head is between them. They're driving down the highway.

ANNIE   —me, my God, it's a great day!

ALVY *(Interrupting)*   Hey, can yuh watch the road? Watch the—

ROB *(Overlapping)*   Yeah, watch the road!

ALVY   You'll total the whole car.

ANNIE *(Laughing)*   Hey, you know, I never even visited Brooklyn before.

ROB   I can't wait to see the old neighborhood.

ALVY   Yeah, the neighborhood's gonna be great.

ROB   We can show her the schoolyard.

ALVY   Right. I was a great athlete. Tell her, Max, I was the best, I was all schoolyard.

ROB   Yes, I remember. *(Annie laughs)* He was all schoolyard. They threw him a football once, he tried to dribble it.

ALVY   Yeah, well, I used to lose my glasses a lot.

EXTERIOR. AMUSEMENT PARK.

Alvy, Annie and Rob move toward the roller coaster on the screen. The area's deserted. Sea gulls are heard.

ALVY   Oh, look, look, there's that . . . that's—that's my old house. That's where I used to live.

ANNIE *(Laughing)*   Holy cow!

ROB   You're lucky, Max—where I used to live is now a pornographic equipment store.
Annie laughs.

ALVY   I have some very good memories there.

ROB   What kind of good memories, Max? Your mother and father fighting all the time.

ALVY   Yeah, and always over the most ridiculous things.

FLASHBACK—INTERIOR. ALVY'S HOUSE.

Alvy's father sits in his chair. His mother is polishing a door while young Alvy lies on the floor playing. Annie, adult Alvy and Rob quietly walk into the scene to watch.

ALVY'S FATHER You fired the cleaning woman?

ALVY'S MOTHER She was stealing.

ALVY'S FATHER But she's colored.

ALVY'S MOTHER So?

ALVY'S FATHER So the colored have enough trouble.

ALVY'S MOTHER She was going through my pocketbook!

ALVY'S FATHER They're persecuted enough!

ALVY'S MOTHER Who's persecuting? She stole!
Alvy's father gets up and gets his hard hat. He sits back down and starts polishing it.

ALVY'S FATHER All right—so we can afford it.

ALVY'S MOTHER How can we afford it? On your pay? What if she steals more?

ALVY'S FATHER She's a colored woman, from Harlem! She has no money! She's got a right to steal from us! After all, who is she gonna steal from if not us?

ADULT ALVY *(Yelling into the scene)* You're both crazy!

ROB They can't hear you, Max.

ALVY'S MOTHER Leo . . . I married a fool!

ROB *(Pointing)* Hey, Max! Who's that?
As the three friends watch Alvy's old living room, the scene has suddenly shifted. A huge crowd stands around the room, laughing, eating, chatting and vibrating with the turns of the roller-coaster ride.

ALVY It-it-it's the welcome-home party in nineteen forty-five, for my cousin Herbie.

ADULT ALVY *(Pointing)* Look, look, there's—there's that one over there, that's Joey Nichols, he was my—*(Young Alvy stands next to Joey Nichols, who's sitting in one of the easy chairs. They smile at each other; people and noise all around)*—father's friend. He was always bothering me when I was a kid.

JOEY   Joey Nichols. *(Laughing)* See, Nichols. See, Nichols! *(Joey shows young Alvy his cuff links and tie pin, which are made from nickels, as Alvy stands with hands on hips, unconcerned. Joey then slaps his hand to his forehead and puts a nickel on his forehead)* Yuh see, nickels! You can always remember my name, just think of Joey Five Cents. *(Laughing)* That's me. Joey Five Cents!
Joey grabs Alvy's cheeks and pinches them.

YOUNG ALVY *(Turning away)*   What an asshole!
A group of women stands near a buffet table eating and listening to Alvy's mother and her sister, Tessie, and a young girl, as the three friends watch.

ADULT ALVY   The one who killed me the most was my mother's sister, Tessie.

ALVY'S MOTHER   I was always the sister with good common sense. But Tessie was always the one with personality. When she was younger, they all wanted to marry Tessie.
She touches Tessie's shoulder. Tessie starts to laugh.

ADULT ALVY *(Pointing, to Rob)*   Do you believe that, Max? Tessie Moskowitz had the personality. She's the life of the ghetto, no doubt.

ALVY'S MOTHER *(To the young girl)* She was once a great beauty.
Tessie nods her head "yes."

ROB Tessie, they say you were the sister with personality.

TESSIE *(Addressing the young girl)* I was a great beauty.

ROB Uh, how did this personality come about?

TESSIE *(Grabbing the young girl's cheek)* I was very charming.

ROB There were many men interested in you?

TESSIE *(To the young girl)* Oh, I was quite a lively dancer.
*Tessie gyrates back and forth imitating a dancer while Annie and the adult
Alvy lean on each other laughing.*

ROB *(Laughing)* That's pretty hard to believe.

EXTERIOR. STREET.

*Alvy and Annie walk contentedly down a street; Alvy's arm is draped
around Annie. People walk by them on the street as they move toward their
apartment building.*

ANNIE Well, I had a really good day, you know that? It was just a real
fine way to spend my birthday.

ALVY Ah? Oh, well, your birthday's not till tomorrow, honey, I hate
to tell yuh.

ANNIE Yeah, but it's real close.

ALVY Yeah, but no presents till midnight.

ANNIE *(Laughing)* Oh, darn it.

INTERIOR. APARTMENT.

*Annie and Alvy sit on the sofa. Annie's unwrapping a gift while Alvy
watches.*

ANNIE *(Making sounds)* This is—*(Making sounds)* Huh?
She pulls out flimsy black lingerie from the box.

ALVY Happy birthday.

ANNIE What is this? Is this a . . . present? *(Laughing)* Are you kidding?

FOUR FILMS OF WOODY ALLEN

ALVY   Yeah, hey, why don't yuh try it on?

ANNIE   Uh, yeah, uh . . . t-t-this is more like a present for you, yeah, but it's—

ALVY   Try it . . . it'll add years to our sex life.

ANNIE   *(Looking up at Alvy and laughing)*   Uh huh. Yeah. Forget it.
Alvy leans over and hands her another box as she puts down the lingerie.

ALVY   Here's a real present.

ANNIE   *(Opening the gift)*   What . . . oh, yeah? What is this, anyway, huh?

ALVY   Check it out.

ANNIE   Let me see. Okay, let's . . . oooh, God! *(She takes out a watch from the box)* Oh, you knew I wanted this . . . *(Laughing)* God, it's terrific, God!

ALVY   *(Making sounds)*   Yeah, I know. Just-just put on the watch, and-and . . . that thing, and we'll just . . .

ANNIE   *(Laughing)*   Oh! My God! *(Making sounds)*
Alvy kisses Annie.

INTERIOR. NIGHT CLUB.

Annie, spotlighted onstage, stands in front of the microphone, smiling. She looks downward and sings "Seems Like Old Times." The audience applauds loudly as the music fades out.

ANNIE *(Laughing)* Thank you.
Alvy sits at the bar, clapping and staring at Annie as she walks over to him and sits down. The low murmur of the night club is surrounding them.

ALVY *(Reacting)* You were—you were sensational. I mean, I—you know, I-I told yuh that if yuh stuck to it, you would be great, and-and, you know, I-I—you-you were sensational.

ANNIE *(Looking at Alvy, smiling)* Yeah, well, we have the, I mean, they were just a terrific audience, I mean, you know, it makes it really easy for me, because I can be . . . huh?
Tony, a famous record personality, pushes through the crowd, moving toward Alvy and Annie. An entourage follows him as he makes his way to their table.

TONY Excuse me.
He shakes hands with Annie, smiling.

ANNIE Oh.

TONY Hi, I'm—I'm Tony Lacey.

ANNIE Well, hi!

TONY Uh, we just wanted to stop by and say that we really enjoyed your sets.

ANNIE *(Laughing)* Oh, yeah, really, oh!

TONY I though it was . . . very musical, and I—I liked it a lot.

ANNIE Oh, neat . . . oh, that's very nice, gosh, thanks a lot.

TONY Are you . . . are you recording? Or do— Are you with any label now?

ANNIE Me? *(Laughing)* No, no, no, not at all.

TONY Uh, well, I'd like to talk to you about that sometime, if you get a chance.
Seated Alvy looks the other way, reacting.

ANNIE Oh. What about?

TONY . . . of possibly working together.

ANNIE *(Looking for the first time at Alvy)* Well, hey, that's, that's nice. Uh. Oh, listen, this is, uh, Alvy Singer. Do you know Alvy? Uh . . . and . . . uh . . . Tony Lacey.

TONY No, I don't—I don't know, but I-I know your work. I'm a big fan of yours.
Tony reaches over and shakes hands with Alvy. The night-club crowd surrounds them all with their low chatter and cigarette smoke.

ALVY Thank you very much. It's a pleasure.

TONY *(Turning to introduce his entourage)* This is, uh, Shawn, and, uh . . . Bob and Petronia.

ANNIE Hi.

ENTOURAGE Hi.

ANNIE *(Laughing)* Hi, hi, Bob . . .

TONY Uh . . . w-we're going back to the Pierre. We're staying at the Pierre . . . and we're gonna meet Jack and Angelica, and have a drink there, and . . . if you'd like to come, uh, we'd love to have you.

ANNIE Yeah.

TONY And we could just sit and talk . . . nothing. Uh, not a big deal, it's just relax, just be very mellow.
Annie and Tony and his entourage turn to look at Alvy.

ALVY *(Fingers to his mouth, reacting)* Remember, we had that thing.

ANNIE What thing?

ALVY *(Staring at Annie and clearing his throat)* Don't you remember we-we-we discussed that thing that we were—

ANNIE *(Overlapping)* Thing?

ALVY *(Overlapping)* —yes, we had, uh . . .

ANNIE *(Looking at Alvy, reacting)* Oh, the thing! Oh, the thing . . . *(Laughing)* . . . yeah . . . yeah.
Annie turns, looks at Tony as he smiles and gestures with his hands.

TONY Oh, well, i-if it's inconvenient, eh, we can't do it now . . . that's fine, too. W-w-w-we'll do it another time.

ANNIE Hey—

TONY Maybe if you're on the Coast, we'll get together and . . . and we'll meet there.
He shakes hands with Annie.

ANNIE *(Reacting)* Oh.

TONY It was a wonderful set.

ANNIE Oh, gosh.

TONY *(Smiling)* I really enjoyed it. *(Looking at Alvy)* Nice to have metcha. Good night.

ENTOURAGE Bye-bye.

ANNIE Nice to see you . . . bye. Yeah. Bye.
She turns and looks at Alvy.

ALVY *(Reacting)* What's . . . you . . . well, what's the matter, wh—
You w-wanna go to that party?

ANNIE *(Looking down at her hands, then up at Alvy)* I don't know, I thought it might be kind of fun, you know what I mean, it'd be nice to meet some new people.

ALVY *(Sighing)* I'm just not . . . you know, I don't think I could take a mellow eve— 'cause I-I don't respond well to mellow, you know what I mean, I-I have a tendency to . . . if I get too mellow, I-I ripen and then rot. You know, and it's—it's not good for my . . . *(Making sounds)*

ANNIE All right, all right, you don't wanna go to the party, so uh, whatta you wanna do?

INTERIOR. MOVIE THEATER.

The screen is projecting the beginning of The Sorrow and the Pity: *a street filled with fleeing cars, belongings tied on top and piled in the back seats. Subtitles pop on:*

> "The Jewish warmongers and
> Parisian plutocrats tried
> to flee with their gold and jewels"

as a narrator explains in German.

CUT TO:

Split screen: Annie and her psychiatrist on the left; Alvy and his on the right. Annie, talking, sits in a white molded chair, as does her doctor. The office is very modern: stark, white and chrome. Alvy, talking to his psychiatrist, lies on a deep leather sofa, the doctor seated away from him. This office looks more like a well-worn den: bookcases overflowing, dark wood. The dialogue is separated in each screen, though no one talks simultaneously.

ANNIE *(To her doctor)*   That day in Brooklyn was the last day I remember really having a great time.

ALVY *(To his doctor)*   Well, we never have any laughs anymore, is the problem.

ANNIE   Well, I've been moody and dissatisfied.

ALVY'S PSYCHIATRIST   How often do you sleep together?

ANNIE'S PSYCHIATRIST   Do you have sex often?

ALVY   Hardly ever. Maybe three times a week.

ANNIE   Constantly! I'd say three times a week. Like the other night, Alvy wanted to have sex.

ALVY   She would not sleep with me the other night, you know, it's—

ANNIE   And . . . I don't know . . . I mean, six months ago I-I woulda done it. I woulda done it, just to please him.

ALVY   —I mean . . . I tried everything, you know, I-I-I put on soft music and my-my red light bulb, and . . .

ANNIE   But the thing is—I mean, since our discussions here, I feel I have a right to my own feelings. I think you woulda been happy because . . . uh, uh, I really asserted myself.

ALVY   The incredible thing about it is, I'm paying for her analysis and she's making progress and I'm getting screwed.

ANNIE   I don't know, though, I feel so guilty because Alvy is paying for it, so, you know, so I do feel guilty if I don't go to bed with him. But if I do go to bed with him, it's like I'm going against my own feelings. I don't know—I-I can't win.

ALVY   *(Simultaneously, with Annie)*   You know . . . it's getting expensive . . . my analyst . . . for her analyst. She-she's making progress and I'm not making any progress. Her progress is defeating my progress.

ANNIE   *(Simultaneously, with Alvy)*   Sometimes I think—sometimes I think I should just live with a woman.

CUT TO:
INTERIOR. APARTMENT.

Alvy and Annie sit close together on the sofa in some friends' apartment. Their friends, another couple, stand behind the sofa in the background. Excited, they talk almost all at once.

WOMAN FRIEND   Wow, I don't believe it . . . you mean to tell me you guys have never snorted coke?

ANNIE   Well, I always wanted to try, you know, but, uh, Alvy, uh . . . he's very down on it.

ALVY   Hey, don't put it on me. You kn— Wh-what is it, I don't wanna put a wad of white powder in my nose 'cause the-the nasal membranes . . .
They all start talking at once.

ANNIE   You never wanna try anything new, Alvy.

ALVY *(Counting on his fingers)* How can you say that? I mean, *(Making sounds)* who said— I-I-I-I said that you, I and that girl from your acting class should sleep together in a threesome.

ANNIE *(Reacting)* That's sick!

ALVY Yeah, I know it's sick, but it's new. You know, you didn't say it couldn't be sick.
Annie laughs, chatters.

WOMAN FRIEND Just come on, Alvy. *(All four are now sitting on the sofa. The male friend starts to prepare lines of cocaine; Alvy and Annie look at each other, reacting)* Do your body a favor. Try it, come on.

ALVY Oh, yeah?

ANNIE Yeah. Come on. It'd be fun.

ALVY *(Moving forward on the couch)* Oh, I'm sure it's a lot of fun, 'cause the Incas did it, you know, and-and they-they-they were a million laughs.

ANNIE *(Laughing)* Alvy, come on, for your own experience. I mean, you wanna write, why not?

MALE FRIEND It's great stuff, Alvy. Friend of mine just brought it in from California.

ANNIE Oh, do you know something—I didn't tell yuh, we're going to California next week.

GIRL Oh, really?

ANNIE Yeah . . .

ALVY . . . I'm thrilled. As you know, uh . . . uh, on my agent's advice I sold out, and I'm gonna do an appearance on TV.

ANNIE *(Interrupting)* No, no, no that's not it at all. Alvy's giving an award on television. Gee, he talks like he's violating a moral issue sitting here.

GIRL You're kidding?

ALVY It's so phony, and we have to leave New York during Christmas week, which really kills me.

MAN *(Interrupting)* Alvy, listen, while you're in California, could you possibly score some coke for me?
Annie laughs.

ALVY *(Over Annie's laughter)*   Sure, sure, I'll be glad to. I-I'll just put it in a-a-a h-h-hollow heel that I have in my boot, you know. *(Alvy picks up the small open gold case of cocaine the man has placed on the coffee table and looks at it, reacting)* H-h-how much is this stuff?

MAN   It's about two thousand dollars an ounce.

ANNIE   God.

ALVY   Really? And what is the kick of it? Because I never . . .
He puts his finger into the drug, smells it and then sneezes. The powder blows all over the room as the man, woman and Annie react silently.

CUT TO:
CALIFORNIA. BEVERLY HILLS STREET—DAY.

It's a warm, beautiful day. Rob, Annie and Alvy in Rob's convertible are moving past the spacious houses, the palm trees. The sunlight reflects off the car. Annie, excited, is taking the whole place in. Background voices sing Christmas carols.

VOICES *(Singing)*   We wish you a Merry Christmas,
We wish you a Merry Christmas
We wish you a Merry Christmas
And a Happy New Year.

ROB *(Over the singing)*   I've never been so relaxed as I have been since I moved out here, Max. I want you to see my house. I live right next to Hugh Hefner's house, Max. He lets me use the Jacuzzi. And the women, Max, they're like the women in *Playboy* magazine, only they can move their arms and legs.

ANNIE *(Laughing)*   You know, I can't get over that this is really Beverly Hills.

VOICES *(Singing)*   We wish you a Merry Christmas
And a Happy New Year.

ALVY   Yeah, the architecture is really consistent, isn't it? French next to—

VOICES *(Singing over the dialogue)*
Oh, Christmas . . . tree,
Oh, Christmas tree,
How bright and green
Our . . .

ALVY —Spanish, next to Tudor, next to Japanese.

ANNIE God, it's so clean out here.

ALVY It's that they don't throw their garbage away. They make it into television shows.

ROB Aw, come on, Max, give us a break, will yuh? It's Christmas.
Annie starts snapping pictures of the view.

ALVY Can you believe this is Christmas here?

VOICES *(Singing)* Oh Christmas tree,
                    Oh Christmas tree . . .
They pass a large house with spacious lawn. Sitting on the lawn is a Santa Claus complete with sleigh and reindeer. Voices continue to sing Christmas carols; Annie continues to take pictures.

ANNIE You know, it was snowing—it was snowing and really gray in New York yesterday.

ROB No kidding?

ALVY Right—well, Santa Claus will have sunstroke.

ROB Max, there's no crime, there's no mugging.

ALVY There's no economic crime, you know, but there's-there's ritual, religious-cult murders, you know, there's wheat-germ killers out here.

ROB While you're out here, Max, I want you to see some of my TV show. And we're invited to a big Christmas party.
They continue driving, now in a less residential area, passing a hot-dog stand. "Tail-Pup" concession; people mill about eating hot dogs.

VOICES *(Singing, louder now)*
                    Remember Christ our Savior
                    Was born on Christmas day
                    To save us all . . . from Satan's power
                    As we were gone astray.
They pass a theater, the marquee announcing "House of Exorcism Messiah of Evil. Rated R. Starts at 7:15."

INTERIOR. TV CONTROL ROOM.

Several monitors line the wall in front of an elaborate console. Rob and Alvy, along with Charlie, the technician, stand in the small room watching the screens showing Rob as a television star on a situation comedy. They chatter, analyzing the footage, over the sounds of the taped television comedy.

ALVY *(Overlapping the chatter)* Oh.

ROB Look, now, Charlie, give me a big laugh here.

ROB ON TV SCREEN A limousine to the track breakdown?

ROB *(Watching)* A little bigger.
TV monitors go black as the technician turns off the monitors to fix the laugh track.

ALVY Do you realize how immoral this all is?

ROB Max, I've got a hit series.

ALVY Yeah, I know, but you're adding fake laughs.
Technicians turn the monitors back on, showing Rob on the screen with another character, Arnie.

ARNIE Oh, I'm sorry.

ROB ON TV SCREEN Arnie.

ARNIE Yeah.

ROB *(Turning to the technician)* Give me a tremendous laugh here, Charlie.

ALVY Look, uh . . .
Loud laughter from the TV monitors.

ROB *(To Alvy)* We do the show live in front of an audience.

ALVY Great, but nobody laughs at it 'cause your jokes aren't funny.

ROB Yeah, well, that's why this machine is dynamite.

ROB ON TV SCREEN You better lie down. You've been in the sun too long.

ROB *(To the technician)* Yeah . . . uh, now give me a like a medium-size chuckle here . . . and then a big hand.
The sounds of laughter and applause are heard from the TV.

ALVY *(Removing his glasses and rubbing his face)*   Is there booing on there? *The monitors show a woman on the screen.*

WOMAN   We were just gonna fix you up with my cousin Dolores.

ALVY *(Overlapping the TV)*   Oh, Max, I don't feel well.

ROB   What's the matter?

ALVY   I don't know, I just got—I got very dizzy . . . *(Coughing)* I feel dizzy, Max.

ROB   Well, sit down.

ALVY *(Sitting down)*   Oh, Jesus.

ROB   You all right?

ALVY   I don't know, I mean, I—

ROB *(Crouching before Alvy, looking at him)*   You wanna lie down?

ALVY   No, no—my, you know, my stomach felt queasy all morning. I just started getting . . .

ROB   How about a ginger ale?

ALVY   Oh, Max . . . no, I—maybe I better lie down.

INTERIOR. HOTEL ROOM.

Alvy lies in bed, one elbow propped up, a doctor sitting next to him looking concerned. The doctor holds out a plate of chicken; Alvy listlessly stares at it. Annie, in the background, is on the phone.

ANNIE *(Talking into the phone)*   Yes.

DOCTOR *(Holding out the food)*   Why don't you just try to get a little of this down? This is just plain chicken.

ALVY *(Taking a piece of chicken and holding it)*   Oh, oh, no, I can't—I can't eat this. I'm nauseous. *(He gasps and makes sounds)* If you could—if you could just give me something to get me through the next two hours, you know I-I have to go out to Burbank . . . and give out an award on a TV show.

ANNIE *(On the phone, overlapping the doctor and Alvy)*   Well . . . H-h huh . . . Oh, good . . . Yes, I'll tell him.

DOCTOR   Well, there's nothing wrong with you actually, so far as I can tell. I mean, you have no fever, no . . . no symptoms of anything serious. You haven't been eating pork or shellfish.
Annie hangs up and moves over to Alvy.

ANNIE *(Sitting on the edge of the bed)*   Excuse me. I'm sorry, I'm sorry, Doctor. Uh, Alvy—Alvy, that was the show. They said everything is fine. They found a replacement, so they're going to tape without you.

ALVY *(Making sounds)*   I'm nauseous. *(He sighs and gasps)* Oh, Jesus, now I don't get to do the TV show?
Reacting, Alvy puts up his hand in disgust, then starts eating the piece of chicken he has been holding. The doctor and Annie watch him, reacting.

ANNIE   Yeah. Listen, Doctor, I'm worried.

DOCTOR   Now, Mrs. Singer, I can't find anything—

ALVY   Christ!

ANNIE   Nothing at all?

DOCTOR   No, I think I can get a lab man up here.

ALVY *(Grabbing the rest of the chicken from the plate)*   Oh, Jesus. Can I have the salt, please?

ANNIE   What do you mean? Do you think he's—

DOCTOR *(Handing the salt to Alvy)*   Yes, excuse me. *(To Annie)*   Perhaps it would be even better if we took him to the hospital for a day or two.
Alvy begins to eat.

ANNIE   Uh-huh . . . Oh, hospital?

DOCTOR   Well, otherwise, there's no real way to tell what's going on.

ALVY *(Making sounds, gasping)*   This is not bad, actually.

EXTERIOR. BEVERLY HILLS STREET. RESIDENTIAL AREA— DAY.

Rob, Annie and Alvy in Rob's car pull into a long circular driveway as an attendant walks over to the car. A sprawling house is seen to the right; a couple moves toward the front door, and the driveway is crowded with other parked cars. Loud music is heard.

ALVY *(Getting out of the car)*   Hey, don't tell me we're gonna hafta walk from the car to the house. Geez, my feet haven't touched pavement since I reached Los Angeles.

INTERIOR. HOUSE.

A Hollywood Christmas party is in session, complete with music, milling people, circulating waiters holding out trays of drinks. It's all very casual. French doors run the entire width of one wall; they are opened to the back lawn, guests move from the room to outside and back in. It is crowded; bits of conversation and clinking glasses can be heard. Two men, California-tanned, stand by the French doors talking.

1ST MAN   Well, you take a meeting with him, I'll take a meeting with you if you'll take a meeting with Freddy.

2ND MAN   I took a meeting with Freddy. Freddy took a meeting with Charlie. You take a meeting with him.

1ST MAN   All the good meetings are taken.

CUT TO:
FULL GROUP SHOT.

A man stands talking, people in groups behind him. Two hornlike gadgets are attached to his shoulders; he's wearing a bizarre space costume.

3RD MAN   Right now it's only a notion, but I think I can get money to make it into a concept . . . and later turn it into an idea.

CUT TO:

Alvy and Rob stand near the French doors leading to the back lawn, eating and drinking and watching the people walking in and out of the house.

ROB   You like this house, Max?

ALVY   M'hm.

ROB   I even brought a road map to get us to the bathroom.

ALVY   Whee, you shoulda told me it was Tony Lacey's party.

ROB   What difference does that make?
Alvy looks into the room, where Annie and Tony Lacey are having an animated conversation.

ALVY   I think he has a little thing for Annie.

ROB   Oh, no, no, that's bullshit, Max. He goes with that girl over there.

ALVY   Where?
Rob nods his head toward a tall woman dressed all in white conversing with a group of people close-by.

ROB   The one with the V.P.L.

ALVY   V.P.L.?

ROB   Visible panty line. Max, she is gorgeous.

ALVY   Yeah, she's a ten, Max, and that's great for you because you're —you're used to twos, aren't you?

ROB   There are no twos, Max.

ALVY   Yeah, you're used to the kind with the—with the shopping bags walking through Central Park with the surgical masks on muttering.

ROB   M'hm.

ALVY   And . . . uh—

ROB   *(Interrupting)*   How do you like this couple, Max?
A couple moves over toward Rob and Alvy. The man's arm is around the woman; they stand very close. In the background, Annie and Tony are still talking.

ROB   And I think they just came back from Masters and Johnson.

ALVY   Yeah, intensive care ward. *(Watching the woman in white)* My God—hey, Max, I think she's . . . I think she's giving me the eye.
As Rob and Alvy observe the guests, the woman in white starts walking toward them.

ROB   If she comes over here, Max, my brain is going to turn into guacamole.

ALVY   I'll handle it. I'll handle it. Hi.

GIRL IN WHITE   You're Alvy Singer, right? Didn't we meet at est?

ALVY   *(Reacting)*   Est? No, no, I was never to est.

GIRL IN WHITE   Then how can you criticize it?

ALVY Oh.

ROB Oh, he—he didn't say anything.

ALVY *(Laughing)* No, no, I came out here to get some shock therapy, but there was an energy crisis, so I . . . He's my-my food taster. Have you two met?

ROB *(Shaking his head)* Hi. How do you do.

GIRL IN WHITE Do you taste to see if the food's poisoned?

ALVY Yeah, he's crazy.
The girl in white laughs.

ALVY *(Looking at Rob and the girl)* Hey, you guys are wearin' white. It must be in the stars.

ROB Yeah. Right.

ALVY Uri Geller must be on the premises someplace.

ROB We're gonna operate together.
Rob and the girl walk off together as the camera moves in on Tony and Annie standing by the buffet table.

TONY We just need about six weeks, in about six weeks we could cut a whole album.

ANNIE I don't know, this is strange to me, you know.

TONY Just . . . that's all you need. You can come and stay here.

ANNIE Oh.

TONY There's a whole wing in this house.

ANNIE *(Laughing)* Oh yeah, stay here? U-huh.

TONY You can have it to use. Why—why are you smiling?

ANNIE *(Laughing)* I don't know. I don't know.
She picks up an hors d'oeuvre.

CUT TO:

The two men still talking about meetings surrounded by other groups of people milling about.

IST MAN Not only is he a great agent, but he really gives good meetings.

2ND MAN M'mm.
Tony, hand in hand with the girl in white, is leaving the party room with Alvy and Annie to show them the rest of the house.

TONY This is a great house, really. Everything. Saunas, Jacuzzis, three tennis courts. You know who the original owners were? Nelson Eddy, then Legs Diamond. Then you know who lived here?

ALVY Trigger.
Annie and the girl in white laugh.

TONY Charlie Chaplin.

ALVY Hey.

TONY Right before his un-American thing.
They stop in a denlike screening room. A man is slouched back on one of the comfortable sofas that fill the room. It is much quieter in here; a contrast to the noise and crowd downstairs.

ALVY Yeah, this place is great.

ANNIE Yeah.

TONY Uh, you guys are still—uh, you're still New Yorkers.

ALVY Yeah, I love it there.

ANNIE *(Laughing)* Yeah.

TONY Well, I used to live there. I used to live there for years. You know, but it's gotten—it's so dirty now.

ANNIE Yeah.

ALVY I'm into garbage. It's my thing.

ANNIE Boy, this is really a nice screening room. It's really a nice room.

TONY Oh, and there's another thing about New York. See . . . you-you wanna see a movie, you have to stand in a long line.

ANNIE Yeah.

TONY It could be freezing, it could be raining.

ANNIE Yeah.

TONY And here, you just—

GIRL IN WHITE We saw *Grand Illusion* here last night.

ALVY AND ANNIE *(In unison)* Oh, yeah?

MAN ON THE SOFA *(Looking over his shoulder at the group)* That's a great film if you're high. *(The group laughs, looking down at the man on the sofa. He looks up at them, smiling, a joint in his hand, and offers them a cigarette)* Hey, you.

TONY *(Shaking his head no)* Come and see our bedroom. We did a fantastic lighting job. Okay?

ANNIE Oh, good. Okay.

ALVY I'm cool.
Tony and the girl in white leave the room, Annie and Alvy following.

ANNIE *(Taking Alvy's arm)* It's wonderful. I mean, you know they just watch movies all day.

ALVY Yeah, and gradually you get old and die. You know it's important to make a little effort once in a while.

ANNIE Don't you think his girl friend's beautiful?

ALVY Yeah, she's got a great-lookin' fa— A pat on the androgynous side. But it's . . .
They pass a man talking on the phone in the hallway.

MAN ON THE PHONE Yeah, yeah. I forgot my mantra.
As they come downstairs, the party is still in high gear. People are looser now; conversations are more animated, some talk quietly in more intimate corners, some couples are dancing. Alvy stands alone sipping a drink near the huge Christmas tree. A tall woman, passing by, shakes his hand, then leaves. He continues to sip his drink, alone, watching Tony and Annie in the center of the room dancing.
The screen shows a plane in flight, Los Angeles far below, then:

CUT TO:
AIRPLANE. INTERIOR.

Annie and Alvy sit, the stewardess behind them serving other passengers. Annie stares out the window holding a coffee cup; Alvy reads. Both are preoccupied, thinking their own thoughts.

ANNIE'S VOICE-OVER *(To herself)* That was fun. I don't think California is bad at all. It's a drag coming home.

ALVY'S VOICE-OVER *(To himself)* Lotta beautiful women. It was fun to flirt.

ANNIE'S VOICE-OVER *(As she sips coffee)* I have to face facts. I—I adore Alvy, but our relationship doesn't seem to work anymore.

ALVY'S VOICE-OVER *(An open magazine lies in his lap)* I'll have the usual trouble with Annie in bed tonight. Whatta I need this?

ANNIE'S VOICE-OVER If only I had the nerve to break up, but it would really hurt him.

ALVY'S VOICE-OVER If only I didn't feel guilty asking Annie to move out. It'd probably wreck her. But I should be honest.
He looks over at Annie.

ANNIE *(Looking back at Alvy)* Alvy, uh, let's face it. You know som—I don't think our relationship is working.

ALVY Tsch, I know. A relationship, I think, is-is like a shark, you know? It has to constantly move forward or it dies. *(He sighs)* And I think what we got on our hands *(Clearing his throat)* is a dead shark.

INTERIOR. ALVY'S LIVING ROOM—DAY.

A lighted Christmas tree stands in the middle of boxes, books, and the general disarray of packing and figuring out what belongs to whom as Alvy helps Annie move out.

ALVY *(Holding up a book)*   Whose *Catcher in the Rye* is this?

ANNIE *(Walking into the room with an armload of books)*   Well, let's see now . . . If it has my name on it, then I guess it's mine.

ALVY *(Reacting)*   Oh, it sure has . . .   You know, you wrote your name in all my books, 'cause you knew this day was gonna come.

ANNIE *(Putting down the books and flipping back her hair)*   Well, uh, Alvy, you wanted to break up just as much as I do.

ALVY *(Riffling through the books)*   There's no-no question in my mind. I think we're doing the mature thing, without any doubt.

ANNIE *(Holding a framed picture and moving about)*   Now, look, all the books on death and dying are yours and all the poetry books are mine.

ALVY *(Looking down at a book)*   This *Denial of Death*. You remember this?

ANNIE   Oh—

ALVY   This is the first book that I got you.
Annie goes over to Alvy. They both look down at the book; the fireplace, burning nicely, is behind them.

ANNIE   —God.

ALVY   Remember that day?

ANNIE   Right. Geez, I feel like there's a great weight off my back. M'mmm.

ALVY   Thanks, honey.

ANNIE *(Patting Alvy's shoulder)*   Oh, no, no, no, no, no. I mean, you know, no, no, no, I mean, I think it's really important for us to explore new relationships and stuff like that.
She walks away.

ALVY   There's no—there's no question about that, 'cause we've given this . . . uh, uh, I think a more than fair shot, you know?
He tosses the book into the carton.

ANNIE *(Offscreen)* Yeah, my analyst thinks this move is keen for me.

ALVY *(Offscreen)* Yeah, and I—an' I tru— you know, I trust her, because my-my analyst recommended her.

ANNIE *(Walking in with another armload of books)* Well, why should I put you through all my moods and hangups anyway?

ALVY Right. And you—and you know what the beauty part is?

ANNIE What?

ALVY *(Holding a small box of buttons)* We can always come back together again. Because there's no—there's no problem. 'Cause . . . Right.

ANNIE *(Overlapping)* Exactly, but . . . exactly. Ooooh!

ALVY You know, I-I-I don't think many couples could handle this. You know, they could just break up and remain friends.

ANNIE *(Taking a button from a box)* Hey, this one's mine, this button. This one, you rem—

ALVY *(Interrupting)* Yeah.

ANNIE I guess these are all yours. *Impeach,* uh, *Eisenhower . . . Impeach Nixon . . . Impeach Lyndon Johnson . . . Impeach Ronald Reagan.*

EXTERIOR. NEW YORK CITY. STREET—DAY.

People milling about on the sidewalk as Alvy walks out of a store and moves toward the foreground.

ALVY *(Into the camera, to the audience)* I miss Annie. I made a terrible mistake.
A couple, walking down the street, stops as the man talks to Alvy.

MAN ON THE STREET She's living in Los Angeles with Tony Lacey.

ALVY Oh, yeah? Well, if she is, then the hell with her! If she likes that lifestyle, let her live there! He's a jerk, for one thing.

MAN ON THE STREET He graduated Harvard.

ALVY Yeah. He may— Listen, Harvard makes mistakes too, you know. Kissinger taught there.
The couple strolls away as an older woman walks up to Alvy while others walk by.

OLD WOMAN Don't tell me you're jealous?

ALVY Yeah, jealous. A little bit like Medea. Lemme, lemme—can I show you something, lady? *(He takes a small item from his pocket to show the woman)* What I have here . . . I found this in the apartment. Black soap. She used to wash her face eight hundred times a day with black soap. Don't ask me why.

OLD WOMAN Well, why don't you go out with other women?

ALVY Well, I-I tried, but it's, uh, you know, it's very depressing.

RECENT FLASHBACK—INTERIOR. ALVY'S COUNTRY KITCHEN.

Alvy's arms and legs fill the screen as he slowly gets up from the floor holding up a live lobster. He puts it on a grill tray.

ALVY *(Pointing to the lobster)* This always happens to me. Quick, g-go get a broom.
His date, a girl wearing short shorts, leans against the sink and lights a cigarette. She makes no move to help.

GIRL DATE *(Smoking)* What are you making such a big deal about? *(As she talks, the lobster drops from the tray to the floor. Alvy jumps away, then gingerly scrapes the tray toward the lobster)* They're only lobsters. Look, you're a grown man, you know how to pick up a lobster.

ALVY *(Looking up in stooped-over position)* I'm not myself since I stopped smoking.

GIRL DATE *(Still leaning against the sink, her hand on her hip)* Oh, when'd you quit smoking?
He gets up off the floor with the lobster on the tray.

ALVY Sixteen years ago.

GIRL DATE *(Puzzled)* Whatta you mean?

ALVY *(Mocking)* Mean?

GIRL DATE You stopped smoking sixteen years ago, is that what you said? Oh, I-I don't understand. Are you joking, or what?

CUT TO:

A solitary Alvy walking along the FDR Drive where he had walked with Annie. The New York skyline is still in the background, the sea gulls go by, the foghorn blows. He walks slowly, moving offscreen.

INTERIOR. ALVY'S BEDROOM—DAY.

Alvy sits on his bed talking on the phone.

ALVY Listen, honey, Central Park's turning green . . . Yeah, I sa—I
saw that lunatic that we—where we used to see . . . with the, uh, uh,
pinwheel hat and, you know, and the roller skates? . . . Listen, I-I
want you to come back here . . . Well, I-I—then I'm gonna come out
there and getcha.

CUT TO:

An airborne plane.

CUT TO:
EXTERIOR. LOS ANGELES AIRPORT.

People milling about as Alvy, in the outside phone-booth center, talks.

ALVY Whatta you mean, where am I? Where do—where do you think
I am? I'm-I'm out . . . I'm at the Los Angeles Airport. I flew in
. . . *(Sniffling)* Tsch, I—well, I flew in to see you . . . *(Muttering)* Hey,
listen, can we not debate this on-on the telephone because I'm, you
know, I-I feel that I got a temperature and I'm-I'm getting my-my
chronic Los Angeles nausea. I-I don't feel so good.
*Alvy's conversation is still heard as the screen shows him behind the wheel of
a car on a busy street; he causes a near-accident by jerking the car too slowly
toward an intersection.*

ALVY'S VOICE-OVER Well, where-wherever you wanna meet, I don't
care. I'll-I'll drive in. I rented a car I'm driving . . . that . . . Whatta
you mean? What—why is that such a miracle? I'm driving myself.

EXTERIOR. OUTDOOR CAFÉ—DAY.

*People sit at umbrellaed tables with checkered tablecloths at a Sunset Boule-
vard outdoor café. Street traffic goes by while they dine. There's a mild
California breeze. The restaurant is somewhat crowded as Alvy makes his
way around the tables looking about. He finally sits down at an empty table;
nearby sits a woman with a younger man. A waitress brings Alvy a menu
and waits for his order.*

ALVY *(To the waitress)* I'm gonna . . . I'm gonna have the alfalfa sprouts
and, uh, a plate of mashed yeast.

Annie, wearing a flowered dress and wide hat, moves into view. Alvy, noticing her, watches as she walks over to his table. He rises and they shake hands.

ANNIE Hi.
Alvy wipes at his nose as he stares. He smiles, the street traffic moving behind him. Annie smiles back.

ALVY You look very pretty.

ANNIE Oh, no, I just lost a little weight, that's all. *(Alvy adjusts his glasses, not exactly knowing where to start; a bit uneasy)* Well, you look nice.

ALVY *(Nodding his head)* You see, I-I've been thinking about it and I think that we should get married.

ANNIE *(Adjusting her sunglasses)* Oh, Alvy, come on.

ALVY Why? You wanna live out here all year? It's like living in Munchkin Land.

ANNIE *(Looking around)* Well, whatta you mean? I mean, it's perfectly fine out here. I mean, Tony's very nice and, uh, well, I meet people and I go to parties and and we play tennis. I mean, that's . . . that's a very big step for me, you know? I mean . . . *(Reacting, Alvy looks down at his hands, then up)* I'm able to enjoy people more.

ALVY *(Sadly)* So whatta you . . . You're not gonna come back to New York?

ANNIE *(Smiling)* What's so great about New York? I mean, it's a dying city. You read *Death in Venice.*

ALVY Hey, you didn't read *Death in Venice* till I bought it for yuh.

ANNIE That's right, that's right. *(Still smiling)* You only gave me books with the word "death" in the titles.

ALVY *(Nodding his head and gesturing)* That's right, 'cause it's an important issue.

ANNIE Alvy, you're incapable of enjoying life, you know that? I mean, your life is New York City. You're just this person. You're like this island unto yourself.

ALVY *(Toying with his car keys)* I can't enjoy anything unless I . . . unless everybody is. I—you know, if one guy is starving someplace, that's . . . you know, I-I . . . it puts a crimp in my evening. *(Looking down at his hands, sadly)* So wanna get married or what?

ANNIE *(Seriously)* No. We're friends. I wanna remain friends.

ALVY *(In disbelief)* Okay. *(Louder, to the waitress)* Check, please. Can I —can I . . . Can I . . . Can I . . .

ANNIE *(Interrupting)* You're mad, aren't you?

ALVY *(Shaking his head)* No. *(Then nodding)* Yes, of course I'm mad, because you love me, I know that.

ANNIE Alvy, I can't say that that's true at this point in my life. I really just can't say that that's true. I mean, you know how wonderful you are. I mean, you know . . . you're the reason that I got outta my room and that I was able to sing, and-and-and, you know, get more in touch with my feelings and all that crap. Anyway, look, I don't wanna— Listen, listen, listen, uh *(Laughing)* h'h, so whatta you up to anyway, huh?

ALVY *(Shrugging his shoulders)* The usual, you know. Uh, tryin' t' write. I'm workin' on a play. *(Sighing)* Jesus. So whatta yuh saying? That you're not comin' back to New York with me?
He nods his head in disbelief.

ANNIE *(Nodding)* No! *(Pauses)* Look, I gotta go.
She starts to rise.

ALVY You mean that . . . *(He gets up and starts following her past diners at other tables)* I-I-I-I flew three thousand miles to see you.

ANNIE I'm late.

ALVY Air miles, you know. I mean, you know what that does to my stomach?
They move down the steps of the café toward the parking lot.

ANNIE If you must know, it's a hectic time for Tony. The Grammys are tonight.

ALVY The what?

ANNIE The Grammys. He's got a lotta records up for awards.

ALVY You mean they give awards for that kind o' music.

ANNIE Oh!

ALVY   I thought just earplugs.
Annie gets into her car. Alvy moves over to his rented convertible.

ANNIE   Just forget it, Alvy, okay? Let's just forget the conversation.
She closes the door, starts the motor.

ALVY *(Yelling after her)*   Awards! They do nothing but give out awards!
I can't believe it. Greatest, greatest fascist dictator, Adolf Hitler!
Annie drives away.
*Alvy gets behind the wheel, starts the motor. Putting the car in gear, he
inadvertently moves forward, hitting a bunch of trash cans with a loud crash.
Putting the car in reverse, Alvy notices a beige car that has just turned into
the parking lot.*
*For a brief moment, the screen shows a flashback of the bumper-car ride at
the Brooklyn amusement park. Alvy's father is on the platform directing
traffic; young Alvy is in a small car bumping others right and left.*
*Alvy, back in the parking lot, backs up his convertible, purposefully smashing
the side of the beige car as another flashback of bumper-car ride appears, this
time—as Alvy's father directs traffic—a Marine in a small car hits the back
end of a soldier's car, and Alvy, back in the parking lot, moves his car over
to another parked car and hits it full force.*
*Another flashback appears: people in the small cars really racing around the
track now, bumping into one another over and over again, Alvy's father
directing the flow, as the film cuts back to the parking lot, where Alvy reverses
the convertible and rams it into the front end of yet another car.*
*He sits behind the wheel as people rush out of various cars and as sirens start
blaring, coming closer and closer, stopping finally as a motorcycle cop gets
off beside Alvy's car and walks over to him)*

ALVY *(Getting out of the car)*   Officer, I know what you're gonna say.
I'm-I'm not a great driver, you know, I-I have some problems with-
with-with—

OFFICER *(Interrupting)*   May I see your license, please?

ALVY   Sure. *(Searching, he finally fishes his license out of his pocket)* Just
don't-don't get angry, you know what I mean. 'Cause I-I have—I
have my-my license here. You know, it's a rented car. And I-I-I-I-
I've . . .
He drops the license and it falls to the ground.

OFFICER   Don't give me your life story *(Looking at the piece of paper on
the ground)*—just pick up the license.

ALVY Pick up the license. You have to ask nicely 'cause I've had an extremely rough day. You know, my girl friend—

OFFICER *(Interrupting)* Just give me the license, please.

ALVY Since you put it that way. *(He laughs)* It's hard for me to refuse. *(He leans over, picks up the license, then proceeds to rip it up. He lets the pieces go; they float to the ground)* . . . have a, I have a terrific problem with authority, you know. I'm . . . it's not your fault. Don't take it personal.

CUT TO:
INTERIOR. JAIL-CELLS CORRIDOR.

A guard moves down the hall to the cell where Alvy stands with other inmates. He unlocks the door and opens it, letting Alvy out.

ALVY So long, fellas. Keep in touch.
He walks down the corridor offscreen.

EXTERIOR. A STREET IN FRONT OF THE COURTHOUSE—DAY.

Policemen are walking up and down the courthouse steps as Alvy and Rob move out the door of the building, down the steps to the street.

ROB Imagine my surprise when I got your call, Max.

ALVY *(Carrying his jacket over his shoulder)* Yeah. I had the feeling that I got you at a bad moment. You know, I heard high-pitched squealing.
They walk over to Rob's convertible and get in.

ROB *(Starting the car)* Twins, Max. Sixteen-year-olds. Can you imagine the mathematical possibilities?

ALVY *(Reacting)* You're an actor, Max. You should be doing Shakespeare in the Park.

ROB Oh, I did Shakespeare in the Park, Max. I got mugged. I was playing Richard the Second and two guys with leather jackets stole my leotard.
He puts on an elaborate helmet and goggles.

ALVY *(Looking at Rob's helmet)* Max, are we driving through plutonium?

ROB Keeps out the alpha rays, Max. You don't get old.

CUT TO:
INTERIOR. REHEARSAL HALL OF A THEATER.

An actor and actress sit on hard wooden chairs in a sparse rehearsal hall. They face each other. The actress resembles Annie; the actor, Alvy.

ACTOR   You're a thinking person. How can you choose this lifestyle?

ACTRESS   What is so incredibly great about New York? It's a dying city! You-you read *Death in Venice.*

ACTOR   You didn't read *Death in Venice* till I gave it to you!

ACTRESS   Well, you only give me books with the word "death" in the title.
The camera pulls back, showing Alvy sitting with two men at a table set up near the actors. A mirror, running the whole width of the wall, reflects the two actors, a script lying on the table between them. It is obvious now that they are rehearsing a scene that Alvy wrote.

ACTOR *(In mirrored reflection)*   It's an important issue.

ACTRESS *(In mirrored reflection)*   Alvy, you are totally incapable of enjoying life.
The camera moves back to actual actor and actress.

ACTRESS   You're like New York. You're an island.

ACTOR *(Rising with emotion)*   Okay, if that's all that we've been through together means to you, I guess it's better if we just said goodbye, once and for all! You know, it's funny, after all the se-rious talks and passionate moments that it ends here . . . in a health-food restaurant on Sunset Boulevard. Goodbye, Sunny.
The actor begins to leave as the actress jumps up from her chair.

ACTRESS   Wait! I'm-I'm gonna . . . go with you. *(The actor comes back. They embrace)* I love you.
The camera cuts to Alvy, who turns and looks straight into the camera.

ALVY *(To the audience, gesturing)*   Tsch, whatta you want? It was my first play. You know, you know how you're always tryin' t' get things to come out perfect in art because, uh, it's real difficult in life. Interestingly, however, I did run into Annie again. It was on the Upper West Side of Manhattan.
Annie, singing "Seems Like Old Times," overlaps Alvy's speech and continues over the next scene, where Alvy, standing in front of a Manhattan theater, shakes hands with Annie and her escort. The theater marquee reads "OPHULS PRIZE FILM THE SORROW AND THE PITY."

ANNIE HALL

ALVY'S VOICE *(Over the theater scene and Annie's singing)* She had moved back to New York. She was living in SoHo with some guy. *(Laughing)* And when I met her she was, of all things, dragging him in to see *The Sorrow and the Pity.* Which I counted as a personal triumph. Annie and I . . . *(Alvy's voice continues over the scene shot through a window of Manhattan café showing Alvy and Annie sitting at a table, laughing and enjoying themselves)* . . . we had lunch sometime after that, and, uh, just, uh, kicked around old times.
A series of flashbacks following in quick succession while Annie continues to sing:

Annie and Alvy going up the FDR Drive, the day they met playing tennis, Annie driving, Alvy holding up partially eaten sandwich.

Annie and Alvy in the Hamptons house kitchen, Annie handing a live lobster to Alvy, who drops it in the pot on the stove.

Annie and Alvy walking side by side by the shoreline.

Alvy at the tennis club, packing his bag, as he looks over his shoulder and sees Annie, hands on her face, then clapping, as she offers him a ride home in her car.

Annie opening the door to Alvy the night he came over to kill the spider; Annie and Alvy in the bookstore buying the "Death" titles; Annie and Alvy in their Hamptons house, Annie reading a school catalogue, the night Alvy puts in the red light.

The memories continue to flash on the screen: Annie and Alvy at a friend's house, Alvy blowing the cocaine all over the sofa; Annie and Alvy playing tennis; Annie and Alvy having a picture taken backstage at the college performance in Annie's hometown; Alvy holding Annie close, the night he came over to kill the spider.

And continue: Annie carrying her luggage and clothes into Alvy's bedroom, Alvy following, the day she first moved into his apartment. Annie holding up her sexy birthday present from Alvy, then leaning over and kissing him; Annie and Alvy walking down a city street, holding each other close; sitting on the park bench, observing the people; and kissing, on the FDR Drive, the New York City skyline behind them.

The music stops.

Returning to the present, the camera, focusing through the café window, shows Annie and Alvy across street. They look about at the city traffic. Lunch is over; it's time.

Alvy and Annie shake hands and kiss each other friendly like. Annie crosses the street, Alvy watching her go. Then he turns, and slowly walks down the street offscreen. His voice is heard over the scene:

ALVY'S VOICE-OVER   After that it got pretty late. And we both hadda go, but it was great seeing Annie again, right? I realized what a terrific person she was and-and how much fun it was just knowing her and I-I thought of that old joke, you know, this-this-this guy goes to a psychiatrist and says, "Doc, uh, my brother's crazy. He thinks he's a chicken." And, uh, the doctor says, "Well, why don't you turn him in?" And the guy says, "I would, but I need the eggs." Well, I guess that's pretty much how how I feel about relationships. You know, they're totally irrational and crazy and absurd and . . . but, uh, I guess we keep goin' through it because, uh, most of us need the eggs.

THE END

DISSOLVES INTO:
BLACK BACKGROUND; credits popping on and off in white.

Credits

Presented by	UNITED ARTISTS ENTERTAINMENT FROM TRANSAMERICA CORPORATION
Production	A JACK ROLLINS–CHARLES H. JOFFE PRODUCTION
Written by	WOODY ALLEN AND MARSHALL BRICKMAN
Produced by	CHARLES H. JOFFE
Associate Producer	FRED T. GALLO
Executive Producer	ROBERT GREENHUT
Directed by	WOODY ALLEN
Edited by	RALPH ROSENBLUM, A.C.E.
Art Director	MEL BOURNE
Costume Designer	RUTH MORLEY
Director of Photography	GORDON WILLIS, A.S.C.

FOUR FILMS OF WOODY ALLEN

Production Manager	ROBERT GREENHUT
1st Assistant Director	FRED T. GALLO
2nd Assistant Director	FRED BLANKFEIN
Location Manager	MARTIN DANZIG
Script Supervisor	KAY CHAPIN
Production Office Co-ordinator	LOI KRAMER
Assistant to Mr. Allen	PATRICIA CROWN
Location Auditor	SAM GOLDRICH
Transportation Captain	WILLIAM CURRY
D.G.A. Trainee	TAD DEVLIN
Production Assistants	CHRIS CRONYN
	BETH RUDIN
	STUART SMILEY
Sound Mixer	JAMES SABAT
Re-recording Mixer	JACK HIGGINS
Camera Operator	FRED SCHULER
1st Assistant Cameraman	THOMAS PRIESTLY
Gaffer	DUSTY WALLACE
Key Grip	ROBERT WARD
Wardrobe Supervisor	GEORGE NEWMAN
Wardrober Supervisor	MARILYN PUTNAM
Makeup Artist	FERN BUCHNER
Unit Publicist	SCOTT MACDONOUGH
Still Photographer	BRIAN HAMILL
Set Decorators	ROBERT DRUMHELLER
	JUSTIN SCOPPA JR.
Propmaster	THOMAS SACCIO
Carpenter	JOSEPH BADALUCCO
Scenic Artist	COSMO SORICE
Construction Grip	JOSEPH WILLIAMS
Film Editor	WENDY GREEN BRICMONT
Assistant Film Editors	SONYA POLANSKI
	SUSAN E. MORSE
Sound Editing	SAN SABLE/MAGNOFEX
Video Services	E.U.E/SCREEN GEMS
Titles	COMPUTER OPTICALS
Casting	JULIET TAYLOR
Extra Casting	AARON BECKWITH
Clothing Designed By	RALPH LAUREN
Animated Sequences	CHRIS ISHII
Miss Keaton's Accompanist	ARTIE BUTLER

ANNIE HALL

Los Angeles Unit:	
Location Manager	DAISY GERBER
Camera Operator	DON THORIN
Sound Mixer	JAMES PILCHER
Gaffer	LARRY HOWARD
Key Grip	CARL GIBSON
Transportation Captain	JAMES FOOTE
Set Decorator	BARBARA KRIEGER
Propmaster	PAT O'CONNOR
Makeup	JOHN INZERELLA
Hair Stylist	VIVIENNE WALKER
Wardrobe Supervisor	NANCY MCARDLE
Songs	"SEEMS LIKE OLD TIMES"
Music by	CARMEN LOMBARDO
Lyrics by	JOHN JACOB LOEB
	"IT HAD TO BE YOU"
Music by	ISHAM JONES
Lyrics by	GUS KAHN

CAST	
Woody Allen	ALVY SINGER
Diane Keaton	ANNIE HALL
Tony Roberts	ROB
Carol Kane	ALLISON
Paul Simon	TONY LACEY
Shelley Duvall	PAM
Janet Margolin	ROBIN
Colleen Dewhurst	MOM HALL
Christopher Walken	DUANE HALL
Donald Symington	DAD HALL
Helen Ludlam	GRAMMY HALL
Mordecai Lawner	ALVY'S DAD
Joan Newman	ALVY'S MOM
Jonathan Munk	ALVY AGED 9
Ruth Volner	ALVY'S AUNT
Martin Rosenblatt	ALVY'S UNCLE
Hy Ansel	JOEY NICHOLS
Rashel Novikoff	AUNT TESSIE
Russell Horton	MAN IN THEATER LINE
Marshall McLuhan	HIMSELF
Christine Jones	DORRIE

FOUR FILMS OF WOODY ALLEN

Mary Boylan	MISS REED
Wendy Girard	JANET
John Doumanian	COKE FIEND
Bob Maroff	MAN #1 OUTSIDE THEATER
Rick Petrucelli	MAN #2 OUTSIDE THEATER
Lee Callahan	TICKET SELLER AT THEATER
Chris Gampel	DOCTOR
Dick Cavett	HIMSELF
Mark Lenard	NAVY OFFICER
Dan Ruskin	COMEDIAN AT RALLY
John Glover	ACTOR BOYFRIEND
Bernie Styles	COMIC'S AGENT
Johnny Haymer	COMIC
Ved Bandhu	MAHARISHI
John Dennis Johnson	L.A. POLICEMAN
Lauri Bird	TONY LACEY'S GIRL FRIEND
Jim McKrell	LACEY PARTY GUEST
Jeff Goldblum	LACEY PARTY GUEST
William Callaway	LACEY PARTY GUEST
Roger Newman	LACEY PARTY GUEST
Alan Landers	LACEY PARTY GUEST
Jean Sarah Frost	LACEY PARTY GUEST
Vince O'Brien	HOTEL DOCTOR
Humphrey Davis	ALVY'S PSYCHIATRIST
Veronica Radburn	ANNIE'S PSYCHIATRIST
Robin Mary Paris	ACTRESS IN REHEARSAL
Charles Levin	ACTOR IN REHEARSAL
Wayne Carson	REHEARSAL STAGE MANAGER
Michael Karm	REHEARSAL DIRECTOR
Petronia Johnson	TONY'S DATE AT NIGHTCLUB
Shaun Casey	TONY'S DATE AT NIGHTCLUB
Ricardo Bertoni	WAITER #1 AT NIGHTCLUB
Michael Aronin	WAITER #2 AT NIGHTCLUB
Lou Picetti	STREET STRANGER
Loretta Tupper	STREET STRANGER
James Burge	STREET STRANGER
Shelley Hack	STREET STRANGER
Albert Ottenheimer	STREET STRANGER
Paula Trueman	STREET STRANGER
Beverly D'Angelo	ACTRESS IN ROB'S TV SHOW
Tracey Walter	ACTOR IN ROB'S TV SHOW

ANNIE HALL

David Wier	ALVY'S CLASSMATE
Kieth Dentice	ALVY'S CLASSMATE
Susan Mellinger	ALVYS CLASSMATE
Hamit Perezic	ALVY'S CLASSMATE
James Balter	ALVY'S CLASSMATE
Eric Gould	ALVY'S CLASSMATE
Amy Levitan	ALVY'S CLASSMATE
Gary Allen	SCHOOLTEACHER
Frank Vohs	SCHOOLTEACHER
Margaretta Warwick	SCHOOLTEACHER
Lucy Lee Flippen	WAITRESS AT HEALTH-FOOD RESTAURANT
Gary Muledeer	MAN AT HEALTH-FOOD RESTAURANT
Sigourney Weaver	ALVY'S DATE OUTSIDE THEATER
Walter Bernstein	ANNIE'S DATE OUTSIDE THEATER

Recorded Music:

"*A Hard Way to Go*"
Performed by Tim Weisberg on A&M Records

Christmas Medley
*Performed by the Do-Re-Mi Children's Chorus
on Vocalion Records*

"*Sleepy Lagoon*"
Performed by Tommy Dorsey on RCA Records

Interiors

Screenplay by Woody Allen

White-lettered credits pop on and off
black screen. There is no sound.

United Artists
Entertainment from Transamerica Corporation

A JACK ROLLINS–CHARLES H. JOFFE PRODUCTION

Copyright © United Artists Corporation 1978

INTERIORS

EDITED BY

RALPH ROSENBLUM, A.C.E.

PRODUCTION DESIGNER

MEL BOURNE

COSTUME DESIGNER

JOEL SCHUMACHER

DIRECTOR OF PHOTOGRAPHY

GORDON WILLIS, A.S.C.

PRODUCED BY

CHARLES H. JOFFE

WRITTEN AND DIRECTED

BY

WOODY ALLEN

CAMERA ABRUPTLY CUTS TO:

A quick succession of almost still-life scenes, starting with the living room of a beach house, a tasteful room illuminated by the bright sun outside. The ocean can be seen beyond the French doors and double windows. There is no sound, no people.
The film quickly cuts to:

Five simple vases on a white mantel in the room. There is no sound. The camera then moves abruptly to:

The beach-house dining room and its entranceway. It is quiet; no one is around. The sea and brush can be seen outside the French doors. And, again, an abrupt cut to:

A painting on the wall. Joey's face can be seen, reflected in the painting's glass. She is walking into the room. There is still no sound.

The camera moves closer to Joey. She is slowly walking around the beach-house living room. She is in darkness; outside, it is very bright. She leaves the room and walks up the stairs of the house. There is still no sound; Joey looks very pensive, thoughtful. She moves over to an upstairs window, looking out at the waves, the brush. As she gazes out, the film cuts to:

A brief flashback. A young Joey and her two sisters play ball on the sand behind the beach house. They seem to laugh and squeal, though there is still no sound.

The film moves back to Joey, still looking out the window, remembering. The movie then quickly cuts to:

Renata, looking out the window in the same pensive pose. She raises her hand and presses the glass pane with her fingers. There is still no sound.

CUT TO:
INTERIOR. OFFICE IN NEW YORK CITY—DAY.

Arthur, his back to the camera, is looking out a picture window at a panoramic view of the New York City skyline.

ARTHUR   I had dropped out of law school when I met Eve. She was very beautiful. Very pale and cool in her black dress . . . with never anything more than a single strand of pearls. And distant. Always poised and distant.
The film dissolves into the brief flashback of the three young sisters playing in the sand in back of the beach house. Arthur continues to speak.

ARTHUR'S VOICE-OVER   By the time the girls were born . . . it was all so perfect, so ordered. Looking back, of course, it was rigid.
The film moves back to Joey, staring out the window of the beach house.

ARTHUR'S VOICE-OVER   The truth is . . . she'd created a world around us that we existed in . . . where everything had its place, where there was always a kind of harmony.
The camera moves back to Renata, still staring out the window, pressing her fingers on the glass pane.

ARTHUR'S VOICE-OVER Oh . . . great dignity. I will say . . . it was like an ice palace.
The film returns to Arthur's office. His back is still to the camera; he is in the same pose as before.

ARTHUR Then suddenly, one day, out of nowhere . . . an enormous abyss opened up beneath our feet. And I was staring into a face I didn't recognize.

CUT TO:
INTERIOR. JOEY AND MIKE'S MANHATTAN APARTMENT— DAY.

A spacious, modern apartment done in pale woods and white; a long counter separates the kitchen from the dining area. Mike sits at a large white dining table dictating information into a tape recorder. Notes are piled up next to him. He is deep in thought.

MIKE *(Speaking into the microphone while looking down at his notes)* The basic popularity and appeal of Mao . . . for so-called American Marxists— This is supposed to go in the sequence, in under the sequence in reel two about South Africa. Um . . . what we want to do is get two examples. But the ideas, his style, was Marxist-Leninist. Mao's style was Marxist-Leninist, but that he was accessible to the lower classes because of his use of homilies. An example would be that "The hardest thing is to act properly throughout one's whole life." What the hell does that mean? Or "Even worse than the—
The doorbell buzzes. Mike gets up, sighing, annoyed at the interruption; he moves offscreen to answer the door.

MIKE Eve. I wasn't expecting you.

EVE *(Also offscreen)* I hope I'm not disturbing you.

MIKE No, I just couldn't imagine who it was.

EVE Is Joey here? Where's Joey?

MIKE Joey's in the shower.
Eve, in a pale-blue sweater coat, carrying a shopping bag, and Mike move onto the screen into the dining area.

MIKE Can I get you anything?

EVE Oh, just some coffee . . . if you don't mind.

MIKE   No, it's no trouble at all.
Eve places her shopping bag on the table while Mike walks to the kitchen area to prepare the coffee.

EVE   I think I found a very nice vase for the foyer.

MIKE *(Absently, getting the coffee materials together)*   Uh huh.

EVE *(Taking out a box from the shopping bag and opening it)*   You'll probably think it's an extravagance, but it's not, all things considered. These pieces are becoming increasingly rare. *(Holding up a delicate blue vase)* Isn't that exquisite? *(Mike, filling a kettle of water at the sink, looks up at Eve; she walks toward the foyer)* I hope you like it, because it's perfect for what I have in mind for the foyer.

MIKE *(Placing the kettle on the range)*   We already have a vase in the foyer, Eve.

EVE *(Speaking from the foyer)*   Yes, but this will never look right when we redo the floors.

MIKE *(Preparing a tray with jar of instant coffee and sugar bowl)*   I never understood why the floors have to be redone.
Eve is busy rearranging a basket of dried flowers on the cabinet in the foyer next to the vase she's just bought; she holds the vase that had been there in her hand.

EVE   Why, we've discussed all that, Michael. Don't you remember? You agreed.

MIKE *(Bringing the tray to the dining table)*   You know, it costs money to have these things done and redone two or three times over.

EVE *(Walking back into the dining area)*   But the— It's such a large floor space. That's why we agreed that the paler tones would make a more subtle statement. The pale woods would be lovely.

MIKE   I never agreed about anything! I'm always being told.

EVE   Well, I wouldn't put it that way.

MIKE   Well, how would you put it, Eve? I mean, first the living room was finished, then it wasn't. Then the, uh, bedroom needed more work. Now the floors have to be stripped again. You picked a sofa, then you hated it.

EVE   It was a lovely piece. It just was the wrong scale, that's all. It's not an exact science. *(Fidgeting with the collar of her suit)* Sometimes you just have to see it . . . then you get the feel of it. *(Glancing at a lamp sitting on a cabinet in the dining area)* You didn't like that in the bedroom?

MIKE *(Looking at the lamp)*   I knew you were gonna say something. I get better use out of it here.

EVE *(Walking over to the lamp)*   Well, if you utilized it in here, that's fine. It's meant to be used. It's just that it was part of what we were trying to do in the bedroom. *(Pointing at the lampshade)* It's the shade and the bedspread. They set each other off so nicely, I thought.

MIKE   How much is the vase?

EVE *(Looking down)*   Uh . . . they're asking four hundred dollars.

MIKE   Uh! Give me a break, Eve!

EVE *(Fingering her forehead and hairline, still holding the small vase from the foyer)*   All right, Michael, I'll return it. Would you mind closing the window? The street noises are just unnerving.
Joey, in a white bathrobe, enters the dining area.

JOEY   I hope you two aren't having another argument.

EVE *(Sitting down at the table)*   Not at all.

JOEY   Oh, I love that suit. It's a unique color.

EVE   Renata calls it ice-gray.

JOEY   Well, it makes you look very beautiful. Isn't she beautiful, Michael?

MIKE *(Bringing the kettle with boiling water and a carton of milk to the table)*   Very lovely.

EVE   Well, I don't feel lovely. I'm exhausted. I've been running up and down Second Avenue all day.

JOEY *(Walking into the foyer, seeing the new vase)*   Oh, wow! Is this for us? It's exquisite!

EVE   No, I was just showing it to Michael.

MIKE   It's too expensive, Joey.

JOEY Really? Well, that's too bad.
Joey comes back into the room holding the new vase.

MIKE Eve, let's keep it.

EVE No, no, no, no.

MIKE Yeah, let's keep it. It's . . . it's very beautiful. We'll work something out.

EVE *(Fingering the vase Joey has placed on the table)* No, I was just . . .
carried away by it. I don't know why. I guess because it's so unique.
But it *is* an extravagance. I'll just look for something along the same
lines at a better price. But I have to point out one thing. *(Looking over
at the lamp on the cabinet)* This really belongs in the bedroom, because
it's too insignificant a piece for in here. The shade is just wrong
against all these slick surfaces.
Eve walks over to the lamp. She unplugs it.

MIKE I'll put it back.

EVE No, I'll do it. I just want to try it in a different spot in there. I
can fix . . . something for you. Uh, something more inexpensive. I've
seen some nice pewters. Em, I should have done that. And I can
make the shade in a smoother fabric if you prefer.
*Eve, holding the lamp, walks into the bedroom. Joey and Mike are still
standing by the dining-room table.*

EVE *(Offscreen)* But we should stick with my beiges and my earth
tones.

MIKE *(Mimicking in low tones)* "My beiges and my earth tones . . ."

JOEY *(Overlapping)* Oh, stop picking on her.

MIKE *(Taking a deep breath)* Nobody's picking on her.

JOEY She's a sick woman.
*The film cuts to Joey and Mike's bedroom, where Eve is turning on the lamp
she brought in from the other room. She steps back to see the effect.*

JOEY *(Coming into the bedroom with a coffee cup in her hand, seeing the lamp)*
That's great.

EVE *(Turning)* Yes, it's nice.
*Eve takes a deep breath and tugs her coat around herself. She sits down on
a bench and leans back. The background is stark white.*

JOEY So, uh . . . how do you feel?

EVE I'm fine. I'm just a little tired, that's all.

JOEY *(Holding out the cup to Eve)* Your coffee.

EVE *(Taking it)* Oh, thank you.

JOEY *(Sitting down next to Eve on bench)* You're welcome.

EVE *(Sipping her coffee)* Umm. Oh, it takes so many jobs. It's just exhausting.

JOEY Yeah, I know. I don't—I can't get over how you sort of jump right in and do it.

EVE Well, I like it. I like to be busy. And I think by now I can say that my comeback is over the shaky period. Wouldn't you say?

JOEY Yeah. I think so. I think your work is better, in fact, than it's ever been.

EVE Do you?

JOEY Yeah.

EVE Well, I have to admit that I have received some . . . rather special compliments lately.

JOEY Oh, yeah?

EVE Um huh. Yes. Well, my spirits are high, and . . . I'm feeling good about myself. Not to say that I don't run into . . . an occasional setback. But I haven't . . . really felt so confident in a long time.

JOEY I can see it. I mean, you look better than you have in ages.

EVE Oh. Oh, have you talked to Dad lately?

JOEY No. I— He's still in Greece.

EVE Mmm. Well, when he comes back I hope he'll corroborate the state of my well-being.
She absently pulls a string off Joey's robe.

JOEY Of course.

EVE I've pulled . . . I certainly pulled myself together in a way that he never thought possible.

JOEY Um unh. I mean you're really impressive.

EVE *(Smiling demurely)* Oh. Well, maybe a reconciliation can finally be discussed. Think so?

JOEY Well . . . I mean, it hasn't been that much time. Uh, I really don't —I don't know.

EVE Tsch. *(Pausing)* Why are you always so negative about it?

JOEY *(Looking down)* I don't think that was negative.

EVE Well, you're always reluctant to encourage me. I don't know why.

JOEY *(Leaning forward)* Mother, I know that you're optimistic, but it's really important for you to be realistic too.

EVE Oh, is there something you know that you're not saying?

JOEY No.

EVE Well, Dr. Lobel doesn't think it's unrealistic . . . to hope that your father and I might reconcile. It's just a goal, that's all.

JOEY Fine. I didn't say it—anything to . . . uh, get in the way of that.

EVE You just always make it sound as though it's impossible.

JOEY *(Yelling)* Mother, I didn't say it was impossible!

EVE *(Overlapping)* Yes, you did. You imply that a lot. Renata thinks it's . . . going to happen.

JOEY *(Turning her head away from her mother)* I'm sure she didn't say that.

EVE Yes, she did. She implied that.

JOEY Well, maybe you read it into what she said.

EVE No, I didn't! She's just a person who looks on the bright side.

JOEY Oh, great!
She stands up and walks off the screen. Eve alone sits on the bench, the stark white background behind her, as they continue to talk.

JOEY I think that's wonderful. I just don't think you should delude yourself, either.

EVE Oh, you don't think there's any chance that your father will ever want to live with me again?

JOEY   I didn't say that! I believe—

EVE *(Interrupting)*   Well, Renata thinks that there's a good chance.

JOEY   Just wait and see.

EVE   You just refuse to encourage me, don't you?

JOEY *(Still offscreen)*   Why don't you discuss it with Renata?!

EVE *(Pulling her coat closer around herself)*   I will, thank you. I will.

CUT TO:
INTERIOR. TAXI CAB—DAY.

A Manhattan street, seen through the window of a taxi, busy with people and activity. Traffic noise is heard as the camera pulls away from the street to show the interior of the moving cab; Eve, staring silently, sits in the back.

CUT TO:
INTERIOR. EVE'S APARTMENT—DUSK.

She enters her apartment and turns on the foyer light. She walks into a stark, tasteful dining room; a large table sits in the middle of the room in front of a pale classic mural on the wall; a silver dish is the table's only ornament. Eve turns on the dining-room light and drops her shopping bag onto the table. She throws down her gloves and begins fumbling in her purse.

CUT TO:
INTERIOR. PSYCHIATRIST'S OFFICE—DAY.

Renata is sitting in a chair, a lamp on a small end table illuminating her face. She looks directly at the camera, as if talking to her doctor. She lights a cigarette and takes a puff.

RENATA   Mother paced all the time. She ... *(Sighing, then weeping)* Um ... she was an insomniac. You could, um ... always hear her upstairs ... pacing in the middle of the night. But ... that was more when she ... got back from the hospital. *(Weeping)* I, uh, I—I saw her ... the first day that they brought her back. Um ... she'd had all this ... electric shock therapy and ... her hair looked gray, and I couldn't believe there was—it was like ... she was a stranger.
As Renata talks, the scene shifts to a flashback at the beach house. It is day. A younger Eve, almost in silhouette, dark against the brightness of the room, is staring intently at a painting leaning on the wall and backboard of a bed.

She moves over to the painting and adjusts it slightly. She touches the bed-spread. Then she walks over to three vases, filled with white roses, standing on a night table. Eve stares at them, then moves them about, changing their position. She takes one away. Satisfied, she walks out of the room. As Eve moves about on the screen, Renata's voice is heard.

RENATA'S VOICE-OVER   Uh . . . After that she was always sort of . . . um . . . *(Sighing)* coming in and . . . going out. I guess you . . . you never knew. Before her breakdown, she was a very successful woman. She was . . . very demanding. She, uh, she put Dad through law school and she financed the start of his practice. So in a sense it was like he was her creation.

The camera moves back to the psychiatrist's office, where Renata is still sitting in the chair, in the same pose as before.

RENATA *(Smoking)*   We kept getting shuffled around to aunts and cousins. And I guess, uh, Joey had the worst of it, 'cause . . . as a kid Joey was very high-strung. She was a bright kid, you know. She . . . she was very sensitive.

The film dissolves into a flashback, again at the beach house. A young Joey and Arthur sit eating at the dining-room table while, through the French doors, a young Renata and her sister Flyn are seen playing outside. Renata continues to speak over the scene.

RENATA'S VOICE-OVER   We'd spend some time with Dad. *(Sighing)* Mostly, um, long Sunday breakfasts. I always resented his relationship to her, you know. I always felt that he favored Joey.

The film moves back to the psychiatrist's office.

RENATA *(Smoking)*   It just seemed like that they were very close, and that I was left out.

The movie cuts to a more recent flashback at the beach house. Arthur sits at one end of the dining-room table, Eve at the other. Renata and Joey sit at opposite sides. They are all eating breakfast.

EVE   I like Frederick. He has dignity . . . and promise . . . as a writer. My own strength is visual. Your images are visual, Renata. And in all candor, I much prefer Frederick to Mike.

JOEY   That's fine, Mother.

EVE *(Grinning)*   Well, he uses a very strong aftershave. *(Renata laughs)* It permeates the house.

JOEY *(Looking down)*   I don't want to talk about it.

EVE Do you think that if I bought him another kind of cologne that he would switch?

JOEY *(Fingering her food)* Could we talk about something else?

EVE Well, let me give him some. Then we won't have to talk about it. It'll just be my gift.
Renata, smiling, puts her napkin alongside her plate; she lights a cigarette.

JOEY Could we please talk about something else?!

ARTHUR Look, I want to say something. I'm gonna be very direct. I think the occasion calls for it. I've done . . . a lot of thinking about this matter, and a great deal of soul-searching. Now that the girls are all on their own, I feel that for my own self . . . I must come to this decision, though I don't take it lightly. I feel I've been a dedicated husband, and a responsible father. And I haven't regretted anything I've been called upon to do. Now . . . I feel I want to be by myself for a while. So, consequently, I've decided to move out of the house. Now, I don't know how I'll feel about it when I finally do it, and it's not irrevocable. But I feel it's something that I have to try. *(Eve listens to him, hands on chin, reacting. She fidgets with her fingers)* Well, as I say, it's . . . not an irrevocable situation. It's a separation. It may be for the best . . . it may not. But I'm going to lay it on the table . . . in front of everyone so that . . . everything is open and as direct as possible.
Joey, reacting, puts her hand to her mouth and begins to breathe slightly more heavily. Arthur, finished with his speech, takes a sip of coffee. Renata continues to smoke her cigarette.

EVE *(To Joey, about to cry herself)* Will you please not breathe so hard. *(Pausing, visibly upset)* I'll move out.

ARTHUR What does that mean?

EVE I don't want to live in this house anymore.

ARTHUR *(Moving his hands under the table)* Eve, think about it.

EVE *(Gritting her teeth)* I'll move out!

ARTHUR Look, it's not irrevocable. It's a trial separation.

EVE I can't be alone.

ARTHUR Eve . . .

EVE *(Touching her eyes, her forehead, and beginning to cry)* I don't want to discuss the details just now. Well, it's a very bad time for me.
The film moves back to the psychiatrist's office, to Renata.

RENATA My impotence set in a year ago. My paralysis. I suddenly found I couldn't bring myself to write anymore. Rather, I mean, I shouldn't say "suddenly." Actually it started happening last winter. Increasing thoughts about death just seemed to come over me. Um . . . these, uh . . . a preoccupation with my own mortality. These . . . feelings of futility in relation to my work. I mean, just what am I striving to create, anyway? I mean, to what end? For what purpose? What goal? *(Sighing)* I mean . . . do I really care if a handful of my poems are read after I'm gone forever? Is that supposed to be some sort of compensation? Uh, I used to think it was. But now, for some reason . . . I—I can't, I can't seem to . . . I can't . . . seem to shake this . . . the real implication of dying. It's terrifying. *(Sighing, crossing her arms in front of her)* The intimacy of it embarrasses me.

CUT TO:
INTERIOR. MIKE AND JOEY'S APARTMENT—NIGHT.

Mike, sprawled out on a cushioned couch with a notebook in his hand, is talking to Joey. She sits on a beige sofa, fingering a large pillow on her lap.

MIKE *(Looking at Joey)* What's the matter? You still thinking about your mother?

JOEY I can't believe Renata encourages her. And she fills her full of false hope.

MIKE She's just trying to keep her spirits up.

JOEY *(Shaking her head)* I want to quit my job.

MIKE *(Sighing)* Oh, Joey!

JOEY I can't keep my mind on it. I—I can't concentrate. I sit there all day reading other people's manuscripts, and halfway through I lose interest. I get headaches from the, uh, words. And then I'm supposed to sit down and write a . . . an opinion. It's not fair to the authors.

MIKE A month ago you said you finally found something you enjoyed.

JOEY Well, I was wrong. I think about going back to acting. *(Pausing, with a sigh)* I—I'm not an actress. Can't do that again. Flyn's the actress in this family.

MIKE   Why don't you work with me?

JOEY *(Scratching her forehead)*   Because political activity is not my interest. I'm too self-centered for . . . that.

MIKE *(Nodding)*   That's my whole point. It would get you off yourself.
He gets up from the couch and walks into the kitchen area to get a soda.

JOEY *(Talking almost to herself, upset and confused)*   Sometimes I think if
we had a child . . .   Oh, God! I . . . and-and that really makes me
anxious. I mean . . . it's totally irrevocable.

MIKE *(Sipping a soda)*   Whatever happened to your photography? You
have so much potential. You used to be so hot on that.

JOEY *(Still pulling at the threads of the pillow)*   I hate it. It's stupid. I feel
a real need to express something, but I don't know what it is I want
to express . . . or how to express it.

CUT TO:
INTERIOR. DRESS BOUTIQUE—DAY.

*Renata and her husband Frederick are looking at blouses and dresses on racks
in smart-looking shop.*

RENATA *(Sighing)*   It's always so difficult getting Mother a birthday
present. It's—uh, it's impossible.

FREDERICK   Hey, please, let's not stay forever at the party. I really
wanna get home and finish proofreading those galleys.

RENATA *(Browsing through a rack)*   Oh, come on, Frederick, really. I
really—I really . . . I hardly ever see Mother. I hardly ever spend any
time with her at all. And besides, it's not going to be so terrible. Flyn
will be there.

FREDERICK   Hah! Terrific! We'll get caught up on the latest Hollywood gossip.

RENATA   Oh, come on, Frederick, you know Flyn likes you. And don't
behave condescendingly, because I think she sort of senses that you
talk down to her.

FREDERICK   No, I don't talk down to Flyn. I love hearing about her
hair and her weight and her latest piece of TV junk she's done.

RENATA *(Snickering)*   Well, I don't know, that's her life. And anyway,
you have to admit that she is a sexy little girl.

FREDERICK   No, Flyn is the opposite of sexy. Hey, what about a scarf?
They walk to the opposite side of the store, passing the display window holding baskets of scarfs.

RENATA *(Barely glancing at the display)*   No.

FREDERICK   Flyn suffers from the same thing my last book suffered from. *(Laughing)* She's a perfect example of . . . form without any content.
He continues to laugh.

RENATA *(Laughing as she browses)*   That's very profound. And you haven't even started drinking yet.

FREDERICK *(Moving behind Renata and putting his hand on her shoulder)*
Yeah, I am profound. But I'm not the award-winning writer. You're the one who's supposed to be giving me insights into sex and other world-shattering phenomena.
He kisses her.

RENATA   Ooooh.

FREDERICK   Mmn. Really.

RENATA   Really, come on, let's go. Look, Frederick . . .

FREDERICK *(Overlapping)*   I wanna—
He kisses her again, pulling her to him; she pushes him away and walks off.

CUT TO:
INTERIOR. EVE'S APARTMENT—NIGHT.

The camera moves with Flyn as she walks through the living room greeting Eve. Frederick, Renata, Joey and Mike are in the background, chattering.

FLYN   You look fabulous, Mother. But the main thing is that you're feeling well.

EVE   Yes, but I tire so easily.

FREDERICK *(To Eve)*   Can I help you with something?

RENATA *(To Eve)*   Joey tells me that you're thinking about taking up some decorating projects again, Mother.

EVE   Yes, Joey pushes me. But I'm not going to accept anything until I'm sure I can maintain the level that I expect of myself.

RENATA Oh.

FLYN (*Gazing around the room*) Mother, I can't believe this room. It's
—it's just beautiful.
She walks over to the window and looks out; Eve joins her nearby.

EVE I'm getting used to it.

FLYN (*Looking out the window, absently*) Mmm.

EVE I miss the sea.

FLYN (*Nodding*) Yeah.
*While Eve and Flyn talk by the window, Frederick and Joey stand near the
dining-room table, looking across the room at Flyn; Frederick is opening a
bottle of champagne.*

FREDERICK I can't get over how sexy Flyn got.
He laughs.

JOEY Yeah. She looks beautiful, doesn't she?
The camera moves back to the window, to Eve and Flyn.

EVE (*Leaning against the wall next to the window*) Your new film is in
Arizona?

FLYN (*Looking at Eve*) No, it's in Denver. I leave tomorrow morning. I have to be ready to shoot on Monday. I have so many lines to learn. But it's just a television movie.

EVE Did you speak to Dad?

FLYN Ah, yeah, I spoke to him on the phone once.

EVE Did he mention anything?

FLYN Well, he said he visits you.

EVE Mm. Just now and then.
She leans her elbow on the window sill and brings her hand to her forehead; she bites her lip.

FLYN (*Turning, seeing Eve about to cry*) Mom . . .

EVE (*Grimacing, tears in her eyes*) I have nothing to live for anymore.

FLYN Come on, Mom, don't say that.

EVE (*Crying now, a handkerchief to her face*) It's true.

FLYN (*Trying to calm her*) You know that's not true. Mother . . . well, it—it's all right, Mom.

RENATA (*Walking over to the window*) What's the matter?

FLYN Nothing. She's fine. Come on, Mom. Mom, it's a trial separation.

RENATA Of course it is, Mother. I mean, you've been through this before. It just takes time. Everything'll work out.
Joey enters the scene, putting her hand on Eve's shoulder and glaring at Renata.

JOEY (*Disapproving, annoyed at what she's just heard*) Renata.

RENATA (*Aside, to Joey*) It's her birthday. Let her enjoy it.

JOEY Well, I don't think that's exactly the right way.
Renata looks away as the scene changes to the dining-room table, where Eve sits at its head, opening her presents.

EVE (*Taking a blouse, Renata and Frederick's gift, out of the box*) Ah!

RENATA Do you like it?
Eve laughs gaily.

MIKE   Oh, that's beautiful.

FREDERICK   That's beautiful.

EVE   Oh, now, that's lovely. That's—

JOEY *(Interrupting)*   Oh, I adore it.

EVE   —lovely.

FLYN   It probably'll be good for you.

MIKE   That's great.

JOEY *(To Flyn)*   It's exactly like yours . . . *(Fingering another blouse, another gift, on the table)* Very nice. *(Laughing at Flyn's teasing)* Thanks.

FLYN *(Laughing)*   It's lovely.

EVE *(Still holding the blouse)*   It's lovely.

RENATA.   Oh, I'm so glad. I hope it fits. I think it—   I'm pretty positive it will.

The group has now regathered in the living room. Eve sits on one couch; Renata on the sofa opposite Eve's; Frederick stands, his arms crossed, in front of a cabinet. While Renata speaks, Mike sits down next to her on the couch.

RENATA *(To Eve)* Well, Frederick has finished what I've already told him is his best work by far.

FREDERICK *(Laughing)* That's what she said about the last one.

RENATA *(Looking up at Frederick)* No, but I—I really feel that this one comes off. I mean, it's terribly precise.
Frederick picks up a bottle of champagne and begins refilling everyone's glasses as he replies to Renata.

FREDERICK Yeah, you said the same thing.

RENATA No, I didn't.

FREDERICK Uh, "precise" . . . "Sparing," you said.

RENATA *(Shrugging)* Oh, well.

FREDERICK Anyway, you couldn't think of anything you really liked about it, so you had to call it something.

RENATA Okay.

FREDERICK *(Overlapping)* Precise, sparing, gripping, meaning.

RENATA *(Lighting a cigarette)* Okay, okay. Well, you just can't handle a compliment, that's all.

FREDERICK Yeah, I know, I guess I can't.

JOEY *(Standing next to Renata)* We gotta go.

RENATA *(Looking up at Joey)* Oh, really? We hardly had any chance to speak.

JOEY I know.

RENATA *(Smoking her cigarette)* Well, so how are you doing? You seem . . . you look okay.

JOEY *(Smiling)* I'm good.

RENATA Good.

JOEY Ah, I read something of yours in a magazine. *New Yorker*, I . . . think. A poem called "Wondering." It was very beautiful.

RENATA (*Shrugging, smoking her cigarette*) It's an old poem. I redid it. And now when I reread it, I find it much too ambiguous. Na. I may redo it again.
The camera moves to Eve's bedroom, where Flyn is putting on her jacket in front of a mirror. Frederick enters the room to get his coat.

FREDERICK We're starting our drive back. Can we drop you someplace?

FLYN (*Still adjusting her jacket in front of the mirror*) I have to catch a plane real early tomorrow morning.

FREDERICK (*Putting on a raincoat*) Right. I heard you're shooting a movie in those cold Rocky Mountains of Colorado.

FLYN (*Leaving the mirror and picking up her purse*) Couldn't be someplace like Acapulco, huh? That's my idea of fantasy. Lie around on the beach, get waited on hand and foot.

FREDERICK (*Laughing*) Really. I can't take Mexico. I always think I'm gonna get shot just walking down the street.
The sound of a door buzzer interrupts them.

FLYN (*Reacting*) Oh, what was that?
The camera moves back to the living room, where Eve has opened the door, receiving a box of white roses. She smiles as she holds up the flowers and a card. The group gathers around her.

EVE (*Reading*) "Happy Birthday. Love, Arthur."

RENATA They're beautiful!

EVE (*Sniffing the roses, still smiling*) Ah. Well . . . I like white roses better than any other flower on earth.

FLYN (*Coming in from the bedroom*) There you are, Mother. See, I knew he wouldn't forget.

RENATA Oh, Mom—and you were worried?

EVE They're a good sign . . . don't you think?

CUT TO:
INTERIOR. RENATA AND FREDERICK'S HOUSE IN THE COUNTRY—NIGHT.

Renata walks into the bedroom, yanking a brush through her hair. She looks at herself in a full-length mirror; Frederick lies in bed, listless, a drink in his hand.

RENATA *(Angrily)* Well? Are you getting dressed, or what? Frederick! Are you talking to me?

FREDERICK We said everything.

RENATA *(Sighing)* Don't blame me. I mean, I've been nothing but understanding.

FREDERICK You don't help by patronizing me.

RENATA I wasn't patronizing you! Your work is . . . great! And who cares what the critics think?!

FREDERICK That's easy for you to say. You get nothing but encouragement. You're just their little darling.
Renata sits down at the vanity table and starts putting on her shoes.

RENATA *(Bending down)* Well, they're lenient with me obviously because I'm a woman.

FREDERICK Huh. It's because you're so damn good.

RENATA But so are you! All right, I mean, the book didn't get the response that it deserved. I hate to tell you how often they've missed the boat.

FREDERICK All right, stop lying to me! I count on you for honesty, not flattery!

RENATA I'm not lying! I'm not lying! *(Standing up to look in the mirror over her vanity)* And who cares what anybody thinks?!

FREDERICK I think what I think. My work won't show promise, and I haven't been able to deliver. It's as simple as that.

RENATA *(Turning away from the mirror to look at Frederick)* Your work is not fashionable, Frederick. You should . . . be thankful for that, for God's sakes! I mean, what are you after? The—the superficial acclaim of some little book reviewer in some room somewhere? I mean, we've always talked about fine work that means something in the long run.

FREDERICK *(Getting up from the bed to stand next to Renata by the mirror)* I don't care about fine work! I don't wanna wait twenty-five years to be appreciated. I wanna be able to knock somebody over now!

RENATA They're stricter with you because you attempt more. Don't you understand that? They refuse to take that into consideration!

FREDERICK (*Yelling*)   Stop looking for excuses! All right, I'm not writing for a time capsule. They won't give me an inch! And half the stuff that's written is garbage they praise sky-high!
Renata walks quickly out of the room. She returns, talking while she puts on her jacket at the vanity-table mirror.

RENATA   The baby-sitter will be here in a minute.

FREDERICK (*Sitting on the edge of the bed*)   I told you I'm not going!
He takes off one of his boots and flings it across the room.

RENATA (*Turning to look at him*)   We can't not go! What is the matter with you?!

FREDERICK (*Standing up now, looking at Renata's reflection in the mirror*)
I'm not in the mood for your lesbian friends and a lot of vacuous gossip about New York poetesses.

RENATA   Will you stop hitting yourself so much?! It's nauseating. I'm going.
When she starts to leave the room Frederick grabs her by the arm.

FREDERICK   Look, why can't you just once in a while . . . consider my feelings and my needs?!

RENATA   I'm sick of your needs! I'm tired of your idiosyncrasy and your competitiveness! I have my own problems!
Renata walks out and begins descending the hallway steps. Frederick follows her, standing at the top of the stairs.

FREDERICK   There'll be a lot of superficial chitchat about the nature of poetry. Your symbolism, your imagery, your contribution to whatever!

RENATA (*Looking up at Frederick from the middle of the staircase*)   We never see Marion and Gail! I don't understand. You used to like them.

FREDERICK   I can't stand 'em! They're so enthusiastic. College kids. I get embarrassed.
He begins to walk down the stairs.

RENATA   Oh, well, don't get embarrassed. Don't come. Stay home and drink yourself unconscious. That's one of the clichés of being a novelist you've had no problem with!
She walks down the stairs.

FREDERICK *(Holding up his drink in a mock toast)*   Yeah . . . I sure can drink.

RENATA   Oh, yes, you're fine as long as I keep everything going!

FREDERICK *(Walking down the stairs)*   What do you mean, keep everything going?

RENATA   Sssh.
They both stand at the bottom of the staircase now, arguing.

FREDERICK   You talking about that check that arrives from Daddy every month so that you can write yourself into immortality?

RENATA   I also raised the family that you wanted, or the family that you *thought* that you wanted!

FREDERICK   Hey! You made some noises about experiencing motherhood. I'm sure you thought it was great potential raw material.

RENATA *(Overlapping)*   It—

FREDERICK *(Interrupting)*   Well, now you got another human being . . . three of us!

RENATA   It wasn't my idea! And I'm not ashamed to be subsidized, either! I turn things out!
She turns and walks into the living room. Frederick sits on the bottom step and looks down at the floor.

FREDERICK *(Whispering)*   Yeah, you do. You turn things out. You're incredible.
Renata walks back into the hallway; she kneels down in front of Frederick.

RENATA *(Softly)*   Frederick . . . *(Sighing)* Frederick, you have so much to offer. I wanna help—uh . . . not hurt.

FREDERICK   I can't go out. I-I-I'm not in the mood. I'm liable to kill somebody.
Renata gets up, resigned.

RENATA   I'm going. 'Night.
She walks out.

CUT TO:
INTERIOR. EVE'S LIVING ROOM—NIGHT.

Arthur sits on the edge of a chair, a cup of coffee in his hand; Eve sits across from him on the sofa, also drinking coffee.

ARTHUR   Well, you look as good as I've seen you in a long time.

EVE *(Smiling)* Oh.

ARTHUR   And in no time at all, you've turned this place into . . . a lovely home.

EVE   I saw Joey last week. I may be working on her apartment. Mike seems amenable. He isn't really what I had in mind for Joey. But I'm getting more used to him.

ARTHUR   She has no direction. I expected such great things from her. She was an extraordinary child.

EVE   And how are you getting along, Arthur?

ARTHUR *(Taking a sip of coffee)*   Fine. I'm fine. Busy. Tsch. It's important to keep busy.

EVE   Did you like the Matisse drawing? It was on sale at Parke Bernet.

ARTHUR   Oh, yes. It's lovely. It's so . . . delicate.
Eve smiles and sips her coffee. Arthur puts down his coffee on the table; he stands up.

ARTHUR   Tsch. Well . . . We'll talk, Eve. *(He bends over Eve and kisses her on the forehead.)* Good night.
An abrupt cut to Eve's hands putting wide black masking tape around the borders of her apartment windows, her doors. She reaches the end of the black tape roll; she breaks off the end and finishes the job with white adhesive tape. Eve's hands work methodically, exactingly; the noise of the pulling and tearing of tape is the only sound over this scene.
When the windows and doors are all sealed, Eve goes into the kitchen. Again, the camera shows only her hands as first one, then two, then all four knobs on her stove are turned on.
Finished, Eve re-enters the living room. The camera shows her full figure now; she is dressed in an elegant robe. She stares at the couch for a moment; she sits down and, finally, lies down full length. It is very quiet.
The jarring sounds of a siren cuts through the quiet as an ambulance is seen tearing down Park Avenue.

CUT TO:
INTERIOR. HOSPITAL ROOM—DAY.

Eve is lying in a hospital bed; Arthur sits in a nearby chair, his hand is over her folded ones on the sheet. When Eve stirs, Arthur takes away his hand. The camera then cuts first to Renata, sitting at the window watching Eve, then to Joey, who is standing up near the bed, anxiously looking down at her mother.

CUT TO:
INTERIOR. HOSPITAL CORRIDOR—DAY.

Arthur is walking out of Eve's room, putting on his coat. He sees Renata leaning against a stretcher; they walk down the corridor together, discussing the situation.

ARTHUR   She's got to go back to the sanitarium for a while at least.

RENATA *(Nodding)*   I know. I just . . .   Oh, poor Joey. Poor Joey. *(Sighing)* She spends so much time with her, and I don't know, but—   What's the point? I mean, we can't watch her constantly. There's no way you can be with her all the time.

ARTHUR   How is Joey? I worry about her. She's . . . she seems to be floundering.

RENATA *(Shrugging)*   I don't know. I—I guess she hasn't found herself yet.

ARTHUR   Couldn't you help her? She looks up to you.

RENATA   Well, I do, Dad. I try. I try to su—   I try to be supportive. I try to encourage her.

ARTHUR   I'm not . . . criticizing, but . . . it just seems to me there's always been an antagonism between you two.

RENATA   Well, you know Joey. She tends to be competitive with me. I'm . . . I don't know.

ARTHUR   Well, you're very successful. I think you kind of hold that over her.

RENATA   Oh, come on, Dad, that's not true!
They walk over to the elevator; Renata presses the down button.

ARTHUR   Now, Renata, I'm not blind. I see what's going on. You—you seclude yourself in Connecticut, acting out the part of the aloof artist. And no one can get near you.

RENATA   I don't want to discuss this right now, Dad, okay? Can we just . . . avoid the subject? I'm upset. You're upset.

ARTHUR   Joey had such potential. And . . . now it's come to nothing.

RENATA   Uh! It's so typical. It's so typical. As usual you're obsessed with Joey while Mother is lying in . . . a hospital room.

ARTHUR *(Angrily)*   Now, don't blame me for that! That's nobody's fault.
They enter the elevator and the film cuts to:

EXTERIOR. SANITARIUM GROUNDS—DAY.

Joey, Renata and Eve are walking toward the camera. It is very bright; there is snow on the ground and the three women are bundled in winter coats.

EVE   How's Frederick?

RENATA   Oh, fine. He's going to be teaching at Barnard.

EVE   Oh, how nice.

JOEY   I read something he wrote recently in, uh, the Sunday *Times Book Review,* I think. It was very nasty *(Laughing)* but very funny.
The camera changes position, showing now the backs of the women as they walk through the sanitarium grounds chatting.

JOEY   It's a giraffe . . . enormous. Cory would love it. Uh, eh, it's probably way too much money, but I'd really like to buy her one.

RENATA   She's so cute. She sits and has conversations with the television set.

EVE   *(Chuckling)*   Oh, she's such a pretty thing.
The film cuts to Joey and Renata walking together away from the sanitarium. Renata is smoking a cigarette; Joey has her hands in her coat pockets.

RENATA   *(Taking a drag on her cigarette)*   How's Mike?

JOEY   Fine.

RENATA   Good.

JOEY   You know, we'd, uh, love to get together with you and Frederick.

RENATA   Oh, well, that'd be great, but I—I, you know, it's been sort of a rough week for me.

JOEY   Well, it doesn't necessarily have to be this week.

RENATA   *(Sighing)*   You know, I mean, I gotta give Frederick a chance to get settled in at Barnard.

JOEY   Rennie, why do you keep pushing me away?

RENATA   *(Reacting)*   Well, I don't.

JOEY   Yeah, yeah, you do. I mean, it's like you don't even want me near you.

RENATA   Oh, Joey, come on! You know, I mean, I . . . I—you know that I've been having some work problems. I need isolation. I need to be alone. The . . . the creative thing is a very— It's very delicate. It's—

JOEY *(Interrupting)*   Well, that's great, isn't it? I mean, you're hiding behind your work, Flyn's never here, and I inherited Mother.

RENATA   Well, I-I-I see Mother, too. I phone her.

JOEY   Yeah. But you're in Connecticut, and I end up with all the dirty work.

RENATA   Look, Joey . . . I can't help it if you feel guilty about your feelings toward Mother. I mean, you-you-you can't seem to do enough to make up for it.

JOEY *(Looking at Renata)*   Hey, what's that supposed to mean?

RENATA   You know what it means. You could never stand her.

JOEY *(Upset)*   I-I don't believe this. My whole life I've only wanted to be her.

RENATA   Yeah . . . well, for a while there you were her, weren't you?

JOEY (*Shaking her head*)   I don't know what you're talking about.

RENATA   Oh, Joey, you know what I'm talking about! All those head-aches every time she'd come home from the hospital. You never wanted her to come home.

JOEY   This is incredible. I mean, you twist everything I say. I-I-I give up!

CUT TO:
INTERIOR. RENATA AT HOME—DAY.

Renata is sitting intense at her desk in the semidark. She has written a couple of poetry lines on a yellow lined pad; she crosses out one word with her pencil and writes another above it. She is fingering her face in concentration.

RENATA (*Reading the lines she wrote*)   Hhm.
She crosses out the new word, her pencil poised to add a new one. Instead, she shakes her head and rips off the sheet of paper. She crumbles it and gets up. She sighs and walks over to the window. She sits down on the ledge, closing her eyes, then opening them to look out at the branches of the trees surrounding the house. It is very quiet. Renata sighs again, her breathing becoming labored. She stares at the trees, perspiration breaking out on her forehead. She wipes away the sweat, then walks into the bathroom, still breathing heavily. She walks over to the sink.

RENATA (*Washing her face*)   Ohhh.
Renata now walks into the hallway. She turns and sees her daughter, Cory, contentedly playing with some stuffed animals on the floor near the staircase railing. The sunlight through the windows almost silhouettes Cory. Renata stares at her daughter for a moment, her breathing still labored.
The film cuts to the stairs and the trees outside the windows; Renata, walking down the steps, abruptly blocks the view. The camera follows her as she walks into the foyer, then the living room, where Frederick, sitting on the couch, is busily looking through some photographs.
Breathing hard, Renata sits down next to her husband.

FREDERICK (*Looking up*)   You okay?

RENATA (*Sighing deeply*)   I just experienced the strangest sensation.

FREDERICK   Well, you look kind of pale.

RENATA (*Gasping*)   It was as if I had a sudden . . . clear vision where everything seems . . . sort of awful . . . and predatory. (*Sighing and gesturing)* It was like—it was like I . . . was here, and the world was out there, and I couldn't bring us together.

FREDERICK *(Putting his hand on Renata's thigh, comfortingly)* Could you maybe have dozed off and had one of those dreams?

RENATA *(Shaking her head)* No. No, because the same thing happened last week when I was reading upstairs. *(Sighing)* I suddenly became hyper aware of my body. Uh . . . I could feel my heart beating, and I began to imagine that— *(Sighing)* I could . . . feel some blood sort of coursing through my veins, and . . . my hands and in the back of my . . . neck. Oh . . . I felt precarious. It was like I was a machine that was functioning, but I could just conk out at any second.
Frederick leans over and puts his arm around Renata. He kisses her on the cheek.

FREDERICK Hey . . . you're not gonna conk out.

RENATA *(Softly)* No.

FREDERICK You gotta put those kinds of thoughts out of your head.

RENATA Yeah. *(Sighing)* It frightens me, too, you know, because . . . I'm not that far from the age when my mother began showing signs of strain.

FREDERICK You're not your mother. You're not, you're not. You've been under some kind of stress, and you haven't been sleeping well, and things like that, that's all.
Frederick hugs her tightly.

RENATA Oh . . . um . . . um. *(She breaks away, reaching for the photographs on Frederick's lap. She glances through them)* Oh . . . What are these? Uh, are these Joey's photographs, these?

FREDERICK Oh, yeah.

RENATA Let me see them.

FREDERICK They're not very good, I'm afraid.

RENATA No, she doesn't really have an eye.

FREDERICK Uhm. She's gonna wanna know what you think, so you better get ready.

RENATA Poor Joey. She has all the anguish and, uh, anxiety, the artistic personality, without any of the talent. And, naturally, I'm put in the position of having to encourage her.

FREDERICK Na, tell her the truth. Get it over with. Don't lead her on.

RENATA I don't lead her on. But, I mean, God, I can't break her heart. And you know how competitive she is with me.
She gets up and goes over to the window.

FREDERICK I always think it's better to level with a person. I wish you'd done that with me more often.

RENATA (*Looking out the window, her hands stretched out on top of her head*) I did.

FREDERICK No, you didn't. You flattered me, and I liked it.

RENATA (*Lowering her arms, still looking out the window*) Frederick, you're good, and I've never hesitated to say it.

FREDERICK There's something missing from my work. I don't know. (*Sighing*) I don't know if I lost it or I never had it, or what.

RENATA (*Turning to look at Frederick*) You're capable of being extraordinary, and you stop for spite!

FREDERICK (*Turning to look at Renata, who is now standing with her back to him*) No, not for spite! (*Pausing and picking up the photographs*) I'll get back to it someday.

RENATA (*Turning to look at Frederick again*) You throw everything away to spite me!

FREDERICK (*Looking down at the photographs*) Let's not talk about it, okay?!

RENATA (*Sighing, looking out the window again*) Fine.

FREDERICK What are you gonna say to Joey?

RENATA She should just marry Michael, and stop her obsessive worrying about being so damn creative! Sometimes she just annoys me.
She walks out of the room.

The film cuts to Joey and Eve driving on a New York highway. Joey's behind the wheel; Eve is staring out her window at the barren landscape; she rolls up the window, continuing to stare out.

INTERIORS

CUT TO:
INTERIOR. EVE'S BEDROOM—NIGHT.

Eve is in bed, watching a religious show on television. Absorbed in the program, she absently picks up a glass of red wine from her night table and sips; the television is heard over the scene, though the screen is never actually seen.

MAN'S VOICE   Praise the Lord. Oh, Jesus . . . It's an exciting thing to be a Christian. Now, I have a gentleman who's a friend of mine . . . a fairly new friend, but, uh, our friendship goes way back to the cross at Calvary. Roy Schwartz . . . uh, it's a delight to have you here today. Now, Roy, you are by birth what nationality?

ROY'S VOICE   A Hebrew.

MAN'S VOICE   A Hebrew. When I was talking about God's chosen people, and you're probably very aware, and you studied your history, you're involved in this, what part did the Jewish people and the nation of Israel have in God's time piece today?

CUT TO:
INTERIOR. DECORATOR AND DESIGN BUILDING—DAY.

Joey is seen entering the building through the outer glass door; she is walking quickly. As she goes through the building, she sees Mike, who's been waiting for her. They both walk briskly to the elevator bank.

MIKE   You're late.

JOEY   I'm sorry.

MIKE   It's forty-five minutes.

JOEY   The traffic was unbearable. I'm sorry.

MIKE   Well, you should take that into account. Your mother's been waiting for over an hour.

JOEY *(Overlapping)*   Could we drop this please?! My head is splitting.

MIKE   What's the matter?

JOEY   Well, what do you think? I'm pregnant.

MIKE   Thought you might be.

JOEY   I'm goddamned annoyed!

MIKE   It's all right. We'll take care of it.
They stand at the elevators, waiting for one to open, arguing, while busy passers-by move in and out of the scene.

JOEY *(Staring at the closed elevator door, her hands in her pockets)*   Well, naturally, we'll take care of it. You don't think I'm gonna have a kid, do you?!

MIKE *(Overlapping)*   Joey, I said we'll take care of it! It's nothing.

JOEY *(Shaking her head)*   I'm so stupid! How can I be so careless?!

MIKE   All right, it happens. You know, we could have a kid. It wouldn't be the end of the world.

JOEY   For you maybe. For me it'd be the end of the world.

MIKE   I'm sorry you feel that way.

JOEY   Oh! Michael, I've thought about it. It's absurd. I mean, how could we have a kid? I don't even know where my life is going.

MIKE   Maybe it's not such a great idea.

JOEY   You don't think so either?

MIKE   I guess not.

CUT TO:
INTERIOR. RUG SHOWROOM—DAY.

Eve stands in the middle of a large rug showroom; she looks up from some samples as Joey and Mike enter the room.

EVE   Well, what happened to you?

JOEY   Nothing. I'm sorry.

EVE   Oh, we found something wonderful for the bedroom.

MIKE   This won't be too expensive, I hope.

EVE   Well, it's a little more than we planned, but—

MIKE *(Interrupting)*   Eve, we had this discussion already.

JOEY *(Overlapping)*   Can we not get into a financial dispute?

EVE   It's right over here. I think you'll like it. *(Eve and Joey move through the rug showroom, away from Mike, to an area where rug samples hang in racks)* Your father's back from Greece.

INTERIORS

JOEY Is he?

EVE Well, you know he's back from Greece. You're having dinner with him tomorrow at Renata's. Renata told me. Were you not going to tell me?

JOEY. Yes. I just know how you are on that whole subject.

EVE Will you talk to him, Joey? He listens to you.

JOEY He's a grown man! He makes his own decisions.

EVE Yes, but he puts great store by what you have to say.

JOEY If he wants to move back in with you, he will. If he doesn't, he won't!

EVE Why are you so reluctant to help me?!

JOEY Reluctant?! I do nothing but cater to you!

EVE Joey, it's as though you don't care whether we get back together or not.

JOEY You're crazy. Why wouldn't I want you to be happy? I just think you shouldn't delude yourself.

EVE Will you tell him how well I've been doing? That my work is finally flourishing again, and that my mood swings are less rapid.

JOEY He doesn't care!

EVE He just wants to know that I'm on an even keel, that's all, and I have an inner tranquillity, and that I wouldn't—

JOEY *(Interrupting, turning to leave)* Leave me alone.

EVE *(Overlapping)* Joey!

JOEY *(Yelling)* Just leave me out of this!
She runs out of the showroom.

EVE *(Loudly)* Joey, where are you going?!

CUT TO:
INTERIOR. TAXI.

Mike and Joey are sitting in the back seat, talking.

MIKE Joey, maybe it wouldn't be such a bad idea to have a child.

JOEY Oh, please!

MIKE I mean, sometimes it's just taking an action—

JOEY I can't, okay?!

MIKE You mean you won't.

JOEY Why do you stay with me? I-I don't understand you. I give you nothing but grief.

MIKE I think you should take the job at the advertising agency, and we should maybe, uh, think about getting settled.

JOEY Yeah, right, that—that's all I need. I start writing copy and having kids, I'd never get out of it. Be swallowed up in some anonymous life style! I want to do something with my life! God, now I'm guilty 'cause I left Mother standing there.
Mike folds his arms around himself and turns to look out the window.

MIKE She'll be fine.

JOEY Oh, a lot you care!

MIKE It's your mother that can't stand *me.*
It's later that night. Mike is in bed, sound asleep under the covers. Joey, in pajamas, still wearing her glasses, is sitting up, staring into space. She runs her hand through her hair and turns to look at Mike. Impulsively, she reaches over to him and leans her head against his back. She then puts her arm around him. Mike wakes up and rolls over; Joey kisses him.

CUT TO:
INTERIOR. RENATA'S HOUSE—DAY.

The camera moves with Renata as she walks through her foyer with Cory in her arms. A book is held up against her arm and torso. She chats with her daughter while sounds of company in the living room are overheard.

MIKE *(Offscreen, in the living room)* Well . . .

RENATA *(To Cory)* I hope the cat isn't in the kitchen.
Renata walks into the living room, where Mike, Joey and Frederick sit talking. She puts Cory down, and as she speaks, puts the book she was holding back in the overstuffed bookcase.

RENATA Cory's gonna go upstairs and play for a while. *(To Cory)* Okay, Cory? I'll see you later, all right?

CORY   Okay.

RENATA   All right. Good-bye.
Cory leaves the room.

FREDERICK *(Resuming the conversation)*   I mean, I think I could get them all out in about a month and a half.

MIKE   And then . . . you wouldn't have anything left to say, right?
The doorbell rings; Frederick goes off to answer the door.

JOEY *(Expecting the new guest to be her father)*   Dad.

RENATA *(Rearranging her bookshelves)*   He was so excited when I spoke to him. He saw that terrible movie that Flyn was in on the plane.
The camera stays focused on Joey's face. She is sitting on the sofa, looking expectantly at the doorway. She hears her father talking to Frederick in the hallway.

ARTHUR *(Offscreen)*   Hello, how are you?

FREDERICK *(Offscreen)*   Come in.

ARTHUR *(Offscreen)*   Nice to see you.

FREDERICK (Offscreen)   It's good to see you.

ARTHUR *(Still offscreen)*　I'm sorry I'm late. The traffic in this town is getting impossible.
Joey's smile turns to shock as Arthur enters the room. Her face stays frozen in surprise as the camera pulls back, revealing the cause of her stare. Arthur stands near the sofa, his hand outstretched to greet everyone. And next to him is Pearl, in a red dress and black fur stole.

ARTHUR *(To the group)*　Hi . . .　Hi, Mike. Hi, Joey.

JOEY *(Composing herself)*　Hi, Daddy.

ARTHUR *(Nodding)*　Renata.

RENATA　Hello, Dad.

ARTHUR　Hi. This is Pearl.

MIKE　Hello.

PEARL *(Nodding)*　Hi.

MIKE　I'm Mike. This is Joey.

PEARL　Glad to meet you. Hi.

MIKE *(Gesturing to Renata)*　Renata.

RENATA　Hello.

FREDERICK　I'm Frederick.

PEARL　Hi.

RENATA　Um . . . Would you like anything to drink?

PEARL　Well, uh, whatever Arthur's having is fine.
Arthur sits down on the sofa.

FREDERICK *(To Pearl, gesturing toward the couch)*　Here, uh . . . why don't you sit down there. It's probably the only comfortable place in the house.
Arthur holds his hand out to Pearl, who sits down next to him.

ARTHUR　Ah, it's good to be back.

FREDERICK *(After a pause)*　Well, I'm sure you must have enjoyed Athens.

ARTHUR　Oh, you can't beat the Greek islands for sand and blue water.

PEARL (*Putting her hand on Arthur's wrist*)   And the food! I could eat lamb six times a day.
Pearl laughs and the camera quickly cuts to Joey, reacting to Pearl's hand on Arthur's wrist, to this surprise, as Pearl and Arthur talk.

PEARL (*Offscreen*)   And this one with the ouzo . . .
The way she pronounces the Greek liqueur—"isuzu"—it sounds more like a Japanese car.

ARTHUR (*Offscreen*)   The only problem I had was nobody spoke English.
The film moves back to Arthur and Pearl. Renata hands them each a drink.

PEARL (*Taking the offered drink*)   Oh, it didn't matter. Everybody understood what was important.

JOEY   Did you get a chance to see any of the temples . . . architecture?

ARTHUR   Oh, yes. Oh, it's so wonderful. You're steeped in history. We saw some great examples from the fifth century B.C. Remember that little island with the temple?

PEARL   Yeah.

ARTHUR   Beautifully preserved.

PEARL (*Touching Arthur*)   To tell you the truth, I prefer the beaches.
She laughs.

ARTHUR (*Laughing with Pearl*)   She could sit in the sun all day.

PEARL   Oh, that's enough ruins. You . . . how many ruins can you see? Oh, but that hot sand and that blue water, that's for me.

RENATA   Well, I don't wanna rush anyone . . . but maybe we should continue this, uh, conversation in the other room.
They all get up from their seats and start walking into the dining room.

PEARL (*To no one in particular*)   First time I went to Europe—with my first husband . . . *many* years ago—all we saw was churches. One cathedral after another. Don't misunderstand. They were beautiful. But . . . so you see two or three, that's enough already. All the day—

JOEY (*Aside, to Renata*)   Did you know he was bringing someone?

RENATA   Yes. Didn't I mention it?

CUT TO:
INTERIOR. DINING ROOM—NIGHT.

The camera is focused on Pearl, sitting on Arthur's left. She is eating and drinking heartily, talking to the group animatedly.

PEARL *(Shaking her head)*   Give me a good sirloin anytime. Charcoaled. They talk about club steaks and porterhouse. Sirloin, charcoaled and blood-rare.

ARTHUR *(Sipping his wine)*   Pearl's husband was something of a chef.

PEARL *(Touching Arthur's arm)*   Hm. He was an amateur chef. Actually, he was in the jewelry business. My first husband, may he rest in peace. Adam, my second, was an orthodontist.

RENATA *(Making a face)*   How many have you had?

PEARL *(Sipping her drink)*   Two. Adam had a massive coronary. Rudy was an alcoholic. *(To Arthur)* Would you like some more gravy?

ARTHUR   Oh, no, no, no. It's too heavy.

PEARL *(Passing him the gravy saucer)*   Oh . . . what are you worried about? It's delicious. Try it.

MIKE   Where are you from, Pearl?

PEARL   Florida. Oh, we lived all over the place when I was younger. But I—I prefer a warm climate. I even lived in Australia for a year. *(Chewing a piece of food)* Mmm. With my sister Fay, when Adam died. I went nuts. It's dead there.

MIKE   I was in, uh, Sydney, Australia, once.

PEARL   Oh . . . Well, was I lying? Did you like it?

MIKE   Well, it was just a vacation, you know. I was only there a couple of days.

PEARL *(Eating)*   Lucky! Oh, it's like a morgue. Nothing to do at night, no pizzazz. I couldn't take that.

ARTHUR *(Laughing)*   Here's a woman who could go dancing every night.
He touches Pearl's shoulder affectionately, then takes her hand in his.

PEARL *(Talking with food in her mouth)*   Well, you know what I say. You only live once. But once is enough if you play it right.

RENATA Do you have any children, Pearl?

PEARL *(Chewing her food)* Oh, yes, I have two sons. Lewis and John. Lewis is in real estate. John runs an art gallery.

RENATA Oh?

PEARL *(Nodding)* In the lobby in Caesars Palace in Las Vegas. Well, it's not—not exactly a gallery. It's more a . . . a concession.

JOEY *(Sarcastically, sipping her wine)* Paintings of clowns on black velvet?

PEARL That's right. Junk. Oh, I tell you, it's pure junk. But people like it. They get a kick out of it. He does very nicely.

ARTHUR Pearl collects African art.

PEARL Oh, oh, I . . . love black ebony. Mmm. I own some statues. Actually, they-they're-they're from Trinidad. Oh, I-I love those real primitive statues with the big hips and the big breasts. I even have some voodoo masks. I believe in that stuff. I could tell your fortune, but I need a deck of cards. Later, maybe.
Everyone is now eating dessert. The camera has left Pearl and now encompasses the group (except Renata) sitting around the table as a whole. The film catches them in the middle of a conversation about a new play.

ARTHUR Uh, this couple we met in Aegina that were raving about it. So I cabled right away to the office to get two tickets. I'm glad I did. It was fabulous.
Renata walks into the scene, carrying a pitcher of cream. She places it on the table and takes her seat at its head.

RENATA *(Sitting down)* Yeah, I know, I know. We thought it was very interesting too.

FREDERICK But depressing as hell. I mean, it was pessimistic to the point of futility.

ARTHUR Passion with pessimism is all the rage nowadays.

FREDERICK When they sentenced those Algerians to death, I thought that was a good imaginative ending.

RENATA See, I don't know. I mean, you call it fashionable, but it's hard to argue that in the face of death, life loses real meaning.

PEARL *(With a puzzled expression on her face)* It is?

RENATA   Well . . . *(Laughing)* I mean, I can't argue it succinctly, but I suppose if you've read Socrates or Buddha or Schopenhauer, even Ecclesiastes . . . they're very convincing.

PEARL   Well, they should know. I don't read that much.

MIKE   What struck me was the way the terrorists . . . only killed if they absolutely had to, never wantonly, just if they had to, to achieve their own aims. I was very moved when that, uh, Algerian boy said he killed in the name of freedom. Yeah, it gave me chills.

RENATA   It's still killing for an abstraction.

MIKE   Why? You—you value the life of a single person over the lives of thousands of others?

RENATA   *(Smoking a cigarette)*   Well, I don't know. I mean, who are those thousands? It's another abstraction.

FREDERICK   To me, eh . . . uh, the conflict over the getting of the information between the French doctor and the Algerian wa-was the best part of the play.

JOEY   I know. I—uh . . . The writer argued both sides so brilliantly you didn't know who was right.

PEARL *(Looking confused)*   I didn't get that. I mean, uh, to me it wasn't such a big deal. One guy was a squealer, the other guy wasn't. I liked the guy that wasn't.

FREDERICK *(Laughing)*   Well, it was a little more complex than that, don't you think?

PEARL   Why? You liked the squealer? Did I miss something?

JOEY   That's what made me anxious about the play. I mean . . . *(Sighing)* How do you figure out the right thing to do? How do you know?

PEARL *(Still looking puzzled)*   How do you know? I don't know. You just . . . know. I mean, you feel it. I mean . . . you just don't squeal. I don't know.
She shrugs her shoulders.

FREDERICK *(After a pause)*   Anyway, it was a good evening in the theater for a change.
The camera moves closer to Pearl and Arthur.

ARTHUR   I'd love another piece of cheese cake, but, uh—

PEARL (*Interrupting*)   Well, have it. Oh . . . what are you worried about? You'll live to be a hundred if you give up all the things that make you want to.
Pearl cuts him another piece of cake and hands it to him. Arthur licks some cheese cake off Pearl's fingers, then kisses her hand, laughing.

JOEY (*Reacting to the scene in front of her*)   Am I the only one, or is it hot in here? Can we open a window?

CUT TO:
INTERIOR. RENATA'S LIVING ROOM—NIGHT.

It is later that evening. Pearl, more comfortable now, sits on the couch; Mike sits next to her, fascinated, as she starts showing him a card trick. Frederick, a drink in his hand, leans on the back of the couch, observing the two of them.

PEARL (*To Mike, holding her deck of cards*)   Okay. Ready?

MIKE (*Nodding*)   Mm huh.

PEARL   Okay, pick a card. Anyone. Anyone.
She laughs.

MIKE (*Picking a card*)   Okay. Here you go.

PEARL   Okay, put it back.

FREDERICK   Let me see it.
Mike shows the card to Frederick; he starts to put it back in the deck, but he can't make up his mind where it should go.

PEARL (*Urging*)   Anyplace, anyplace.

MIKE   Okay.
He finally puts the card back in the deck.

PEARL   All right. Okay.

FREDERICK   I'm ready.

PEARL (*Shuffling the cards*)   All right. Now we shuffle.

MIKE (*Watching her, confused*)   What do you . . .? All right.

PEARL   What?

MIKE   No, nothing. Just go ahead.

PEARL   All right. (*Turning over a card*) Is it that?

MIKE *(Shaking his head)*   No, no.

PEARL *(Turning over another card)*   That?

MIKE   No.
Pearl turns over yet another card, laughing.

PEARL   That?

MIKE   No, no.

PEARL   Okay. It's none of those three, right?

MIKE and FREDERICK   None of those three.

PEARL   Okay. *(She turns over a card and places it on the sofa between herself and Mike)* Not that one. *(Turning over a second card)* Not that one.

MIKE *(Shaking his head)*   No.

PEARL *(Smiling, pausing slightly)*   That one.
Frederick and Mike laugh, acknowledging Pearl's success.

FREDERICK   That was great.

MIKE   How did you do that?

PEARL *(Gesturing)*   Oh, what's the difference?

MIKE   That is a miraculous card trick. And I was watching really closely this time. Where did you learn that?

PEARL   Oh, I'm a gal that's been around. I've picked up a lot of useless information.

MIKE   You tell fortunes . . . you do, uh, card tricks. You do seances, too?

PEARL   Oooh. Not me. I figure whatever's out there, it's their business. Besides, you—you think I want to bring back my ex-husbands?
Pearl spreads the cards out on the couch to show another trick while Mike and Frederick look on, laughing.
The scene abruptly changes to Renata's upstairs bedroom. While Pearl is showing card tricks to Mike and Frederick, Renata, Joey and Arthur are having a serious discussion. Arthur sits on Renata's bed; Renata, smoking a cigarette, sits in a nearby chair; Joey stands against the wall, her arms folded across her chest.

ARTHUR   As soon as possible, Pearl and I are going to get married.

JOEY   Oh, God. (*Sighing*) Well, that's gonna sink Mother.

ARTHUR   She'll have a hard time at first, but she'll get over it.

JOEY   Well, that's easy for you to say.

ARTHUR   It's not easy!

RENATA   Well, how long have you known her, Dad?

ARTHUR   Now, a month.

JOEY   A month? Uh, isn't that a little hasty?

ARTHUR   We've spent a lot of time together.

JOEY   That's a lot of time? Four weeks?

ARTHUR   Now, I expect you all at the wedding. Flyn, too. I insist that Flyn fly in and meet Pearl and be there when we're married.

RENATA (*Lighting a cigarette*)   Well, I must admit that the whole thing does seem a little bit fast.

ARTHUR   Now, it's gonna be fine. She's a nice woman. She's kind. She's affectionate. Christ, I'm sixty-three years old. I wanna relax. I'm happy just to lie on the beach with her. (*Joey groans, reacting*) And I like it that she's full of energy, and demonstrative and open.

JOEY (*Angrily*)   You just met her! She's a—a widow, and you're a wealthy man.

ARTHUR   What's that supposed to mean? She's after my money?

RENATA (*Trying to calm Arthur*)   She's not saying that.

JOEY   Why? Is that so far-fetched?

ARTHUR (*Angrily*)   I won't dignify that.

RENATA   Don't get upset. It's just a man in your position has to be careful.

ARTHUR   You don't know her yet. She's a fine woman, and I love her.

JOEY   Okay, all right. But it's going to be the worst possible thing that could happen to Mother.

ARTHUR   I can't believe she still imagines we're gonna get back together after all this time.

JOEY *(Pointedly)* Of course she imagines it, because everyone *except me* leads her on!

RENATA *(Gesturing)* I don't wanna hear that old story.

JOEY Oh, well, it's true! *(Turning to Arthur)* And from the day you moved out, all that talk about a trial separation! You were never coming back.

ARTHUR I wanted to let her down easily! She's such a fragile thing.

JOEY Oh! Well, she is not a thing. I mean—well, we all treat her like a patient in a hospital. She's a human being!

RENATA Oh, your idea of treating her like a human being is always to throw cold water on her hopes all the time!

JOEY *(Putting her hands in her pockets)* What hopes? Now look what's happening.

RENATA It was bound to happen sooner or later, Joey. The most that we could do was . . . postpone it a little bit.

JOEY Well, all she lives for . . . She's accustomed to—

ARTHUR *(Interrupting)* Don't give me that responsibility.

JOEY And now you're to abandon her for this . . . this—

ARTHUR *(Pointing his finger)* Joey! Don't you go any further.

RENATA *(Smoking a cigarette)* All right . . . Dad, don't get upset. Don't get all riled up.

ARTHUR *(Pointing his finger at both Renata and Joey)* And don't think I don't notice the both of you looking at her in a very judgmental superior way.

RENATA Now you're imagining things.

JOEY *(Crossing her arms)* Uh, we knew . . . er—about your affairs when Mother was in the hospital, but your choices were just a little more discreet!

RENATA *(Anxiously)* Joey! Shut up! Dad . . . she's upset.

ARTHUR Joey, why do you do this to me? You know how much your opinion means to me.

JOEY *(Loudly)* She's a vulgarian!

RENATA   Joey, be quiet.

ARTHUR *(Getting up from the bed)*   I don't wanna discuss this.

RENATA *(Standing up and going to Arthur)*   I think you should do as you feel with our blessing.

ARTHUR *(Standing at the doorway, pleading)*   Joey, I count on you!

JOEY *(Still standing against the wall, her arms crossed)*   I'm sorry. I—I can't help it.
She shakes her head.

RENATA *(Leaning now on her closet door)*   Will you tell him it's okay?! Obviously it's your approval he needs.

JOEY   He certainly had no trouble getting yours!

RENATA *(Coldly, her arms crossed)*   Clearly, it doesn't mean as much as yours.

ARTHUR *(Walking around the room)*   I want the support of all my daughters! I'm not just here to make sacrifices and foot the bills! It's time you thought of me!
The film abruptly cuts to Joey and Mike driving home. Mike is behind the wheel; Joey sits looking out her window. The only sound is the traffic outside. And as Joey and Mike ride home, the scene shifts to Renata sitting on the edge of her bed; Frederick is next to her, under the covers and looking at her with half-closed eyes. She sighs and takes a pill from the bottle on the night table. She swallows it with some water, staring straight ahead at nothing in particular.

CUT TO:
INTERIOR. CATHEDRAL—DAY.

The camera shows a dim, candlelit cathedral. The voices of Eve and Arthur are heard, but the screen does not show them yet. All that can be seen is the sprawling, immense church, its pews and its altar becoming more distinct as the camera moves down the aisle. The figures of Eve and Arthur are discerned as the camera gets closer to them; they are walking down the aisle of the church.

EVE *(Offscreen)*   I'm sorry to have hurried you through lunch, but I wanted you to get here and see this before the place gets cluttered up with people. *(Eve and Arthur are clearly seen now, standing near the front of the main altar)* When you wrote from Greece . . . you were telling me about the—the mosaics in the Orthodox churches.

ARTHUR   Hmm.

EVE *(Gesturing)*   But look at this. All these mosaics, there behind the altar, and in a Romanesque church. *(Laughing)* Isn't that amazing?

ARTHUR   It is amazing.

EVE   And look at that. *(Pointing to the windows)* And here in New York. It's really incredible.

ARTHUR   Quite surprising.
They sit down in a pew.

EVE *(Sighing)*   Oh, it makes me homesick for our trips. All those churches. You must have seen a lot when you were there.

ARTHUR   Yes.

EVE   Oh, it would be so marvelous just to forget everything and take a nice slow trip to the Far East. It would get us back on the right . . . right track.

ARTHUR   Eve, I said I—I had something I wanted to say to you?

EVE *(Looking at Arthur, reacting)*   What?

ARTHUR   I think we should finalize our divorce.

EVE *(Looking away from Arthur)*   You do?

ARTHUR   Yeah, I think sooner or later we've got to . . . face reality and try to make new lives for ourselves.

EVE   You know it's very funny, because I thought that's what might be on your mind.

ARTHUR   It's not the end of the world.

EVE *(Her voice quavering)*   It's not? I think it's pretty goddamn terrible.

ARTHUR   Now, Eve, everything's going to be just fine.

EVE *(Her hand on her forehead, trying to gain control)*   Oh, I know that it's a little . . . soon perhaps to talk about a reconciliation, but I don't see why we have to finalize a divorce. I don't see why we can't just go on the way we are.

ARTHUR   W-we should each of us be free to make other plans.

EVE   Like what, what kind of plans?

ARTHUR Well, in the event that . . . we meet other people—

EVE *(Interrupting)* Oh!

ARTHUR —become involved.

EVE *(Her voice rising)* Well, what are you saying? You want to re-marry, is that it?

ARTHUR I'm not discussing that.

EVE Have you met someone?

ARTHUR No.

EVE Ooh, you're lying. Of course you've met someone. Why don't you be honest about it?

ARTHUR Yes, I have, but you're going to make much too much out of it.

EVE *(Standing up)* Oh, never mind, just don't talk anymore about it. I don't want to hear any more.
She walks to the front of the altar, where many red candles burn in their holders; Arthur follows her.

ARTHUR I talked with your doctor. He feels you can handle this.

EVE You've talked to Dr. Lobell about this behind my back?

ARTHUR Not behind your back. Discreetly.

EVE *(Putting her hand to her head)* You've discussed this with Dr. Lobell . . . behind my back. It's so humiliating.

ARTHUR Now, Eve, it's your doctor and myself. Now, how private can one be?

EVE *(Sighing, looking at Arthur)* And he assured you that I can handle this. Is that what he— H-h-how humiliating.

ARTHUR You're not humiliated.

EVE *(Putting her hand to her face)* Oh!! I just want to die!

ARTHUR Now, stop that!

EVE *(Sighing)* I just hate myself . . . !
She sweeps her arm across the burning candles, smashing them off the altar; amid the harsh sound of breaking glass, Arthur grabs Eve's arm and pulls her away from the altar.

Arthur puts his arm around Eve's waist and begins pulling her out of the dark cathedral, their voices trailing after them.

EVE I'm fine . . . I'm fine. *(Arthur mumbles, desperately trying to hurry Eve out of the church)* Oh, I hate myself, I hate myself, oh no!

CUT TO:
INTERIOR. EVE'S LIVING ROOM—NIGHT.

Eve, drink in hand, stands in front of her fireplace. She sips, then walks across the room. It is very quiet.
The silence is broken by a quick cut of the ocean at the beach house, the waves crashing on the sand.
The camera moves inside the house. Flyn, just arrived, walks into the living room. She is wearing her sunglasses as she greets Renata and Joey—who is totally obscured behind her older sister.

JOEY Flyn!

FLYN Uh, hi!

RENATA *(Overlapping)* Flyn, how are you?

FLYN Oh, oh, God, it's good to see you. How are you?

RENATA Oh, it's good to see you.

JOEY Flyn, you look great.

FLYN *(Overlapping, to Renata)* Oh, you look terrific!

RENATA *(Laughing)* Hmm.

FLYN *(To Renata)* You really do. Oh, and that's a great sweater.

RENATA *(Looking down at her sweater)* Oh, no.

FLYN No, it really is. It's nice.

RENATA Not really.

JOEY *(Agreeing)* It's a great sweater.

RENATA You've seen this sweater before.

FLYN Oh, no, I haven't. It's terrific!

RENATA *(Shrugging)* Ah, hmmm.

FLYN *(To Renata)* Are you tan, Rennie? Have you been somewhere?

RENATA *(Touching her face)* Why? Why, do I have on too much make-up?

JOEY You're the one that looks great, Flyn.

FLYN *(Looking at Joey)* Well, I don't know. Oh, no, I don't.

JOEY You do!

FLYN I'm heavy. No, I've gained weight.

JOEY *(Ignoring Flyn's protestations)* Great.

FLYN Oh, and my plane flight was so bumpy I thought I was gonna die! I made such a fool of myself with the man next to me.
She takes off her sunglasses; Joey laughs offscreen.

FLYN I really did.

RENATA Have you met Pearl?

FLYN Yes. She's not what I expected.
Joey takes a sip of her wine.

RENATA No. God. God, isn't it strange being back in the house again.

FLYN Yeah.

RENATA Have you spoken with Mother?

FLYN Oh, yes, we're gonna have dinner one night this week. How's she holding up?
As the three sisters talk, Frederick and Arthur can be seen in the background, outside the glass doors; Mike is seen standing alone at the dining-room table.

RENATA I don't know. Better than we all expected. Isn't that right, Joey?

JOEY *(Sitting down on the living-room couch)* She took it very badly at first. But after the initial shock she seemed to come out of it.

RENATA *(Walking to the window to look out at the beach)* Joey feels that all of her Jesus Christ nonsense is actually somewhat of a help.

FLYN Well, whatever works.

MIKE *(Coming into the room)* Hello, Flyn.

FLYN Michael! Gosh, hi-iii!
They embrace.

MIKE   Nice to see you.

FLYN   *(Breaking the embrace)*   Oh, it's good to see you too! Ooh! Oh, lis— Joey, you have to tell me what you're up to.

JOEY   *(Still sitting on the couch, toying with a glass on the end table)*   Yet another job . . . with an ad agency.

FLYN   Oh, that's fabulous!

JOEY   *(Shaking her head)*   No, but it's temporary.
   Pearl enters the living room carrying a tray of tiny hot-dog hors d'oeuvres.

PEARL   Here we are. I made some cocktail franks, and meatballs.

MIKE   It's about time, too. I'm starved.
   He claps his hands; he and Flyn each take a hot dog.

PEARL   Oh, there's plenty to eat and drink. We have everything your little heart desires.

FLYN   *(Overlapping)*   Hmmm.

MIKE   *(Nodding)*   Good.

FLYN   Um . . . are you and Dad gonna be staying on here, or are you gonna take a place in town?

MIKE   *(Still nibbling hot dogs)*   It's good.

PEARL   Well, it's a little quiet out here, but Arthur loves it. 'Course it means redoing so much of the house.

JOEY   *(Reacting, still sitting on the sofa toying with her glass)*   In what way?

PEARL   *(Putting down the tray on a side table)*   Oh, I don't know. It's just the two of us, and it's . . . kind of pale. Besides, I have so much furniture of my own, and pictures and knickknacks. *(Laughing)* This place would look like a warehouse. Would you like to hear some music?
   She walks out of the room. Mike and Flyn stare at her back, reacting. And the film cuts to the beach. It is later. Renata and Flyn are walking along the shoreline, waves crashing behind them. They wear sweaters; the wind whips.

RENATA   *(Hugging herself)*   Do I look older?

FLYN   *(Hands in her pockets)*   Older?

RENATA   Yeah, I mean it. Do you think I look older?

FLYN   No. Why would you think that?

RENATA   I don't know. I don't know. I, uh—

FLYN *(Interrupting)*   Why?

RENATA   I look in the mirror every day, and I feel discouraged. And look, now I see you, and you don't change at all.

FLYN   Ha, ha! Bless you.

RENATA *(Putting her hands on Flyn's face)*   No, you don't change. Your skin is like cream. Look at your skin. I'm so envious.

FLYN   I work at it.

RENATA   No. I don't think that's it.

FLYN   I have a few good years, then—

RENATA *(Interrupting with a sigh)*   Aah.

FLYN   —my youth will be frozen on old celluloid for TV movies.

RENATA   Oh, come, Flyn, you're more than just beautiful. You know you have a lot of talent.

FLYN   Don't pump me up, Rennie.

RENATA   What!? Why do you say that?

FLYN   I know what I am. Look, I'm not treated seriously. When really classy parts come along, I get passed over. If it wasn't for the stupid television industry, I wouldn't make enough to live.

RENATA   You know something? You have always been so self-deprecating, Flyn. You know that.

FLYN   No. *(Pausing)* No, you're the gifted one in this family, Rennie.

RENATA   Oh—

FLYN   *(Interrupting)*   Well, I'm proud of you.
The two sisters put their arms around each other as they walk.

RENATA   You know, I wish you lived here, I mean, I really do.

FLYN   Rennie, I—

RENATA *(Interrupting)*   Every time I see you, i-it just reminds me how much I do miss you.
She laughs and sighs. The sisters take their arms from around each other and continue to walk; they are silent for a few moments.

FLYN   How's Frederick?

RENATA   He's angry. He's teaching, when he really wants to be writing. Teaching's something that can't be taught, anyway. Now he's taking his rage out in these critical pieces under the guise of high standards. I don't know, I guess I . . . I don't think I've been very good for him.
They stop walking, facing each other for a moment.

FLYN   Oh, Rennie, he idolizes you.

RENATA   No.

FLYN   Rennie, what time is it? We ought to get back.

RENATA   No, I think I'm gonna stay a while longer.

FLYN   Okay. I'll see you back there.

RENATA   Okay. I'll be in soon.
Flyn turns and starts walking back to the house; Renata sits down on the sand and stares out at the ocean.

CUT TO:
INTERIOR. BEACH HOUSE—DAY.

Arthur stands at a window, looking out at the waves. Joey walks over to him and puts her arm around his waist. She, too, looks out at the surf. They stand almost in silhouette, the only light furnished by the bright sun outside the window.

JOEY   Hi. You know I want you to be happy. I want you both to be happy.

ARTHUR *(Looking at Joey, his arm around her shoulder)* Tell her. Tell Pearl. I know she puts on a gay façade, but . . . she knows how you feel. Tell her. Will you?

JOEY Okay.
The film moves to the beach where Renata is still sitting, still staring at the ocean. Her hair blows in her face; her arms hug her knees. The waves crash. She covers her face with her hands briefly, then stands up, ready to walk back to the house.
The film cuts to a bedroom in the beach house, where Frederick, drink in hand, paces back and forth across the floor. He pauses in front of a full-length mirror, staring at his reflection. Flyn enters the scene, standing in the doorway, half smiling, watching Frederick looking at himself.

FLYN Well, you look deep in thought.

FREDERICK *(Laughing, turning away from the mirror)* No, I'm deep in vodka.
Flyn walks into the room and sits on the edge of the bed.

FLYN Would you help me get my boots off?

FREDERICK *(Smiling)* That's the best offer I had all year.
He kneels near the bed, pulling off one of Flyn's boots and dropping it on the floor.

FLYN I paid two hundred bucks for these boots and they kill my feet. Uhh.

FREDERICK *(Looking down for a moment)* I did a terrible thing last week. I wrote about this friend's book . . . not a very good book . . . and I pointed that out . . . *(Sniffling)* which is what I was getting paid to do. But I was extremely cruel about it. And I took great pleasure in my cruelty. *(He begins to lift Flyn's other foot)* My anger scares me. I don't like what I'm becoming.

FLYN *(Smiling, looking directly at Frederick)* Well, I happen to think you're a very impressive person.
Frederick pulls off her other boot.

FREDERICK Oh . . . I think you have very impressive feet.
Flyn laughs and leans forward, close to Frederick's face.

FLYN And I happen to think you're very drunk.

FREDERICK Come on. Not yet.
Flyn stands, her boots off, and pats Frederick on his head.

FLYN Yes. Thank you.

Flyn leaves as Frederick, still crouched on the floor, finishes his drink.

FREDERICK Uh-hum.

CUT TO:
INTERIOR. BEACH-HOUSE BEDROOM—NIGHT.

Arthur stands in front of a mirror, putting on his suspenders. Pearl comes into the room and helps him clip them to his pants. She then puts her hand to his face tenderly; he touches her arm. There is no sound.

CUT TO:
EXTERIOR. BEACH-HOUSE BALCONY—NIGHT.

Flyn, in a slip, comes out onto the balcony. She brushes her hair, staring at the ocean. The crashing waves are heard but not seen.

CUT TO:
INTERIOR. BEACH-HOUSE BEDROOM—NIGHT.

Frederick is sitting on the edge of his bed fixing his tie; Renata, too, sits on the bed. She is putting on her watch. The couple, busy with their tasks, do not talk or look at each other.

CUT TO:
INTERIOR. BEACH-HOUSE LIVING ROOM—NIGHT.

The camera shows Joey's profile as she watches the wedding ceremony in front of her. The judge's voice is heard over her concentrating face.

JUDGE *(Offscreen)*   We are gathered together here, in the presence of this company, to join this man and this woman in the bonds of matrimony. Arthur . . . will you have this woman as your wedded wife, to live together in the ordinances of the state of matrimony? Will you love her, comfort her, honor and keep her, in sickness and in health, and forsaking—
The camera pulls back, revealing now Joey, Mike and Renata in sharp focus. The judge continues to speak over this scene as the ceremony continues.

JUDGE *(Offscreen)* —all others, keep you only unto her, so long as you both do live?

ARTHUR *(Offscreen)*   I will.

JUDGE *(Offscreen)*   Pearl, will you have this man as your wedded husband, to live together in the ordinances of the state of matrimony? Will you love him, comfort him, honor and keep him, in sickness and in health, and forsaking all others, keep you only unto him, so long as you both do live?

PEARL *(Offscreen)*   I will.
The camera pulls back even farther, revealing now Joey, Mike, Renata, Frederick and Flyn as the ceremony proceeds offscreen.

JUDGE *(Offscreen)*   Inasmuch as Arthur and Pearl have consented together in wedlock, and have witnessed the same before this company, and thereto have pledged each to the other, and have declared the same by the joining of hands, I, in accordance with the authority vested in me by the law of the State of New York, pronounce that they are . . . husband and wife.
The camera moves now into the dining room, where the table is elaborately set with glasses, champagne and wedding cake. The camera stops at the doorway; the judge's back is seen through the doors leading into the living room. Pearl and Arthur, Flyn, Renata and Frederick, and Joey and Mike are now seen full-face.

JUDGE   You may kiss the bride.
Arthur and Pearl kiss. The others gather around them, congratulating the couple.

ARTHUR Okay.

JUDGE Well . . . Arthur . . . friends.
*The music starts. Everyone moves about in both the dining room and the
living room. Frederick, in the dining room now, stands by himself, sipping
a drink. Renata is sitting at the table, smoking a cigarette, and watching
Arthur and Pearl dancing in the living room.*

RENATA *(To Frederick, without looking up)* Jesus, I don't think I've ever
seen him dance before in his life.
*Pearl, in a full-skirted print dress, and Arthur, in a dark suit, are dancing
animatedly. Mike and Flyn dance near them; Renata and Frederick continue
to watch from the dining room. Pearl, flushed with excitement, takes off her
earrings and gives them to Arthur.*

PEARL *(Laughing)* Ow. Wait. Ow. Wait. *(Arthur, smiling, puts the earrings in his pocket)* All right, don't forget.
*As Arthur and Pearl dance by Mike and Flyn, Pearl takes Mike's hand and
starts dancing with him. The film quickly cuts to the judge, sitting alone on
a bench drinking champagne, then moves back to Pearl and Mike dancing.
Pearl is smiling and chattering; Renata and Frederick dance in the background.*

MIKE *(To Pearl, laughing)* I'll go get you some champagne.
He leaves Pearl; she sashays over to Flyn, trying to get her to dance.

PEARL *(Gesturing)* Come on, baby. Oh, my!
*Flyn laughs. She and Pearl dance over to Renata and Frederick. Flyn starts
dancing with Frederick; Pearl, still swaying, dances over to Arthur and Joey,
who are dancing and talking. She tries now to get Joey to dance; Joey shakes
her head, moving away. Arthur takes Pearl's arm and they start to dance;
Frederick and Flyn dance past them, chattering.*
*The film cuts to Joey, standing at the dining-room table, drinking a glass of
champagne. Mike stands near her at the buffet table. They are both staring
out at the dancers in the living room.*
*Frederick and Flyn continue to dance, as do Arthur and Pearl; Joey, sipping
her champagne, continues to watch her father and his new wife. A quick cut
shows Renata, leaning against the door between the two rooms, drink in hand.
She is touching her forehead and breathing heavily.*
*The music abruptly changes to a louder beat. Pearl and Arthur, hearing the
new tempo, stop for a moment before continuing to dance. Joey continues to
watch them, drinking her champagne, as Pearl swings around out of Arthur's*

grasp and begins dancing by herself. Arthur sits down, watching Pearl, but unlike Joey, who watches as well, he is smiling as he sips his champagne. Frederick and Flyn, no longer dancing, look on bemused as Pearl does a little shake by herself. She sashays near a Parsons table that holds white roses in three elegant vases. She's smiling, enjoying herself in her own little world. She twirls around as the others look on, sipping champagne; she moves jauntily, side to side, to the beat. Suddenly she starts to get dizzy, losing her balance. As she puts her hand to her forehead, she knocks off one of the vases, filled with the white roses, from the Parsons table. As it crashes to the floor, Joey leaps up from her chair.

JOEY Jesus Christ! Be careful!
Pearl looks on, reacting, while Mike walks over to Joey and takes away her champagne glass.

MIKE (*Aside, to Joey*) You've had too much to drink.

JOEY (*Loudly, still furious*) I'm not drunk . . . just because I don't act like an animal!

ARTHUR (*Reacting*) That's enough!

JOEY (*Running out of the room*) Oh, leave me alone. Just leave me alone!
Renata watches Joey leave the room. She takes a sip of her champagne. Flyn, too, continues to sip her drink while Frederick, nearby, eyes her. Pearl, chagrined, looks down, and the film cuts to the back of the beach house. It is dark; the sounds of the waves fill the screen. Renata is seen walking along the beach, deep in thought, the ocean almost at her feet.
The sound of the waves continues as the film moves back into the house, into the living room, where Joey sits alone on the couch sipping a drink. She stares into space, lost in thought.
The sound of the waves stops as the scene abruptly changes to the darkened garage of the beach house.
Flyn walks into the garage and gets into a car on the driver's side. She slides over to the passenger seat and opens the glove compartment. She reaches in and takes out a small vial of cocaine. She pours some of the powder onto a small spoon and snorts some in each nostril.
Frederick comes into the garage, walking over to the car, as Flyn, finished, is putting back the cocaine into the glove compartment. He is chuckling, amused at what he'd just witnessed. He takes a sip of the drink in his hand and gets into the car. He leans over to Flyn and begins to kiss her.

FLYN   Un-uh. *(She pulls away from the kiss)* Oh, Frederick, you're drunk.

FREDERICK   Un-uh. Come on. You're always flirting with me.
He starts to kiss her again.

FLYN *(Pulling away)*   No.

FREDERICK   Yes. You flirt. You like to be looked at. All right. You don't exist . . . except in somebody else's eyes.
He continues to try to kiss her.

FLYN *(Trying to get away)*   Stop it, Frederick. You're drunk.

FREDERICK   No, I'm celebrating. You got a new mother. She's a hot number. *(Laughing)* Don't you feel the heat?
He pulls Flyn to his side. She pulls away.

FLYN *(Angrily)*   Frederick.

FREDERICK   It's been such a long time since I made love to a woman that I didn't feel inferior to. Or am I being . . . tactless?

FLYN   Oooh!
She pushes away from Frederick. She tries to get out of the car, but he holds her back. She manages to break away finally, and she opens the car door. Flyn runs out on the passenger side, trying to get away from Frederick, who, grunting, grabs her and pushes her down on the back of the car. He starts to kiss her.

FLYN *(Sighing)*   No.

FREDERICK   Flyn.
Flyn once more struggles out of Frederick's grasp and runs away. She trips over a nearby rowboat. She picks herself up and starts to run again, but Frederick corners her. He forces Flyn back, picking up her legs and pushing up her skirt. Flyn, breathing heavily, flips Frederick to the floor. She runs around the rowboat and out of the garage.
Frederick, also breathing heavily from his unsuccessful struggle, picks himself up from the floor.

CUT TO:
INTERIOR. ARTHUR'S BEDROOM IN BEACH HOUSE—NIGHT.

Arthur and Pearl are in bed, under the covers. Pearl rubs Arthur's bare chest; they embrace.

CUT TO:
INTERIOR. BEACH-HOUSE LIVING ROOM—NIGHT.

Joey is still sitting in the dark, in an armchair, sipping her drink. She hears footsteps; she leans forward to listen better, then gets up and walks slowly to the glass-paneled door leading into the room.

JOEY   Mother? Is that you? *(Sighing, after a pause)* You shouldn't be here. Not tonight. I'll take you home. *(Eve stands, her face in shadow, behind the door; she looks into the living room while Joey continues to talk)* You look so strange and tired. I feel like we're in a dream together. *(Joey walks to a straight-backed chair, near the fireplace, and sits down)* Please don't look so sad. It makes me feel so guilty. *(Sighing)* I'm so consumed with guilt. It's ironic . . . because, uh, I care for you so . . . and you have nothing but disdain for me. *(Joey takes a sip of her drink. Her mother, now in the living room, stands by a window, leaning her head against the pane; her face is still in shadow)* And yet I feel guilty. I think you're, uh . . . really too perfect . . . to live in this world. I mean, all the beautifully furnished rooms, carefully designed interiors . . . everything so controlled. There wasn't any room for—uh eh, any real feelings. None. I . . . uh, between any of us. Except Renata . . . who never gave you the time of day. You worship Renata. *(Eve, reacting, looks intently at Joey, her face still in shadow)* You worship talent. Well, what happens to those of us who can't create? What do we do? What do *I* do . . . when I'm overwhelmed with feelings about life? How do I get them out? I feel such rage toward you! Come on, Mother—don't you see? You're not just a sick woman. That would be too easy. The truth is . . . there's been perverseness—and willfulness of attitude—in many of the things you've done. At the center of—of a sick psyche, there is a sick spirit. But I love you. And we have no other choice but to forgive each other.
She looks down, her speech finished. Pearl, wearing a robe, enters the room.

PEARL   Are you talking to someone?

JOEY *(Turning)*   Yes . . . I—

PEARL   I thought I heard voices.
She looks around the room; she sees no one.

JOEY *(Ignoring Pearl)*   Mother?

PEARL   Yes?

JOEY   What?

PEARL Uh, you said "Mother," and I said "Yes."

JOEY (*Anxiously*) Mother?
The camera moves outside, to the beach, where Eve is walking toward the crshing waves; the wind is blowing her coat. She walks into the water, a black speck in the white waves, deeper and deeper.
Joey runs down the beach after her.

JOEY (*Screaming*) Mother!
Joey stops at the water's edge, watching her mother swallowed by the waves.

JOEY (*Screaming*) Mother!
Joey runs into the water. Pearl, who's run from the house, watches Joey struggling in the waves, trying to reach Eve. Mike rushes from the house and jumps into the surf trying to get to Joey before she drowns. Pearl watches Mike and Joey struggling in the water; the crashing sound of waves is heard.
The film quickly cuts to Renata, asleep in her bed, then to Flyn, also fast asleep beneath the covers. The sound of waves continues as the camera moves back to the drama on the beach, where the surf crashes over Joey's and Mike's heads as he grabs her and tries to drag her back to the shore.
For a moment, the film cuts to Arthur, asleep in his bed, then it moves back outside where Mike has managed to pull Joey out of the surf to the safety of the shore. Pearl runs to the shoreline and helps Mike drag Joey to the dry sand. An abrupt cut shows Renata, still in bed, suddenly lift her head from the pillow; Flyn, in her bed, opens her eyes, startled, as back on the beach Pearl kneels down in front of Joey's still body and begins to give mouth-to-mouth resuscitation; Mike, also kneeling, presses on Joey's stomach in rhythm with Pearl's first aid. The waves continue to crash over the sounds of Pearl's breathing.
Joey begins to cough. Pearl stops her mouth-to-mouth resuscitation. Mike takes Joey in her arms and hugs her tightly. He gets up and carries her back to the house.
No one is left on the beach. The ocean is desolate. The film quickly cuts to the back of the house. It is early morning; the wind blows through the brush and the sounds of the waves are heard.

INTERIOR. ARTHUR'S BEDROOM IN THE BEACH HOUSE—DAY.
Arthur, dressed in a black suit, is sitting on the edge of his bed; his head is down. Pearl walks into the room, picks up her coat from the bed and puts it on. She takes her purse from a nearby low chest and walks over to Arthur. She takes his hand. He gets up from the bed and they walk out of the room.

CUT TO:
EXTERIOR. BEACH HOUSE—DAY.

Arthur, Pearl, Frederick and Renata leave the beach house, walking past the brush and the sand in the back of the house.

CUT TO:
INTERIOR. CHURCH—DAY.
A mahogany coffin is seen, illuminated by a stained-glass window. Arthur enters the scene, carrying a single white rose. He places it on top of the closed coffin, then leaves.
Renata enters. She pauses over the coffin, then places a white rose on top of the coffin. She sighs and begins to cry, then leaves.
Joey walks into the scene, placing one white rose on the coffin. She leaves, and Flyn, tears streaming down her face, walks in, placing her single white rose on the coffin.
The film cuts to Renata and Joey walking up the church aisle together. Once at the door, Joey touches Renata's back; Renata turns to her. They cry, then hug each other.

JOEY   Rennie.
Renata sighs.

CUT TO:
INTERIOR. BEDROOM—NIGHT.

Joey's hands can be seen; she is writing in a notebook on her bed.

JOEY'S VOICE (*As she writes*)   After the funeral service . . . we all re-turned to the beach house. We couldn't help experiencing some very nostalgic memories . . . naturally of my mother . . . and pleasantly of the few warmer moments we'd known.

The film shows a flashback of Eve and Arthur, dressed to go out, and the three small sisters, all gathered in a bedroom; they are framed by the bedroom's doorway, the staircase banister partially hiding the view.

JOEY'S VOICE-OVER   I recalled how beautiful she was . . . dressing to go out for the evening with my father.

The film cuts to a second flashback. Eve is standing in the living room, showing a small Renata an elegant new vase that she'd just taken out of a box on the sofa.

JOEY'S VOICE-OVER   And of how Renata looked up to her . . . and her ideas about art.

The movie shows a third flashback. Through the open doors separating the living room and the dining room, the entire family is seen gathered around a large Christmas tree. The young girls watch as Eve adjusts the bulbs on the tree.

JOEY'S VOICE-OVER   And how Flyn was so . . . impressed as a tiny girl when Mother decorated a Christmas tree.
The film moves back to Joey writing in her notebook on her bed.

JOEY'S VOICE-OVER   I felt compelled . . . to write these thoughts down. They seemed very powerful to me.
She closes the notebook as the film cuts to some windows in the beach house. It is daylight. The white room is very bright. Renata, dressed in black, walks over to one of the windows and stands, gazing at the ocean. Joey, also dressed in black, enters the room and stands next to her.

JOEY *(Looking out the window)*   The water's so calm.

RENATA *(Looking out the window)*   Yes. *(Sighing)* It's very peaceful.
Flyn, also in black, walks over to them as Renata speaks. The three sisters stare out the window as the film

FADES OUT TO:

A black background with white credits popping on and off the silent screen.

(Starring in alphabetical order:)

KRISTINE GRIFFITH
MARYBETH HURT
RICHARD JORDAN
DIANE KEATON
E. G. MARSHALL
GERALDINE PAGE
MAUREEN STAPLETON
SAM WATERSTON

Executive Producer
ROBERT GREENHUT

Production Supervisor
JOHN NICOLELLA

Casting
JULIET TAYLOR

Production Manager	JOHN NICOLELLA
1st Assistant Director	MARTIN BERMAN
2nd Assistant Director	HENRY MLOTT
Location Coordinator	CARL ZUCKER
Script Supervisor	KAY CHAPIN
Production Office Coordinator	BARBARA DE FINA
Production Accountant	MARC G. GREENBERG
Transportation Captain	EDWARD IACOBELLI
D.G.A. Trainee	IRA HALBERSTADT
Production Assistants	PATRICK MCCORMICK
	MARGARET HUNNEWELL
	CHARLES ZALBEN
	ANGELA VULLO
	SONYA SONES
	SETH SCHULTZ

INTERIORS

Camera Operator	HERB WAGREICH
Sound	NAT BOXER
Rerecording Mixer	JACK HIGGENS-
	MAGNO SOUND
1st Assistant Cameraman	JAMES HOVEY
Still Photographer	BRIAN HAMILL
Gaffer	DUSTY WALLACE
Key Grip	ROBERT WARD
Propertymaster	JAMES MAZZOLA
Wardrobe	CLIFFORD CAPONE
Make Up	FERN BUCHNER
Hair Stylist	ROMAINE GREENE
Unit Publicist	SCOTT MACDONOUGH
Design Coordinator	KRISTI ZEA
Set Decorators	DANIEL ROBERT
	MARIO MAZZOLA
Carpenter	JOSEPH BADALUCCO
Scenic Artists	JAMES SORICE
	COSMO SORICE
Extras Casting	AARON BECKWITH
Assistant Film Editors	SUSAN E. MORSE
	SONYA POLONSKY
Sound Editing	BERNIE HAJDENBERG-
	MAGNOFLEX
Assistant Sound Editor	WILLIAM SCHARF
Titles	COMPUTER OPTICALS INC.

Recorded Music:

"Keepin' Out of Mischief Now"
performed by Tommy Dorsey on RCA Records

"Wolverine Blues"
performed by The World's Greatest Jazz Band
on Project III Records

(emblem)

I.A.T.S.E. Camera and lenses by Panavision® MOTION PICTURE
(seal) Prints by Technicolor® ASSOCIATION
OF AMERICA
#25289

FOUR FILMS OF WOODY ALLEN

KRISTIN GRIFFITH	*Flyn*
MARYBETH HURT	*Joey*
RICHARD JORDAN	*Frederick*
DIANE KEATON	*Renata*
E. G. MARSHALL	*Arthur*
GERALDINE PAGE	*Eve*
MAUREEN STAPLETON	*Pearl*
SAM WATERSTON	*Mike*
MISSY HOPE	*Young Joey*
KERRY DUFFY	*Young Renata*
NANCY COLLINS	*Young Flyn*
PENNY GASTON	*Young Eve*
ROGER MORDEN	*Young Arthur*
HENDERSON FORSYTHE	*Judge Bartel*

The Producers gratefully acknowledge
the cooperation given by:

The City of New York
Stark Carpet Corporation
The Pace Collection
The Village of Southampton
The Caristo Family

Manhattan

Screenplay by Woody Allen
and Marshall Brickman

The words "United Artists, a Transamerica Company," appear in white over a silent black screen, cutting almost immediately and suddenly to a series of shots of the New York City skyline. As "Rhapsody in Blue" is heard over the scenery, the images flash on and off: the skyline at dawn, the sun silhouetting the Empire State Building, jutting skyscrapers, parking lots, crowded streets, the Brooklyn Bridge, neon lights advertising Broadway, Coca-Cola, various hotels, the snow-covered and lamp-lit streets of Park Avenue and Central Park, the garment district, an excited demonstration downtown . . .

As the music swells over the Manhattan scenery, Ike's voice is heard, as if reading aloud from his writings.

IKE'S VOICE-OVER   "Chapter One. He adored New York City. He idolized it all out of proportion." Uh, no, make that: "He—he . . . romanticized it all out of proportion. Now . . . to him . . . no matter what the season was, this was still a town that existed in black and white and pulsated to the great tunes of George Gershwin." Ahhh, now let me start this over. "Chapter One. He was too romantic about Manhattan as he was about everything else. He thrived on the hustle . . . bustle of the crowds and the traffic."

As Ike continues to talk, more Manhattan scenes are shown: sophisticated women walking down Fifth Avenue; construction men drilling on the streets; the docks; a ferry moving into port; children running down the steps of a private school, finished for the day. Accenting Ike's words, the images continue to flash: a fish market, presided over by a man in a smudged apron; two elderly women, bundled in winter coats; a fruit stand; high school boys playing basketball in a fenced-off court; joggers in the Park; the Plaza Hotel; garbage piled up on the streets; building fronts of such landmarks as Gucci and Sotheby Parke Bernet; the Guggenheim Museum; people, young and old; trafficked streets; three men loitering on a corner; the crowded lower level of the 59th Street Bridge. The "Rhapsody in Blue" score continues very softly in the background.

IKE'S VOICE-OVER   "To him, New York meant beautiful women and street-smart guys who seemed to know all the angles." Nah, no . . . corny, too corny . . . for . . . my taste *(Clearing his throat)* . . . I mean, let me try and make it more profound. "Chapter One. He adored New York City. To him, it was a metaphor for the decay of contemporary culture. The same lack of individual integrity to cause so many people to take the easy way out . . . was rapidly turning the town of his dreams in—" No, it's gonna be too preachy. I mean, you know . . . let's face it, I wanna sell some books here.

"Chapter One. He adored New York City, although to him, it was a metaphor for the decay of contemporary culture. How hard it was to exist in a society desensitized by drugs, loud music, television, crime, garbage." Too angry. I don't wanna be angry. "Chapter One. He was as . . . tough and romantic as the city he loved. Behind his black-rimmed glasses was the coiled sexual power of a jungle cat." I love this. "New York was his town. And it always would be."

While Ike finishes his recitation, "Rhapsody in Blue" loudly fills the screen as the pictures of New York City life continues to appear on and off the screen: a man and a woman kissing on a balcony; a lighted Broadway; Yankee Stadium at night, its lights illuminating the crowds; two actors performing on the Delacorte Theatre stage; Radio City Music Hall; and ending with a spectacular view of the Manhattan skyline at night, firecrackers flashing over the buildings and dark sky, as the music reaches a crescendo and abruptly stops and the film cuts to:

EXTERIOR/INTERIOR. ELAINE'S CAFÉ—NIGHT.

The camera shows the word "Elaine's" drawn on the glass of the restaurant, and moves inside, past patrons being shown to their seats, past the crowded, noisy, smoky tables, to Issac (Ike) Davis' table, where he sits with his date, a young girl named Tracy, his good friend Yale Pollack, an intellectual teacher-critic, and Yale's wife, Emily. Yale is in the midst of an intense discussion as the camera moves in closer to his face.

YALE   I think the essence of art is to provide a kind of working through the situation for people, you know, so that you can get in touch with feelings that you didn't know you had, really.

IKE   Talent is luck. Tsch. I think the important thing in life is courage.

EMILY *(To Tracy, chuckling)*   They've had this argument for twenty years.

IKE   Listen to this example I'm gonna give. If the four of us *(Smacking his lips together)* are walking home over the bridge *(Inhaling)* and then there was a person drowning in the water, would we have the nerve, would one of us have the nerve to dive into the icy water and save the person from drowning?

YALE *(Overlapping)*   Jump into the water and save the drowning man.

IKE Because . . . that's a—that's a key question. You know, I—I, of course, can't swim, so I never have to face it.
He puts a cigarette in his mouth and lights it, staring at Tracy, looking only at her and humming, while Emily and Yale talk in the background.

IKE *(To Tracy, mumbling)* I don't know.

YALE *(To Emily)* No, no. Which of us would do it.
He chuckles.

EMILY *(To Yale, chuckling)* I don't know.

YALE *(Giving Emily a forkful of his food)* You want a little more?

EMILY No.

YALE Come on. *(Chuckling)* You really do.

EMILY *(Taking the food)* Thanks.

IKE *(Puffing on his cigarette, still looking at Tracy)* Mm. Oh, man, that is so great!

YALE *(To Emily, overlapping)* Mm.

TRACY *(To Ike, chuckling)* You don't smoke.

IKE I know I don't smoke. I don't inhale because it gives you cancer. But *(Exhaling)* I look so incredibly handsome with a cigarette—

TRACY *(Interrupting)* Oh.

IKE —that I can't *not* hold one. I know this. *(Still smoking the cigarette)* You like the way I look?

TRACY Mm-hm.
She nods her head yes while Yale chuckles with Emily in the background.

IKE *(Looking at Tracy)* I know.

YALE *(To Emily)* Provocative.

IKE *(To Tracy)* I'm getting through to you, right?

TRACY *(Overlapping)* Yup. You'll have to excuse me.
She gets up from the table.

YALE *(Looking at Tracy as she walks away)* Jesus, she's gorgeous.

IKE *(Drinking his glass of wine and nodding his head)* Mm, but she's seventeen. *(Smacking his lips together)* I'm forty-two and she's seventeen. *(Coughing)* I-I'm dating a girl wherein I can beat up her father. It's the first time that phenomenon ever occurred in my life.

EMILY *(Shaking her head)*   He's drunk.

YALE   You're drunk. You know, you should never drink.

IKE *(Still drinking his wine)*   Tsch. Did I tell you *(Exhaling)* that my ex-wife—

EMILY *(Interrupting)*   Who, Tina?

IKE *(Shaking his head and holding up two fingers)*   —mm-mm-my second ex-wife—is writing a book about our marriage and the breakup?

EMILY   That's really tacky.

IKE *(Puffing on his cigarette)*   It's really depressing. You know, she's gonna *(Sighing)* give all those details out, all my little idiosyncrasies, and my quirks and mannerisms and—and, mm, mm, not that I have anything to hide because, you know . . . *(Smacking his lips together)* but there are a few disgusting little moments that I regret.
Yale sighs.

YALE   It's just gossip, you know. Gossip is the new pornography. We have it in the daily newspapers.

IKE *(Overlapping)*   I should never let her threaten me.

YALE   I know.
Tracy comes back to the table and sits next to Ike, who is laughing drunkenly.

YALE *(Chuckling)*   You should never let yourself drink.

IKE   I know, my head.

TRACY *(Looking at Ike)*   You know, we ought to go 'cause I've got an exam tomorrow.
A man and a woman pass their table, talking together.

MAN *(To the woman)*   A regular plan for . . .

IKE *(To Tracy, overlapping)*   Oh, do you? *(To Emily and Yale)* The kid's gotta get up and . . .
The man and woman continue to talk near their table; Tracy sighs and laughs at Ike and the situation.

WOMAN   Eleven-forty.

MAN   Eleven-forty.

IKE *(To Yale, chuckling)*   She's got homework. I'm dating a girl who does homework.
Tracy continues to sigh as the film leaves the noisy restaurant and cuts to:

EXTERIOR. STREET—NIGHT.

Emily and Tracy trail behind Ike and Yale as they walk along the sidewalk, illuminated by the street lamps. Ike casually holds his sweater over his shoulder as he talks to his old friend.

IKE   What is it? What's the matter with you? You—you—you, where is your—where are you now?

YALE *(Sighing)*   Oh.

IKE   Your mind is like a million miles away someplace.

YALE   Yeah, I have something I wanna talk to you about. I, uh, I just didn't know quite how to . . . get into it. Um . . . I, uh, I, uh, uh, uh, about seven or eight weeks ago, I, uh, I went to this dinner party. And, uh, I met a woman there. And *(Sighing)* tsch, and I-I-I-I've— I've got kind of involved with her. Um, um . . .

IKE   You're kidding?

YALE   It started out very casually, you know. I mean—

IKE *(Overlapping)*   Un-huh.

YALE   —we had lunch a couple of times. And now, it's . . . you know, it's—it's getting out of hand, and I don't know what to do about it. I mean, I'm . . . it's scary.

IKE   Well, what—who is she? What are—what are the details, hm?

YALE   Well, she's a journalist.

IKE   Ah-ha.

YALE   She's very—

IKE *(Interrupting)*   Is she married too?

YALE   No, no, no. She's very beautiful.

IKE   Um-hm.

YALE   She's very—you know, kind of nervous, high-strung . . . illusive.

IKE   Oh, great. It sounds wonderful.

YALE   *(Chuckling)*   Oh, she's, she is wonderful. I mean, I just, she's—she's on my mind *all* the time.

IKE   S-so, wh-what are you telling me—that your, uh, that your marriage is, you . . . ? I mean, how serious is it?

YALE   *(Looking over his shoulder at Emily, then shrugging)*   I don't know. I'm—but it's pretty serious. I mean . . .

IKE   *(Interrupting)*   But you haven't said anything to Emily?

YALE   *(Looking over his shoulder again)*   No, God, no.

IKE   *(Touching himself on his chest)*   It's amazing. I'm stunned because I—of all the people that I know, I always . . . thought for sure that you and Emily had one of the best marriages.

YALE   We *do*. You know, I mean, I love her.
Yale mumbles to himself.

IKE   *(Overlapping)*   Yeah, but you're seeing, but you—

YALE   *(Interrupting)*   I—I know it. I know, but I just—I mean, in all the years that we've been married, I've—you know what, I've had, what, o-one or two very minor . . . things with other women. I mean—I mean, very . . . listen . . . I hate the whole idea of it. I hate myself when I'm doing this sort of thing.

IKE   Well, I don't know.

YALE   But this is just, you know, this is not like that. I—

IKE   *(Interrupting)*   This is terrible. I, uh, you know, I listen, you shouldn't ask me for advice. I . . . *(Yale sighs)* When it comes to relationships with women, I'm the winner of the August Strindberg Award.
The camera cuts to Yale and Emily entering their darkened apartment. They discuss the evening while Emily switches on the light.

EMILY   Well, I don't think seventeen is too young. Besides that, she's a bright girl.

YALE   *(Chuckling)*   Well, uh, you—you get no argument from me. I think she's terrific. He—he could do a lot worse. He has done a lot worse. *(Chuckling again)* I just think he's wasting his life. You know, he writes that crap for television.

Yale walks into the living room, taking off his jacket and turning on the light. Emily talks to him from the kitchen.

EMILY *(Offscreen)* Yale . . . have you ever thought any more about having kids?

YALE Oh, my God, kids. Listen, I've got to get this O'Neill book finished. It's never gonna get done. I've got to get the money together to get this magazine started, huh. Kids.
He walks into the kitchen. Emily puts down the dish she was holding. They put their arms around each other.

EMILY Well, we always talk about getting a place in Connecticut. *(Yale sighs. She adds, smiling)* You could do it there.

YALE Connecticut.

EMILY Yeah.
Yale kisses Emily.

YALE I can't go to Connecticut. It's not practical. Look, all my stuff's here. *(Chuckling)* My work's here. It's just the wrong time. What about Isaac? I mean, we can't abandon him, you know. *(Chuckling)* He can't function anywhere other than New York, you know that. Very Freudian.

EMILY *(Nodding her head)* Mm-hm.
They kiss again.

The film moves to the bright exterior of the Time-Life Building, where Jill, Ike's ex-wife, has just left through the revolving doors. She walks quickly, tossing her long blond hair, and practically bumps into Ike, who's been standing in the doorway of another building, waiting for her to pass. They start walking together, Jill staring straight ahead and moving quickly, and Ike, gesturing and arguing and looking directly at her.

IKE Are you writing a book about our marriage?

JILL Will you leave me alone?

IKE Are you writing something about our breakup? Just tell me.

JIL We've said everything that needs to be said to each other.

IKE Well, I happen to know you are, because I have a friend at Random House, okay?

JILL *(Overlapping)* You know, I'm free to do as I please.

IKE Yeah, but this affects me.

JILL I'm in a rush.

IKE So you're gonna tell everybody everything, right? Our life, our sexual life, our—all the details, right?

JILL *(Overlapping)* What do you do? Do you spy on me?

IKE No, I don't have to spy. I was at a party and a guy said he read a-a-a-an advance chapter of a book that my wife was writing. And it was hot stuff. He said it . . . was hot stuff.
Jill laughs.

IKE *(Gesturing)* I spilled my—I spilled wine on my pants.

JILL *(Looking at Ike)* Well, I don't care to discuss it.

IKE You don't care to discuss it. How's Willie?

JILL *(Looking away)* Fine.
They stop near some fountains in front of a Sixth Avenue building, still talking.

IKE Well, give me some details, will you? What do you mean "fine"? I mean, does he play baseball? Does he wear dresses? What?!

JILL He doesn't wear dresses. You'll find out all the details when it's your turn to see him.

IKE Hey, don't write this book. It's a humiliating experience.

JILL It's an honest account of our breakup.
They continue walking again at their quick pace.

IKE Jesus, everybody that knows us is gonna know everything.

JILL Look at you, you're so threatened.
Jill walks off as Ike continues to talk.

IKE *(Stopping in his tracks, yelling after Jill's receding figure)* Hey, I'm not threatened because I, uh, of the two of us, I was not the immoral, psychotic, promiscuous one. I hope I didn't leave out anything.

CUT TO:
INTERIOR. IKE'S APARTMENT—NIGHT.

Tracy sits on a couch in the living-room area, reading a book, while Ike, carrying two wine glasses, walks down a nearby spiral staircase into the hallway. He talks to Tracy as he walks into the kitchen to put away the glasses. Mood music plays in the background.

IKE Are you telling me that-that-that I'm—that-that you've had three affairs before me? That's really hard to believe. You know, it's mind-boggling. When I was your age, I was still being tucked in by my grandparents.

TRACY Oh, well, they were really immature boys. I mean, they were nothing like you.

IKE Yeah, what does that mean?

TRACY Well, I told you before. I think I'm in love with you.
Ike leaves the kitchen and walks over to the couch. He sits down beside Tracy, pushing aside her sprawled-out legs to make room.

IKE Hey, don't get carried away, okay? This is—this is a terrific thing *(Pushing aside Tracy's legs)*—move over, love—'cause you know, and then it's a wonderful . . . you know, we're having a great time and all that. But you're a kid, and—and I never want you to forget that, you know. I mean, you're gonna meet a lot of terrific men in your life and . . . You know, I want you to enjoy me, my—my wry sense of humor and *(Chuckling)* astonishing sexual technique, but never forget that, you know, you've—you've got your whole life ahead of you.

TRACY Well, don't you have any feelings for me?

IKE *(Gesturing)* Well, how can you ask that question? What do you— of course, I've got nothing but feelings for you, but, you know . . . you don't wanna get hung up with one person at your age. It's . . . tsch, charming, you know, and *(Clearing his throat)* . . . erotic. There's no question about that. As long as the cops don't burst in, we're—you know, I think we're gonna break a couple of records . . . you know. But you can't, uh, you can't do it. It's not, uh, it's not a good thing. You should think of me . . . sort of as a detour on the highway of life. Tsch, so get dressed because I think you gotta get outta here.
He gets up from the couch and takes Tracy by the hand.

TRACY Don't you want me to stay over?
Reluctantly she gets up from the couch. They walk hand in hand up the spiral staircase as they talk.

IKE   I—I don't want you to get in the habit, you know, because the first thing you know, you stay over one night and then two nights and then, you know, then you're—you're living here.

TRACY   You know, that doesn't sound too bad.

IKE   Mm, no, no, it's not such a great idea. You won't like it. Believe me, I'm—I'm tough to get along with. Tomorrow we'll go to the Bleecker Street Cinema and I'll show you the Veronica Lake movie, okay?

TRACY   All right. Veronica Lake's the pinup with the red hair?

IKE   No, that's Rita Hayworth. Tell me, do we—do we have to go over this all the time?
As Ike and Tracy walk up the stairs they leave the screen; their voices are still heard.

TRACY *(Walking offscreen)*   Who, Ri-Rita who?

IKE *(Walking offscreen)*   Rita Hayworth. Are you joking with me? I mean, I never know when you're teasing.

TRACY *(Offscreen)*   Of course I'm joking! Do you think I'm unaware of any event pre–Paul McCartney or something?
The music stops and the film dissolves into the Guggenheim Museum, where Tracy, in shirt and jeans, and Ike study some photographs. It is crowded; people walk by them, talking and looking.

IKE   You see, I find these photographs interesting, you know. I mean—

TRACY *(Interrupting)*   Yeah, so do I.

IKE   Have you—do you ever use the camera that I got you?

TRACY   Oh, yeah, I use it all the time. I was taking pictures in our drama class.

IKE   Were you?

TRACY   It's fun. It's really neat, yeah.

IKE   You know who you sound like when you talk? The mouse in the *Tom and Jerry* cartoons.

TRACY *(Laughing)*   Are you kidding me?

IKE   No, no, I figured it out.

TRACY You should talk! You have a whiny voice.
She chuckles.

IKE You sound—you sound exactly like the mouse. It's really an art.

TRACY *(Chuckling)* Oh, well. Thanks.

IKE I know, I'm a whiner. You know—
Ike stops talking and looks through the doorway. Both he and Tracy stand there, looking offscreen, as they greet Yale, who is not yet seen.

IKE *(To Yale)* What are you doing here?

TRACY *(Overlapping)* H-hi.

YALE *(Offscreen)* Hi.

IKE How-how long have you been here?

TRACY *(To Yale)* Really, we were just talking about you.

IKE *(Gesturing)* Oh, that's hilarious.

TRACY Ha.

IKE *(Overlapping, to Yale)* What're you—what're you, uh, what're you —were—what are you—you walking around behind us or what?
Tracy laughs while Yale walks through the doorway into the photography room.

YALE *(Chuckling, to Ike)* How are you? *(To Tracy)* Hi.

IKE Okay, good. That's so funny. We were talking about—you know, we're—we're all gonna go to that Shakespeare in the Park thing this weekend. See if we can go ahead and do that.

YALE Oh, yeah, right. *(Mary Wilke walks through the doorway and stands beside Yale)* I wanna do that. *(Turning to Mary)* Issac Davis and Tracy.

MARY *(Shaking Ike's hand)* Well, hello, hi.

IKE Hello, how do you do? How are you?

MARY Nice to meet you.

IKE You, too. You, too.

TRACY Hi.

IKE *(Chuckling nervously)* We were downstairs at the Castelli Gallery. We saw the photography exhibition. Incredible, absolutely incredible.

TRACY Oh, it's really good.

MARY Really, you liked that?
Yale sighs, not participating in the conversation.

IKE The-the photographs downstairs . . .

MARY Yes, downstairs.

IKE *(Overlapping)* . . . Castelli Gallery . . . great, absolutely great.
(Pausing) Mm-hm, did you?

MARY Huh? No, I—I really felt it was very derivative. To me, it
looked like it was straight out of Diane Arbus, but it had none of the
wit. It was—

IKE *(Interrupting)* Really? Well, you know, we—we didn't like 'em as
much as the—the Plexiglas sculpture, that I will admit. I mean,
it—

MARY *(Interrupting)* Really, you liked the Plexiglas, huh?

IKE You didn't like the Plexiglas sculpture either?

MARY *(Sighing)* Oh, it's interesting. *(Shrugging)* Nah, I—uh, I, uh,
tsch.

IKE It-it was a hell of a lot better than that—that steel cube. Did you
see the steel cube?

TRACY *(Overlapping)* Oh, yeah, that was the weirdest.
Ike laughs nervously.

MARY Now, that was brilliant to me, absolutely brilliant.

IKE The steel cube was brilliant?

MARY Yes. Uh, to me, it was—it was very textural. You know what
I mean? It was perfectly integrated and it had a-a-a marvelous kind
of negative capability. The rest of the stuff downstairs was bullshit.
*Ike raises an eyebrow, reacting, as the film moves outside the museum to the
sidewalk where Ike and Tracy, Yale and Mary walk in the sun, four abreast,
talking.*

YALE *(To Ike)* You wanna go see the Sol LeWitts?

IKE Sure, that'd be fun. *(To Tracy)* You wanna see Sol LeWitts too?

MARY *(Overlapping)* You know, he's having an opening at the Modern soon. I was gonna, uh, do a piece on Sol for *Insights.* Do—do you know that magazine? It's a—you know, it's one of those little magazines. I mean, they're such schmucks up there. *(Chuckling)* Really mired in thirties radicalism. *(Looking at Tracy)* What do you do, Tracy?

TRACY I go to high school.

MARY *(Chuckling and nodding)* Oh, really, really, hm. *(Aside, to Yale)* Somewhere Nabokov is smiling, if you know what I mean.

YALE *(Laughing, to Ike)* I think LeWitt's overrated. In fact, I think he may be a candidate for the old Academy.

MARY *(Interrupting)* Do you? Oh, really? *(Laughing)* Oh, that's right, we—

YALE *(Interrupting)* Mary and I have invented the, uh, Academy of the Overrated—

MARY *(interrupting)* That's right.
She laughs.

YALE —for, uh, such notables as . . .

MARY *(overlapping)* Such people as, uh . . .

YALE *(Laughing)* Gustav Mahler.

MARY And Isak Dinesen and Carl Jung . . .

YALE . . . Scott Fitzgerald and . . . *(Chuckling)* uh—

MARY *(Interrupting)* Lenny Bruce. We can't forget Lenny Bruce—now, can we?

YALE *(Laughing)* Lenny Bruce.

MARY And how about Norman Mailer and Walt Whitman and—

IKE *(Interrupting)* I think those people are all terrific, everyone that you mentioned.

MARY What? What?

YALE *(To Mary)* Who's that guy you had? You had a great one last week.

MARY *(Overlapping)*   No, no, I didn't have it. It was yours. It was Heinrich Böll, wasn't it?

YALE *(Laughing)*   Oh, God.

IKE *(Looking incredulous)*   Overrated?

YALE   Anyway, we don't wanna leave out ol' Heinrich.

IKE   Hey, what about Mozart? You guys don't wanna leave out Mozart—I mean, while you're trashing people.

MARY *(Chuckling)*   Oh, well, how about Vincent Van Gogh *(Pronouncing it "Goch")* . . . or Ingmar Bergman?

IKE *(Overlapping)*   Van Goch? *(Aside, to Tracy)* Did she say "Van Goch"?

MARY *(To Yale)*   How about Ingmar Bergman?

IKE *(Overlapping, shaking his head)*   Van Goch.

YALE *(Overlapping to Mary)*   Oh, you—you'll get in trouble with Bergman.
He sighs.

MARY   What do you mean?

IKE *(Overlapping, looking at Mary)*   Bergman? Bergman's the only genius in cinema today, I think. I just mean—

YALE *(Interrupting, to Mary)*   He's a big Bergman fan, you know.

MARY *(Looking at Ike, gesturing)*   Oh, please, you know. God, you're so the opposite! I mean, you write that absolutely fabulous television show. It's brilliantly funny and his view is so Scandinavian. It's bleak, my God. I mean, all that Kierkegaard, right? Real adolescent, you know, fashionable pessimism. I mean, the silence. God's silence. Okay, okay, okay, I mean, I loved it when I was at Radcliffe, but, I mean, all right, you outgrow it. You absolutely outgrow it.

YALE   Ah, I think I've got to go with him and Ingmar.
He laughs hesitantly.

IKE *(Aside, to Tracy)*   Get her away from me. I don't think I can take too much more of her. She's really a cr-creep.

MARY   Oh, no, no, no, no, don't you see—don't you guys see that it is the dignifying of one's own psychological and sexual hangups by attaching them to these grandiose philosophical issues? That's what it is.

Ike clears his throat. The group stops walking.

YALE *(Pointing to a nearby apartment building)*   Here we are.

IKE *(Fumbling)*   Uh, listen, I . . .

MARY *(overlapping)*   Oh.

IKE *(To Mary)*   It was very nice meeting you.

MARY   Well.

IKE *(Shaking Mary's hand)*   It was—it was a pleasure and a—

YALE *(Interrupting)*   Oh.

IKE   —sincere sensation, but we have to go—

MARY   Yeah, well.

IKE   —because we gotta get some—we gotta do some shopping. I forgot about it.

MARY *(Laughing nervously)*   Hey, listen. Hey, listen, I don't even wanna have this conversation. I mean—really, I mean, I'm just from Philadelphia. You know, I mean, we believe in God, so—uh, uh, okay?

IKE *(Gesturing)*   What the hell does that mean?

MARY *(Frowning, confused)*   Is it?

IKE *(Gesturing)*   What is it—what—what'd you—what'd you—what'd she mean—what do you mean by that there?

MARY   Well, what—

IKE *(Interrupting)*   "I'm from Philadelphia." "I believe in God." What-what does . . . *(Mary laughs nervously)* Does—does this make any sense to you at all? I . . .

CUT TO:
INTERIOR. DEAN AND DELUCA'S FOOD SHOP—DAY.

Tracy and Ike are picking up some groceries. While Tracy calmly looks at the foodstuff, a wire basket in her hand, Ike talks and gestures rapidly.

IKE *(Sighing)* What a creep! Could you believe her? I mean, she was really—

TRACY *(Interrupting)* Oh, she seemed real nervous.

IKE Nervous? She was overbearing. She was, mm, you know, mm, terrible. She was all cerebral *(Sighing and pointing to his head)* you know. Wh-was—where the hell does that little Radcliffe tootsie come off rating, mm, Scott Fitzgerald and Gustav Mahler and then Heinrich Böll?

TRACY *(Putting a can in her basket)* I don't understand why you're getting so mad.

IKE I'm mad because I don't like that pseudointellectual garbage. And she was pedantic. Van Gogh. *(Prouncing it "Goch")* Did you hear that? She said "Van Goch." I couldn't— Like an Arab she spoke. I couldn't . . . and if she had made one more remark about Bergman, I would've knocked her other contact lens out.
He makes a fist in the air.

TRACY *(Putting a container of cocoa in her basket)* Oh, is she Yale's mistress?

IKE *(Shaking his head)*   That will never cease to mystify me. I mean, he's got a wonderful wife and he prefers to—to, mm, diddle this little yo-yo that—that . . . you know. Uh, but—but he was always a sucker for, uh, th-th-those kind of women, you know, the kind, uh, who'd involve him in discussions of existential reality, you know. They probably sit around on the floor with wine and cheese and mispronounce "allegorical" and "didacticism."
He sighs.

TRACY   Well, I get the feeling that Yale really likes her.

IKE   Well, I'm old-fashioned. I don't believe in extramarital relationships. I think people should mate for life, like pigeons or Catholics. *They walk to the cashier. Tracy takes out her parcels and places them on the counter.*

TRACY   Tsch. Well, I don't know, maybe people weren't meant to have one deep relationship. Maybe we're meant to have, you know, a series of relationships of different lengths. I mean, that kind of thing's gone out of date.

IKE   Hey, don't tell me what's gone out of date, okay? You're seventeen years old. You were brought up on drugs and television and the pill. I-I-I was World War Two. *(Sighing)* I was in the trenches.

TRACY *(Chuckling)*   Oh, you were eight in World War Two.

IKE   That's right. I was never in the trenches. I was caught right in the middle. It was a very tough position.
Tracy laughs.

IKE *(Looking away, gesturing)*   Get the groceries, will you?

CUT TO:
INTERIOR. TELEVISION STUDIO—DAY.

Technicians and cameramen scurry around a raised set where a comedic Interviewer sits with his guests, Gregory and Caroline Payne Whitney Smith. She has long blond hair; she remains motionless, staring into one of the television cameras. Her husband is much more jittery; he wears a turned-around baseball cap on his head. Audience laughter is heard over the skit as the Interviewer or his guests say or do something funny.

INTERVIEWER   Good morning and welcome to *Human Beings Wow!* We're talking this evening with, uh, Gregory and Caroline Payne

Whitney Smith, who are very close friends of the Carter family, isn't that right?

GREGORY *(Nodding and laughing)* And we're just normal people, just ordinary people just like you are, in debt.

INTERVIEWER *(Chuckling)* Except for the fact that Mrs. Payne Whitney Smith is a catatonic. Isn't that correct?

GREGORY Well, we don't consider her a catatonic. We just kind of consider her quiet.

INTERVIEWER Oh, that's very . . .
The camera moves to the control booth, where Ike stands near the window looking down on the studio set. Television monitors display the interview skit going on below; a man sits behind the control console while Dick, the show's director, sits near him; Paul, the show's producer, stands between them, almost totally offscreen except for his wristwatched arm. The skit continues over the voices of the men in the booth.

INTERVIEWER *(Over the television monitors)* . . . beautiful. She's a wonderful, wonderful person and you take very good care of her too.

TECHNICIAN IN CONTROL BOOTH I said "Slide seven." See slide seven.

IKE *(Overlapping, reacting)* Jesus, this is terrible. This-this is really embarrassing to me. I mean, I—I mean, this is so antiseptic. It's nothing like what we talked about.

DICK No, no, wrong, wrong. That's not antiseptic.

IKE I mean, this isn't—this has nothing . . .

DICK That's—that's very chancy material. I mean, who fights—

IKE *(Interrupting)* How do you see this as chancy?

DICK —who fights more with the censor?

IKE *(Sitting down on the edge of the console)* It's empty.

TECHNICIAN IN CONTROL BOOTH Slide three.

IKE What-what has the—what has the censor got to do with it? It's empty. There's not, uh—there's not, uh, uh, any substance to the comedy.

PAUL No, no, you don't find this insightful here?

IKE   Well, it's worse than not insightful. It's not funny. There's not —there's not a legitimate laugh in that.

DICK *(Pointing to the monitor)*   Oh, it's— That's funny. That's funny! Funny.

IKE   Why do you think that it's funny?

PAUL *(Gesturing)*   Look at the audience.

IKE   There's not a—

DICK *(Interrupts, pointing to the audience below the control booth)*   Look at —look at the audience there.

IKE *(Listening to the audience laughter coming from the monitor)*   You're going by the—you're going by audience reaction to this? I mean, this is an audience that's raised on television. Their-their standards have been systematically lowered over the years. You know, these guys sit in front of their sets and the-the gamma rays eat the white cells of their brains out. Uh, you know, um, ya, I'm— I quit.
He stands up and leans over the console, picking up his jacket from a chair.

DICK   All right. Just relax. Take a lude. Take a lude.

IKE *(Overlapping)*   No, no, no, no, no, I quit. I can't write this anymore. I can't . . . I don't want a lude.
The men in the control booth are quiet for a brief moment; the audience laughter and the interview dialogue continues over the monitor in the silence.

IKE *(Putting on his jacket and breaking the pause)*   All you guys do is-is, uh, drop ludes and then-then take Percodans and angel dust. Naturally, it seems funny.

DICK   You know, just relax, relax.

IKE *(Gesturing)*   Anything would if you're—if you're . . . You know, we, y-y-you should abandon the show and open a pharmaceutical house.

DICK   Look, you—

IKE *(Interrupting)*   I quit.

DICK   Relax—

IKE *(interrupting)*   I quit. I quit.

DICK　—Ike, you're being silly.
Ike turns and walks away while the audience laughter continues over the monitor. The camera moves closer to the monitor screen, where Gregory has just put his arms around Caroline's neck and, twisting her head, cracks her neck. The audience is roaring with laughter over the accompanying dialogue.

GREGORY *(With his arms around Caroline's neck)*　See, look at this. I'll just do this. We-we-we-we've talked a little about this. We consider. We figure . . .

INTERVIEWER *(Interrupting, on the television monitor screen)*　Yeah. Now, don't—don't break her neck there. Oh, good.

GREGORY *(Twisting Caroline's head, on the television monitor screen)*　No, I won't . . . Well, that's fine . . .

The film fades to the fairly crowded Rizzoli bookstore, where Yale is browsing through the shelves while Ike stands nearby, gesturing and talking, more intent on the conversation than the books.

IKE *(Shaking his head)*　Tsch. What did I do? I made a terrible mistake.

YALE *(Scanning the shelves)*　Ike, will you stop it? This is the first smart thing you've ever done for yourself.

IKE No, I've screwed myself up completely. You know, for about thirty seconds, I was a big hero. And then—and now it's directly to unemployment.

YALE If you need to borrow any money, I'll take care of it.

IKE *(Following Yale to another bookshelf)* That's not the point. Money, what's money got to do . . . ? I've got enough for a year. If I—if I, uh, live like Mahatma Gandhi, I'm fine. My accountant says that I did this at a very bad time. My stocks are down. I, uh, I-I-I'm cash-poor or something. I got no cash flow. I'm not liquid or, uh, something's not flowing. I know it. But they got a language all their own, those guys.

YALE *(Turning from the books to look at Ike)* Well, we discussed this. I mean, it's difficult to live in this town without a big income.

IKE Yeah, plus I got two alimonies and I got child support and I got . . . you know, I gotta cut down. I'm gonna have to give up my apartment, I'm not gonna be able to do the tennis lessons, I'm not gonna, um, pick the checks up at dinner or . . . you know. I won't be able to take the-the Southampton house.

YALE *(Sighing)* Oh.

IKE I mean, you know, oh . . . plus I'll probably have to give my parents less money. You know, this is gonna kill my father. He's gonna—he's not gonna be able to get as good a seat in the synagogue, you know. *(Yale sighs and straightens himself up. He turns and looks at Ike)* This year he's gonna be in the back, away from God, far from the action.

YALE *(Chuckling)* What about Tracy? Have you said anything to her?

IKE Oh, but, uh, what is it *(Shaking his head)* I'm, uh, I gotta get out of that situation. She's a—she's a young girl. What am I—I'm *(Sighing)* . . . You know, it's ridiculous. I mean, I, uh, uh . . . *(Sighing)* Hey, and wha-wha-what happens if the year goes by and, uh, and my book doesn't come out?

YALE *(Putting his hands on Ike's shoulders)* Your, hey, your book is gonna come out. Your book is gonna be wonderful. I mean, the worst thing that can happen to you is that you're gonna learn something about yourself, right? Listen, listen, I'm really proud of you. I mean, this is a very good move.

CUT TO:
EXTERIOR. MUSEUM OF MODERN ART'S SCULPTURE GARDEN
—NIGHT.

Bella Abzug, wearing a large hat, stands in the middle of a large crowd; she holds a microphone in her hand.

BELLA ABZUG *(Talking into the microphone)* This is a wonderful turnout . . . and the Museum of Modern Art has been very generous. And the proof of . . . the strength of the Equal Rights Amendment is that so many of you who would never do it before put on black tie tonight. *(The crowd applauds and laughs)* We love you for it. We need you and you've come through. And now, no more talk, enjoy yourselves.

She gestures expansively with her hands as the crowd, applauding, begins to break up into small groups, chattering and laughing. Background music is heard as Jerry, in a black tuxedo, drink in hand, approaches Ike. They shake hands.

JERRY Ike, nice to see you.

IKE Hi, what're you doing here? So—congratulations on your book. I thought it was terrific.

JERRY Ah, thanks.

IKE Absolutely terrific.

JERRY Thanks. Thanks.

IKE It's nice to see you.

Jerry turns to the group he'd been talking to: Helen, Dennis, Mary and Polly.

JERRY Listen, good people, I'd like you to meet my friend Isaac Davis.

IKE *(To Helen)* Hi, howd'you do.

HELEN *(To Ike)* Hi, how're you.

MARY *(Startled, to herself)* Isaac Davis?

HELEN *(Shaking Ike's hand now)* Hello, Isaac.

IKE *(To the entire group)* Isaac Davis. Hi.

MARY *(Chuckling)* Isaac, hello. Hi, what—

IKE *(Equally startled to see Mary)* Hi. *(Chuckling)* Wha-what're you doing here?

MARY   Well, uh, I'm here, of course, I'm here, are you kidding?

IKE   *(Shaking his head)*   What a f-f-funny coinci—   *(To Dennis, who is standing next to Mary, not yet introduced)*   Uh, excuse me—Isaac Davis.

DENNIS   *(Shaking Ike's hand)*   Hi.

IKE   *(Overlapping)*   Hi, how are you?   *(To Dennis, pointing to Mary)*   We met before. We met.

MARY   Yeah.

JERRY   You know her?

IKE   *(Looking at Jerry)*   We know one another.

MARY   It's funny.

JERRY   I-I-I'm sorry.

MARY   *(Laughing)*   No, no.

IKE   *(Laughing)*   No, no, it's all right.

JERRY   *(Chuckling)*   I-I heard you, uh, you, uh, uh, quit your job.

IKE   I, uh—y-yeah, a real self-destructive impulse. You know, I wanna write a book so I—so I . . . *(Sighing and changing the subject)* Ha-has anybody read that the Nazis are gonna march in New Jersey, you know? *(Helen and Polly shake their heads no)* I read this in the newspaper. *(Waving his fist)* We should go down there, get some guys together, you know, get some bricks and baseball bats and really explain things to 'em.

JERRY   There was this devastating satirical piece on that on the Op-Ed page of the *Times*. It was devastating.

IKE   W-e-e-elll, a satirical piece in the *Times* is one thing, but bricks and baseball bats really gets right to the point down there.

HELEN   *(Overlapping)*   Oh, but really biting satire is always better than physical force.

IKE   But true physical force is always better with Nazis, uh . . . because it's hard to satirize a guy with, uh, shiny boots on.

HELEN   Oh, you get emotional, I know, but—

DENNIS   *(Interrupting)*   Excuse me—

IKE *(Nodding)*   It's—it's all right.

DENNIS *(Overlapping)*   —we were talking about orgasms.

MARY *(Chuckling, reacting)*   Oh, no, please wait, no.

IKE *(Overlapping)*   Oh, really? I'm sorry. I didn't mean to—

DENNIS *(Interrupting)*   Really?

MARY *(Overlapping)*   Give me a break, Dennis.

DENNIS *(Defensively)*   Well, we were.

MARY   No, I'm from Philadelphia. We never talk about things like that in public.

IKE *(Chuckling)*   Yeah, you said that the other day.

DENNIS   I'm, uh—

IKE *(Interrupting, to Mary)*   I didn't know what the hell it meant then, either.

DENNIS   I'm just about to direct a film—

IKE *(Interrupting)*   Ah-ha.

DENNIS   —uh, of my own script and, um . . . the premise is: This guy screws so great—

IKE *(Interrupting)*   Screws so great?

DENNIS   —screws so great that when . . . he brings a woman to orgasm, she's so fulfilled . . . that she dies, right? Now, this one . . . *(Looking at Mary)* excuse me, finds this hostile.

MARY *(Shaking her head)*   This one? Hostile . . . God, it's worse than hostile. It's aggressive-homicidal.

DENNIS   I beg your—

IKE *(Interrupting, reacting)*   She dies?

MARY *(To Ike, laughing nervously)*   You-you-you have to forgive Dennis.

DENNIS *(Musing over everyone's reactions)*   He might not.

MARY   He's Harvard direct to Beverly Hills.

IKE *(To Dennis)*   Is that where you're from?

DENNIS (*Nodding*)   Yeah.

MARY   It's, uh—

IKE (*Interrupting, incredulous*)   Is that where you're from?

MARY   It's Theodor Reik with a touch of Charles Manson.

DENNIS (*Nodding*)   Yeah, right.

POLLY (*Speaking for the first time*)   I . . . uh, I finally had an orgasm and
my doctor told me it was the wrong kind.
There is a slight pause while everyone digests Polly's words.

IKE (*To Polly, breaking the pause*)   Tsch. Did you have the wrong kind?
Oh, really? I've never had the wrong kind—

POLLY (*Interrupting, shrugging*)   Yes?

IKE   —ever, never. Uh, my worst one was right on the money.

POLLY (*Staring at Ike*)   Oh, was it?

CUT TO:
EXTERIOR. STREET—NIGHT.

*A taxi drives up the street and stops at a curb. Its back door opens and Ike
and Mary get out, bending down to peer through the car door at Dennis and
the others.*

IKE (*Waving*)   Good night. It was nice to meet you.

DENNIS' VOICE (*Inside the taxi*)   Same here.

IKE (*To the others still in the cab*)   Nice meeting you.

MARY (*Waving*)   Bye, bye.

DENNIS' VOICE   Bye.
(Mary closes the cab door and the taxi pulls away.

IKE (*Shouting*)   Bye!

DENNIS' VOICE (*Inside the moving taxi, shouting*)   Bye, bye!

HELEN'S VOICE (*Inside the moving taxi, shouting*)   Goodbye!
*Ike and Mary start walking down the street, looking in the shop windows
and talking.*

IKE   Oh. (*Sighing*) It—it's an interesting group of people your friends
are.

MARY   Oh, I know.

IKE   It's like a cast of a Fellini movie.

MARY   They're such fun. They're such wonderful people and Helen is really a good friend. She's a very brilliant woman, you know.

IKE   Mm-hm. Is she?

MARY   She's really a genius.

IKE   Mm-hm.

MARY   I met her through my ex-husband, Jeremiah.

IKE   Yeah, how come you guys got divorced? I—I—I mean, that's something I never—

MARY *(Interrupting)*   Well, I don't understand.

IKE   —you know.

MARY *(Overlapping)*   What do you mean how come we got divorced? Uh—

IKE *(Interrupting)*   Well?

MARY   —what kind of a question is that? Uh, I don't even know you at all.

IKE   No, you don't have to tell me if you don't—   I'm just curious, you know.

MARY *(Crossing her arms)*   Oh, well, I—we had a lot of problems. We fought a lot and *(Sighing)* I was tired of submerging my identity to a very brilliant, dominating man—

IKE *(Interrupting, reacting)*   Mm-hm.

MARY   —'cause he's a genius.

IKE   All right, he was a genius and Helen's a genius and Dennis is a genius. You know a lot of geniuses, you know. Uh, you should meet some stupid people once in a while. You know, you could learn something.

MARY   Well, okay, tell me, why'd you get a divorce?

IKE   Why?

MARY   Yeah.

IKE I got a divorce because my ex-wife left me for another woman. Okay?

MARY *(Reacting)* Really?

IKE *(Nodding his head)* Mm-hm.

MARY God, that must've been really demoralizing.

IKE *(Shrugging)* Tsch. Well, I don't know, I thought I took it rather well under the circumstances.

MARY *(Still reacting, shaking her head)* Phew-wee.

IKE I tried to run 'em both over with a car.

MARY I can imagine. I mean, that's incredible sexual humiliation. It's enough to turn you off of women.

IKE *(Shrugging)* Well . . .

MARY And I think it accounts for the little girl.

IKE Well . . . Hey, the little girl is fine. Jesus, she's— What's with— what's with "the little girl"?

MARY Oh, sure, I understand, believe me. Sixteen years old and no possible threat at all.

IKE Uh-huh, she's seventeen. She's gonna be eight— You know, sometimes you have a-a losing personality, Mary.

MARY Hey, I'm honest. What do you want? I say what's on my mind. And if you can't take it—well, then, fuck off.

IKE And I like the way you express yourself too.
Mary laughs. The sounds of traffic are heard as they continue to walk through the lamp-lit streets.

IKE You know, it's pithy, yet degenerate. You get many dates? I don't think so.

MARY (*Nodding her head for emphasis*) Well, I do. I actually . . . Now I do. Uh, you'll never believe this, but I never thought I was very pretty. Oh, what is pretty anyway? I mean, I hate being pretty. It's all so subjective anyway.

IKE Oh, yeah?

MARY I mean, the brightest men just drop dead in front of a beautiful face. And the minute you climb into the sack, if you're the least bit giving, they're so grateful.

IKE Yeah, I know I am—

MARY (*Interrupting*) Hm.

IKE —you know.

MARY Do you have any kids or anything like that?

IKE Me, yeah, I got a kid who's—

MARY (*Interrupting*) Really?

IKE —being raised by two women at the moment.

MARY Oh, well, you know—I mean, I think that works. Uh, they made some studies I read in one of the psychoanalytic quarterlies. You don't need a male. I mean, two mothers are absolutely fine, just fine.

IKE Oh, really? Because I always feel very few people survive one mother.

MARY (*Turning to look at Ike*) Hm. Well, listen, I gotta get my dog. Uh, you wanna wait? I gotta walk it. Ar-are-you—you in a rush or something like that?

IKE *(Shaking his head)*   Oh, no, no, sure. Wha-what kind of dog you got?

MARY *(Chuckling)*   The worst.

IKE   Really?

MARY   It's a dachshund.

IKE   Oh, really.

MARY   You know—I mean, it's a penis substitute for me.
They stop walking. Ike scratches his chin and raises an eyebrow, reacting.

IKE   Oh, I would've thought then, in your case, a Great Dane.

MARY *(Laughing)*   Really? Oh.
The scene shifts to a street near Mary's apartment. It's a bit later that night, and Ike and Mary are walking her dog, Waffles. An orchestration of "Someone to Watch Over Me" plays over this scene, stopping after the film moves to an all-night luncheonette where Mary, Waffles in her arms, and Ike stand by the counter; they wait for some just-grilled hamburgers to be put into takeout containers by the man behind the counter. Mary is laughing happily.

IKE   So, are you serious with Yale or what?

MARY   Serious?

IKE *(Nodding his head)*   Mm-hm.

MARY *(Shrugging)*   Mm, yeah. You know, I mean, he's married. *(Chuckling)* Tsch, oh . . .

IKE *(Shrugging)*   Mm, yeah, so what?

MARY   I don't know. I guess I— *(Sighing)* I guess I should straighten my life out, huh? Well, I mean, Donny, my analyst, is always telling me—

IKE *(Interrupting)*   You call your analyst Donny?

MARY *(Laughing)*   Yeah, I call him Donny.

IKE *(Overlapping, incredulous)*   You call him Donny, your analyst?

MARY   Yes.

IKE   I call mine Dr. Chomsky . . . you know.

MARY   Oh, well.

IKE *(Raising and lowering his hand in demonstration)*   Yeah, or—uh, he hits me with the ruler. *(Mary laughs)* Donny? That's a first name?

MARY *(Ignoring Ike's remarks)*   Anyway, Donny tells me that I get involved in these situations and that it's deliberate, you know. I mean, es-es-especially with my ex-husband, Jeremiah. You know, I mean, I—I was his student and, um—

IKE *(Interrupting)*   Really? You married your-your-your teacher?

MARY   Yeah, yeah, of course, I mean . . .

IKE *(Overlapping)*   That's very . . . very, uh—

MARY *(Interrupting)*   All right, listen to that, he failed me and I fell in love with him. It's so perfect, right?

IKE *(Nodding)*   Well, that's perfect, yeah, that's—yeah, that is, yeah.

MARY   I know, I mean, I was sleeping with him and he had the nerve to give me an F. So.

IKE   Really?

MARY   Yeah, really.

IKE   No kidding? Not even an Incomplete, right? Just a straight F? *He sighs.*

MARY *(Laughing)*   You know, you've got a good sense of humor. You actually do.

IKE *(Gesturing)*   Hey, hey, thanks, thanks. I don't need you to tell me that, you know.
Mary laughs.

IKE   I've been—yeah, no, I've been making good money off it for years—

MARY *(Interrupting)*   Oh.

IKE   —till I quit my job to write this book. And now I'm very . . . very nervous about it, you know.

MARY *(Nodding)*   Uh-huh. Oh.

IKE   But, you know, I'm—
The waiter puts the takeout bag in front of them, interrupting Ike's speech. Ike reaches into his pocket and takes out some money.

MARY Listen, do you wanna—? *(Stopping her speech as she sees Ike take out his money)* Oh, you don't have to pay for it, really.

IKE Oh, that's okay.

MARY *(Gesturing and chuckling)* No, no, I'm serious. You wanna walk by the river? We can—

IKE *(Interrupting)* You know what time it is now?

MARY What do you mean what time is it?

IKE Well, if I don't get at least sixteen hours, I'm a basket case.

MARY *(Sighing)* Oh. Well, I'd like to hear about your book. I—I—and I'm— I really would, you know. I'm—I'm quite a good editor.

IKE Yeah?

MARY *(Nodding her head)* Uh-huh.
  Ike picks up the takeout bag. The sounds of "Someone to Watch Over Me" begins again as Mary and Ike walk out of the luncheonette, deep in discussion. Their voices are heard as they leave; the camera stays focused on the almost empty coffee shop.

IKE *(Offscreen, walking out of the luncheonette)*   Well, my book is about decaying values. It's about . . . See, the thing is, years ago, I wrote a short story about my mother called "The Castrating Zionist." And, um, I wanna expand it into a novel.

MARY *(Offscreen)*   That's good.

IKE *(Offscreen)*   You know, I could talk about my book all night.
"Someone to Watch Over Me" is still playing as the film switches to the 59th Street Bridge. It is almost dawn and the scene has a nearly perfect feel of light and beauty to it. Mary and Ike, their backs to the camera, are sitting on a bench looking out over the water. Waffles is curled up at their feet.

MARY *(Contentedly)*   Isn't it beautiful, Ike?

IKE   Yeah, it's really—really so pretty when the light starts to come up.

MARY   Oh, I know. I love it.

IKE   Boy—

MARY   Hm.

IKE *(Sighing)*   —this is really a great city. I don't care what anybody says. It's just so—really a knockout, you know? It's—

MARY *(Interrupting, sighing)*   Yeah. I think I better head back. I have an appointment with Yale for lunch later on.

IKE *(Sighing too)*   Hm.
They get up from the bench and walk away. The music stops.

CUT TO:
INTERIOR. YALE'S BEDROOM—MORNING.

Yale, lying in bed, rests on his elbow as he picks up his ringing phone. As he talks he grabs his wristwatch from a nearby night table. He checks the time, then puts the watch back on the table.

YALE *(Into the telephone)*   Mm, hi . . . *(Coughing)* No, no, no, I'm awake . . . Jesus, what're you—what're you doing? It's seven-fifteen . . . Oh, yeah . . . Really? You did—at the museum? . . . Yeah, well, she's— uh, very active in the feminist movement. *(Emily walks into the bedroom. She moves around the bed, picking up a newspaper)* Uh, so—so you're gonna go a-apartment hunting with Tracy? . . . Yeah, well, you know, you should be able to find something. *(To Emily)* It's

Isaac. *(Into the telephone)* Yeah, I don't think you'll have any trouble. *(He looks up at Emily as she leaves the room)* Yeah, well, I knew you'd —I knew you'd *(Sighing)* see she's a terrific woman if you spent some time with her, you know.

The film cuts to Ike on his end of the phone. He is in a crowded phone-booth area.

IKE *(Into the telephone)*   And—and you still—you still feel the same way about her? You still feel as hung up on her? 'Cause I know you hadn't mentioned it in a while . . . So you . . . Yeah . . . Mm-hm, tsch . . . Yeah. *(He holds the telephone receiver away from his ear and, reacting, grimaces; he shakes his head knowingly, then puts the receiver back to his ear and nods affirmatively)* Mm-hm . . . Right . . . No, I know. She's great, I know, great . . . So, uh . . . No, I gotta go apartment hunting today 'cause I have to get something cheaper. I can't keep living—*(Sighing)* you know, yeah, where I do, it's just . . . tsch.

The film cuts to Bloomingdale's main floor. It is crowded; people pass by, going up and down the escalators. There are bells ringing over the chatter of the crowds. The camera moves to a cosmetic counter where Mary, standing and talking to Yale, is in the midst of purchasing some makeup.

YALE   Isaac's terrific, isn't he?

MARY *(Checking her wallet for her credit card)*   Mm, yeah.

YALE   He said he had a great time with you.

MARY   Did he really?

YALE   Mm-hm.

MARY *(Handing her card to the saleslady behind the counter)*   That's good. That's funny 'cause I always think that he's uncomfortable around me.

YALE   Oh, come on. *(Chuckling, lowering his voice)* I missed you so much.

MARY   Oh, Yale.

YALE   It's terrible.

MARY   This is—it's just ridiculous. It's—you're married. I can't . . . Listen to me, I'm beginning to sound like I'm one of those women. I—it sounds terrible. I hate it.

YALE   Look, why don't I just move out?

MARY   No! Oh, no, I don't—I don't want you to do that. I'm—I don't want to break up a marriage yet. Besides, I'm really—I'm not looking for any big involvement here. It's just . . . I don't—*(Sighing)* It's crazy. It's crazy! I think about you when you're not around.

YALE *(Smiling)*   Well, wha-what do you want me to do?

MARY   Nothing. I don't know. I really don't know. I just—I guess I should be seeing someone who's not married.

YALE *(Starting to kiss Mary)*   God, you are so beautiful.

MARY *(Reacting and pulling away)*   Oh, Yale, stop it.

YALE   You make me crazy.

MARY   Please stop it. We're in the middle of Bloomingdale's. *(Yale laughs)* And someone's gonna see us. Oh, did I tell you? I think I may have an interview with Borges. I-I-I told you that we met before when he was here. And he seems to feel very comfortable around me.

YALE   Let's go somewhere and make love.

MARY *(Laughing)*   What do you mean? Not now.
Yale continues to laugh as the saleslady behind the counter hands a sales slip and the credit card to Mary.

MARY *(Signing the slip)*   Not now. Jesus! You've got—anyway, you've got a—a writing class in an hour. Your students are gonna know. You're gonna have this—this big grin on your face.
Mary hands the slip back to the saleslady.

YALE   And I don't wanna go to your house 'cause I can't stand the dog—

MARY *(Sighing and motioning to Yale to be quiet)*   Oh. Shush. Well, can't you . . . ?

YALE   —and the telephone ringing all the time.
The saleslady hands Mary her package.

MARY *(To the saleslady)*   Thank you. *(Yale puts his arm around Mary; they begin walking through the crowded, noisy store.)* Can't you just hold me? Does your love for me always have to express itself sexually? What about other values, like warmth and spiritual contact? A hotel, right? Jesus, I'm a *(Laughing)* pushover anyway.

Their voices fade as the sounds of the department-store bells and chatter fill the screen.

CUT TO:
INTERIOR. JILL'S APARTMENT—DAY.

Connie, Jill's companion, opens the front door.

CONNIE   Oh, hi, Isaac.

IKE   Hi, is Willie ready?

CONNIE   Yeah, come on in.
Ike, casually dressed in T-shirt and slacks, follows Connie into a large living room.

JILL *(Offscreen)*   He'll be right down.

CONNIE   How you been, Ike?

IKE   Good. How you been?

CONNIE   I've been terrific.

IKE   Yeah?

CONNIE   Yeah, I've been getting a lot of work done. Things are going really well.
Jill is standing near a dining-room table, yet to be cleared from a recent meal, and framed by a large quilt hanging on the wall. She looks up.

JILL   You want some coffee or something?

IKE   Uh, no.
Connie walks out of the room; Jill begins stacking and clearing the dishes off the table.

IKE   So how's Willie doing?

JILL   Willie's fine. He's beginning to show some real talent in drawing.
Connie comes over to the table and begins to help Jill.

IKE   Yeah, where—where does he get that? 'Cause you don't draw and I don't draw.

CONNIE *(Looking up from the dish-clearing at Ike)*   I draw.

IKE *(Reacting)*   Yup, but there's no way that you could be the actual father.

JILL *(Ignoring Ike's remarks)* I'm hoping that you'll take Willie the weekend of the sixteenth 'cause Connie and I are thinking of going to Barbados.

IKE Okay, let me ask you something. Are you still gonna write that stupid book? I mean, are you serious about that?

JILL I'm very serious about it. It's an honest book and you have nothing to be ashamed of.

CONNIE Excuse me.
She begins to walk offscreen, up the stairs. Jill and Ike continue to talk, their voices rising.

IKE Can—can I talk to you for a minute? *(To Connie, who is halfway up the stairs)* Will you excuse me for a minute? *(To Jill)* Let me ask you something. Here's what I still don't understand.

JILL I'm late.
She starts fussing nervously, walking in and out of the kitchen, stacking dishes, clearing the table, tossing her hair. Ike follows her, gesturing excitedly.

IKE Wh-what the—what're you—where're you running? All the times I come over here, I can't understand how you can prefer her to me. I mean—

JILL *(Stopping her activity for a moment)* You can't understand that?

IKE No, no, it's a mystery to me.

JILL Well, you knew my history when you married me.

IKE Yeah, I know, my analyst warned me, but you were so beautiful that I—that I got another analyst.

JILL Tsch. *(Sighing and shaking her head)* Do you think we can be ever just friends?

IKE You're gonna put all the details in the book, right? You're gonna put 'em—

JILL *(Interrupting)* No, I'm not gonna dwell on the part where you tried to run her over with a car.

IKE Wha—I tried to run—I tried to run her over with a car? What're you talking about?

JILL That's what I said.

IKE It was late at night. I . . . you know I don't drive well. It was raining. It was—it was dark.

JILL What were you doing lurking around outside the cabin anyway?

IKE I was spying on you guys 'cause I knew what was happening in there.

JILL Obviously.

IKE You were—you were falling in love.
Jill walks over to a closet and takes out three brass candlesticks. She brings them to the table and places them at its center. She sits down, flinging back her hair, and looks up at Ike, who has continued to follow her around the room.

JILL *(Sighing)* So you felt that you *(Sighing)* had to run her over with a car?

IKE *(Gesturing)* Do I look like the type of person that would run someone over in a car?
Jill continues to sigh; she looks down.

IKE You know how slowly I was going?

JILL Not slowly enough that you didn't rip the whole front porch of the cabin off.

IKE *(Pointing over his shoulder)*   Get the kid. I can't . . .   Get the kid 'cause I can't have this argument with you every time I come over.
Upbeat music begins playing, a transition from Jill's dining area to the front door opening, Ike and his son, Willie, stepping animatedly outside. Willie is holding a basketball; they run along the sidewalk taking turns dribbling the ball.
The music continues as they stand in front of the F.A.O. Schwarz window; the camera is inside, facing out at the display and the two of them on the sidewalk. Two toy sailboats, one rather large, one much smaller, are prominently displayed. Willie keeps pointing to the large boat, mouthing that he wants it. Ike continues to point to the small one, mouthing, "No. That one." They continue to point to their choices, both stubbornly refusing to back down, until Ike finally hits Willie playfully on the head. It does no good. Willie still points to the large boat. Resigned, Ike takes some money out of his pocket, and after one last look at the boats in the window, follows Willie into the store. The music continues over the entire scene.
The movie shifts to the Russian Tea Room, where Willie and Ike are standing in line, waiting to be seated. Two tall beautiful models stand in front of them, chatting. A headwaiter comes over to Ike and hands him a jacket to wear over his T-shirt.

IKE *(To Willie, pointing to the jacket)*   The stupidest thing, you know.

WILLIE   You look funny in that jacket.
The upbeat music finally stops, the sounds of the busy restaurant taking its place.

IKE *(Putting his hands on Willie's shoulders)*   I know, I know. I had hoped for something in gabardine, but . . . It's crazy, isn't it? So, do you miss me?

WILLIE   Yeah, do you miss me?

IKE   Of course I miss you. I love you. That's why I—you know, that's why I come and get you all the time.
The headwaiter hangs up a nearby telephone; he walks over to the two models and, carrying two menus, motions them to follow him.

MODEL *(To the headwaiter)*   Oh, all right.

WILLIE *(Overlapping the model's words)*   Why can't we have frankfurters?

IKE   Because this is a Russian tea room. I mean, you wanna have, you know, you wanna have a blintz or something. A frankfurter gives

you cancer, anyhow. And besides, did you see those two women here? *(He points to the two models, who are walking away behind the headwaiter, offscreen)* They have very beautiful women that eat here. You know, we could—we could do very well. I think we could've picked up these two if you were a little quicker. I'm serious. I think the brunette liked you.
Ike and Willie both stare offscreen.

CUT TO:
INTERIOR. MARY'S APARTMENT—DAY.

Mary, distraught and nervous, is standing in the middle of her disarrayed living room. Books and papers are everywhere. Waffles is barking in the background. Mary lights a cigarette and finally sits down in an easy chair. She picks up the phone and begins to dial.

MARY *(Sighing and talking to herself)* Oh, boy. I'll call him. *(Into the telephone)* Hello, Yale? . . . Um, I'm sorry for calling . . . Well, no, no, nothing—nothing's wrong. I've . . . Well, I don't know. I just thought that it's, you know, it's Sunday out and I—*(Sighing)* and I thought maybe if you could, uh, get away, we could go for a walk or . . . Mm, mm-hm, mm-hm . . . *(Inhaling her cigarette smoke)* Oh, that's right, yeah, you mentioned that . . . *(Sighing)* Well, okay, it was just a shot . . . Yeah . . . Tsch . . . Yeah . . . Well, I won't keep you . . . Okay. *(Ending abruptly)* Bye, bye.
She gets up from the chair and puts down the receiver. She stares into space, still smoking.

CUT TO:
INTERIOR/EXTERIOR. IKE'S APARTMENT/TERRACE—DAY.

Through his interior Levolor blinds, the slats opened, Ike is seen sitting in a chair in his garden terrace. Surrounding plants are framing the blinds in the window. The phone rings and Ike picks it up, the Sunday paper on his lap.

IKE *(Into the telephone)* Hello? . . . Oh, hi. Hi, how you doing? . . . No, no, not at all. I was—I was just sitting around looking through the, uh, the magazine section . . . Uh, no, no, no . . . *(Chuckling)* No, no, I-I-I was, uh, I didn't read the, uh, the piece on China's faceless masses. I was—I was checking out the lingerie ads . . . Yeah, I can never get past them. They're really erotic.
The film cuts back to Mary's apartment, where she stands, leaning in her patio doorway, with the telephone receiver resting on her shoulder.

MARY *(Into the telephone)* You wanna go for a walk? Well, eh, I don't know. I mean, I've gotta get out. I'm going stir- *(Chuckling)* crazy here and Yale's with Emily's parents. Eh—it's such a beautiful Sunday.
The sound of thunder is heard as the movie cuts to Central Park, where Ike and Mary run down a path, trying to get out of the rain. The sky is dark and ominous in contrast to the bright sun a few hours before. Ike and Mary shout to teach other over the thunder and lightning.

IKE Come on, it's an electrical storm. You wanna wind up in an ashtray?

MARY It was such a beautiful day out.

IKE Yeah, wonderful. *(Reacting to some close thunder)* Jesus, I think I heard the Chrysler Building blow up.

MARY Oh, no! Thunder scares me.

IKE *(Reacting to the worsening storm)* Oh, come on.
The rain is coming down in torrents, soaking their hair and light clothing. Mary hands Ike a piece of newspaper she's been holding.

MARY Here.

IKE *(Responding to Mary's previous comment)*   Yeah, it's not my favorite sound either.

MARY   Oh, God. Do you know that every year, one or two people get killed during an electrical storm in Central Park?

IKE   Yeah, yeah, why don't I run up ahead and we'll talk later in the week.
Ike and Mary continue to run through the rain, the papers over their heads providing poor shelter from the storm. They manage to race up the steps of the Hayden Planetarium; they rush into its entrance. They stand inside near the door, laughing and making futile attempts to dry off. People browse at the planetarium exhibit in the background as Ike and Mary talk.

IKE   Jesus Christ, I'm soaking wet. This is awful.

MARY *(Laughing)*   You look ridiculous, you know that?

IKE   Oh. Next time you want someone to go for a walk with you on a Sunday, get somebody else.

MARY *(Chuckling)*   Hey, you know, I've never seen anybody react so strongly to a little bit of rain, a little bit of water like that.
Mary walks over to a garbage can and throws away their soaking wet newspapers.

IKE *(Following her)*   It was not the water. It was the electricity. I don't want to get hit by lightning. I—I'll turn into one of those guys that sells comic books outside of Bloomingdale's.
They walk farther into the planetarium, becoming silhouetted in the darkness by a huge illuminated photograph of a nebula.

MARY *(Sighing)*   What do you think? You think I look terrible? What do you think?

IKE   Let's see.

MARY   How—how do I look?

IKE *(Trying to see her in the dark)*   I can't see.

MARY *(Laughing)*   You should see your face.

IKE   You look kind of nice, actually. You're sort of pretty.
They walk farther into the planetarium's interior, passing through a moon exhibit. It is dark, the only illumination coming from an enormous moon-scape, realistically portrayed with its craters and rock sculptures, as Mary

and Ike are first only heard, then finally seen as they walk deeper into the exhibit, still silhouetted by the dark and the moonscape's spot lighting.

MARY *(Offscreen)*   You know, I'm really annoyed with Yale.

IKE *(Offscreen)*   Why?

MARY *(Walking in front of the moonscape exhibit)*   He was supposed to see me today, and then he couldn't. We had tickets to this Vivaldi concert last night. He had to cancel on me, of course.

IKE *(Walking in front of the moonscape exhibit)*   Well, you know, that's what happens when you're—

MARY *(Interrupting)*   I know, when you're having an affair with a married man. What a terrible way to put it.

IKE   Hey, I didn't put it that way.

MARY   My husband was—no, my ex-husband was having an affair while we were married. And I never—

IKE *(Stopping and looking at Mary)*   Oh, really?

MARY   Yeah, he was, at least one that I know of. But I never mentioned anything because *(Sighing)* I felt that I was deficient in some way, that I was bad in bed, or I wasn't bright enough, or that I was *(Sighing)* physically unattractive. But I'll tell you something. In the end, he was just a louse.

IKE *(Moving away from the moonscape)*   Yeah, I know, an intellectual louse.

MARY *(Following Ike)*   Oh, God, was he brilliant. I was so crazy about him. He really opened me up sexually. He taught me everything. Women found him devastating.
They stop and look at each other and the film cuts to a large photograph of Saturn, complete with ring. Ike and Mary, still in shadow, walk in front of it, still talking; they stand in front of the photograph, dramatically lit by its glow as they continue their conversation.

MARY   Oh, look, there's Saturn. Saturn is the sixth planet from the sun. How many of the satellites of Saturn can you name? T-there's Mimas—uh, Titan, Dione, Hyperion, of course, uh . . .

IKE   Nah, I can't name any of them and—and, fortunately, they never come up in conversation.

MARY *(Sighing)* Facts. Yeah, I've got a million facts on my fingertips.

IKE That's right. And they don't mean a thing, right? Because nothing worth knowing can be understood with the mind . . . you know. E-e-e-everything really valuable has to enter you through a different opening . . . if you'll forgive the disgusting imagery.

MARY I really don't agree at all. I mean, where would we be without rational thought? Come on.

IKE No, no, you-you-you-you, you—you rely too much on your brain. It's a . . . the-the-the brains is the most overrated organ, I think. *The film goes black as Ike and Mary leave Saturn and walk through one of the exhibit corridors. Their voices are heard in the dark; their forms take a dim shape in the gloom as they pass in and out of some spotlighted areas.*

MARY *(Offscreen)* I know, you-you probably think I'm too cerebral.

IKE *(Offscreen)* Well, you are, *(Sighing)* you know, kind of on the brainy side. *(Chuckling)* Oh, what's the difference what I think about you? God knows what you must think about me. *Ike's form is dimly seen in the gloom.*

MARY *(Talking in the dim shadows, her form seen on the screen)* No, I think you're fine. Are you kidding? *Once again, Mary and Ike walk offscreen as they pass through the exhibit.*

MARY *(Offscreen)* I mean, you do have a—a tendency to get a little hostile, but I find that attractive.

IKE *(Offscreen)* Oh, yeah? *(Sighing)* Well, I'm glad you do. *They stand now in close profile, backlit by hundreds of stars, a replica of space.*

MARY So you think I have no feelings, is that it?

IKE Oh, well—you—I . . . You're so sensitive. Jesus, I never said that. *(Mary sighs)* That doesn't . . . I think you're terrific. Really, I think, you know, I—I just . . .

MARY Yeah, well . . .

IKE *(Overlapping)* You're very insecure. I think—I really think you're wonderful, really.

MARY *(Sighing)* Tsch. Well, what do you think? It's probably stopped raining. Um . . . you wanna grab a bite or something like that?

IKE *(Sighing)*   I gotta see somebody this evening.

MARY *(Looking down)*   Mm.

IKE *(Overlapping)*   I don't know if it's such a great idea.

MARY   Right. Well . . . so what about sometime next week? I might give you a call or—   Do you have any free time?

IKE *(Sighing)*   Uh . . . I'm—I'm not gonna have—   I don't think I'm gonna have any free time, you know, 'cause . . .

MARY   Mm.

IKE   I don't think it's such a great idea for me. I'm, you know, I'm working on this book.

MARY   Hm.

IKE *(Overlapping)*   And it's—and it's, uh, you know, it takes a lot of my energy up.

MARY *(Nodding)*   Okay. Okay.
The screen abruptly leaves the dark stars of the planetarium and cuts to an off-ramp of the George Washington Bridge. Yale and Emily are driving down the Henry Hudson Parkway, the back of Yale's convertible to the camera.

YALE *(Laughing)*   Well, your parents were in a good mood. I almost had a good time.

EMILY *(Laughing)*   Who was that you called after dinner?

YALE   Oh, uh, uh, Da-David Cohen. He wants me to review the new book on Virginia Woolf. He's written another one. Can you believe it?

EMILY   Are you okay?

YALE   Yeah, I'm fine. What do you mean?

EMILY   Well, you seem sort of nervous.

YALE   Nah, I'm not. I feel good. I was gonna . . . ask you—

EMILY *(Interrupting)*   No, I'm okay.

YALE   —how you felt. You seemed a little strange at dinner.

EMILY   Well, I just . . . More thoughts about kids.

YALE Oh, come on. Listen, I told Cohen I'd stop by and pick up the book. Is that okay with you?

EMILY Yeah.

CUT TO:
INTERIOR. JOHN'S PIZZERIA—DUSK.

Ike and Tracy are seated across from each other in the popular and noisy Greenwich Village eatery.

TRACY *(Looking around)* Hey, it's not too crowded.

IKE No, not bad for Sunday. I thought it would be jammed.

TRACY So did I.

IKE Gee, I'm glad you could get out tonight, you know, 'cause—uh, I really did want to see you a lot.

TRACY *(Smiling)* You know, I like it when you get an uncontrollable urge.

IKE Yeah, I know, it's my best feature . . . *(Sighing)* my boyish impetuosity. My— You look adorable.
Tracy smiles quickly.

TRACY So I have a chance to go to London and study with—with the Academy of Music and Dramatic Arts.

IKE Really? When did this happen?

TRACY Mm, the other day. I got a letter in the mail.

IKE *(Reacting)* Well, that's great. You have a— That's terrific.

TRACY Well, I don't wanna go without you.

IKE Hey . . . I can't go to London and study. I mean, you know, it's crazy, especially Shakespeare. You know, I-I don't look good in leotards or anything like that.

TRACY I'm serious.

IKE Of course you should go. I mean, it's great. You'll have a great time in London. It's a great town and you're a wonderful actress. And it's a terrific place to study. You know, it's—uh, uh, you know, you'll be the toast of the town. You'll have a good time. Really, you shouldn't—you shouldn't pass that. So . . .

TRACY   So what happens to us?

IKE   Well, you know, we'll always have Paris. *(Sighing)* I'm kidding . . . You—   What kind of question is that? You know you can't think of that now.

TRACY   You won't take me seriously, just because I'm seventeen.

IKE   Yeah, exactly, because you're seventeen. I mean, look at it, I mean, it's ridiculous. When you're seventeen now . . . when you're thirty-six, I'll be . . . um . . .
Ike pauses, trying to figure out the mathematics.

TRACY *(Smiling)*   Sixty-three.

IKE *(Nodding his head)*   Sixty-three, right. Thank you. You know, it's absurd. You'll be at the height of your sexual powers. Of course, I will, too, probably, but, mm, you know, I'm a late starter.
He shakes his head from side to side as a waiter comes over to the table with two pizza pies.

WAITER   Who ordered a plain pie?

IKE   Uh, me.
Tracy sighs as the waiter puts the plain pie in front of Ike.

WAITER *(To Tracy)*   So you must be anchovies, sausage, mushrooms, garlic and green peppers.

TRACY *(Nodding)*   Mm-hm.
The waiter puts down Tracy's pie and walks off.

IKE *(Looking at Tracy's pizza)*   You forgot the coconut. So what do you wanna do tonight? Anything. We'll go to the movies, we'll . . . I'll take you dancing if you want. Whatever it is, it's your night.

TRACY   Anything, huh?

IKE   Absolutely anything.

TRACY   Okay, I know what we can do.

IKE   Get that filthy look off your face.

TRACY   Shut up. *(Laughing and smiling)* It's not filthy.

CUT TO:
EXTERIOR. CENTRAL PARK—NIGHT.

A horse-drawn carriage ambles down a tree-lined park path. Ike's and Tracy's voices are heard over some romantic background music and the sounds of the horse's hooves against the cobblestones.

IKE'S VOICE-OVER   This is so corny. I—you know, I can't believe this. Is this what you wanted to do? Is-is this your one wish?

TRACY'S VOICE-OVER   *(Chuckling)*   I don't think it's corny. I think it's fun, I really do.

IKE'S VOICE-OVER   Well, it is fun. But, I mean, I did this when I was a kid, you know, uh . . .

TRACY'S VOICE-OVER   Yeah, well, I've never done it. I think it's great.

IKE'S VOICE-OVER   Hm. *(Tracy laughs happily)* Geez, on my prom night, I went around this park five times, six times. *(Tracy laughs again)* If I had—if I had been with a girl, this would've been a-an incredible experience.
Tracy continues to laugh as the camera moves closer to the carriage where the couple is sitting, their arms around each other, in the back seat. They kiss.

TRACY   *(Breaking away from the kiss)*   Quit fighting it. You know you're crazy about me.

IKE   *(Gesturing and pointing to the sky)*   I am. You-you-you're . . . look, you're—you're God's answer to Job . . . you know. You would've ended all—all argument between them. I mean, H-H-He would've pointed to you and said, you know, "I do a lot of terrible things, but I can also make one of these," you know. *(Ike points to Tracy; she chuckles, then buries her head in his shoulder. He kisses her hand)* And then —then, Job would've said, "Eh, okay—well, you win."
The camera pulls back and once again the horse-drawn carriage in its idyllic setting is seen on the screen. The romantic music continues to play as the film cuts to:

INTERIOR. MARY'S APARTMENT—NIGHT.

The music suddenly stops. Mary is walking rapidly through her apartment. She goes back and forth from her kitchen to her living room, carrying first a bottle of wine, then a plate of cheese. Yale is behind her, following her as she walks to and fro. They are in the midst of a heated conversation.

MARY *(Rapidly and nervously)*   Now, look, this is crazy. I mean, I just can't do this anymore. It's really bullshit! You know what I mean? You're married! You're married! And I expected to see you this weekend and I sit around. I got nothing to do. So—so I called Isaac. We went for a walk. Well, it was just lucky he was free.

YALE   I know, I know. I'm sorry.

MARY   Oh, it's—it's not your fault. What the hell. It's a no-win situation. I . . . It's just—I'm beautiful and I'm bright and I deserve better!

YALE   Oh, I know. Wh-what if I took some-some action?

MARY   No! I'm not, oh, I'm not a home wrecker! *(The telephone rings just as Waffles starts to bark. Mary walks to the ringing phone)* Fuck it! I still —I just don't know how I got into this situation. I guess we met at the wrong time or something like that! It happens. *(Into the telephone, fingering her face)* Hello? . . . Oh, hi. Oh, hi, Harvey, how are you? . . . Uh, what? . . . Well, um, why don't you—why don't you bring it by on Thursday and I'll—I'll read it then, okay? . . . Yeah, yeah, yes, okay . . . Right. I'll talk to you later . . . Oh, okay. Bye, bye. *(Mary hangs up the telephone and sighs; the dog continues to bark)* God.

YALE *(Overlapping)*   Look, what do you want me to do?

MARY *(To Waffles, who is barking down around her legs)* Waffles! *(To Yale, looking up from the floor)*   Nothing! I mean, it's just . . . it's just we're going— *(Interrupting herself, to Waffles)* Waffles, will you please stop that now? *(To Yale)*—we're just going no place. Just excuse me. *Distraught, Mary picks up the wine bottle and opens it while Yale continues to talk over the barking dog.*

YALE   Look, I know it's terrible. I mean, I'm sitting up at Sneden's Landing with Emily and her parents, and I love her! And I-I-I'm sitting around thinking about you all the time. And I wanted to call you.

MARY *(Turning to Yale, overlapping)*   Yeah, well, I—I don't want . . . *(The telephone rings again; the dog continues to yelp in the background)* Oh, Christ! I mean, I don't wanna hear about that! I'm from Philadelphia. *(Gesturing as she walks to the ringing telephone)* My—my family's never had affairs. My parents have been married forty-three years. Nobody cheats at all! *(Picking up the telephone receiver)* Hello? . . . Oh, uh, Donny, hi. *(Looking at Yale for a moment, her hand over the receiver)* It's my analyst. *(Into the telephone again)* Hello. *(Sighing, touching her*

face) Uh, um, no, uh . . . Well, I—no, I think that'd be impossible
. . . Uh, okay—Well, why . . . Probably later in the week . . . Okay
. . . All right . . . All right, I'll get back to you. *(Chuckling)* Oh, okay
. . . Okay, bye. *(She hangs up the telephone, then covers her eyes with her hands. The dog still barks. She says to herself, sighing)* Relax. *(To Waffles)* Waffles, please. *(To Yale, exasperated, reacting to his attempted touch)* Don't, please. Please just don't.

YALE *(Still trying to touch her, comforting)* Mary.

MARY This is really a bad time—*(To Waffles, interrupting herself)* Waffles . . . *(She bends down and picks up Waffles; he has not stopped barking)*—a bad time for me. Just . . . I've gotta think things through here.
She rushes through her disarrayed living room, the dog in her arms.

YALE *(Calling after her)* Well, obviously I shouldn't have come here, right?

MARY *(Offscreen)* Well, no, probably not.
The dog continues to bark as the camera stays on Yale's intense face, looking offscreen at Mary through the doorway.

CUT TO:
INTERIOR. IKE'S NEW APARTMENT—DAY.

As upbeat jazz music is played, Ike is seen through the doorway of his new, cheaper apartment. He is standing in a living room filled with unpacked cartons, looking around the room as he supervises three huge, burly, T-shirted movers, as first one comes through the doorway carrying a chair, then the second and third, who plunk huge cartons down on the floor at Ike's feet. Finished, they walk toward Ike at the doorway; one of the men wipes the back of his neck with a cloth while another mover hands Ike a slip of paper. They all look somber, almost menacing; they tower over Ike, standing almost on top of him. Ike quickly signs the paper and hands it back.
The music stops and the film moves to Ike's new bedroom, a small room with barely enough space for the bed—which is almost flush against the white venetian-blind–covered window; a solitary candle rests on the window sill. Ike and Tracy are lying in bed, under a sheet; strange clanging noises are heard over the scene.

IKE *(Sighing, reacting to the noise)* Listen to that. What am I— How am I gonna get— What is it? What's that sound? Can you hear that? *(He reaches over and picks up his glasses lying on the night table. He puts them on, then sits up, resting on his elbow)* Just-just listen. Where's it coming from? It's like—it's like, uh, it's like somebody's playing the trumpet. Like a guy who's . . . *(Moving his hand as if sawing something)* where-where somebody's sawing, um, like a man sawing a trumpet in half. Right? Right? Well, it's like—

TRACY *(Interrupting, resting on her elbows and looking at Ike)* Let's fool around.

IKE *(Pointing to the ceiling)* Do you hear that sound? Do you?

TRACY Let's fool around. It'll take your mind off it.

IKE H-hey. How many times a night can you . . . How-how often c-can you make love in an evening? *(Distracted by noise)* What is that?

TRACY *(Overlapping)* A lot.

IKE Yeah, I can tell. A lot. That's . . . Well, a lot is *(Chuckling)* my favorite number. *(Chuckling)* Gee, really, can you?

TRACY Yeah, well, let's do it in some strange way that you've always wanted to do, but nobody would do with you.

IKE *(Hitting his chest, then touching Tracy on her chin)* I'm shocked. What kind of talk is that from a kid your age? *(Tracy mumbles under her breath while Ike continues to talk)* I'll get—I'll get my scuba diving equipment and we'll—I'll really show you an in—

TRACY *(Interrupting)* Take me seriously.

IKE I do take you seriously, but, you know—*(Reacting to a strange, rumbling sound)* Listen to this. Can you hear this? Am I crazy? *(Tracy sighs. Ike slaps his forehead)* What . . . ? *(Gasping)* I— That's a rumbling. Listen to that goddamn . . . Where the hell is that coming from?
He gets out of bed and walks out of the room.

TRACY *(Talking a bit louder so Ike can hear her)* It's probably just the elevator shaft.
Ike's shadow is seen as he walks in and out of the room, pacing.

IKE It's not the elevator shaft! It's coming from the walls someplace. It's a strange . . . Let's—let's . . . Could we check into a hotel? I don't wanna sleep here—

TRACY *(Interrupting)* You're crazy.

IKE   —tonight. I can't sleep here.
He walks out of the room again; Tracy sighs, resigned.

IKE *(Still pacing, walking in and out of the room)*   I can't. Where's the aspirin? I mean, wha-wha-what'd you do with the aspirin?

TRACY *(Ignoring his whining)*   I could help you fix this place up if you'd give me a chance.

IKE *(Loudly, talking from the bathroom offscreen)*   I don't wanna fix it up. And I don't want you living here. Tonight is a special occasion. It's —it's my first night in the apartment, so, you know, I—I . . . it was okay. I wanna break in the place and I was afraid to sleep alone tonight. *(Muttering to himself as he turns on the bathroom faucet)* Hey, what is this? *(Loudly, to Tracy)* There's brown water.

TRACY *(Loudly, to Ike offscreen)*   The pipes are rusty.

IKE *(Overlapping)*   There's brown water coming out of the tap. What is this, Tracy?

TRACY *(Loudly, exasperated)*   Eh, the pipes are rusty.

IKE *(Still talking loudly)* Tracy, look at this. *(His shadow is seen as he walks into the room, to the foot of the bed)* It's brown water. I'm paying seven hundred dollars a month. I've got—I've got rats with bongos, and a—and a frog, and I got brown water here. Look at this.
He sits down on the bed. He holds up a glass of brown water.

TRACY *(Ignoring Ike's glass of water)*   What's gonna happen to us?

IKE *(Ignoring Tracy's remark)*   This is disgusting. I like colorless liquid.

TRACY   Listen. You keep ignoring me. What's gonna happen with us?
Ike puts down the glass of brown water and turns his body to Tracy.

IKE *(Pointing to his chest)*   Tsch. What do you mean, what's gonna happen with us? What . . . uh, do you have a good time with me? Are-aren't I a load of laughs and fun?

TRACY   Yes.

IKE *(Overlapping)*   Can't you tell from this evening? So—and that's it, and then, you know, and we have, we have fun. And then, you're gonna go to London exactly as we discussed it. You're gonna take advantage of that opportunity *(Sighing)* and study acting over there, you know. And—and you'll think of me always as a fond memory. *(Pointing to his head)* Now be nice.

CUT TO:
EXTERIOR. STANHOPE CAFÉ—DAY.

Mary and Yale sit across from each other at a white-clothed table in the crowded outdoor café; they talk over the sounds of the nearby city traffic.

YALE   You know we have to stop seeing each other, don't you?

MARY *(Sighing)*   Oh, yeah, right . . . right. I understand. I could tell by the sound of your voice over the phone. Very authoritative, you know . . . like the Pope or the computer in *Two Thousand and One.*

YALE   Look, it's not fair to you and I don't know what the hell I'm doing.

MARY *(Overlapping)*   Right. Right.

YALE   I mean, come on, don't be angry. I mean, you-you-you brought this up to begin with. You're not happy the way things have been going.

MARY *(Shaking her head)*   I'm not angry. I'm just—it's just that I knew it was going to end this way. But now that it's happened, I'm upset, okay?

YALE *(Pounding on the table for emphasis)*   Oh, look, y-y-y-you don't wanna make a commitment. And I don't wanna break up my marriage and then find out that—that we're no good together. I-I've-I've gotta start thinking about Emily.

MARY   Okay, you made your point. It's very clear. I'm—I'm just glad that one of us, uh, had the nerve to end it.

YALE   Will you be all right?

MARY *(Crying for a brief moment)*   Yeah. *(Sighing, holding herself tightly with her arms)* Of course I'm gonna be all right. What do you think I'm gonna do, hang myself? I'm a beautiful woman, I'm—I'm young, I'm highly intelligent, I got everything going for me. The point . . . the point is—is that, uh, I don't know. I'm all fucked-up. I'm just . . . shit. The point is: What the hell am I doing in this relationship anyway? *(Gesturing now, reacting to Yale's news)* M-my phone never stops ringing. I could go to bed with the entire faculty of M.I.T. if I wanted to. It's just . . . I don't know, I'm wasting myself on a married man. So I don't . . . *(Sighing)* Listen, I think I'd better go now. I think it's . . . I—I just want you to have this. I had . . . I got these tickets to see Rampal tonight. *(Handing them to Yale)* Here—

YALE (*Overlapping, shaking his head no*)   Oh, Mary.

MARY (*Overlapping*)   —you take them. (*Reacting to Yale's protestations*) What?

YALE   Listen, this is very hard on me too, you know.

MARY   No, please, why don't you just take them and go with your wife?

YALE   Mary, come on, you love Rampal. I mean, call somebody up. Take Isaac.

MARY (*Staring at Yale and sighing*)   Ya—   Fuck off, Yale!
Mary tears up the tickets and the film cuts to Ike's apartment. Through a doorway, Ike is seen filling a glass with brown water at the kitchen sink. He talks to a guest in his living room as he leaves the kitchen and walks into the living-room area. The camera cuts to Mary, his guest, looking distraught and depressed.

IKE   Tsch. Um, you . . . I know you're gonna think the water's a little brown, but you can drink it. You know, it's—it's, uh . . . don't get —don't get thrown by this, you know.

MARY   I'm really sorry for bothering you. You know what I mean?
She takes a pill out of the bottle she is holding.

IKE   No problem. Really, it's no . . .
He hands her the glass of brown water.

MARY (*Overlapping, sighing*)   I—   It's just I didn't know . . . (*Reacting to the water*) God, this is brown, isn't it?

IKE   This . . . yeah, yeah, it is on the brown side. No question about it. But it—but it, you know, you get used to it after a while.
Mary puts the pill in her mouth and drinks some water.

MARY   I didn't know who to call, that's all.

IKE   I don't think you should take those Valium, you know, 'cause I think it causes cancer.
He walks off again; he can be seen going into his bedroom, fussing and straightening, as he talks to Mary over his shoulder.

MARY (*Offscreen, from the living room*)   No, half a Valium?

IKE   Yeah, yeah, abdominal cancer, I think.

MARY   When did they find that out?

IKE   Oh, uh, the . . . uh, th-that's just my theory. But I think it's correct. I-I got tissues someplace.

MARY   Well, I guess I deserve everything I get.

IKE   (*Offscreen, from the bedroom interior*)   Oh, come on!

MARY   (*Still offscreen, from the living room*)   It's true . . . it's really true! I mean, I knew it couldn't possibly work out.
Ike is busily going from room to room throughout his apartment; he switches the lights on and off as he enters each interior. He talks to Mary over his shoulder as he walks on and off the screen. The camera stays focused on the empty hallway, showing Ike as he walks in and out of various rooms.

IKE   (*Offscreen*)   Yeah, you—you pick a married guy and then—(*Onscreen*) then, when it doesn't work out, it confirms (*Offscreen*) your worst feelings.

MARY   Well, what worst feelings?

IKE   (*Still walking from room to room*)   You know . . . your feelings about men and marriage and that nothing works—

MARY   (*Interrupting*)   Oh.

IKE   —you know, all that junk.

MARY   Oh, please, don't psychoanalyze me. I re—   I pay a doctor for that.

IKE   (*Offscreen, reacting to Mary's remark*)   Hey.
Mary sniffles.

IKE   (*Sticking his head into the hallway from the kitchen*)   Uh, you-you call that guy that you-you talk to you a doctor? I mean, like y-y-y-you don't get suspicious when-when your analyst calls you up at three in the morning and weeps into the telephone?
Ike pulls back into the kitchen; the camera moves back to Mary in the living room.

MARY   All right, so he's unorthodox. He's a highly qualified doctor.
She sits down in an easy chair. Ike enters the room holding a huge wad of paper toweling.

IKE   He's—he's done a great job on you, you know. Your-your self-esteem is like a notch below Kafka's. (*Handing Mary the paper toweling*) Here, then you can blow your nose.
A strange noise is heard above their heads.

MARY Uh, what is that noise?

IKE *(Pointing to the ceiling)* Yeah, it's incredible, isn't it?

MARY Yeah.

IKE *(Looking around and gesturing)* There's a—there's—there's a guy upstairs. I don't know what the hell it is! I get this every day. *(The strange noise is heard again)* It's like he's—he's up there strangling a parrot or something. I can't stand it.

MARY Look, how can you stand it? It's terrible! It's awful.

IKE *(Standing in front of a large framed picture, gesturing)* I know. I used to have a great apartment, but I can't afford it. You wanna go for a walk? 'Cause it's quieter in the street.

MARY *(Crying softly)* No, I think I'll just go home.
Ike walks over to her.

IKE Nah, come on.

MARY *(Crying)* This is ridiculous. *(Sniffling)* Well, he led me on! That's the point of it. Why am I reluctant to criticize him?
Ike takes the glass of brown water that Mary had been clutching in her hand; he walks her across the living room to the front door.

IKE Hey, relax. Yale would not lead you on.

MARY Oh, please—

IKE *(Interrupting)* He's not that kind of a guy.

MARY *(Blowing her nose)* —don't defend him. You guys all stick up for each other.

IKE Yale has his problems as we all do, you know. *(Mary continues to sniffle)* I-I'm starting to sound like Rabbi Blitzstein here.

MARY Well, listen, thanks for letting me come over. I really do appreciate it. It was very nice of you.

IKE You know, Tracy and I are going out tonight if you wanna come along and you got nothing to do.

MARY *(Sniffling)* Oh, no, no, I'll be fine, I'll be fine, I'll be okay.

IKE Yeah?

MARY   Yeah.

Ike opens the front door while looking down at the huge wad of paper toweling in Mary's hand.

IKE *(Chuckling)*   That's a nice healthy piece of towel paper you got.

MARY *(Laughing)*   Oh, Jesus, God. Well, good-bye and thanks a lot.
She leaves; Ike closes the door.

CUT TO:
INTERIOR. IKE'S BEDROOM.

And it's later that night. Ike and Tracy are in bed together. They are eating Chinese food out of white containers and watching television. The camera stays focused on them in the bed; the television screen's variations of light flicker on their faces.

MAN'S VOICE-OVER ON TELEVISION   Yeah, but my—my point is, Does a
—does a cab driver . . . does he make enough money to send all the brothers and sisters through medical school?
The voice continues to be heard in the background as Ike and Tracy talk.

IKE *(Eating the Chinese food)*   Mm, mm, this is good. Mm, oh . . .
(Pointing to the television set) look at that—look at that guy's toupee.

TRACY *(Chuckling)*   Hm.

IKE   That's unbelievable.

TRACY   That's really weird.

IKE   That is hilarious. *(Sighing and pointing)* Mm, there's a-a-a-an inch of cheesecloth. You can see it. *(Tracy giggles)* I don't know why his, you know, his loved ones don't tell him. *(Raising and lowering his hand to indicate a falling motion)* Tsch. It looks like the-the toupee dropped on his head from a-a window ledge or something when he was walking, you know, and no one—

TRACY *(Interrupting, chuckling and eating)*   No, but look at his wife. It looks like her face has been lifted about eight thousand times.

IKE *(Pulling back the skin on his face)*   Yeah, I know, it's so plastic, mm, and it's so tight.

TRACY   I hate that.

IKE   Her flesh is—

TRACY *(Interrupting)* I just hate that. I wish ... Why can't they just age naturally instead of putting all that junk on?

IKE I know, it looks ... You know, old faces are-are-are nice—

TRACY *(Interrupting)* Yeah.

IKE *(Overlapping)* —you know? *(Picking at the food in his container)* Mm.

TRACY *(Nibbling her food)* Just great.

IKE *(Enjoying his food)* Mm, mm, hey, be careful.
Tracy chuckles as Ike begins to fuss, looking down at the bed and picking up his napkin.

IKE I think I got black—black-bean sauce in the bed. We're gonna sleep in that tonight.

TRACY *(Ignoring Ike's last remark, pointing to the television set)* Oh, look, it's great. The Late Show's a W. C. Fields film.

IKE Mm.

TRACY Oh, great. We gotta watch that.
*Ike sighs. He leans over and kisses Tracy on the shoulder.
And the film cuts to:*

INTERIOR. UPTOWN SQUASH CLUB—DAY.

Yale, wearing tennis shorts, and Ike, in long pants, work up a sweat playing squash; they talk while they rally, smashing the ball against the wall.

YALE *(Sighing)* Oh! Oh, God. Boy, I really feel good, you know. I've got my life together finally.

IKE Yeah?

YALE Yeah, you know *(Sighing)* I just had to cut this thing off finally. I'm not the type for affairs. You know, I finally figured it out.

IKE Do you—do you ever hear from Mary or see her or anything?

YALE No, no, we just— *(Sighing)* you know, cut it off. I think it's easier that way, you know?

IKE *(Breathing hard, hitting the ball)* Ah-ha.

YALE *(Overlapping)* She's a terrific person. She deserves more than a fling with a married guy.

IKE   Yeah, she's great. She's a little screwed up but great.

YALE   Yeah, well, that's right up your alley, you know. I think you oughta call her.

IKE   I—I should call her?

YALE   Yeah.

IKE   Why should I call her?

YALE   Because she likes you. She told me she did.

IKE   You're crazy.

YALE   No, I'm not. She said she finds you attractive.

IKE   She said she found me attractive?

YALE *(Missing a shot)*   Yeah.

IKE   Yeah, when was this?

YALE   Oh, she said it when she first met you.

IKE *(Missing a shot)*   I didn't know. I can't.

YALE *(Laughing at Ike's miss)*   Sorry about that.

IKE *(Overlapping)*   I can't. I always think—I always think of you two guys as together. *(Sighing)* I—I don't think that I could.

YALE *(Shaking his head)*   Nah, it's over, it's over. Unless you're serious about Tracy. Are you serious about Tracy?

IKE *(Hitting the ball)*   No, Tracy's too young.

YALE *(Missing a shot)*   Well, then call her up. Listen, she's an unhappy person, you know. I mean, she-she needs something in her life. I mean, I think you guys would be good together.

IKE *(Sighing)*   I think I could be a good influence on her. *(Catching his breath)* I think that under my personal vibrations, I could put her life in-in-in some kind of good order. You know what I mean?

YALE *(Laughing)*   Yeah, that's what you said about Jill, you know. And under your personal vibrations, she went from bisexuality to homosexuality.
Their game finished, Ike and Yale walk to the glass doors of their court.

IKE *(Catching his breath)*   Yeah, but I gave it the old college try there *(Laughing)* for a while.

YALE *(Laughing)*   Listen, really, you should call her up.

IKE   You're kidding. What-what'd she say about me?
They go through the glass doors into a crowded stairwell, talking above the surrounding chatter and laughter.

YALE   She said that, uh, she likes you very much. She thinks you're smart. She thinks you're—

IKE *(Interrupting)*   Keep going, don't stop.

YALE *(Laughing)*   —attractive.

IKE *(Laughing)*   She said that, really? No kidding.

YALE   Yeah.
They walk up the stairs, offscreen, and the film cuts to the exterior of a movie theater, its marquee saying: "Inagaki's Chushingura; Dovzhenko's Earth." Light, breezy music is heard as the entrance of the theater opens, letting out a departing audience. Among the exiting viewers are Mary and Ike. They stand outside the movie house in an animated discussion; they then walk along the crowded sidewalk, gesturing and talking as the film cuts to Mary's apartment. The couple continue their discussion as Mary opens the door and turns on her hallway light.

IKE   You see, to me, a great movie is with W. C. Fields. That's what I like. *Grand Illusion*, that's—that—I see that every time it's on television if I—if I'm aware of it. *(Ike follows Mary into the kitchen, a large white room only partially seen by the camera, which stays in the doorway. While Mary takes out some crackers from a cupboard, Ike examines the contents of her refrigerator, offscreen, blocked from view by the doorway)* So what've you got to eat here? Nothing, right? You got—

MARY *(Making a face, overlapping)*   Well.

IKE *(Offscreen)*   Oh, Jesus, what is this? You got a-a corned-beef sandwich here from nineteen-fifty-one, I think. *(He walks over to Mary, holding half a corned-beef sandwich)* Look at this.

MARY *(Laughing)*   Yeah, I—

IKE *(Interrupting)*   Look at this. I mean, it-it should-should-should—

MARY *(Interrupting, moving about her kitchen)*   I know, I know, I . . . Listen, I don't have time to cook.

IKE (*Looking at the sandwich and shaking his head*)   Corned beef should not be blue, you know. There's just . . . ugh, it's really terrible. Hey.

MARY   What?

IKE   Come here.
Mary walks over to Ike. They kiss, then look at each other; Ike's hands are touching Mary's face.

MARY (*Reacting*)   What? What're you doing?

IKE   What am I doing? You have to ask what I'm doing? I was kissing you flush on the mouth.

MARY (*Nodding her head*)   Oh, Jesus, I don't know. I . . . I—boy, I cannot get my life in any kind of order. It's just—

IKE (*Interrupting*)   Well, it's something I wanted to do for the longest time, you know, and . . . and—

MARY (*Interrupting, nodding her head*)   Yeah, I know.

IKE   Do you?

MARY (*Nodding*)   Uh-huh.

IKE (*Overlapping*)   'Cause I-I-I thought I was hiding it. I was trying to be real cool and casual.

MARY   Oh, I thought you wanted to kiss me that day at the planetarium.

IKE   Yeah, I did.

MARY   Yeah, I thought so.

IKE   But . . . but you were—you were—you were going out with Yale then.

MARY   Mm-hm.

IKE   And I would never in a million years, you know, interfere in anything like that. I just . . . well, did you want me to kiss you then? I mean—

MARY (*Interrupting*)   Mm, I don't know what I wanted. I was so angry at Yale that day.
She pulls away from Ike and walks to another area of the kitchen.

IKE *(Framed by the doorway, looking offscreen at Mary)*   But you were so sexy, you know. You were all soaking wet from the rain, and I had a mad impulse to throw you down on the lunar surface and commit interstellar perversion with you.

MARY   I can't go from relationship to relationship. It's senseless. I can't do it.

IKE   Well, what-what's it? Are you—are you still hung up on Yale? Is that the problem?

MARY   Oh, I've got too many problems. I'm—I'm just really . . . I'm not the person to get involved with. I'm trouble.

IKE   Hey, honey, trouble is my middle name.
Mary stops fussing about in her kitchen to look at Ike.

MARY *(Laughing)*   Tr—   What're you saying?

IKE *(Walking over to Mary and holding her head)*   It is. Actually, my middle name is Mortimer. But, uh . . . *(Mary laughs. They kiss. Saxophone music begins playing in the background)* . . . I-I'm kidding.
The film cuts to the Whitney Museum. The saxophone music continues in the background as Ike and Mary are seen walking through the various gallery rooms. As they talk and study the various sculptures and paintings, they pass a man and a woman.

MARY   My problem is I'm both attracted and repelled by the male organ.

IKE *(Pointing to the man and the woman)*   Sssssh.

MARY   Oh, you know, so . . . I mean, it doesn't make for very good relationships with men, that's all. What about you, what about your relationships with women? You never really told me much about your first wife.
They stop in front of a metal sculpture.

IKE *(Clearing this throat and staring at the sculpture)*   My first wife was a kindergarten teacher, you know. She—she got into drugs and she, uh, moved to San Francisco and went into est . . .

MARY *(Interrupting)*   Yeah.

IKE   . . . became a Moonie.
Mary chuckles; she is also looking at the sculpture.

IKE She's with the William Morris Agency now.

MARY *(Gesturing to the sculpture)* Do you like that?

IKE *(Sniffling)* This—this, I think, has a—has a kind of wonderful otherness to it, you know.

MARY *(Overlapping)* An otherness.

IKE *(Gesturing)* It's kind of got a marvelous negative capability—

MARY *(Interrupting, chuckling)* Okay.

IKE —a kind of w-w-w-wonderful energy to it—

MARY *(Continuing to chuckle)* Uh-huh.

IKE —don't you think?

CUT TO:
EXTERIOR. WEST SIDE HIGHWAY—NIGHT..

A taxi drives down the highway; traffic and city lights roll by in the dark. Mary's and Ike's voices are heard over the traffic sounds and the continual saxophone music.

MARY'S VOICE-OVER Mm, I thought that wine was wonderful, didn't you think? And I—it just made my face all flushed and hot.

IKE'S VOICE-OVER Yeah. You look so beautiful I can hardly keep my eyes on the meter. *(Mary laughs)* It's—it's fourteen bucks to go to Brooklyn.

MARY'S VOICE-OVER I know, but it was a great restaurant. Didn't you love it?

IKE'S VOICE-OVER Mm, yeah, I love seafood. *(Sniffling)* Of course, I'm drunk. *(Chuckling)* Ha, I don't know if you can tell or not. *(Sighing)* Hey, y-y-you know, it was—it was the only time in my life I ever had Chianti from Warsaw. *(Mary chuckles)* Give me a kiss.

MARY'S VOICE-OVER Okay.
The sounds of kissing are heard as the film moves to Mary's apartment. It's later that evening and Mary is sitting on Ike's lap. They are kissing, illuminated by a single lamp on a nearby table. As they embrace, Mary leans over and shuts off the light. The screen goes pitch-black; Ike sighs in the darkness.

MARY *(Sighing)* What're you thinking?

IKE *(Sighing)* Uh, I-I was just thinking there must be something wrong with me because I've never had a relationship with a woman that's lasted longer than the one between Hitler and Eva Braun.

MARY *(Chuckling)* I think you're still drunk.
They kiss in the dark. The music stops. And the film cuts to:

EXTERIOR. THE DALTON SCHOOL—DAY.

Ike, wearing a striped jacket, is leaning against a fence in front of the school. Various students are leaving, walking down the stone steps and chattering; the camera shows this scene in an almost panoramic view as Tracy walks out of the school in jeans and T-shirt. She doesn't see Ike; she walks down the steps and onto the sidewalk. Ike catches up with her and taps her on the shoulder. Tracy is surprised. She puts her arm around him and gives him a kiss. As they stroll down the street, Tracy hands Ike a present. He gives her a kiss. The camera continues to stay far away from the couple; their speech is indistinguishable, seeming more like pantomime because of the distance.
They are now in a soda shop, sitting at the counter in the crowded, noisy room. Ike is looking at a harmonica, the present Tracy gave him, as she sips an ice cream soda through a straw.

IKE *(Looking at the harmonica)* Tsch. I-it's great. It's-it's . . . I don't play the harmonica, but it's an incredible *(Sighing)* harmonica is what it is.

TRACY Well, you said you wanted to learn. I'm trying to open up that side of you.

IKE Tsch. Tracy, Tracy, you're throwing away an enormous amount of real affection on the wrong person.

TRACY It's not wrong for me.
A young woman walks up to the counter and places an order in the background while Ike and Tracy talk.

IKE *(Sighing)* You see, I don't—I-I-I don't think we should keep seeing each other.

TRACY Why not?

IKE Because I think you're getting too hung up on me, you know? Hung up on me. I'm starting to s-sound like you when I talk.

TRACY I'm not hung up on you. I'm in love with you.
The camera moves closer to their faces.

IKE You can't be in love with me. We've been over this. You're a kid. You don't know what love means. I don't know what it means. Nobody out there knows what the hell's going on.

TRACY We have laughs together. I care about you. Your concerns are my concerns. We have great sex.

IKE (Sighing) You-you're—but you're seventeen years old. By the time you're twenty-one, you're gonna have—you'll have a dozen relationships, mm, believe me, far more passionate than this one.

TRACY Well, don't you love me?

IKE (Sighing) I . . . (Sighing again) . . . Well, the truth is that I love somebody else.

TRACY You do?

IKE Hey, come on, will you? We—you—we . . . This was supposed to be a temporary fling, you know that.

TRACY You met someone?

IKE Don't stare at me with those big eyes. Jesus, you look like one of those barefoot kids from Bolivia who need foster parents.

TRACY Have you been seeing someone?

IKE (Shaking his head no, then nodding yes) No . . . yes, uh, someone older. Yeah, I mean, y-y-you know, y-y-you know, old, not as old as I am . . . but in the same general ball park as me.
The camera moves closer to Tracy's face; it stays tight on her features, showing her expressions, throughout most of the remaining scene.

TRACY (Reacting, sighing) Gee, now I don't feel so good.

IKE (Offscreen) It's—it's not right. You—you know, y-y-you shouldn't get hung, I mean, you should open up your life. You should see . . . you know, you've got to.

TRACY (Sighing) You keep stating it like it's to my advantage when it's you that wants to get out of it.
The camera moves briefly to Ike's face.

IKE Hey, don't be so precocious, okay? I mean, don't be so smart. I-I'm forty-two years old. My hair's falling out. I'm starting to lose some hearing in my right ear. Is that what you want?

TRACY   I can't believe that you met somebody that you like better than me.

IKE *(Looking down)*   Why should I feel guilty about this? This is ridiculous. I've always encouraged you to—to go out with g-guys more your own age, guys, kids from your class. I mean, mm, mm, Billy and Biff and Scooter and, mm, mm, you know, little Tommy or Terry.
Tracy's face once again fills the screen. She begins to cry. Ike's hand reaches over and touches her shoulder and neck.

IKE *(Offscreen)*   Hey, come on, don't cry. *(Tracy continues to cry)* Don't cry. Come on, don't cry. Tracy . . . Tracy, don't—come on, don't cry, Tracy. Tracy.

TRACY *(Sighing)*   Just leave me alone.
Ike's hand wipes a tear from Tracy's face.

TRACY *(Reacting, still crying)*   Leave me alone.

CUT TO:
INTERIOR. IKE'S BEDROOM—NIGHT.

Ike is sprawled on his bed, writing. Sighing, he stops and picks up the harmonica lying next to him on the bed. He plays a few notes, stops, and looks at it. Then he puts the harmonica back down on the bed; he stares off into space, reflecting.

CUT TO:
EXTERIOR. COUNTRY ROAD—DAY.

An orchestral rendition of " 'Swonderful" is heard as Mary and Ike drive down an idyllic country road in a car; Ike is behind the wheel. As the music continues, the camera moves to a peaceful waterfall scene, complete with lush trees and a wooden bridge. After a moment Mary and Ike are seen strolling on the bridge. They pause, looking down at the water. They embrace.

CUT TO:
INTERIOR. COUNTRY INN'S BEDROOM—NIGHT.

Over a pitch-black screen, Mary's and Ike's voices are heard.

MARY'S VOICE-OVER   That was wonderful.

IKE'S VOICE-OVER   Yeah, I'll say.

MARY'S VOICE-OVER   I love being in the country.

IKE'S VOICE-OVER   Mm, it's very relaxing.
Mary switches on the light; Mary and Ike are revealed now, lying in bed together, a wooden headboard behind them.

MARY   I know.

IKE   Of course, the mosquitoes have sucked all the blood out of my left leg. *(Mary chuckles as Ike reaches over to the night table for his glasses and puts them on)* Of course, apart from that I'm . . . in good shape.

MARY   Doesn't it make you feel better? I feel better about myself.

IKE   Yeah, you were dynamite. Except I did get the feeling that, for about two seconds in there, you were faking a little bit.

MARY *(Reacting)*   What're you . . . ?

IKE *(Overlapping)*   Not a lot. You were just overacting—

MARY *(Interrupting)*   No, I didn't.

IKE *(Touching his neck)*   Yes, when you dug your nails into my neck. I thought you were just giving it a little—

MARY *(Sighing and shaking her head)*   Uh, no . . . no, I don't know.
She shrugs.

IKE   Were you?

MARY   I guess I'm a little nervous around you still.

IKE   Really, still?

MARY   Well, yeah, I think—

IKE *(Interrupting)*   It's so crazy.

MARY   Because I really—I would like everything to work out.

IKE   It's gonna, it will. It will work out. You should leave everything to me. I'll make everything happen. You don't—you don't have to worry.

MARY   You promise? Do you really promise?

IKE *(Nodding)*   Mm-hm, mm-hm.

MARY   Because I do, I like you a lot. I feel good around you.

IKE *(Chuckling)*   Yeah, I don't blame you.

MARY (*Laughing*)   Yeah, I mean, I don't know. Yale was—yeah, he was great. He was absolutely great, but he was married. And Jeremiah, look at Jeremiah, my ex-husband. He was just this oversexed br- brilliant kind of animal.

IKE   Hey, what am I, Grandma Moses? (*Chuckling and pointing to him- self*) What do you mean?

MARY (*Shaking her head*)   No, not at all.

IKE (*Overlapping*)   You know. Hm?

MARY   No, no, no, you're much different, you're much different. You're—

IKE (*Interrupting*)   Yeah?

MARY   Yes, you're someone I could . . . uh, I could imagine having children with.

IKE   Really?

MARY   Yeah.

IKE (*Pointing to the lamp*)   Well, well, hit the lights. Go ahead.

MARY (*Reaching over to the lamp switch*)   Hm.

IKE *(Taking off his glasses)*   Turn 'em out again. *(Sighing)* We'll—we'll trade fours.

Mary turns the light off. The room goes dark and dissolves into Mary's apartment, where she and Ike are dancing cheek to cheek around her paper-and-book–filled living room. The light is dim; romantic music plays in the background.

The music continues over the next view of Mary and Ike. They are now in a rowboat on the Central Park lake. Mary sits with her elbow on the edge of the boat smoking a cigarette. Ike, leaning back, sticks his hand in the water. He takes it out and finds his entire hand covered with mud and dirt. He grimaces.

And still the music plays, this time while Ike and Mary stand in front of Zabar's window, pointing at and discussing the delicacies displayed. People go in and out of the store. When Ike notices three African men in native dress weighted down with Zabar shopping bags walking out of the store, he nudges Mary with his elbow. She stops talking and stares, smiling, at the men, as amazed as Ike.

The music stops as the film cuts to a Brooklyn Heights street where Emily and Ike stand by the wall of a brick building. They look offscreen where Yale is haggling over the price of a Porsche up for sale.

EMILY   Well, we never see you anymore.

IKE *(Sighing)*   Well, 'cause I've been working on my book. I'm submerged, dedicated.

EMILY   It's that girl you're seeing. Serious, isn't it?

IKE   Well, it's serious, you know.

EMILY   Well, when are we gonna get a chance to meet her?

IKE   Well—

EMILY *(Interrupting)*   I'm sure Yale would like to meet her.

IKE   Then we should go out sometime, you know.

EMILY *(Nodding)*   Yeah, that's fine.

IKE *(Gesturing)*   I don't understand. Why-why-why does he need a car? A sudden urge to get a car. It's so—

EMILY *(Interrupting Ike, shrugging)*   He just wants it, what can I tell you?

IKE —crazy.
He and Emily walk over to Yale where he stands, near the curb, talking to two men; the Porsche is parked near them.

ONE MAN *(To Yale)*   The roof—the roof's custom-made.

IKE *(To Yale, overlapping)*   Look . . . uh, is there nothing I can do to dissuade you from this?

ONE MAN *(To Yale)*   The roof—the roof's custom-made. *Yale continues to bargain with the men.*

ONE MAN *(To Yale)*   Oh, okay.
Yale and Ike move a few feet away from the Porsche and the others. They continue to talk while the two men continue to sell their car to Emily.

IKE *(To Yale)*   It's so crazy. They should—they should ban all cars from Manhattan. I mean, this is—this crazy . . . Listen, Emily wants to know why, I mean, you know, I never bring Mary around.

ONE MAN *(To Emily, overlapping)*   The car's in perfect condition. The roof's custom-made.

YALE *(To Ike)*   You know, why don't you bring Mary around?

ONE MAN *(To Emily, overlapping)*   The tires are in good shape.

IKE *(To Yale)*   Well, I don't know. Is it awkward for you or what?

YALE   Oh, are you kidding?

IKE   Look, I spoke to her about it. It's no problem for her, either.

EMILY *(To one of the men, overlapping Ike's and Yale's speech)*   Oh, yeah?

YALE *(To Ike)*   Well, why aren't we doing it?

ONE MAN *(To Emily, overlapping)*   You like this Porsche?

EMILY   I guess.

IKE *(Overlapping Emily's remark, pointing to the car and speaking to Yale)*   Well, you know. Hey, don't get this thing, 'cause this is—   You know, I hate cars.

YALE *(Laughing)*   Oh, Isaac, you're gonna love it.

IKE   You know, it just . . . it screws up the environment and—

YALE *(Interrupting)* It's a work of art.

IKE Yeah.

CUT TO:
INTERIOR. YALE AND EMILY'S APARTMENT—NIGHT.

Mary and Ike enter Yale and Emily's apartment. They stand in the doorway, looking offscreen at Emily and Yale.

IKE Hi.

YALE *(Offscreen)* Hi.

EMILY *(Offscreen)* Hi.

IKE *(Overlapping)* Hi. This is—this is . . . uh, Emily.
The camera cuts to Emily and Yale, greeting their guests.

EMILY *(To offscreen Mary, shaking her hand)* Hello, nice to meet you.

IKE *(To Mary)* This is Yale.

YALE *(Shaking hands with Mary)* Hi.

MARY Hi, Yale.
The camera now shows the four of them standing in the doorway, looking at one another in a brief pause.

IKE *(Coughing, breaking the pause)* So, shall we go?

EMILY *(Looking at Yale)* Yeah, let's go.

YALE *(Smiling at Emily and sighing)* Sure.

CUT TO:
INTERIOR. CONCERT HALL—NIGHT.

Ike, Mary, Yale and Emily sit watching and listening to the concert music. Ike turns his head and looks at Mary. She looks at him, reacting; he looks away. He steals a quick second glance at her, then turns back to watch the stage. Yale then turns and looks at Mary. He, too, turns away quickly, then turns back to look at Ike, who bends down, pulling up his socks, and turns back to the stage. Emily sits oblivious to the tension of the others, absorbed in the concert, and the film cuts to:

A wrecking site. It's daylight. Ike and Mary are walking along a crowded sidewalk. Ike looks at all the construction, reacting.

IKE   Look at that. That building is almost completely torn down.

MARY   Well, can't they have those things declared landmarks?

IKE   Yeah, I once—I once tried to block demolition. You know, getting some people to lie down in front of a building . . . and some
policeman stepped on my hand. The city's really changing.
They walk to a storefront and enter a stark, trendy men's clothing store.
Mary and Ike immediately start browsing through a rack of shirts. Jeremiah,
her ex-husband, is also shopping in the store; he is short, chubby and balding.

IKE *(Chuckling, browsing through the clothing)*   No, I need something, you
know, that I can wear around the house that doesn't make me look
too Mexican.

MARY *(Sighing)*   Ugh. This is—

JEREMIAH *(Interrupting)*   Mary?

MARY   Oh, my God—   *(Laughing nervously)* Jeremiah! Well . . .

JEREMIAH   Hi.

MARY   Um. *(Chuckling)* Jeremiah, this is my friend, uh, Isaac Davis.

JEREMIAH *(Shaking Ike's hand)*   Hi.

IKE   Hi.

JEREMIAH   Glad to meet you. Hi.

MARY *(Overlapping, laughing)*   God.

JEREMIAH *(To Mary)*   God, this is so incredible.

MARY   I-it's incredible, I know.

JEREMIAH   I'm just in town for a few days.

MARY   Yeah?

JEREMIAH   There's kind of a symposium on semantics.

MARY   Oh, well . . .
Jeremiah steps in front of Mary, subtly pushing Ike away offscreen

JEREMIAH   And you're just looking so great. I just, uh—

MARY *(Interrupting)*   You, you're so thin. You lost a lot of weight,
didn't you?

JEREMIAH   Well, uh, I have an exercise machine.

MARY   Just fabulous-looking . . . Well, you really look good . . . *(Jeremiah sighs)* . . . really good.

JEREMIAH   God, well, I'm a bit late, but . . . uh, it's just so nice seeing you. And, uh—

MARY *(Interrupting)*   It's great—

JEREMIAH *(Interrupting)*   You know, I read an article by you in, uh, the *Atlantic*—

MARY *(Interrupting)*   Oh, shit.

JEREMIAH   —on Brecht.

MARY   I know, I know . . . Brecht *(Pronouncing it "Bresht")*. Well, you know—I mean, I always was a sucker for Germanic theater. *Jeremiah laughs.*

MARY *(Sighing)*   Well . . .

JEREMIAH *(Sighing)*   Okay. Well . . .

MARY *(Overlapping)*   Just great. Well . . .

JEREMIAH *(Waving good-bye)*   God. Okay, so long.

MARY *(Overlapping)*   Bye. Bye, Jeremiah.

JEREMIAH *(To offscreen Ike)*   Bye, bye.

IKE *(Offscreen)*   Bye.
Jeremiah leaves the store.

MARY *(Walking over to Ike)*   Oh, what a surprise! I cannot get over it. My ex-husband. And he does—

IKE *(Overlapping)*   Mm-hm.

MARY   —he really does look a lot thinner. He looks great.

IKE *(Reacting to Jeremiah's appearance)*   Yeah, well . . . well, y-you certainly fooled me. I mean, I was shocked—

MARY *(Interrupting)*   What do you mean?

IKE   —'cause that's not what . . . this is not what I expected.

MARY   What did you expect?

IKE *(Looking down and clearing his throat)* I don't know. You said, you know, you had always led me to—and you said that-that he was a great ladies' man—

MARY *(Interrupting)* Yeah, I did.

IKE —and that he opened you up sexually, you know.

MARY So, sooo?

IKE And, you know, and then this—this little homunculus, you know . . . I, uh—

MARY *(Interrupting, sighing)* He's quite devastating.

IKE *(Shaking his head)* Really? Well, it's . . . you know, I—it's amazing how subjective all that stuff is.

MARY *(Sighing)* I don't know what you're—

CUT TO:
INTERIOR. IKE'S APARTMENT—DAY.

Ike is sprawled out on his bed, writing. He is seen through the doorway of his bedroom. The sound is heard of Mary typing in the living room.

IKE *(Looking up from his work)* Boy, you're really typing away in there.

MARY *(Offscreen)* Yeah, it's a cinch.

IKE *(Writing again)* Yeah, are you still reviewing *The Tolstoy Letters?* *The camera moves to Mary, seated at a typing desk in the living room. She has a cigarette in her mouth.*

MARY No, no, I finished that two days ago. I'm—I'm on that novelization.
The camera stays in the hallway, moving back and forth between Ike in the bedroom on the left side of the screen, and then cutting to Mary at her typewriter in the living room on the right side of the screen.

IKE I mean, what-what do you waste your time with a novelization for?

MARY Why? Because it's easy and it pays well.

IKE It's, mm, you know, it's like another contemporary American phenomenon that's truly moronic—the, uh, um, novelizations of movies. I mean, you're much too brilliant for that. You know, you should be doing other stuff.

MARY *(Taking a puff on her cigarette)* Like what?

IKE You know, like fiction. I've seen your fiction. It's terrific.
The telephone rings. Mary picks it up.

MARY *(Into the telephone)* Hello?
The film cuts briefly to Yale in a Park Avenue phone booth; the traffic zooms by.

YALE Mary, hi. It's Yale. I was hoping you'd pick up. Listen—uh, could we meet for coffee?
The film cuts back to Mary in Ike's apartment.

MARY *(Hunching over the phone)* Well—why, why? What is it? Wha—?
Yale is seen for a moment.

YALE Well, you know, I miss you and I thought—thought maybe we could talk.
The camera is back at Ike's place.

MARY *(Sighing)* No, I don't think that would be possible, really. I don't think that would be possible at all. I'm sorry, I just, uh . . . no, I-I'm sorry, I've gotta go.
Mary hangs up, reacting. She leans back in her chair, shaking. Ike, sharpening a pencil on his bed, looks up for a moment.

IKE Who was that?

MARY What?

IKE Who was that on the phone just now?

MARY *(Slumping back in her chair, still shaking)* Uh, dance lessons.

IKE Dance lessons that was?

MARY *(Biting her nails)* Yeah, do we want free dance lessons.

IKE *(Chuckling)* Right. They give you one free lesson, and then they hook you for fifty thousand dollars' worth.
And the film cuts back to the Park Avenue phone booth where Yale hangs up the receiver and walks onto the crowded sidewalk. Traffic continues to go by; horns bonk and he quickly disappears into the crowd.

CUT TO:
INTERIOR. YALE AND EMILY'S APARTMENT—DAY.

Ike and Emily, backs to the camera, stand talking in front of some bookshelves in the living room.

IKE *(Turning to Emily)* Viking loved my book.

EMILY Oh, good.

IKE They loved the first four chapters, which is all I gave 'em. But they—they said it was amusing and they were, you know, they were really complimentary.
Emily walks into the kitchen; Ike follows her.

EMILY Yeah, well, Yale had read them and he thought they showed a great deal of promise.

IKE Yeah, I know, but Yale's family, you know, so of course he's always enormously encouraging. But Viking is, you know—they're the ones who gotta shove up the money.

EMILY Yeah, well, maybe it'll inspire Yale to finish his O'Neill biography. I mean, he's been talking about it long enough.

IKE I know, for ages.

EMILY Yeah.
She walks back into the living room, Ike still following her.

IKE Well, Mary—Mary read the stuff and she—she was just laughing out loud. And I-I respect her judgment, you know, though she's doing a think piece on a rock star, which really is—
Ike is interrupted by the sound of the front door opening and closing.

YALE *(Offscreen, calling from the doorway)* Hello?

IKE *(Ignoring Yale's entrance)* You know, she's getting—

EMILY *(Interrupting Ike, to Yale)* Hey, where were you? You were supposed to be home an hour ago.

YALE *(Entering the living room)* Uhhh, I bought the car.

EMILY Oh, no—you did?

YALE *(Laughing)* I know, I know, I know it's a meaningless extravagance—
Ike sighs.

YALE   —but I had to have it. It was too beautiful.

IKE   Did you get that-that thing that we saw?

YALE *(Nodding his head)*   Yeah, yeah.

IKE   Oh!

EMILY   Did you hear about Ike?

YALE   Huh?

EMILY   Viking Press loved the first four chapters of his book.

IKE *(Nodding)*   Mm-hm.

YALE *(Overlapping)*   Oh, really?

IKE   Yeah, they were real complimentary about it.

YALE   All right, next week I get the car. We'll take it out and we'll celebrate.

IKE   Okay.

EMILY *(To Ike, smiling)*   In our new car.

CUT TO:
EXTERIOR. TAPPAN ZEE BRIDGE—DAY.

Yale, Emily, Ike and Mary are crammed into Yale's new Porsche. Yale is driving through the traffic while light music plays in the background. The film abruptly cuts to a quaint shopping street in Nyack, New York. Yale and Ike are seen leaving an antique shop. As they walk down the sidewalk, Mary and Emily are seen leaving a different store. Mary hands Ike a framed picture she's just bought him. Ike gives her a kiss, and as the group continues down the street, he falls back and quickly throws it into a nearby garbage can, then catches up with the others. The music continues.

It's a bit later; the group is passing in front of a Nyack bookstore. The camera is in the display window, focusing out on the group. While Yale and Emily pass by the window quickly, something catches Ike's and Mary's attention. Ike lights a cigarette and points at the window. Yale and Emily quickly walk back onscreen. The foursome stare at the window; the light music continues to play. The camera moves outside the store; it is focused on the window, showing the object of their surprise and shock:

There, prominently displayed, is Jill's book, Marriage, Divorce and Selfhood. *Several of the books show the title; others are turned over to show a full cover photograph of Jill herself. The music stops and the film cuts to:*

EXTERIOR. NYACK WATERFRONT—DAY.

Boats are in the harbor; the bay touches the dock; seagulls fly over Mary, Ike, Yale and Emily as they walk past the dock. Yale, holding Jill's book, reads out loud.

YALE *(To the group)*   Jesus, listen to this. "Making love to this deeper, more *(Laughing)* masterful female made me . . . *(Laughing)* made me realize—"
Ike covers his ears.

YALE   "—what an empty experience, what a bizarre charade—"
Ike sighs.

YALE   "—sex with my husband was."
Emily laughs.

IKE   Please, that is so nauseating. *(Sighing)* I—oh . . .

YALE *(Overlapping)*   Oh, God Almighty.

EMILY *(Chuckling)*   Is this true? Did you make love with Jill and an-other woman?

IKE   Uh, she put that in there?
Emily takes the book from Yale; they both laugh.

IKE *(Putting his hands in his pockets)*   Christ. I mean, she-she wanted to, I think. You know, I-I was—I didn't wanna be a bad sport.

YALE   Did you have a good time?

MARY   And then there's the one where—where—

IKE *(To Yale, interrupting Mary)*   No, I didn't have a good time.
Yale and Emily continue to laugh: they both read the book, Emily still holding it.

MARY *(Turning around to look at Yale and Emily)*   Did you hear the one where he tried to run her—her lover over?

YALE *(Looking at Mary)*   Oh, yeah.

IKE *(To Mary)*   Whose side are you on?

MARY *(Looking at Ike)*   What do you mean?

IKE *(Ignoring Mary's question)*   No, I didn't try and run her over. It was raining out. The car lurched. Jesus, now every-everybody in town is gonna know all—

EMILY *(Interrupting)* I can't believe it.

IKE —these details. Everybody, all my friends and—

EMILY *(Reading from the book now)* Hey, listen to this: "He was given to fits of rage, Jewish, liberal paranoia, male chauvinism, self-righteous misanthropy, and nihilistic moods of despair. He had complaints about life but never any solutions."
The foursome walk off the screen. Their voices are still heard over the peaceful scene; the sea gulls continue to fly overhead.

EMILY *(Offscreen, continues to read)* "He longed to be an artist but balked at the necessary sacrifices. In his most private moments, he spoke of his fear of death, which he elevated to tragic heights when, in fact, it was mere narcissim."
The film cuts to a close-up of Ike's angry face. He has just entered Jill's apartment.

IKE I came here to strangle you.

JILL *(Offscreen)* Nothing I wrote was untrue.
Ike walks across Jill's living room to the table; Connie sits in one of the chairs, listening, while Ike and Jill walk around the room in heated discussion.

IKE What do you mean?! That book makes me out to be like Lee Harvey Oswald!

JILL It's an honest account of our marriage.

IKE That I'm narcissistic?!

JILL Don't you think you're a little self-obsessed?

IKE And—and misanthropic? And self-righteous?

JILL *(Fiddling with some yarn she has picked up from the table)* Well, I— I wrote some nice things about you.

IKE Like what? What?

JILL Like what? Like you cry when you see *Gone With the Wind.*

IKE Oh, Jesus.
Connie laughs.

IKE *(To Connie)* What're you laughing about? You're supposed to be the mature one of the two. You let her write that garbage?

CONNIE Hey, wait a minute. This is between you two.

IKE Uh, do you—do you honestly think that I tried to run you over?

CONNIE You just happened to hit the gas as I walked in front of the car.

IKE *(To Jill)* Gee, I-I—did I do it on purpose?

JILL Well, what would Freud say?

IKE Freud would say I really wanted to run her over. That's why he was a genius.

CONNIE *(Getting up from the table)* All right, listen you two, I'm going upstairs. I got work to do. Don't forget that Willie's at ballet class. *She walks up the stairs.*

IKE *(Mumbling)* Yeah.

JILL Look, I better warn you. I've had some interest in this book for a movie sale.
Ike looks away, incredulous, and the film cuts to:

INTERIOR. IKE'S APARTMENT—DAY.

Ike enters his apartment, closes the door and walks into the kitchen.

IKE *(Calling)* Is anybody home?

MARY *(Offscreen)* Uh-huh.

IKE *(Turning on the light switch in the kitchen)* Yeah? I got an unbelievable story to tell you, absolutely incredible. You okay?

MARY *(Offscreen)* Oh, yeah.

IKE Yeah? Just let me get one glass of brown water . . . and I'll be fine 'cause I'm dying of thirst.
Ike turns on the faucet and fills a glass with brown water.

MARY *(Offscreen, overlapping)* Isaac . . . yeah, I wanna talk to you—

IKE *(Drinking)* Mm-hm.

MARY —first.

IKE *(Not listening to Mary, excitedly)* So I go over to Jill's this morning, right? Because I'm real annoyed over all that junk she printed in the book.

MARY *(Offscreen)* Yeah. Isaac? Mm-hm.

IKE *(Overlapping)* And . . . and I'm, you know—
Ike turns off the kitchen light. Holding his glass of water, he walks into the living room, where Mary is standing.

MARY *(Looking at Ike, interrupting)* Before you get wound up, there's just something I—I wanna tell you.

IKE *(Looking at Mary)* What's the matter? You look—you look . . . pale.

MARY Well.

IKE Well, wha-what's the matter? Hey, what— Is there something wrong? What is it?

MARY *(Hesitating)* I think I'm still in love with Yale.

IKE *(Reacting)* What? You— Are you kidd—? You are?

MARY Yes.

IKE Well, when did this happen? I mean, what . . . ? Well, you are or you think you are?
Mary walks over to a coffee table, its surface holding a bottle of wine and some glasses. She pours herself a glass of wine.

MARY *(Sipping her wine)* I started seeing him again.

IKE When? Since when?

MARY Mm . . . just since today. We're not really . . . That's why I wanted to be open about it.

IKE Jesus, I'm . . . I'm shocked. I'm—I'm . . . shocked. I'm . . . s-surprised.

MARY *(Pacing back and forth, holding her wine glass)* I-I-I think I've always been in love with him.

IKE *(Reacting)* How does he feel about this?

MARY *(Sighing)* Well . . . tsch, he wants to move out of his place so that we can live together.

IKE *(Sitting down on the edge of a chair)* I'm stunned. I'm—I'm . . . I'm in a state of, uh . . . Somebody should throw a blanket over me. You know, I'm—

MARY *(Interrupting)* Well, you see, he called me several times in a very depressed and confused state. And he *(Sighing)* he still loves me.

IKE *(Reacting)*   This-this-this is shaping up like a Noël Coward play, you know. Somebody should go out and make some martinis.

MARY   I don't blame you for being furious with me.

IKE   Well, I'm—I'm too stunned to be furious.

MARY   Well, then, I wish you would. I wish you'd get angry so that we could have it out, so that we could get it out in the open.

IKE *(Pointing to himself)*   Well, I don't get angry, okay? I mean, I have a tendency to internalize. I can't express anger. That's one of the problems I have. I—I grow a tumor instead.

MARY   Well. I told you that-that I was *(Sighing)* . . . trouble from the beginning, from when we first started dating.
Mary stops pacing and sits down on the coffee-table edge, still holding her wine glass.

IKE   So what does—what does your analyst say? I mean, did you speak to him?

MARY   Well, Donny's in a coma. He had a very bad acid experience.

IKE   Oh, that's gr—, that's great. I mean, you know . . . *(Sighing)*   I think you're making a big mistake here.

MARY   Why?

IKE   Why? Because you . . . Why? B-b-because you're preferring Yale to me, that's all. I know that sounds egotistical, but, uh . . . *(Mary sighs. Ike shakes his head)* . . . you know. This guy's been married for twelve years to Emily. You'd . . . what'd you think's gonna happen? He'll be away from her for a month, he'll go crazy. And-and-and if he does commit to you, you know, when you start to feel secure, you'll drop him. *(Snapping his fingers)* I know it. I—I give the whole thing . . . four weeks, that's it.

MARY   Well, I-I-I-I can't plan that far in advance.

IKE   You can't plan four weeks in advance? I mean, what—

MARY *(Interrupting, shaking her head)*   No!

IKE   —what-what kind of foresight is that? *(Sighing)* Jesus. You know, I-I knew you were crazy when-when we started going out. I—you know, I . . . y-you . . . always thinking you're gonna be the one that makes 'em act different, you know, but . . . eh.

MARY   Isaac, I'm sorry.

IKE   Yeah, well . . .

MARY   I really am. I'm really sorry.

IKE   Mm-hm.
Ike mumbles under his breath. He puts down his brown water on the coffee table. He stands up and walks out of the room.

MARY   Isaac? Well . . . I'm sor—   Where are you—where are you going?

IKE   *(Offscreen)*   I gotta get some air.

MARY   *(Reacting)*   Oh.
The camera stays on Mary for a moment; she still sits on the coffee table, one hand on her head, the other holding her glass of wine.
And marching music is heard as the scene shifts to Ike, walking quickly on the New York sidewalks, muttering to himself, gesturing, oblivious to the passers-by. He enters a university, walking past two girls looking at a bulletin board. Still muttering to himself, he marches to a classroom door. He knocks on its small window. Yale, teaching a class, turns and sees his friend. Ike motions to Yale to come over to him; he knocks again. Yale excuses himself to his students and walks out the door. The music stops.

IKE   *(Whispering)*   Psst. I wanna talk to you.

YALE   *(Standing by the door, still holding the knob)*   What're you doing here?

IKE   What do you mean what am I doing here? I spoke to Mary. Weren't you going to say anything?

YALE   *(Softly)*   Oh, damn. I was gonna say something to you, but not—   Ssssh, there's a class in there.

IKE   Yeah, so where can we go and talk?

YALE   *(Motioning)*   Come here. Come here. Come here. Come here.
Yale pulls Ike across the corridor to another classroom door; they continue to speak in low voices.

IKE   Where can we—where can we go speak?

YALE   How'd you get past the security?

IKE   What do you mean? I walked right past.

Ike and Yale walk through the door to an empty classroom. It looks like an ordinary schoolroom, with its wooden desks and blackboard, except for the two skeletons hanging near the door; they seem to be observing the two friends as they talk.

IKE *(Sighing)*   What are you telling me, that you-you're-you're gonna leave Emily—is this true?—and-and run away with the-the winner of the . . . Zelda Fitzgerald Emotional Maturity Award?

YALE   Look, I love her. I've always loved her.

IKE *(Sighing)*   Oh, what kind of crazy friend are you?

YALE   I'm a good friend! I introduced the two of you, remember?

IKE   Why? What was the point? *(Chuckling)* I don't understand that.

YALE   Well, I thought you liked her!

IKE   Yeah, I do like her! Now we both like her!

YALE *(Looking away)*   Yeah, well, I liked her first!

IKE *(Reacting, incredulous)*   "I liked her first." What're you—what're you, six years old?! Jesus.

YALE   Look . . . I thought it was over. You know, I mean, would I have encouraged you to take her out if—if I still liked her?

Ike walks closer to Yale; he now stands next to one of the skeletons. As he talks, he shares the screen with the skeleton's skull, which looks as if it has a perpetual grin. Ike, deep in conversation with Yale, ignores his long-dead scene stealer.

IKE   So what, you liked her. Now you don't like her. Then you did like her. You-you-you know, um, it's still early. You can change your mind one more time before dinner!

YALE   Don't get sarcastic about this. You think I like this?!

IKE   How-how long were you gonna see her without saying anything to me?

YALE   Don't turn this into one of your big moral issues.

IKE *(Reacting, still standing next to the skeleton)*   You could've said—but you-you . . . all you had to do was, you know, was call me and talk to me. You know, I'm very understanding. I'd 'a said, "No," but you'd 've felt honest.

YALE   I wanted to tell you about it. I knew it was gonna upset you. I—uh, uh . . . we had a few innocent meetings.

IKE   A few?! She said one! You guys, you should get your story straight, you know. Don't-don't you rehearse?

YALE   We met twice for coffee.

IKE   Hey, come off it. She doesn't drink coffee. What'd you do, meet for Sanka? That's not too romantic. You know, that's a little on the geriatric side.

YALE   Well, I'm not a saint, okay?

IKE   *(Gesturing, almost hitting the skeleton)*   But you—but you're too easy on yourself, don't you see that?! You know, you . . . you—that's your problem, that's your whole problem. You-you rationalize everything. You're not honest with yourself. You talk about . . . you wanna—you wanna write a book, but—but, in the end, you'd rather buy the Porsche, you know, or you cheat a little bit on Emily, and you play around the truth a little with me, and—and the next thing you know, you're in front of a Senate committee and you're naming names! You're informing on your friends!

YALE   *(Reacting)*   You are so self-righteous, you know. I mean, we're just people, we're just human beings, you know. You think you're God!

IKE   I—I gotta model myself after someone!

YALE   Well, you just can't live the way you do, you know. It's all so perfect.

IKE   Jesus—well, what are future generations gonna say about us? My God! *(He points to the skeleton, acknowledging it at last)* You know, someday we're gonna—we're gonna be like him! I mean, y-y-y-y-you know—well, he was probably one of the beautiful people. He was probably dancing and playing tennis and everything. And—and— *(Pointing to the skeleton again)* and now—well, this is what happens to us! You know, uh, it's very important to have—to have some kind of personal integrity. Y-you know, I'll—I'll be hanging in a classroom one day. And—and I wanna make sure when I . . . thin out that I'm w-w-well thought of!
The camera stays focused on the skeleton, its full form shown now, as Ike leaves, then Yale.

YALE (*Offscreen, calling*)   Ike . . . Isaac, where're you going?
The film stays in the empty classroom a moment longer, the camera focused on the grinning skeleton in the silence. The movie dissolves into:
Ike is sitting at his typewriter, staring into space. It is day. His back is to the camera; he sits in the same place where Mary sat working when she was with him. Ragtime is heard in the background as Ike finally picks up some paper, puts it into the typewriter, turns on a cassette recorder and starts to type.
It is night now. Ike is shown quickly typing away; then, the same ragtime still playing, the camera cuts to Willie carving a pumpkin. It pulls back, showing Ike carving his own gigantic pumpkin.
The ragtime still playing, the scene shifts to a Central Park field where fathers and sons are playing football, chatting and yelling. When the game ends, Ike, his arm around his son, and Willie walk away, their sweat shirts declaring "Divorced Fathers and Sons All Stars."
The music stops as the film cuts to the fairly crowded SoHo Charcuterie. It is day. Ike and Emily sit across from each other, eating lunch.

EMILY   No, I knew Yale had affairs . . . but then, nothing's perfect. (*Sighing*) Marriage is a—requires some minor compromises, I guess.

IKE (*Coughing*)   You know, it's funny because I can't— I, you know, I'm just a noncompromiser. I mean, I can't—I can't see that. You know, I think it's always a big mistake to—to look the other way . . . (*Clearing his throat*) 'cause you always wind up paying for it in the end anyhow, you know . . . but then, you—so it . . . Jill wrote about me in that book, you know. I'm-I-I'm living in the past.

EMILY   How about you? You seeing anybody?

IKE (*Shrugging*)   Uh, uh, y-you-you know, I-I n-n-never had any problem meeting women. I mean, that's . . . you know, but (*Clearing his throat*) I was thinking about this just about a week ago. I think, and I know this sounds strange, but I think I really missed a good bet when I let Tracy go. Do you remember Tracy? Yeah.

EMILY (*Overlapping*)   Yeah, I always liked her.

IKE   Tsch. Yeah. I was—I was just thinking about this at home last week and (*Sighing and looking at his hands*) I think of all the women that I've known over the last years, when I actually am honest with myself . . . tsch, I think I had the most relaxed times and the most, you know, the nicest times with her. She was really a terrific kid, but young, right? So . . . that's that.

EMILY Why don't you call her?

IKE No, I would never do that. I think I blew that one. You know, I—I really kept her at a distance and I just would never give her a chance. And *(Sighing)* she was so sweet. You know she—she called me . . . uh, she left a message with my service about a month ago *(Sighing and looking off into space for a moment)* that I should watch *Grand Illusion* on television . . . *(Emily chuckles; Ike shakes his head and gestures)* . . . you know. And I never returned her call or anything. I—you know . . . *(Smacking his lips together)* 'cause I—you know, I, uh, didn't wanna lead her on or anything. I—uh . . . she really cared about me and I . . .
Ike trails off, sighing.

EMILY *(Shaking her head)* Tsch. You know I was a little pissed-off at you.

IKE *(Raising an eyebrow and pointing to himself)* Me?

EMILY *(Nodding her head)* Yeah. I figured if you hadn't introduced Mary to Yale, this might never have happened.
Ike, reacting to Emily's words, nods his head affirmatively.

CUT TO:
INTERIOR. IKE'S APARTMENT—DAY

The camera shows a tape recorder, the cassette wheels turning inside the case.

IKE *(Offscreen)* An idea for a short story . . . *(Sighing)* about, um, tsch, people in Manhattan who, uh, who are constantly creating these real, uh, unnecessary neurotic problems for themselves 'cause it keeps them from dealing with, uh, more unsolvable, terrifying problems about, uh, the universe.
The camera pulls back, revealing Ike, sprawled out on his couch, holding the recorder's microphone to his mouth. He continues to talk, fiddling with the microphone's wire as he thinks out loud.

IKE *(Into the microphone, sighing)* Um, tsch—it's , uh . . . well, it has to be optimistic. Well, all right, why is life worth living? That's a very good question. *(Sighing)* Um. *(Clearing his throat, then sighing again)* Well, there are certain things I—I guess that make it worthwhile. *(Sighing)* Uh, like what? *(Sighing again and scratching his neck)* Okay. Um, for me . . . *(Sighing)* oh, I would say . . . what, Groucho Marx,

to name one thing . . . uh, ummmm, and *(Sighing)* Willie Mays, and um, uh, the second movement of the Jupiter Symphony, and ummmm . . . *(Exhaling)* Louie Armstrong's recording of "Potatohead Blues" . . . *(Sighing)* umm, Swedish movies, naturally . . . *Sentimental Education* by Flaubert . . . uh, Marlon Brando, Frank Sinatra . . . *(Sighing)* ummm, those incredible apples and pears by Cézanne . . . *(Sighing)* uh, the crabs at Sam Wo's . . . tsch, uh *(Sighing)* Tracy's face . . .

Ike chuckles softly as sad, romantic music plays in the background. He puts down the microphone on his chest and sighs. He leans up on his elbow, thinking for a moment, then sits up. He puts the microphone on the coffee table and stands up. He walks across his living room to a cabinet. He opens a drawer, then another as, finally, he finds what he was looking for—Tracy's harmonica. He takes the harmonica out of its box, tossing the container onto the nearby dining-room table. He walks back to the couch, hesitating for a moment, then sitting down. Still holding the harmonica, he picks up the phone, then quickly puts it down. He puts down Tracy's present, then, determinedly, he picks up the phone again and dials a number. It's busy. He puts down the phone and, impulsively, gets up, grabbing his jacket from a chair and running out of his apartment.

The music changes to a marchlike orchestration. Ike runs down a crowded sidewalk. He stops at a corner, trying to hail a taxi in the busy street. There

*are no vacant cabs. Exasperated, Ike gestures his disgust with his hands, then
begins to run again.*

*He's now on Second Avenue, in the Yorkville section of Manhattan. He stops
running for a moment to catch his breath. Once again he tries to hail a cab
in the truck-filled street. No luck. He starts to run again.*

*The music continues. The camera shows an empty phone booth; Ike runs over
to it. He puts a dime into the slot and dials. The number is still busy. He
drops the receiver back and leaves the booth quickly.*

*He continues to run, now past Gramercy Park, oblivious to the passers-by,
the traffic, everything but getting to where he desperately wants to go.*

*The camera shows the lobby of Tracy's apartment house, looking outside from
its interior. A limousine is parked at the curb. The music changes to "But
Not for Me" as Ike runs onto the screen. He looks inside the glass doors,
breathing hard. He looks pleased.*

*Tracy, in a trim suit, is standing by the elevators, handing her luggage to
a chauffeur. The driver leaves the building; Tracy takes a brush out of her
purse and begins to run it through her hair. She brushes her hair for a moment,
then stops, brush in hand, as she sees Ike standing outside.*

*Ike walks inside the lobby while the chauffeur puts Tracy's suitcases into the
limousine. Ike walks over to Tracy. The orchestration of "But Not for Me"
is heard in the background. Ike looks at Tracy. She looks at him, playing with
her brush's bristles.*

IKE *(Sighing)* Hi.

TRACY *(Sighing)* Hi.

IKE Tsch, I . . .
He clears his throat.

TRACY What're you doing here?

IKE Tsch. *(Sighing)* Well, *(Clearing his throat again)* I ran. *(Catching his
breath, sniffling)* Tsch, I—I tried to call you on the phone, but, uh
. . . it was busy, so *(Inhaling)* I know that was two hours' worth of
. . . *(Tracy chuckles)* So then I couldn't get a taxi cab, so I ran.
(Breathing heavily) Tsch . . . Where you going?

TRACY London.

IKE *(Reacting, looking away for a moment)* You're going to London
now? You mean if— What do you—what do you mean? If I—if I
got over here two minutes later, you'd be—you'd be—you'd be
. . . going to London? *(Tracy sighs and nods her head; Ike sighs too)* Well,

l-let me get right to the point then. *(Clearing his throat)* I don't think you oughta go. I think I made a big mistake. And I would prefer it if y-you didn't go.

TRACY *(Sighing)* Oh, Isaac.

IKE I—I mean it. I know it looks real bad now *(Chuckling)* but, uh . . . you know—it, uh, uh, are you—are you seeing anybody? Are you going with anybody?

TRACY *(Shaking her head)* No.

IKE *(Sighing and shrugging)* So . . . well . . . you st-st-st— Do you still love me or has that worn off or what?

TRACY *(Sighing, reacting)* Jesus, you pop up. You don't call me and then you suddenly appear. I mean . . . what happened to that woman you met?

IKE Well—well, I'll tell you that—uh, it's—uh, Jesus, yeah, I don't see her anymore. I mean, you know, we say . . . Look, I made a mistake. What do you want me to say? *(Pausing)* I don't think you oughta go to London.
He sighs and takes a deep breath.

TRACY Well, I have to go. I mean, all the plans have been made, t-the arrangements. I mean, my parents are there now looking for a place for me to live.

IKE *(Sighing)* Tsch. W-well . . . uh, ah, do you still love me or—or what?

TRACY Do you love me?

IKE Well, yeah, that's what I—uh . . . well, yeah, of course, that's what this is all about . . . you know.

TRACY Guess what? I turned eighteen the other day.

IKE Did you?

TRACY *(Chuckling and nodding)* I'm legal, but I'm still a kid.

IKE You're not such a kid. Eighteen years old. You know, you can— you can . . . they could draft you. You know that in some countries, you'd be . . . *(Tracy smiles, then laughs softly. Ike moves a strand of hair away from her face)* Hey . . . you look good.

TRACY You really hurt me.

IKE *(Stroking Tracy's cheek)*   Uh, it was not on purpose . . . you know. I mean, I—I . . . uh, you know, I was . . . yeah, I mean . . . you know, it was just—just the way I was looking at things then—

TRRACY *(Interrupting)*   Well, I'll be back in six months.

IKE *(Raising an eyebrow, reacting)*   Six months—are you kidding?! Six months you're gonna go for?

TRACY   We've gone this long. Well, I mean, what's six months if we still love each other?

IKE *(Nodding his head)*   Hey, don't be so mature, okay? I mean, six months is a long time. Six months. You know, you're gonna be— you're gonna be i-in-in-in the— . . . working in the theater there. You'll be with actors and directors. You know, you're . . . you know, you go to rehearsal and you-you hang out with those people. You have lunch a lot. And, and *(Clearing his throat and frowning)* . . . well, you know, attachments form and-and, you know, I mean, you-you don't wanna get into that kind of . . . I mean, you-you'll change. You know, you'll be—you'll be . . . in six months you'll be a completely different person.

TRACY *(Chuckling)*   Well, don't you want me to have that experience? I mean, a while ago you made such a convincing case.

IKE   Tsch. Yeah, of course I do, but you know, but you could . . . you know, you—I mean, I-I just don't want that thing about you that I like to change.
An orchestration of "Rhapsody in Blue" begins in the background, the same music as in the beginning of the film.

TRACY   I've gotta make a plane.

IKE   Oh, come on, you . . . come on. You don't—you don't have to go.

TRACY   Why couldn't you have brought this up last week? Look, six months isn't so long. *(Pausing)* Not everybody gets corrupted. *(Ike stares at Tracy, reacting. He pushes back his glasses)* Tsch. Look, you have to have a little faith in people.
Ike continues to stare at Tracy. He has a quizzical look on his face; he breaks into a smile.
And the "Rhapsody in Blue" orchestration swells. The film cuts to a magnificent skyline of Manhattan, the early-morning sun casting it almost in silhouette; the sun sets in another, a different, skyline, and, finally, Manhattan is

FOUR FILMS OF WOODY ALLEN

shown at night, its buildings and bridges illuminated with thousands of lights. "Rhapsody in Blue" reaches a crescendo as the film cuts to a black background, white credits popping on and off the screen, while music from the film is heard . . .

Directed by	WOODY ALLEN
Written by	WOODY ALLEN AND
	MARSHALL BRICKMAN
Produced by	CHARLES H. JOFFE
Executive Producer	ROBERT GREENHUT
Director of Photography	GORDON WILLIS
Production Designer	MEL BOURNE
Costume Designer	ALBERT WOLSKY
Film Editor	SUSAN E. MORSE

A Jack Rollins-Charles H. Joffe Production
"Manhattan" Copyright © United Artists Corporation
MCMLXXIX
All Rights Reserved

Starring	WOODY ALLEN
	DIANE KEATON
	MICHAEL MURPHY
	MARIEL HEMINGWAY
	MERYL STREEP
	ANNE BYRNE

Featured Cast

KAREN LUDWIG	MICHAEL O'DONOGHUE
GARY WEIS	KENNY VANCE
TISA FARROW	DAMION SHELLER
WALLACE SHAWN	HELEN HANFT
BELLA ABZUG	VICTOR TRURO

Casting	JULIET TAYLOR

MANHATTAN

Music by   GEORGE GERSHWIN

"Rhapsody In Blue"
Performed by
The New York Philharmonic

Conducted by
ZUBIN MEHTA

Music Adapted and Arranged by   TOM PIERSON
Arranger for Buffalo Philharmonic   DON ROSE
Audio Producer for the New York
    Philharmonic   ANDREW KAZDIN
Music Recording Engineers   RAY MOORE
                                                                BUD GRAHAM
"Rhapsody In Blue" Piano Soloist   PAUL JACOBS

The New York Philharmonic
Zubin Mehta, Music Director
Perform   "Rhapsody In Blue"
                                                    "Love Is Sweeping the Country"
                                                    "Land of the Gay Caballero"
                                                            "Sweet and Low Down"
                                                          "I've Got a Crush on You"
                                                                        "Do-Do-Do"
                                                                    " 'Swonderful"
                                                              "Oh, Lady Be Good"
                                                              "Strike Up the Band"
                                                                "Embraceable You"

The Buffalo Philharmonic
Michael Tilson Thomas, Music Director
Perform   "Someone to Watch Over Me"
                                                          "He Loves and She Loves"
                                                                  "But Not for Me"

Production Manager   MARTIN DANZIG
Assistant Director   FREDRIC B. BLANKEIN
Second Assistant Director   JOAN SPIEGEL FEINSTEIN
Unit Supervisor   MICHAEL PEYSER
Script Supervisor   KAY CHAPIN
Production Office Coordinator   JENNIFER OGDEN

FOUR FILMS OF WOODY ALLEN

Assistant to Mr. Allen	GAIL SICILIA
Location Auditor	KATHLEEN MCGILL
Camera Operator	FRED SCHULER
Assistant Cameraman	JAMES HOVEY
Still Photographer	BRIAN HAMILL
Gaffer	DUSTY WALLACE
Key Grip	ROBERT WARD
Property Master	LESLIE BLOOM
Carpenter	JOSEPH BADALUCO
Scenic Artists	COSMO SORICE
	JAMES SORICE
Transportation Captain	JAMES FANNING
Set Decorator	ROBERT DRUMHELLER
Set Dressers	JUSTIN SCOPPA JR.
	MORRIS WEINMAN
Costumer	CLIFFORD CAPONE
Wardrobe Supervisor	C. J. DONNELLY
Hair Stylist	ROMAINE GREENE
Makeup Artist	FERN BUCHNER
Mr. Allen's Wardrobe by	RALPH LAUREN
Sound Mixer	JAMES SABAT
Boom Man	VITO ILARDI
Re-recording Mixer	JACK HIGGINS
Sound Editor	DAN SABLE
Assistant Film Editor	MICHAEL R. MILLER
Assistant Sound Editor	LOWELL MATE
Casting Associates	HOWARD FEUER
	JEREMY RITZER
Extras Casting	AARON BECKWITH CASTING
Unit Publicist	SCOTT MACDONOUGH
Production Accountants	BERNSTEIN AND FREEDMAN
Production Assistants	ROBERT E. WARREN
	CHARLES ZALBEN
	CHERYL HILL
DGA Trainee	LEWIS H. GOULD

Cast

WOODY ALLEN	*Isaac*
DIANE KEATON	*Mary*
MICHAEL MURPHY	*Yale*

MANHATTAN

MARIEL HEMINGWAY	*Tracy*
MERYL STREEP	*Jill*
ANNE BYRNE	*Emily*
KAREN LUDWIG	*Connie*
MICHAEL O'DONOGHUE	*Dennis*
VICTOR TRURO	*Party Guest*
TISA FARROW	*Party Guest*
HELEN HANFT	*Party Guest*
BELLA ABZUG	*Guest of Honor*
GARY WEIS	*Television Director*
KENNY VANCE	*Television Producer*
CHARLES LEVIN	*Television Actor #1*
KAREN ALLEN	*Television Actor #2*
DAVID RASCHE	*Television Actor #3*
DAMION SHELLER	*Ike's Son*
WALLACE SHAWN	*Jeremiah*
MARY LINN BAKER	*Shakespearean Actor*
FRANCES CONROY	*Shakespearean Actor*
BILL ANTHONY	*Porsche Owner #1*
JOHN DOUMANIAN	*Porsche Owner #2*
RAY SERRA	*Pizzeria Waiter*

WAFFLES trained by Dan Animal Agency

Filmed in Panavision®
Prints by Technicolor®

The story, all names, characters and incidents
portrayed in this production are fictitious. No
identification with actual persons is intended
or should be inferred.

This motion picture is protected under the laws
of the United States and other countries and its
unauthorized distribution or exhibition may
result in severe liability and criminal prosecution.

I.A.T.S.E.
(emblem)

(emblem)
MOTION PICTURES ASSOCIATION OF
AMERICA
#25643

The Producers gratefully acknowledge the cooperation of:
The City of New York
Mayor Ed Koch
Nancy Littlefield
Lieutenant Paul Glanzman
Museum of Modern Art
American Museum of Natural History
—Hayden Planetarium
Whitney Museum of American Art
Solomon R. Guggenheim Museum
New York Shakespeare Festival
Hunter College
New York University
Warner Bros. Music/New World
Music
Chapell Music

The
Motion Picture
Code and Rating
Has Rated
This Motion Picture
R
Restricted
Under 17 Requires Accompanying
Parent or Adult Guardian
(emblem)
Motion Picture Association
Of America

THE END

Stardust Memories

Screenplay by Woody Allen

Over a silent black screen, the
words "United Artists, a Transamerica
Company," appear in white. Nineteen-
forties–like jazz begins playing as
white credits pop on and off the screen:

A JACK ROLLINS–CHARLES H. JOFFE PRODUCTION

STARDUST MEMORIES

Starring

WOODY ALLEN

CHARLOTTE RAMPLING

JESSICA HARPER

MARIE-CHRISTINE BARRAULT

TONY ROBERTS

CASTING

JULIET TAYLOR

EDITOR

SUSAN E. MORSE

PRODUCTION DESIGNER

MEL BOURNE

COSTUME DESIGNER

SANTO LOQUASTO

DIRECTOR OF PHOTOGRAPHY

GORDON WILLIS

EXECUTIVE PRODUCERS

JACK ROLLINS AND CHARLES H. JOFFE

PRODUCED BY

ROBERT GREENHUT

WRITTEN AND DIRECTED BY

WOODY ALLEN

The music stops abruptly as the last credit pops off the screen. The film cuts to the interior of a train. It is old, dingy; a loud ticking clock is heard instead of the train engine's rattle. Sandy Bates sits alone in his seat. He looks around at the other passengers. There is an old, somber-looking woman across from him; another woman sits behind him, staring into space, her lips tightly pressed together.

The ticking continues as the camera moves around the train, at the Kent III cigarette poster, looking more out of the past than its brand name implies, at the balding fat man who looks back at Sandy, at the graying man, sitting alone and crying, wiping his nose with his sleeve. A young blond man with a crew cut sits in front of the crying man; he wears wire-rimmed glasses over almost expressionless eyes. Two gypsylike women share a seat; one wears a kerchief around her head.

The ticking continues. Sandy, reacting to the other riders, leans back on his wicker and metal-rimmed seat. He stares out his dirty window at another

train. He watches the passengers partying in their car in silent pantomine, laughing, cavorting and drinking champagne. A well-dressed, suited man hands a blond woman a trophy. She smiles. Her hair is up in a twist; she wears a long sheath.

The ticking continues, louder. Sandy stares around his train's car again. It is still grim, a stark contrast to the partying passengers. The train conductor, pale and sinister-looking, stares back at Sandy; a priest watches. Sandy turns back to the window quickly; the beautiful blonde, holding the trophy, sees Sandy through her window. She kisses the pane with her dark-lipsticked mouth.

The old train's whistle blows; it starts to move. Sandy, panicky, takes his ticket from his jacket pocket and shows it to the conductor, who is plodding down the aisle. The train's engine is heard now, louder, louder, as Sandy mouths his objections to the conductor. He insists he is on the wrong train. The joyous train pulls out of the station. He is too late. Sandy, reacting, gets up from his seat. He runs down the aisle. A blind man is at the car door's window, pressing the window with his hand, trying to get inside. The solemn conductor just stares at Sandy; the old women, the fat bald man, the gypsy women and the priest turn and watch Sandy, almost in unison, their heads bouncing with the train's vibrations. Sandy makes it to the compartment door and tries desperately to open it. The camera flashes quickly to Sandy's mother and father and young sister, looking as they did in earlier times, as they turn their heads to stare at Sandy from their train seats.

The train continues to rattle, louder, faster. Sandy pulls the emergency cord by the door; the cord breaks. Sandy runs back down the aisle, the other passengers following him with their heads, their eyes.

Sandy stops near the middle of the aisle and bangs on a window. While he pounds on the glass a suitcase, filled with sand, begins to fall off an overhead rack. The sand drops out of the suitcase; Sandy continues to pound on the window; the train continues to rattle and sound its loud whistle; and the passengers continue to look, dully, lifelessly, at Sandy. A sallow, dark-haired woman with a large hook nose stares off into the distance; a fat blond woman, sitting next to a sloppy-looking man, puts on coat upon coat of lipstick on her mouth, staring into a compact mirror, her legs splayed. The train rattles; its whistle is heard. Sandy pounds on the window, trying to get out, and the film abruptly cuts to:

EXTERIOR. JUNKYARD—DAY.

Instead of the monotony of the loud train engine, the peaceful sounds of sea gulls are heard over a beach-lot junkyard. The somber-looking passengers from the train, including the conductor, the priest and Sandy walk along the sand. The wind blows as they make their way through the piles of junk, suitcases in hand.

The passengers from the joyous train, including the pretty blonde, walk into the junkyard from the opposite direction. They, too, work their way around the garbage. Sandy stares at the glamorous group, reacting, and the film cuts to:

INTERIOR. PRIVATE SCREENING ROOM—DAY.

The tail end of a piece of film is in the projector; the code numbers flash on the white movie screen, the sound warbles off and, as the film entirely leaves the screen, five silhouetted studio executives, Pabst, Taylor, Smith, Walsh and Kleiner, are seen—black, amorphous shapes against the white background of the movie screen.

PABST *(Over his black form)*   Well, I thought it was terrible. Absolutely terrible. I don't recall seeing anything this bad.

TAYLOR *(Over his black form, clearing his throat)* You're not kidding. This man is sick. I mean, what is this thing?
Walsh, a female executive, appears to be holding a drink in her hand. The others cluster around the screen, their flickering forms appearing stronger, then dimmer, as they pace in front of the movie screen, which is still illuminated by the projector's bright light.

WALSH *(Over her black form)* I thought this was supposed to be a comedy. That was the most horrifying thing I've ever seen!

TAYLOR *(Over his black form)* Sea gulls! Dead cars!

KLEINER *(Over his black form)* Just horrible!

PABST *(Over his black form)* This is a disgrace!

WALSH *(Over her black form)* It's a . . . Hey! I don't get it.

PABST *(Over his black form)* He has no balance left.

TAYLOR *(Over his black form)* Listen, I think the guy's losing his mind.

WALSH *(Over his black form, gesturing)* Somebody please cut that projector.
The projector is shut off. The screen loses its illumination; the executives' voices are heard in the haze created by the camera still focused on them from behind the projector.

KLEINER *(Offscreen)* Something wrong with him.

PABST *(Offscreen)* Well, I say out of balance.

TAYLOR *(Offscreen)* What are we gonna do?

SMITH *(Offscreen, overlapping)* Really nothing.

WALSH *(Offscreen)* It's too bad.

KLEINER *(Offscreen)* Twelve million dollars for that . . .
The camera moves suddenly from behind the haze.

SMITH *(Looking directly into the camera)* He's not funny anymore.
The executives are fully seen now; the room is still fairly dark; the group still paces and gestures, deep in conversation.

KLEINER . . . garbage!

PABST Okay! Okay! Let's not panic.

KLEINER What self-indulgence! I think the man's lost his mind!

TAYLOR   Look, we can take the film away from him! We can reshoot it. We can recut it. Maybe we can salvage something.

WALSH   He's pretentious. His filming style is too fancy. His insights are shallow and morbid. I've seen it all before. They try to document their private suffering and fob it off as art.

TAYLOR   What does he have to suffer about? Doesn't the man know he's got the greatest gift that anyone could have? The gift of laughter?

CUT TO:
EXTERIOR. NEW YORK CITY STREET—DAY.

A white Rolls-Royce fills the screen head-on. Traffic blares and horns honk as the camera cuts to the inside of the car. Sandy is sitting in the back seat, wearing a T-shirt that reads "24" in front. He is talking on a white phone while his chauffeur, George, stares straight ahead at the traffic. A truck's huge grill fills the back window.

SANDY   *(Talking into the telephone)*   Yeah . . . No, I-I don't think I'm gonna make it. We're—we're sitting here in what looks like a truck route or something, you know? I don't know what the hell's goin' on. I— Hold on one second. *(To George)* G-George? That guy's parked, you know. You can just drive around him. You don't have to—*(Without answering, George takes off his cap, still looking straight ahead; Sandy goes back to his telephone conversation)*   You know, it's crazy. The town is jammed . . . I don't know. Is the . . . is the Pope in town, or some other show-business figure?
The film cuts to Sandy's office, where his secretary, a huge woman, sits in a chair behind her desk. The background shows an enormous blown-up photograph of Sandy hanging on the wall. The secretary talks on the telephone to Sandy in his car.

SECRETARY   Oh, my God! Do you know what I forgot? I forgot to cancel your lunch with the editor of *Newsweek.* My fault.
The scene shifts back to Sandy in his Rolls-Royce.

SANDY   *(Talking into the telephone)*   And-and-and, you know, you were supposed to tell me about the, uh, Public Television thing. Uh, you know, I remembered that. And-and-and you were supposed to send the limousine to the airport for my parents.
The camera is back in Sandy's office; his secretary smokes a cigarette and talks on the telephone.

SECRETARY   I know, sweetheart. It's just that the cast came off my finger, so I was at the doctor yesterday. Look, that one's my fault . . . Listen, I made a couple of changes. *(Looking at her desk calendar)* You've . . . the analyst at two instead of three. I moved your tennis lesson up an hour. The chiropodist is at four, and we moved the hair treatment to . . . um, um, Friday. I'm sorry! Wednesday. *(Puffing on her cigarette)* No, Thursday! Thursday at two . . . is the hair . . . treatment.

The film moves to Sandy's penthouse apartment. It is a very white, very spacious apartment, made even brighter by the daylight coming through the floor-to-ceiling windowed terrace doors. Sandy's accountant, a large man in a plaid jacket, is busy talking to Sandy, who is walking around his apartment, still in his "24" T-shirt and loose pants. Sandy's press agent, wearing a neck brace, stands smoking a cigarette and gesturing, busy talking to Sandy whenever the accountant pauses.

Also gesturing and making conversational points is Sandy's manager, an intense man in a plaid three-piece suit, and Sandy's lawyer, a balding man with glasses in a dark three-piece suit. Sandy's doctor, a gnarled, hunched-over old man, is also in the apartment; he doesn't say anything, but he shuffles around, stethoscope around his neck, busily taking Sandy's blood pressure as he talks, gesturing and pacing, to his three employees; a fourth employee, his cook, wearing a uniform, shouts as she walks to the kitchen, where she's presumably working. A large photograph of the My-Lai massacre is illuminated on the entire wall behind Sandy's white table and chairs. The whole background scene seems almost sterile; it is so white that, at times, while the group talks, it is difficult to see where the floor ends and the walls begin.

ACCOUNTANT   Can I please get your signature on this oil-shelter thing?

SANDY   Oil? You told me cattle.

ACCOUNTANT   The cattle died.

SANDY   Did Isobel call?

PRESS AGENT   Has anybody given any thought to *Time* magazine? 'Cause I said I'd get back to them.

COOK *(Walking to kitchen)*   Your cousin called. He needs to borrow more money.

MANAGER   Oh, jeez! Don't bug him about the *Time* cover. He can do it after the weekend.

SANDY *(Overlapping)* Isobel never called? *(He sits down at his white table; his old doctor takes his blood pressure)* Hey, I don't want to go away this weekend. I mean, who-who needs a festival of my old films? It's absurd. It's . . . ridiculous.

ACCOUNTANT *(Handing Sandy a paper)* Sign here, please. And don't worry about that income tax thing. I'll be with you when you go to see the treasury agents.

SANDY *(Signing the paper)* Treasury agents?! Since when is it that serious?

LAWYER *(Overlapping)* Look, Sandy, this is two lousy days. You drive up there, they honor you, they show your films, they ask you a couple of stupid questions, and you go home!

SANDY I don't want to be honored. It's a hype.

PRESS AGENT *(Smoking a cigarette and fiddling with her neck brace)* Don't be ungrateful. She's an important film critic. You promised! They sold a lot of tickets. You can't back out.

LAWYER   You might enjoy it. The nice clean sea air!

MANAGER   Sandy, we've got to talk about the new picture.

SANDY *(Getting up from the table and beginning to pace)*   What do you want me to say? I don't want to make funny movies anymore. *(Gesturing)* They can't force me to. I . . . you know, I don't feel funny. I-I look around the world, and all I see is human suffering.

MANAGER   Human suffering doesn't sell tickets in Kansas City.

SANDY *(Reacting)*   Oh!

PRESS AGENT   They want laughs in Kansas City. They've been working in the wheat fields all day.
The camera passes some bookshelves, then settles on Sandy's press agent as she walks through the open front door; she is seen pushing the elevator button in the bright white hallway. The group continues to chatter.

SANDY   Hey, fellas, I'm getting a headache. Can I please get some privacy?

ACCOUNTANT   Your problem is ya never got over Nat Bernstein's death.

SANDY   Of course I never got over . . . The guy was thirty years old, never sick a day in his life, and then suddenly, out of left field, amyotrophic lateral sclerosis. It was horrible! He was lying there in the hospital, his body degenerated like Lou Gehrig. It was just—

LAWYER *(Interrupting)*   You could use this weekend at the seashore. You know something? You should take a month.

SANDY   I don't want— My mother used to take— When I was a kid, my mother took me to the seashore. Little old decaying hotels and awnings, ya know?

DOCTOR *(Handing Sandy a bottle of pills)*   These are Valium.

SANDY *(Taking the bottle and examining it)*   Oh, great. Just what I— Another show-business tranquilizer. Hey, did-did anybody read on the front page of the *Times* that matter is decaying? Am I the only one that saw that? The universe is gradually breaking down. There's not gonna be anything left . . . I'm not talking about my stupid little films here. I'm— Uh, eventually there's not gonna be any, any Beethoven or Shakespeare, or . . .

The lawyer, the manager, the accountant and the old doctor join the press agent at the elevator; they say their good-byes offscreen to Sandy as they wait for the elevator to come.

PRESS AGENT *(Offscreen)*   Yeah, yeah, go to the seashore.

ACCOUNTANT *(Offscreen)*   Have a nice weekend.

SANDY   Oh, good. Great.
The front door is closed. Sandy stands alone in his now quiet living room; his cook is still offscreen in the kitchen. Sandy, sighing, walks over to his stereo; some brisk guitar music begins playing in the background. Sandy walks forward, closer to the camera, as if looking out a large picture window. He takes off his glasses and rubs his eyes. He stares into space, looking straight ahead.

DORRIE *(Offscreen, from the left)*   What are you thinking about when you look out there?

SANDY *(Sighing while rubbing his chest and staring straight ahead into the camera)*   Just, you know, all those people and *(Sighing)* you know, how unhappy most of them are, and how . . . those terrible things they do to each other and, you know. How everything is . . . over so quickly and *(Sighing)* you don't have any idea . . . was it worth it or not.

DORRIE *(Offscreen)*   Is there any way I can cheer you up?

SANDY *(Sighing)*   No, there's . . . *(Sighing)* What do you have in mind?
Sandy chuckles and walks to the left, to Dorrie. She is staring into space herself a bit, as if she's not entirely there. She is tall, striking, in her black sweater. Sandy puts his arm around Dorrie and rubs her back.

DORRIE *(Looking straight ahead)*   Mmm. You smell nice.

SANDY *(Looking at Dorrie)*   Yeah?

DORRIE *(Staring straight ahead into space)*   That aftershave. It just made my whole childhood come back with a sudden Proustian rush.

SANDY   Yeah? That's 'cause I'm wearing Proustian Rush by Chanel. It's-it's reduced. I got a vat of it.

DORRIE *(Still staring off into space, chuckling)*   Mm. Why don't I just run down and get some food and we'll stay in tonight and I'll cook.

FOUR FILMS OF WOODY ALLEN

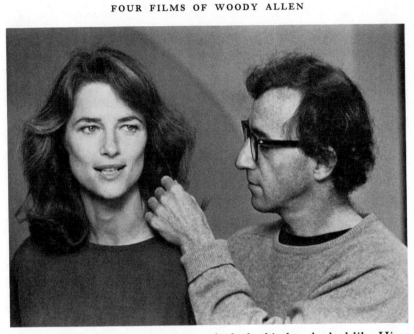

SANDY Well, the last time you cooked, the kitchen looked like Hiroshima.

DORRIE Yeah, we had a good time. I could do my-my mother's recipe for Filet de Boeuf fourre Perigourdine. I could do sweet-potato rum casserole and—

SANDY What? No beverage?
They kiss.

DORRIE Mmmm . . .

SANDY I think they've been putting something wonderful in your lithium.

DORRIE I've stopped taking the lithium.

SANDY Oh, Jesus, you're kidding? Dorrie, that's not a good idea. You-you know, you can't just go on and off it like that. It's not—

DORRIE (*Overlapping*) I don't think it does much good.

SANDY You're wrong. 'Cause I noticed the difference. I . . . you know, you can't keep— It's not all right.

DORRIE It's a pain to keep getting my blood checked. I feel heavy and I feel—

SANDY *(Overlapping)*   I-I'm sure it is. I know, but-but-but you . . . You know, it's better for you. You know, it's not a good thing to just, well . . . really.
Dorrie and Sandy kiss again.

DORRIE *(Chuckling)*   Mmm . . . You are the best kisser.

SANDY *(Chuckling)*   Well, that was my major in college.
Dorrie chuckles; she and Sandy kiss again. As they kiss, the cook screams out, a voice-over transition to the next scene.
The guitar music has stopped. Sandy is standing alone, looking out the picture window, his daydream shattered. He turns, reacting, from the window and runs into the kitchen. His cook, a tiny, birdlike woman, holds a dead rabbit by the ears. She is staring at the oven. It is on fire. She is screaming at the top of her lungs, gesturing.

COOK   Mr. Bates! Mr. Bates, come here at once! Please! Mr. Bates, the stove's on fire!

SANDY   Oh, shit! What's the matter with you?!

COOK   Oh! Put it out! Put it out! Oh! I can't—

SANDY *(Grabbing a towel and hitting the fire with it)*   Where's the—   Will you stop being so hysterical? Every night it's a fire!

COOK *(Overlapping)*   Oh! Oh!

SANDY   Ev—   You don't know how to work this stove yet?

COOK *(Putting the rabbit down on the counter)*   I worked it perfectly. I did just what you said.

SANDY *(Putting down the towel and grabbing a fire extinguisher)*   For God's sake! You do nothing but start fires here!

COOK   I-I did just what you said.

SANDY *(Spraying the oven with the extinguisher)*   Careful.

COOK *(Sighing)*   Ohh!

SANDY   It's a simple stove. And every night you set the apartment on fire.

COOK *(Shielding herself from Sandy's spraying extinguisher)*   Maybe . . . maybe . . . Ahh! Maybe it's defective. Did ya have someone to check it?
Sandy stops spraying; the fire is finally out.

SANDY   All right, relax. And no rabbit! How many times have I told you, no rabbit?

COOK   I thought you only meant just that one time.

SANDY   Not . . . no . . . never. Never. Never. I never want rabbit. I don't eat—I don't eat rodent.

COOK   *(Nodding)*   All right. I-I understand now.

SANDY   It's—   Do you understand that? It's fur-bearing. Never rabbit.

COOK   Never. You never want rabbit. Now that's clear.
Forties type of music begins playing. The camera cuts to the pure white rabbit, nestled among some vegetables on the counter, then to Sandy's face, reacting. The music continues as the film cuts to:

EXTERIOR. STARDUST HOTEL—DUSK.

For a brief moment the Stardust Hotel is seen, a busy structure with towers, pinnacled roofs and a sprawling front path. The camera then moves inside Sandy's Rolls-Royce. Sandy, wearing dark, wire-rimmed sunglasses, is in the back seat. He leans forward, looking out at the mobs of people, reflected in the car's window, who are waiting expectantly for him at the hotel entrance.

The car stops. Vivian Orkin, a large woman with black, carefully coiffed hair, leans down to look at Sandy through the window. People cluster behind her, hoping to catch a glimpse of the back-seat passenger.

VIVIAN *(Peering into the window, gesturing)*   Everyone is just ecstatic that you're here this weekend. The turnout is tremendous. And, you know, these film-culture weekends are just absolutely fantastic. They are getting so popular. Do you know, you're gonna love our screening facilities? When I had my Orson Welles weekend here, you know what he told me? He said that I had the best sound and projection system he'd ever seen, bar none, believe it or not. He did, that's what he—*(Looking to her left for a moment)* Oh! Oh! This is Mr. Payson, our chairman, and Mrs. Payson. They adore you.
The camera shifts to the left, showing Mr. and Mrs. Payson smiling into the car window. Mrs. Payson wears oversized sunglasses and huge rings on her fingers; Mr. Payson is smaller.

MRS. PAYSON *(Smiling and nodding)*   Hi.

MR. PAYSON   We love your work. My wife has seen all your films.

MRS. PAYSON *(Laughing)*   I especially like your early funny ones.
Mr. Payson nods as Dick Lobel, a fat man complete with jowls, a kerchief and chains around his neck and wearing a corduroy blazer, walks in front of them, eager to get his chance.

LOBEL *(Smiling into the car window)*   Dick Lobel. I'm, uh, with the museum, uh, film department. We have a collection of more than twenty thousand prints.
Vivian walks back to the window, pushing away the milling people. She is pulling Libby, a bouncy, chubby woman, over to the window.

VIVIAN   Oh, oh. Th-this is my friend Libby. *(Libby giggles and nods)* She thinks you're a genius. Libby just did a definitive cinematic study of Gummo Marx. *(Vivian overlaps Libby's giggles)* She did!

LOBEL *(Trying still to talk to Sandy)*   Interestingly, he's the one Marx brother that never made any movies.
Sandy is out of the car. He walks down the entrance path, the camera in front of him, showing his fans moving back, making a path for him. They all try to talk at once; they stare, some smiling, some with their mouths open. Some snap their cameras as Sandy walks by them; some reach out with paper for Sandy to sign, hoping to get his autograph or to simply shake his hand. There is almost a forties feel here, a timelessness that doesn't fit in with the modern

eighties. The mass of people look slightly off-kilter, almost carnivorous in their need to see and touch Sandy. The music continues. There is a dark-haired woman who gives Sandy a flirting look; there are couples in coats, complete with bouffant hairdos or balding hairlines. Some people are quite dressed up, decked out in their jewelery; others, plainer, seem to fade into the background. They nod and talk among themselves, shouting out their greetings to the guest celebrity.

SMILING MAN   Hello. Glad to have you here.

MAN *(Pointing his fingers up in a V-for-victory sign)*   Great. You're great. You're great.

PIXIE GIRL *(Giggling)*   Here, read this.

ANOTHER MAN   I think you're absolutely magnificent.

GIRL FAN   Really intense.
The noise of the people suddenly stops; the music is gone. A young Sandy is on the hotel lawn with his mother. He is dressed in a mock Superman costume; he wears little white socks. His mother is fastening a cape to his shoulders. The noise and music returns as the film cuts abruptly back to the grown-up Sandy walking past his fans; some of them snap his photograph.
The film goes back to the young Sandy and his mother; she looks proudly at Sandy, still dressed in his Superman costume, as he flies up into the air, off the screen.
And a grown-up Sandy looks back at the swarms of people, his only escape inside the hotel.

CUT TO:
INTERIOR. STARDUST HOTEL ROOM—DUSK.

The camera is focused on Sandy's bedroom, seen through the doorway of his hotel suite. His arm drops into view, dangling off the edge of his bed. His voice is heard; the screen continues to show only his dangling hand, playing with his sunglasses.

SANDY *(Offscreen, talking on the telephone)*   Hello, Isobel? . . . Isobel, I'm up here. Jeez, I'm goin' crazy. Can you—do you think you can get up here? . . . Well, I miss you! . . . I-in, in English. Sp-speak to me in English . . . Your-your-your English is perfect. Don't-don't worry . . . Wh-what's the matter? You sound . . . You . . . Well, can . . . Do you want me to call you back? . . . Can you not talk? . . . All right, all right. I'll call you back.

Music is heard as the film cuts to the Stardust Hotel auditorium, where a movie is being shown. The camera is focused on the screen, where a tall woman vocalist, wearing a long flowered gown, sings "Three Little Words" to the dancing accompaniment of Sandy and another man. The men are dressed in top hats and tails; they smile while they do a soft-shoe dance step. The audience laughs over the scene.
The song ends; the audience continues to laugh as the screen goes blank. A young woman, wearing glasses and looking solemn, pops up from her seat and addresses Sandy.

YOUNG WOMAN What were you trying to say in this picture?
Sandy, standing behind a podium on the stage in front of the now blank screen, answers her question; Vivian, in a striped dress, sits in a chair next to him, observing him and his audience.

SANDY I was just trying to be funny.
The audience laughs. A young man with a spiky crew cut asks a question from his seat in the packed auditorium.

YOUNG MAN Do you find it very hard to direct yourself?

SANDY *(Scratching his head)* Uh, hard? No, no. I just have to resist, uh, temptation to give myself too many extreme close-ups.
The audience continues to laugh. A fat man, wearing glasses, gets up next.

FAT MAN Have you studied filmmaking in school?

SANDY *(Shaking his head)* No, no, I-I didn't study anything in school. They studied me.
The audience laughs at Sandy's joke as a young girl, wearing huge oval-shaped glasses and a white shirt, stands up from her wooden chair.

YOUNG GIRL I understand you studied philosophy at school.

SANDY *(Gesturing)* Uh, no, that's not true. I-I-I did take—I took one course in existential philosophy at, uh, at New York University, and *(Coughing)* on, uh, on the final *(Sniffing)* they gave me ten questions, and, uh, I couldn't answer a single one of 'em. You know? I left 'em all blank. *(The audience laughs; Vivian, in her seat on the stage, her legs crossed, nods at everything Sandy says. After a pause he adds)* I got a hundred.
The audience continues to laugh; the camera shows some of their faces—a laughing man with a scruffy beard, a woman with pencil-thin eyebrows and lots of make-up, a man with a small mustache—all reacting and staring at Sandy on the stage.

CUT TO:
INTERIOR. STARDUST HOTEL LOBBY—NIGHT.

Sandy is walking through the large Stardust Hotel lobby, his podium stint finished for the night. His fans, the same guests who'd hovered around his Rolls-Royce when he arrived, follow him, chattering and staring, trying to get his attention. Vivian stays close to Sandy, trying to engineer the right distance between him and his effusive fans. Sandy is not seen at first, only the fans who make room for his passage, who talk to him, looking at their offscreen idol.

VIVIAN *(Enthusiastically)* Oh, you are marvelous. You are a genius, Sandy. You're a comedy genius.

WOMAN FAN Good questions! Didn't you think so? I did.

MR. PAYSON You handled them beautifully! You're a genius!

MRS. PAYSON Beautiful! Beautiful!

MALE FAN One of the most intelligent films I've seen in many years . . .

PHOTOGRAPHER *(Holding up his camera)* Can I get a photo, Mr. Bates?

WOMAN WITH A RECORD Hi! I just think you're great, and I-I just wanted to give you this record . . .
She hands Sandy a record, not waiting for an answer, as the fans gather around him. Sandy is seen now, amid the crowds.

SECOND PHOTOGRAPHER *(Holding up his camera)* One more photo, Mr. Bates.
Some fans move away; others take their places as Sandy tries to walk through the lobby. They thrust paper in front of him, hoping for an autograph, hoping for some attention.

WOMAN IN A COWBOY HAT Mr. Bates! Mr. Bates! I'm with the tuberculation . . . uh, Tuberculosis, uh, Association. We're doing a, uh, benefit—

SANDY *(Interrupting, talking to another fan and signing autographs)* Thank you, thank you.

ANOTHER WOMAN FAN Oh, there you are. There you are.

MALE FAN IN LOUD PLAID JACKET Mr. Bates, if I could just have ten minutes of your time, I'd like to ask you a couple of questions, uh—

MAN HOLDING PAPER *(Interrupting)*   Mr. Bates, Mr. Bates, could I have your autograph, please?

SANDY   Sure.

MAN HOLDING PAPER *(Watching Sandy sign his autograph)*   Thank you very much.

MALE FAN IN LOUD PLAID JACKET   I'm doing this piece on the sh-shallow indifference of wealthy celebrities, and I'd like to include you . . . I'd like to include you in my piece.

ANOTHER MALE FAN   Mr. Bates, can I ask you a question, please?
Daisy and Jack, two guests at the hotel, stand by themselves, apart from the group surrounding Sandy. Daisy wears sunglasses; her arms are crossed in front of her. Jack wears an old army jacket.

DAISY *(To Jack)*   I'm starving.

CUT TO:
INTERIOR. SANDY'S APARTMENT—DAY.

A quick memory flash of Sandy's apartment is shown as Daisy speaks to Jack. It is quiet. Dorrie stands in front of a large photograph of herself in a mental-patient hospital gown. She leans against the wall, staring into space, and as Vivian's voice is heard, the film leaves Sandy's mind and goes back to the noisy, crowded Stardust Hotel lobby.

VIVIAN'S VOICE-OVER   Sandy, there's a phone call for you. *(Vivian, now onscreen, leads Sandy to the lobby phones; his fans still follow him, like metal drawn to a magnet)* Let me show you where the phone is, Sandy.
Dr. Pearlman, a large man in a suit, approaches Sandy, interrupting his walk with Vivian to the phones. A smiling woman holds on to the doctor's arm, proudly watching him talk to Sandy.

DR. PEARLMAN   I'm Dr. Paul Pearlman. I did a paper on you and your films at a psychiatric convention.

SANDY *(Looking at the doctor)*   Thank you. Oh, really?

DR. PEARLMAN   It was very well received, you'll be happy to know.

SANDY   Oh, I'm glad to hear that.
Sandy has made it to the house phone on the wall. He signs another autograph as Dr. Pearlman continues to speak, oblivious to the crowds.

MALE FAN *(Looking at the paper Sandy has just autographed)*   Thanks.

DR. PEARLMAN (*Overlapping the male fan*) For my . . . for my own records, would you tell me—

SANDY (*Nodding impatiently*) Yeah. Yeah.

DR. PEARLMAN Have you ever had intercourse with any type of animal?

VIVIAN (*Pushing Dr. Pearlman away from Sandy*) Dr. Pearlman, please!

SANDY (*Picking up the phone receiver as he answers Dr. Pearlman*) With an animal? No, I never . . . (*Talking into the telephone, interrupting himself*) Hello? Yeah?
An old man with a hearing aid approaches Sandy, ignoring the fact that he is talking on the phone. He takes Sandy's hand and begins pumping it up and down, grinning gleefully.

OLD MAN (*Shaking Sandy's hand*) Very good! Very good!

SANDY (*To the old man, while holding the phone receiver to his ear*) Oh, thank you very much. Thank you.

OLD MAN (*Overlapping, still shaking Sandy's hand*) Keep up the good work, and good luck!

SANDY (*Still holding the phone, still talking to the old man*) Thank you. Oh. (*Vivian walks over and drags the old man away while Sandy talks into the telephone*) N-no. I don't think that's fair . . . What?
A giggly girl with very long hair runs over to Sandy, ignoring his attempts to talk on the telephone. She stands next to him and points to her boyfriend, standing a few feet away from her, holding up a camera.

GIRL Please, Mr. Bates, do you mind if we take a picture? Over here, Mr. Bates. (*Sandy turns in the direction the girl requests. He smiles at the camera, still holding the telephone receiver*) Thank you so much. One more picture! One more picture!
The girl and her boyfriend begin to switch places when Vivian's husband walks over and pulls them away; the girl continues to plead to Sandy as she's led offscreen.

SANDY (*Overlapping the girl, into the telephone*) No, I don't want 'em to touch the film . . . No, tell him to come up here tomorrow and we'll talk about it. They can't recut my film! Y-uh!
As Sandy hangs up the phone, Claire, a very prim woman in a suit and a high-necked blouse with a bow at the collar, approaches him.

CLAIRE   I know this is an imposition, but my name is Claire Schaeffer and I do work with the blind.
An elderly woman walks over and hugs Sandy, interrupting Claire.

ELDERLY WOMAN *(Overlapping)*   Oh, Mr. Bates, you're a genius, an absolute genius.

SANDY *(Overlapping the old woman, listening to Claire)*   Oh, yeah? Really? Yes.

CLAIRE *(Nodding)*   And we have a celebrity auction this month.

SANDY *(Overlapping, to the elderly woman)*   Yes, thank you. *(To Claire)* Uh-huh?

CLAIRE   If you could donate something, like an ashtray, or a pair of socks?

SANDY *(Nodding)*   Oh, sure. Be no problem at all, really.
Another fan, a man, approaches Sandy as he talks to Claire; the fan holds a piece of paper.

MALE FAN   Excuse me, Mr. Bates, may I have your autograph, please?

CLAIRE *(Overlapping the male fan)*   Somebody told me you wear a truss. An old truss would just be wonderful.

SANDY *(Reacting)*   Uh. A truss? *(Laughing)* No, I don't wear a truss.

MALE FAN *(Looking at the autograph, interrupting)*   Thank you very much.
The male fan walks off; an old man, wearing a hearing aid, and his wife approach Sandy next. Sandy has not yet been able to move from the wall phone area.

CLAIRE *(Reacting to Sandy's truss remark, with disappointment)*   Oh.

OLD MAN WITH HEARING AID *(Overlapping Claire)*   Say hello to my wife Rash. We were to Israel, and they love you there. They're just crazy about you.
Vivian comes over and drags off the old man and his wife; the old man continues to look back, talking.

SANDY *(To the departing old man)*   Oh.

OLD MAN *(Turning in Vivian's grasp)*   Shalom!
Jack walks over to Sandy as a woman fan, wearing a peasant dress, holds up a flash camera and takes Sandy's picture.

JACK (*Holding out his hand to Sandy*)   I'm Jack Abel.

SANDY (*Shaking Jack's hand*)   Hi. How are you?

JACK   I teach screenwriting at Columbia.

SANDY (*Reacting to the flash from the woman fan's camera*)   Hey! Geez, what is this? (*Laughing*) It's unbelievable.
The woman fan walks off; Jack continues to speak, one hand in his army jacket pocket.

JACK   If I could get you to come up and lecture to my students, it would make me a hero.

SANDY   Oh, I'm not the type that lectures. It's just . . .
Sandy is interrupted by a gypsylike woman who thrusts a large salami in his face.

WOMAN WITH SALAMI   For your enjoyment, with my genuine affection.

SANDY (*Nodding, taking the salami*)   Thank you very much. I really appreciate this. It's exactly what I need.
As the salami woman walks away, Grimsby, a nondescript-looking man in a suit, takes her place. He holds out a piece of paper.

GRIMSBY   Mr. Bates, people are always telling me how much we look alike. So, if you could take my name, maybe next time you do a—

SANDY (*Interrupting, looking at Grimsby*)   So I . . . you—I can see that. Okay.
Sandy laughs. Vivian once again appears and drags Grimsby away. Jack looks on, reacting.

JACK   This is a madhouse.

SANDY (*Looking at the salami in his hand*)   I've got a suggestive item of food here.
Vivian rushes over and takes the salami.

VIVIAN   Let me take this salami.

SANDY (*Holding out the record he'd been given earlier*)   Can you take this? I—
He laughs as Vivian takes the gifts and walks off. Daisy, who's been leaning against a wall, walks over to Jack and Sandy.

JACK (*Gesturing to Daisy*)   Daisy and I were going to go grab a beer. If you'd like to come with us—

SANDY *(To Daisy, interrupting Jack)*   Hi.

DAISY *(Nodding)*   Hi.

JACK   —we'd love to have you.

SANDY   Oh, God, I would love it.

JACK   Would you?

SANDY   Yeah.

JACK *(Overlapping)*   'Cause I know a roadside place about a quarter of
a mile from here.
They start walking through the lobby, to the main entrance of the hotel.

SANDY *(Reacting, gesturing around the lobby)*   I don't believe this. I don't
know what's going on.
*Simon, a small man in a sweater, rushes over to Sandy before the group have
a chance to walk out of the hotel. He grabs Sandy's arm and gestures excitedly.*

SIMON   Can I talk to you about an idea for a film I have?

SANDY *(Trying to shrug him off)*   Oh, this is not the place. Really.

SIMON *(Pleading)*   Do you have a moment, please?

SANDY *(Shaking his head)*   No, no, no, no.

SIMON *(Overlapping)*   It's a comedy.

SANDY *(Overlapping, reacting)*   Please.

SIMON *(Overlapping)*   Uh, uh, based on that whole Guyana mass suicide thing.

SANDY   Oh, great.
*The threesome walk away from Simon, who continues to talk about his idea
to Sandy's departing figure. The group almost makes it to the doors; the lobby
is still crowded with smoke and people. Just as they are about to walk outside,
an old, hunched-over man who used to be in vaudeville walks over to them.*

VAUDEVILLIAN   Sandy, this is what I did in vaudeville years ago. I did
this in vaudeville.

SANDY *(Looking over his shoulder at the old man)*   What?

VAUDEVILLIAN *(Singing)*   Give me the spotlight, give me the stage and
leave the rest to me . . .

SANDY (*Nodding, reacting*)   That's great.

The old man continues to sing and dance, following Jack, Sandy and Daisy until they finally make it outside; other fans, still milling about in the lobby, watch them go. Someone takes a picture of Sandy's back, and the film cuts to Jack's car driving down a neon-lit suburban highway. Music is heard; an old, German-like voice sings "Brazil."

The movie cuts to the singer, performing on the stage of a dark roadside club. She is a fading Lili Marlene-type cabaret singer, chubby and wearing a sequined dress. An aging pianist sits at his piano, sharing her spotlight.

The woman continues to sing as the camera cuts to the audience, clustered around small tables in the dark club. It moves close to the small round table where Sandy, Jack, and Daisy sit, talking over the woman's singing. Daisy is still wearing her sunglasses; she is silent, looking down, while Jack speaks to Sandy. The camera circles the table, moving closer and closer, as they talk.

JACK   Comedy is hostility.

SANDY (*Nodding*)   Uh-hmm.

JACK   It's rage.

SANDY (*Nodding*)   Uh-hmm.

JACK   I don't have to give you that clichéd speech. What is it the comedian says when his jokes are going well? "I murdered that audience"... "I killed 'em"... "They screamed"..."I broke 'em up."

SANDY   Yeah. So-so what are you saying? Are you saying that someone like-like myself or (*Coughing*) or Laurel and Hardy, or-or Bob Hope are furious?

JACK   Furious or latent homosexual.
Sandy laughs.

JACK   It's hidden behind the jokes.
Daisy laughs.

SANDY   I can't speak for those guys, but—

DAISY (*Interrupting Jack*)   Jack, I think that's a little—

JACK (*Interrupting Daisy*)   It's only theory . . . we're only theorizing.

SANDY (*Laughing, turning to Daisy*)   What do you do, Daisy? Are you a teacher too?

DAISY (*Shaking her head, fumbling with a cigarette pack*)   No, no, I don't . . . uh . . .

JACK (*Overlapping*)   She's a brilliant violinist.

SANDY   Really? Is that so?

DAISY (*Shrugging*)   Well, that's an exaggeration. I mean—

JACK (*Interrupting*)   She's with the Philharmonic.

DAISY   Yeah, but . . .

SANDY (*Reacting, overlapping*)   No kidding. That's very impressive.

DAISY   Well, I sit way in the back. You know, it's one of those things.
*The woman is still singing "Brazil." Jack turns to Daisy and takes her empty
cigarette pack. He stands up.*

JACK (*To Daisy*)   Get you some Camels? (*To Sandy*) Excuse me.
Jack walks off.

DAISY (*To Jack's retreating back*)   Yeah, thanks. (*Taking off her sunglasses,
looking at Sandy*) So, um, can I ask you a question? Um, is it my
imagination or . . . or, um, have you been kinda looking at me all
night? Um, I mean, tell me if I'm wrong . . . I don't know . . .

SANDY (*Sitting down in Jack's vacant seat*)   Does it bother you?

DAISY   No, no, no. I mean—I mean, I was just wondering, you know
. . . What-what's so interesting?

SANDY   I-I can—I've never seen such a sexy classical violinist before.
(*Daisy laughs as a waiter walks by, carrying a tray of drinks*) I mean it.
Uh, usually they're escaped Hungarians.

DAISY   No, I'm from Winnetka, Illinois.

SANDY   Are you?

DAISY (*Looking down*)   Yeah.

SANDY   Funny, 'cause you remind me of somebody. It's the strangest
thing. Mm-hmm. Yeah. I . . . I mean, i-i-i-it's not that you look like
her, or anything. I-it's just that there's some kind of odd . . . sense
that I have. It . . .
*Daisy laughs; the female singer finishes her song, and as the audience, includ-
ing Daisy and Sandy, applauds, an announcer introduces the next act offscreen.*

ANNOUNCER VOICE-OVER   And now the Brooklyn Boys' Club is happy
to present the amazing Sandy.

*Daisy and Sandy, still clapping, look offscreen at the stage, and the film cuts
to the darkened stage where a young Sandy, wearing a magician's cape,
stands blowing kisses to an adoring audience. A young girl with long blond
curls assists Sandy, introducing him to the audience with a wave of her hands.
She walks offstage as Sandy turns to a small table holding a white globe. He
moves his hands over it; the globe begins to rise. Eastern-like music plays in
the background.*

*The camera moves briefly to the audience staring in amazement at the young
Sandy and his magic trick. They murmur enthusiastically.*

A MALE AUDIENCE MEMBER   Incredible.

*As Sandy continues to wave his arms over the floating globe, the blond
assistant crosses the stage, gesturing, encouraging the audience to applaud
more. She walks over to Sandy and makes an "okay" sign to him, smiling.
The music continues in the background.*

*The camera goes back to the audience, to a sophisticated group, consisting of
an Italian couple, Marina and Dimitri, and Judith Crist, clustered around
a round table, smoking cigarettes and watching with cool appreciation. They
are dramatically backlit, as if sitting in black space.*

MARINA   *È straordinario e divino.*

DIMITRI (*Nodding his head*)   *È vero. Magnifico.*

JUDITH CRIST   The boy's a natural. I've never seen anything like it. A born magician.
The camera cuts to Sandy's mother, sitting at another table and looking directly at the camera.

SANDY'S MOTHER   Well, he should be. He sits in his room alone and practices for hours.
A man talks to her offscreen, as if he were an interviewer.

MAN'S VOICE   You sure he's not doing something else?

SANDY'S MOTHER   Oh, he does that, too. *(She holds up several photographs of half-nude women in erotic poses in front of her face)* I found these pictures hidden in his drawer.
While the rest of the audience chatters in the background, the camera moves to the table where Sandy's analyst sits, a distinguished-looking man with a pointy gray beard.

SANDY'S ANALYST *(Looking directly into the camera)*   It causes him great guilt. I don't know if I can ever cure him. I've been treating him for years already.
The camera is back on the stage. The young Sandy, looking serious in his glasses, holds up a cane. He moves his hand down its stem and the cane turns into a bouquet of flowers; his assistant stands in the back of the stage holding another cane and a deck of oversized cards. The audience gasps and applauds in pleased amazement.
The music stops and the film cuts back to the Stardust Hotel lobby. It's a bit later. Sandy, Daisy and Jack are walking inside, returning from their night at the roadside club. The lobby looks deserted; its décor, seen finally without the constant stream of people, looks nineteen-fortyish, like a white stucco Southern California villa. A large coffee table in the center of the room holds a huge urn of flowers; the staircase leading to the other floors is closed off by floor-to-ceiling columns that create an archlike effect to the stairs; the staircase and its balustrades look dramatically framed, resembling an old-time glamorous Hollywood movie set. The group's footsteps are heard on the empty tiled floor; they stop near the staircase to say good night.

SANDY   Well, thanks for a nice, uh, a nice time.

DAISY   Sure.

SANDY   I'll see you guys.

DAISY See you around.

JACK Bye.
As Daisy and Jack make their way up the stairs, Sandy starts walking across the lobby to the doorway leading to his suite of rooms. He is stopped in his silent ambling by a young actor in a rumpled plaid shirt who's been waiting in a lobby easy chair.

ACTOR *(Running up to Sandy)* Hey, Sandy! I hate to hassle you or anything, but I just—I got to tell you . . . I love you.
Sandy laughs; the actor starts walking next to him, gesturing and talking.

ACTOR I mean, I love your work.

SANDY Oh, thank you. Thank you.

ACTOR I'm an actor. Right now I'm working as a busboy, but really I am an actor.

SANDY *(Nodding)* Ah-hah, ah-hah.

ACTOR Anyway, I don't want to bug you or anything, I just want to give you a picture for your files.
The actor digs into a manila envelope and hands Sandy a photograph.

SANDY *(Looking at the photograph)* Ah-hah. You-you should mail this to my office—

ACTOR *(Handing Sandy another photograph, interrupting)* Here's another picture.

SANDY *(Nodding tiredly)* —you know. You should—you should—

ACTOR *(Interrupting, handing Sandy yet another photograph)* Here's a composite I have of myself.

SANDY *(Sighing)* Yeah, well, you should send this stuff all to my office.

ACTOR *(Ignoring Sandy's protestations, handing him a paper)* And a résumé.

SANDY Yeah, I-I'm gonna go to sleep now. You know, I—

ACTOR *(Interrupting)* If you don't mind, they'll be just-just a second.
They walk through some windowed lobby doors into the hallway leading to Sandy's suite. Sandy mutters to himself; the actor continues to talk.

ACTOR *(Nervously)*   I could give you . . . well, here's some of the reviews . . . on the things that critics have said about me. That's from, uh, that's from the Jersey *Journal.*
He laughs.

SANDY *(Sighing)*   You know, I shouldn't take this, actually. I . . . right. That's great. *(Laughing)* Oh, but you—

ACTOR *(Interrupting)*   Here's a picture of me as Tevye in *Fiddler on the Roof.* I did that in high school.

SANDY   Really? Oh. Did you? Did you?

ACTOR   Let's see . . . *(Sandy stops, resigned and looks back through the glass-paned doors to the lobby staircase. Framed by one of the arched windows are Jack and Daisy, walking up the stairs arm in arm. They stop and kiss passionately. Sandy stares at them intently as the actor, offscreen, continues to hustle his wares)* . . . here's a résumé. That's where I did Ensign Pulver. I worked in regional theater. Ensign Pulver in *Mister Roberts* there.
The film cuts to a beach. It is daylight; the waves can be heard hitting the sand. The wind is blowing a film crew's equipment slightly as cameramen, technicians, production assistants and actors walk busily on and off the screen, setting up a scene for a movie.
Dorrie sits, her legs crossed, on a director's chair behind some scaffolding. She is intently reading a book and gently pushing away some hair that has blown in her face from the wind. Sandy's voice is heard offscreen.

SANDY'S VOICE-OVER   Hey, I'm-I'm crazy about you.

DORRIE *(Looking up from her book, smiling)*   You don't even know who I am.

SANDY'S VOICE-OVER   Yeah, but you-I've just been looking at you all morning. And you-you're—I gotta tell you—you-you're incredibly beautiful, whoever you are.

DORRIE *(Slightly nodding, looking offscreen at Sandy)*   Yeah, well, it's true I am. I guess I'm a little on the beautiful side.

SANDY'S VOICE-OVER   Yeah, but . . . and you're real interesting. I mean, I've been watching you all morning and you just . . . just sittin' off by yourself and reading. You got a real strange quality.

DORRIE *(Smiling)*   Go on, keep going. You're getting through.

SANDY'S VOICE-OVER   Yeah? Ha-how long you been acting?

DORRIE *(Pushing away some windblown hair)*   Oh, I guess I'm always acting.

SANDY'S VOICE-OVER   Yeah?

DORRIE   Mm-hmm.
Sandy moves on to the screen; he walks over to Dorrie and pulls over a wooden crate next to her chair. He wears a large army jacket and a woolen cap. A group of male extras, dressed as sailors, sit down in the background; a group of female extras, wearing swimsuits, walk by chatting.

SANDY *(Staring at Dorrie, sitting down on the crate)*   Can I sit next to you?

DORRIE   Sure. Be my guest.

SANDY   Yeah? So tell me about yourself. Who are you? Give me-give me a lot of personal information immediately 'cause uh, don't hold anything back. I mean, are you married? Are you living with somebody?

DORRIE   Mmm . . . I just —I'm fascinating, but I'm trouble.

SANDY *(Laughing)*   Trouble?

DORRIE *(Smiling)*   Yeah.

SANDY   Yeah? You said the right thing. I—   So, so are you free for dinner, or what? Uh, what are your plans later? Don't feel obligated to say yes because I'm the director of the film.

DORRIE *(Laughing and shaking her head)*   It's just . . . I mean this is a big coup for me. I'm a-I'm a nobody with a one-line part and I-and I managed to impress you just by sitting around speed reading Schopenhauer.

SANDY *(Pointing at the book on Dorrie's lap)*   Yeah, do you understand any of that stuff?

DORRIE   No, but I can fake my way through most situations.

SANDY *(Staring at Dorrie)*   Yeah?

DORRIE *(Staring at Sandy)*   Yeah.

SANDY   Well, I gotta tell ya, I'm fatally attracted to you, so don't blow it. Because . . . you know . . .

DORRIE *(Overlapping)* Well, I'll . . . do my best. And it hasn't failed me yet.

Some romantic jazz is heard as the film cuts to Dorrie and Sandy standing in front of a spinning carousel. It is dark, raining. Sandy holds an umbrella over their heads. They look at each other as the camera moves backwards, revealing a movie crew, complete with lights and camera, filming the romantic couple in the rain.

*The music continues as daylight at the beach is seen on the screen. Sandy walks over some dunes, on the other side of an iron fence. He walks over to Dorrie, who is standing with her back to him. He spins her around; she slaps him. Sandy takes off his glasses and rubs his eyes; he gestures negatively to someone offscreen. A hand holding a movie slate board moves in front of the fenced-in scene. The slate, reading "Suppression/Scene 42/Director—*SANDY BATES*/ Cameraman—*L.* CHAPIN*/Date-5/11/81/Producer—R.* POLL*," is clapped. The hand moves offscreen. Dorrie laughs and rubs Sandy's face where she'd slapped him and the film cuts to:*

INTERIOR. SANDY'S PENTHOUSE APARTMENT—DAY.

The white table is set for dinner; the mural projected on the wall behind the table shows the Marx Brothers bigger-than-life. Sandy, in a plaid shirt, is standing at the table as Dorrie, wearing a white lace slip, comes into the room from the kitchen. She is towel-drying her just-washed hair as she walks over to him. She pours herself some wine.

DORRIE Your spaghetti could have used another twenty minutes.

SANDY You said *al dente*. I was giving you my best shot here. Wh-what do . . . you don't want a—

DORRIE *(Interrupting)* *Al dente* . . . that was so crispy.

SANDY God! Come on, you don't want a limp noodle, do you? *(Dorrie laughs, sipping her wine)* You know, my spaghetti with a nice Czechoslovakian sauce, that's-that's my specialty, and I—

DORRIE *(Interrupting)* I suppose it's different.

SANDY Yeah. It's a congealed, disgusting spaghetti. Where did you learn so much about wine?

DORRIE My father's an expert.

SANDY *(Laughing)* Oh, her father. This is incredible. I mean, what is this guy not an expert in? He's-he's a tennis player, and-and a—a-an

antique connoisseur, and-and a wine expert, and-and he's probably
gorgeous, right? With the graying temples, and the aquiline profile.

DORRIE He's a great-looking man.
*She walks into the living room of the apartment. She talks to Sandy without
looking at him, sipping her wine and staring into space instead.*

SANDY *(Offscreen)* Yeah, I'll bet.

DORRIE Whenever Mother was away in the sanitariums, the ladies,
they flocked around him.
*Sandy walks over to Dorrie and puts his hands on her shoulders, massaging
her.*

SANDY Yeah? And what about you? Tell me, did you-did you have a
little crush on him? You can admit this to me if you like.
*Dorrie moves her shoulder with the back rub, but still stares into space,
sipping her wine.*

DORRIE Sure. We had a little flirt every now and then.

SANDY You had a little—a little small flirt? Your mother away getting
shock treatments and the only beautiful daughter home . . . long,
lingering breakfasts with Dad? Is this getting nauseating?

DORRIE Yeah. But I was no competition for my mother because she
was very beautiful.

SANDY Your mother?

DORRIE Yes.

SANDY Your back is . . . is—

DORRIE *(Interrupting)* I know, it's very tense.

SANDY —really knotted up. What . . . what was your mother diag-
nosed as? Was she schizophrenic? Or—?

DORRIE *(Interrupting)* She was schizophrenic, she was depressive, she
was–
*Dorrie stops in midsentence and moves away. Sandy, still talking, walks over
to the couch. He sits down, putting one foot on the coffee table; a glass door
leading to an outside terrace is behind him.*

SANDY Oh, I see. The full complement of uh . . . nasties. It's funny,
because in my family nobody ever committed suicide, nobody . . .
this was just not a middle-class alternative, you know? I— My

mother was too busy running the boiled chicken through the deflavorizing machine to think about shooting herself or anything. God . . . *(Sighing)* So—did-did you always want to be an actress? *Dorrie walks over to Sandy. Holding a bottle of wine, she sits down on the edge of the coffee table and tries to open the bottle.*

DORRIE *(Opening the wine, her head down)* No, I'm not really an actress.

SANDY *(Touching Dorrie's back with his foot still on the coffee table)* You're good, Dorrie. You have a real— You do. You have a real interesting quality on the screen.

DORRIE No, you're just saying that.

SANDY No, you're wrong. You have . . . it's not so . . . you have a real charming quality. You got a real— You're a natural. Yeah.

DORRIE I'm a natural. I'm a natural at everything I do and then I wind up not being able to do anything.

SANDY No, you're wrong. You've got real, genuine charisma on the screen. It's true. You're sexy; you got no confidence, of course, but-but you got a real charming quality. *Sandy stops talking and moving his foot. He gasps as a pigeon flies in through the glass door of the terrace.*

DORRIE *(Looking up at the fluttering bird)* Oh! What was that thing? It's a pigeon. *Sandy, excited, stands up and begins throwing magazines from the coffee table at the pigeon.*

SANDY *(Flinging the magazines)* What was that? What was that?

DORRIE Hey, that's so pretty. A pigeon!

SANDY *(Running after the pigeon, trying to catch it)* Geez . . . no, it's not pretty at all. They're . . . they're . . . they're rats with wings. *He runs out of the room. Dorrie, standing up, watches the pigeon fly circling the ceiling.*

DORRIE They're wonderful. No! It's probably a good omen. It'll bring us good luck.

SANDY *(Offscreen, from the kitchen)* No . . . no, get it out of here. It's probably one of those killer pigeons. *Sandy runs back into the living room carrying a fire extinguisher. He runs around, trying to shoot the pigeon with the extinguisher's spray.*

DORRIE *(Reacting to Sandy's extinguisher attempts)*   No, get something for it to eat. We can coax it down! What are you doing? Hey, wait!

SANDY   You see, it's got a swastika under its wings.

DORRIE   It's wonderful. *(Laughing)* Not that.
Dorrie walks over to the frantic Sandy, his back to her, watching the pigeon. She puts her arms around him.

SANDY   I just . . . I just want to guide it out of the apartment. Geez. I don't want a winged thing in my house.
He mumbles; Dorrie turns him to her. They kiss.
As they embrace, the pigeon flies back outside through the terrace doors, and the film is once again at the Stardust Hotel. For a brief moment the screen shows the exterior of the hotel, the pathway leading to its main entrance, its twinkling night lights, and then the film quickly cuts to Sandy's suite, its passageway leading to a partially seen desk holding a desk lamp. The memory's background music stops and Sandy walks into the scene, going down the passageway into his bedroom. He turns on his bedroom light and sees a hippyish-looking girl, Shelly, who is wearing a T-shirt with Sandy's picture, sitting up in his bed. Sandy, startled, reacts by turning the light back out.

SANDY   Oh, I'm sorry. Forgive me, I'm in the wrong room.

SHELLY   *(Giggling)*   No, no, no, no, you're right. This is your room.

SANDY   I'm—

SHELLY   *(Interrupting, turning the light back on)*   Isn't this fun? I-I tipped the porter so I could meet you.

SANDY   *(Throwing his keys down on the four-poster and walking to the other side of the room)*   Oh, Jesus, you're kidding. You're telling me they let you in here?

SHELLY   Well, I know you get this all the time, I—

SANDY   *(Interrupting, gesturing)*   No, I don't.

SHELLY   No—but, you know, I have a psychic, and-and I asked-asked her about you, and she told me that we were destined to make it together.
Sandy walks around the room, taking off his jacket and trying to prepare himself for bed.

SANDY   *(Reacting)*   Look, whoever you are, please, I'm tired. Go away.

SHELLY Well, I won-I won't stay over. I mean, I-I just know you're a Sagittarius and, and Sagittarians get along really well with Pisces, 'cause I'm a Pisces.

SANDY (*Stopping for a moment at the bed*) Yeah?

SHELLY And I think that-that—

SANDY (*Interrupting*) Will you get out of the bed, please?
Shelly turns her head and pulls a package of brownies out from under the bed covers.

SHELLY Uh, well, wait here. And I drove all the way from Bridgeport to make it with you.

SANDY (*Taking the brownies*) Yeah? Oh, what is this? The-the traditional brownies with hash? Is this what you're giving me?
Shelly hands Sandy another smaller package in a plastic bag.

SHELLY No, no. Look, here's the hash on the side because I didn't know how much you took.

SANDY (*Reacting*) How much I took? What is it, hollandaise sauce? What do you mean, how much I took?

SHELLY (*Shrugging*) Well . . . well . . . I mean, you—

SANDY (*Interrupting*) You-you got in a car and you drove a-a-a long distance to go through mechanical sex with a stranger. Is this what you—what you do?

SHELLY Well, my husband drove me. We-we have a van.

SANDY (*Gesturing, walking into the bathroom*) Your husband? You're kidding. Is your-is your husband here?
The camera stays focused on an empty area of the bedroom. Sandy, in the bathroom, and Shelly, in the bed, talk to each other offscreen.

SHELLY Oh, he would be so honored if I could tell him that we made it. He's-he's a—he's a great fan of yours. He's got—he's got all your albums. He sees every movie. He talks about you all the time. You're one of his heroes.

SANDY I'm sure. Oh, yeah. He's not insanely jealous?
Sandy walks into camera view; he starts opening closets, talking all the while.

SHELLY No, we never have any problems with that.

SANDY   And exactly where is your husband right now?

SHELLY   Oh, he's sleeping in the van downstairs.
The camera moves back to the bed, where Shelly is still sitting up, leaning against the four-poster's wooden headboard.

SANDY *(Sighing)*   Hey, look, I don't feel that well. I'm tired. I don't want to go through an empty experience. I've had—

SHELLY *(Interrupting)*   Listen, empty sex is better than no sex, right? Come on, don't be so angry.
Shelly moves over and turns off the light. Melodramatic music begins over the darkness and the film cuts to the movie screen in the Stardust Hotel's auditorium. A scene taking place in a snowy Central Park is projected on the screen. A group of police, snapping bloodhounds, Sandy (as Sydney) and Sandy's analyst are running through the snow. A radio announcer's voice is heard over the action.

RADIO ANNOUNCER'S VOICE *(In Walter Winchell style)*   We interrupt this program to bring you a special bulletin. Sydney Finklestein's hostility has escaped. Finklestein, a short man with glasses, told police that he had been fighting to hold his anger in for years. And he's very embarrassed that it broke loose while he napped. Police are combing the countryside and warn all citizens to stay indoors.
The group begins passing a number of bodies lying in the snow.

SANDY AS SYDNEY *(Pointing to all of the sprawled bodies, reacting)*   My God, look. That-that's my schoolteacher, Miss Reilly. *(Pointing to other prone bodies)* Oh, geez, look. That's my ex-wife and her-her alimony lawyer. And my brother Alvin. Geez, he-he's the one that-that they taught to speak up. He-he'd always come downstairs and recite. *(Pointing straight ahead)* Look. That's my mother.
The hostility monster, a huge beast covered in fur, is tossing Sandy's mother up and down in the snow. She is screaming; the monster is roaring. The group stares at the monster, unable to move, except for the pointy-bearded analyst who walks closer to the beast, trying to talk in reasonable tones to him.

SANDY'S ANALYST *(Gesturing with his pipe)*   Please, uh, we don't want to hurt you. We want to reason with you. *(Sandy's mother goes on screaming, still in the monster's arms)* I'm a psychoanalyst. *(Holding out his pipe)* This is my pipe. *(The audience in the auditorium laughs)* I want to help you.

The melodramatic music stops; the camera moves from the screen to the audience; the crowd is laughing, reacting to the action that had been on the screen. A man in the audience, wearing a leisure suit, asks the first question.

A MAN IN THE AUDIENCE *(Standing up, asking the first question)* Your films are always psychological, never political. Where do you stand politically?
Sandy is once again standing at the podium on the stage. Vivian is sitting proprietorially next to him, wearing print lounging pajamas and listening to every word he says. Reporters and photographers stand off to the left of the stage.

SANDY What can I say to that? I'm-I'm for uh, total, honest democracy. You know. And I also believe the American system can work.
The audience laughs; some of the people in the packed auditorium chatter to each other.

A WOMAN IN THE AUDIENCE *(Raising her hand)* A lot of people have accused you of being narcissistic.
The audience laughs.

SANDY No, I know people think that I'm egotistical and narcissistic, but it's not true. I-I . . . uh, I—as-as a matter of fact, if I did identify with a Greek mythological character, it would not be Narcissus.

ANOTHER MAN IN THE AUDIENCE Who would it be?

SANDY Zeus.
The audience continues to laugh as the film cuts to the Stardust Hotel lobby. A cancer-society representative, wearing an elaborately veiled hat, approaches an offscreen Sandy; she fills the screen.

CANCER REPRESENTATIVE Mr. Bates?

SANDY *(Offscreen)* Uh-huh.

CANCER REPRESENTATIVE I'm with the Cancer Society—

SANDY *(Offscreen; interrupting, distracted)* Right.

CANCER REPRESENTATIVE —and it would mean so much to so many people if you could appear at our benefit.
The camera moves back, revealing Sandy, once again trying to walk through the room, followed by his entourage of eager fans trying to talk to him, touch him, or get his autograph.

SANDY   I would be glad to. Just call me when I get back into town. I do 'em—I do it all the time.
Vivian is standing behind Sandy, trying to keep the fans away. A Russian man, wearing an ascot, approaches Sandy as the cancer representative finishes her conversation.

CANCER REPRESENTATIVE *(Walking away)*   Thank you.

SANDY *(To the cancer representative)*   Really.

RUSSIAN MAN *(Walking with Sandy)*   So, did you know that as we speak, Russian scientists are being forcibly detained in insane asylums?

SANDY   Yeah, well, I'm on a committee for that. You know what I mean? So I've signed petitions and all that.

RUSSIAN MAN *(Holding out a piece of paper)*   Oh, good. Terrific. You know what? Would you sign this autograph? It's for my wife.

SANDY *(Signing the paper)*   Yeah. Oh, yeah, sure.

RUSSIAN MAN *(Looking at Sandy as he signs his autograph)*   Uh, to Hilda.
Jerry Abraham points his finger at Sandy. He wears a printed shirt and gestures excitedly.

JERRY *(Overlapping the retreating Russian man)*   Sandy Brockman from Flatbush Avenue. Jerry Abraham!

SANDY   I-I know! I remember!

JERRY   We went to school together, right? You used to dress as Superman—you tried to fly . . .
More fans approach Sandy and he signs autographs for them as he continues to talk to Jerry.

SANDY *(Signing autographs, to Jerry)*   I remember. I remember.

JERRY   Look, I know you're busy now. When can we talk?

SANDY   I'll be here all weekend.

JERRY *(Waving)*   Okay, take care.
Jerry walks off as a man in a white shirt gives Sandy a manila envelope.

SANDY *(Looking at the envelope in his hand)*   What-what is this?

MAN IN WHITE SHIRT   Don't read it now. Wait until later. My son wrote it . . . it's-it's-it's-it's perfect for you. It's a spoof on jockeys.
Sandy sees Jack and Daisy in the background. He waves at them.

SANDY   How ya doing? *(To the man in white shirt)* On jockeys?

MAN IN WHITE SHIRT *(Gesturing with his hands)*   Yes, a spoof on jockeys
. . . little jockeys . . .

SANDY *(Walking away from the man in white shirt and other milling fans)*
Little tiny jockeys? Sounds great.

MAN IN WHITE SHIRT *(Calling after Sandy's retreating figure)*   Yes. Call.
Call. Okay?

VIVIAN *(Trying to disperse the milling fans)*   Would you go ahead please?
Yes, please.
*The film cuts to the hotel grounds. It is day. Sandy is standing near a pagoda,
surrounded by shrubbery. Guests walk by; the scene is peaceful, quiet. For
once, Sandy is without his hordes of fans. A man, fairly heavyset and wearing
a T-shirt, comes over to Sandy, trying to get his attention.*

MAN *(Giving Sandy a slip of paper)*   Sandy! Can I have your autograph?

SANDY *(Signing the paper)*   Oh, sure. There you go.
Sandy hands the paper back to the man.

MAN *(Solemnly)*   I was a Caesarean.

SANDY *(Laughing)*   Oooh, that's great.
*Old-time big-band jazz music begins playing in the background. Sandy turns
and looks down the hotel's long path. There is Isobel, blond and slightly
plump, walking toward him carrying an overnight bag. The camera stays
focused on her as she gets closer and closer until, the music still playing, she
greets a surprised Sandy.*

SANDY   Isobel, my God, what are you doing here?

ISOBEL *(Laughing)*   But you called me. You were lonely.

SANDY   I know, but what a surprise. What a— What a treat! Oh.
Jesus.
*They embrace on the hotel's garden path; a fat girl in pigtails interrupts them,
waving to Sandy, ignoring their private moment.*

FAT GIRL *(Overlapping)*   Sandy! Hey, Sandy, hi. I really loved your last
film.

SANDY *(To the fat girl, but looking at Isobel)*   Oh, thank you.

ISOBEL *(Overlapping)*   J'ai quelque chose très importante à te dire.

SANDY   Isobel . . . In English. Speak to me in English. I had . . . I had a very erotic dream about you last night. You know, I-I hope you brought your, your little tiny white cotton socks that I like, you know, because it's—

ISOBEL *(Interrupting)*   Listen . . . I left my husband.

SANDY *(Reacting)*   Oh. Really?

ISOBEL *(Nodding)*   He knew I was having an affair, and I did not want to lie to him.

SANDY *(Putting his hand to his chest, reacting)*   I'm . . . I'm stunned.

ISOBEL   That makes you . . . nervous, no?
Sandy and Isobel start walking down the path, still deep in conversation.

SANDY *(Chuckling and gesturing)*   I'm—   No-no-no, I-I'm not nervous. I-I-I-I'm just so . . . I just—

ISOBEL *(Interrupting)*   You don't have to—

SANDY *(Overlapping)*   I know we talked about it, I just—
He is interrupted by another female fan, a dark-haired woman who looks at him with the same yearning eyes as the first time she'd seen him, when he was getting out of his Rolls-Royce at the hotel at the beginning of the seminar.

FEMALE FAN *(Smiling coyly)*   Sandy, I knitted this sweater for you myself.

SANDY *(Taking the sweater, nodding)*   Oh, thanks, yeah, thanks very much. Thank you.
The girl walks off; Sandy and Isobel try to resume their conversation.

ISOBEL *(Overlapping Sandy's words to his fan)*   You know, you don't have to—

SANDY *(Interrupting Isobel)*   I just didn't think it would happen . . . I mean—

ISOBEL *(Interrupting)*   You don't have to worry about it. I just—I'm just going to take care of myself.

SANDY   No, I'm not worried about it. I'm just—I know, that's— What has that got to do— What does that mean, you're gonna take care—
Once again Sandy and Isobel are interrupted by Sandy's adoring and oblivious fans. This time it's two athletic-looking young men in T-shirts, shouting out their greetings as they walk by.

FIRST YOUNG MALE FAN *(Loudly)* We've seen all your films.

SECOND YOUNG MALE FAN *(Loudly)* They suck.

SANDY *(Reacting to the fans' words)* Oh.

FIRST YOUNG MALE FAN They're terrific.
The men stare at Sandy for a while in the background. Sandy and Isobel resume their conversation, ignoring the fans.

ISOBEL *(Rubbing Sandy's face)* Because I know your face, I know, I know you are going to be sick—

SANCY *(Interrupting)* I'm not going to be sick.

ISOBEL —to your stomach in one minute.

SANDY I'm just so stunned. I can't—I— You know, we discussed it, and—and I, and I, uh—

ISOBEL *(Interrupting)* Well, I think I am going to stay in a hotel, and find an apartment.
Sandy stops walking. He turns and looks at Isobel. The two male fans have gone away.

SANDY Honey, you're not staying in a hotel. The whole point was that you would leave your husband and stay with me. That we would live together, or-or-or marry, but-but be together.
A man in a suit approaches Sandy and Isobel, holding out a pad and pencil.

MAN Can I have your autograph?
Sandy takes the piece of paper and signs it; he continues to talk to Isobel, not really looking at his fan.

SANDY That's the point of it. You're not gonna stay at a hotel.

ISOBEL No, I—

SANDY *(Interrupting)* That's ridiculous.

ISOBEL Oh, I think it would be okay to live like that.
Sandy gives the autograph back to the man.

MAN *(Overlapping Isobel's speech)* Thank you.
The man walks away; Sandy does not look at him, intent instead on his conversation with Isobel.

SANDY *(To Isobel, reacting to her words)* No.

ISOBEL We could marry, but . . . there is no pressure.

SANDY Hey, I don't feel pressure. It's—i-i-i-i-it's funny. I had salmon for breakfast, you know.

ISOBEL Ah. Oh.

SANDY *(Rubbing his forehead)* And I . . . and I feel nauseous a little bit. It's— You know, they never . . . they never serve it fresh.

ISOBEL You know—you know something? I just brought up a wonder-ful bottle of wine, and my-my white socks. You know, the ones you like.

SANDY Uh. Ugh. Oh, I'm so— Gee, Isobel, I . . . *(Laughing)* Gee, I feel like such a fool.

ISOBEL *(Laughing)* Poor boy.
The interruptions still come. This time a woman, in white sunglasses, and her husband, in wire-rimmed glasses, come over, thrusting a pad and pencil in front of Sandy.

HUSBAND Excuse me, Mr. Bates, could I have your autograph, please?

SANDY *(Nodding to the couple)* Oh, yeah.

HUSBAND I've seen all of your films. You're a—you're a master of despair.

SANDY *(Nodding, signing his autograph)* Uh huh. Here.
He gives the paper back to the couple.

WIFE Such a touch of Kafka.
The eyeglassed couple walks away. Once again, Sandy and Isobel try to talk; Sandy still holds the hand-knit sweater.

ISOBEL Will you give me fifteen minutes? I'm going to have a bath, and you will come to the room.

SANDY Oh, gee. Iso— But what about the children?

ISOBEL *(Smiling)* But they're okay. They will come tomorrow.

CUT TO:
INTERIOR. STARDUST HOTEL AUDITORIUM—DAY.

The theater is dark, in contrast to the bright sunlight outside. For once, it's empty. Daisy, in her dark sunglasses and zippered sweatshirt, walks in and sits down in the front row. She turns as Sandy approaches.

SANDY *(Offscreen)* Hi.

DAISY *(Turning her head)* Hi.

SANDY *(Offscreen)* What are you doing here?

DAISY I just came in to be alone for a minute to think. What are you doing here?

SANDY *(Offscreen)* Oh, yeah? Oh, I— That's exactly what I was doing. I was sitting around, thinking . . . trying to get away. *Sandy walks onto the screen; he walks over to Daisy.*

DAISY What are you—what are you thinking about?

SANDY *(Sitting down next to Daisy)* Me? Oh . . . sss . . . Well, I was thinking about should I change my-my movie? Should I change my life? You know, all kinds of . . . you know . . . serious—

DAISY *(Laughing, interrupting)* Mmm-hmm. Yeah?

SANDY *(Laughing)* I am, I'm surprised.

DAISY You know, I had a dream about you last night.

SANDY Did you?

DAISY Yeah.

SANDY What did you dream?

DAISY *(Shaking her head)* I can't tell you.

SANDY Oh, come on, you can tell.

DAISY *(Smiling)* No, it was really, it was really embarrassing.

SANDY It really was? Really? Was it one of those?

DAISY No, I can't . . . *(Laughing)* Yeah, it rea— It was.

SANDY God, that's terrible.

DAISY Mm-hmm. Maybe if I get to know you better, I'll tell you. But I can't. No.
Daisy laughs. A teen-age girl, her hair in a long ponytail, approaches them from the second row.

SANDY *(Laughing)* Yeah? That sounds ver—

TEEN-AGE GIRL IN PIGTAILS (*Giggling and interrupting; handing Sandy a piece of paper and a pencil*)   Hi! Can I have your autograph?
The upbeat music, begun when Isobel had come to the hotel, stops as a second teen-age girl comes over to the group from the right-hand side of the front row. Both girls stare at Sandy, giggling, excited, hovering over him as he tries to talk to Daisy.

SANDY (*Reacting to the eager fans who'd found him in the dark auditorium*)   Oh, you're kidding. What—what do you guys do?

SECOND TEEN-AGE GIRL (*Handing Sandy another pad and pencil*)   Me, too.

SANDY (*Shaking his head; signing his autograph for the two girls*)   What do you guys do, follow me around?
The teen-age girl with the pigtails laughs.

SECOND TEEN-AGE GIRL (*Giggling, nodding*)   We follow you around.

TEEN-AGE GIRL IN PIGTAILS   Oh, we think you're so sexy.

SANDY (*Reacting*)   I'm sexy?

SECOND TEEN-AGE GIRL   So sexy . . .

TEEN-AGE GIRL IN PIGTAILS (*Overlapping*)   Yes, you really are.

SANDY (*Overlapping, to Daisy*)   They think I'm sexy.
Daisy laughs as the film cuts to Sandy's darkened penthouse apartment. For a brief moment, bright light from the hallway illuminates the room as Sandy and Dorrie enter the apartment, a flashback to the past.

SANDY   Come on, Dorrie.

DORRIE (*Taking off her coat*)   Don't lie to me. You're attracted to her.

SANDY   I'm not . . . I'm not attracted to her. What are you talking about?
Dorrie walks quickly into the bedroom, turning on the light. Sandy turns the light on in the living-room area, revealing a large newspaper-headlined mural about "Incest" behind the dining-room table.

DORRIE (*Offscreen from the bedroom*)   You keep staring at her all through dinner. Giving each other looks.

SANDY   Aw, what are you so— Oh, stop it. She's fourteen years—

DORRIE (*Interrupting, offscreen*)   Well, don't you think I see it?
Dorrie leaves the bedroom; she continues walking quickly, agitated, into the living room, the kitchen and dining area.

SANDY *(Calling after Dorrie's rushing form)* She's not even fourteen. She's—she's thirteen and a half.

DORRIE I don't care. I used to play those games with my father, so I know. I've been through all that.

SANDY What-what kind of games? I'm-I'm— You think I'm flirting with your kid cousin?

DORRIE Well, you can't take your eyes off her.

SANDY *(Walking toward the kitchen, where Dorrie is pacing; trying to placate her)* But she was sitting opposite me.

DORRIE Well, you smile at her.

SANDY Ye— I smile at her. I'm a friendly person. What do you want? She-she's a kid. This is stupid. I don't want to have this conversation.
Dorrie walks out of the kitchen and stands next to Sandy, who has been talking to her in its doorway.

DORRIE Don't tell me it's stupid. I used to do that with my father across the table. All those private jokes. I know.
She resumes her brisk pacing.

SANDY *(Gesturing, following Dorrie)* Do . . . do what? What private jokes? We were talking about movies. She-she likes funny movies. So we were-we were discussing it. *(Dorrie has stopped her wild pacing. Sandy walks past the newspaper-headline mural and faces her; they are framed by a circular interior window as Sandy continues to talk)* What-what—hey, what's the matter with you? Dorr-Dorrie, what's the matter with you? What's— You-you've-you're nuts. You-you know how—you know how ridiculous this sounds? What are you-what are you saying? That I'm—hey, hey, we used to— and I'm flirting with your kid cousin? I mean, doesn't that sound— It's-it's-it's absurd. Come on . . .
And the film cuts back to the present, to the living-room interior of a suburban house where Debbie, Sandy's sister, lives with her husband, Sam. Debbie, a black-haired woman in oval eyeglasses, is opening the door. The camera stays on her face, showing her surprised reaction to her guest. Clustered behind her, and coming forward as they see who's just entered, is a group of women friends, mostly overweight, in various muumuus, sweatshirts and jewelery. The walls of the living room are covered with a splashy wallpaper. A buffet, holding candlesticks and fruit, leans against the wall.

DEBBIE (*Opening the door, reacting*) Oh, my God.

SANDY (*Offscreen*) I was in the neighborhood. I had to say hello.

DEBBIE (*Walking backward into the living room as an offscreen Sandy comes forward*) Why didn't you call me?

SANDY (*Offscreen*) I-I-I'm appearing right near here. Right next—

DEBBIE (*Interrupting*) What a surprise! Come on in.

SANDY (*Offscreen, overlapping*) Oh, this is Isobel. This is my sister.

ISOBEL (*Offscreen as well*) Hi.

DEBBIE (*Gesturing*) Hello, Isobel. Oh, my God, Sam's gonna die. Come on in. Girls! My brother! Do you believe this?!
Debbie is well into the living room by now; her women friends are gathered behind her, beaming their smiles in Sandy's direction. An Indian guru, in suit and turban, stands with the group of women, smiling and nodding as well. The camera continues to stay focused on Debbie and her friends. Sandy and Isobel remain offscreen; the group of women friends look as if they are talking and smiling into the camera as they direct their speech and looks at the offscreen Sandy.

SANDY (*Offscreen, overlapping*) Wha-what are you shouting for?

DEBBIE (*Gesturing, overlapping*) This is my brother Sa— We're relaxed. We're all relaxed, Sandy.

SANDY (*Offscreen*) Did-did I come at a bad time?

DEBBIE No, you didn't come at a bad time. We're all doing yoga. We're all relaxed. Come on. You know everybody. I know you know Irene.
Irene moves closer to Debbie. She is a small, fat woman with a blond ponytail; her ample T-shirt says "Sexy" in elaborate script in front. As she nods and smiles at the offscreen Sandy, the camera stays focused on her face, marred by a half-concealed black eye and numerous bruises. The other yoga women continue to chatter excitedly, smiling and nodding, in the background.

IRENE (*To Sandy*) Hi. Remember?

SANDY (*Offscreen*) Oh, hi. Oh, yeah. (*Noticing Irene's bruised face*) What happened, Irene?

DEBBIE (*Gesturing*) It's so ironic. Look at her face.

IRENE (*Overlapping*) Ohh, no, you don't wanna know.

SANDY *(Offscreen)*   It's . . . it's . . . okay.

DEBBIE   We moved here to get away from the crime and garbage . . . and look what—   Look at this face.
A yoga woman friend in a muumuu interrupts Debbie.

YOGA WOMAN *(Interrupting, to Sandy)*   Oh, I just have to have your autograph.

SANDY *(Offscreen)*   Okay.

IRENE *(Talking over the yoga woman's request, gesturing)*   Oh, please.

DEBBIE   Someone broke into her house last week. They robbed her. They raped her and they beat—   Isobel, they raped her over and over again.

SANDY *(Offscreen)*   Up in the suburbs? Really?

IRENE   I wish that— *(Sighing, shaking her head)* It was horrible . . . just horrible.

DEBBIE   They tied her to the bed. Do you believe it?

IRENE *(Nodding)*   With my scarfs.

SANDY *(Offscreen)*   Really? That's—

IRENE *(Interrupting)*   I didn't even resist.

SANDY *(Offscreen)*   I'm sure you didn't resist, knowing you, Irene, you . . . you . . .

DEBBIE *(Interrupting, shaking her head and reacting)*   I gotta get outta here.

IRENE *(Overlapping)*   I didn't resist. Oh.

DEBBIE   I'm going crazy. Well, come on in. How about a drink? Isobel? Coffee? Tea?
Sandy and Isobel walk into view. They mill with the group of yoga women friends; Sandy shakes Irene's hand.

SANDY   Irene, you feel all right?

DEBBIE   Sa-Sandy, you gotta go see Sam. He's in the—he's in the bedroom and he's meditating and he's exercising.

IRENE *(To Sandy, overlapping Debbie's speech)*   Oh, I'm feeling better.

SANDY *(Shaking the guru's hand)*   Hello.
As the various women gather around Sandy, waving to him, smiling, and chattering among themselves, Sandy finally answers Debbie's earlier request.

SANDY   Sam. I will. I'll see Sam. *(To one of the women)* Hi. How are you?
One of the yoga friends hands Sandy a pad and pencil.

YOGA FRIEND   Would you, please?

SANDY *(Nodding, taking the pad and pencil)*   Yeah.

YOGA FRIEND *(Watching Sandy sign his autograph)*   To Kevin and Mendel.

DEBBIE *(Overlapping)*   Oh, don't bother him. He hates this. He hates this.

SANDY *(To the yoga friend)*   Kevin and Mendel? What are they, children?

YOGA FRIEND *(Nodding)*   Yes. They're my chil—

DEBBIE *(Interrupting)*   He—
The film abruptly cuts to Debbie's bedroom, where Sam, her husband, is busily working out on his exercise bicycle and talking to an offscreen Sandy. At first, the camera shows only Sam's feet pedaling away, around and around, accented by a tinny exercise bell that keeps ringing; the camera eventually moves back, revealing Sam's entire hefty body.

SAM   I had two heart attacks before I got the bicycle.

SANDY *(Offscreen)*   Um-hmm. And since then?

SAM   I also had two.
> *The camera cuts to Sandy, leaning against the wall, watching Sam and reacting.*
> *The film then moves back to the wallpapered living-room area. Debbie and Isobel are sitting at the dining-room table, looking through a photograph album. A huge metal coffee urn sits on a nearby buffet. The yoga women walk around in the background; one carries a bottle of wine.*

DEBBIE *(Pointing to a photograph in the album)*   Oh, this is-that's where we used to go to the seashore every summer.

ISOBEL *(Leaning her head on her elbow, looking at the album)*   It's cute. *(Pointing)* Oh . . . this is Sandy?

DEBBIE *(Nodding)*   That's Sandy.

ISOBEL   And you were . . . yeah.

DEBBIE *(Pointing)*   That's me as a baby.

ISOBEL *(Nodding)*   Oh . . . right . . . nice baby.

DEBBIE   Yes . . . yeah, my father stayed in the city . . . I think he fooled around. *(Pointing to a picture)* There he is.

ISOBEL   And your mother?

DEBBIE *(Pointing to another photograph)*   That's my mother. Oh, they were always fighting, always screaming at each other. Once the police had to come. *(Leafing through the album)* Oh, here's Sandy in the Hebrew school play.

ISOBEL *(Laughing)*   Oh, baby.

DEBBIE   My God, I haven't seen this picture in ages.

ISOBEL   He's so cute.

DEBBIE   Yeah. Glasses, skinny . . . look how skinny he is. Really skinny.

ISOBEL *(Laughing)*   Oh, yeah.
> *The camera moves closer to the photograph album. Old-time movie music begins as the film cuts to a school auditorium stage where a young Sandy in a robelike biblical costume fights with another costumed child. A rabbi comes onto the stage, trying to pull the children away from each other. Another*

rabbi comes along to help, then another and another. They move in rapid old-time movie motion and the music continues to play. Debbie's and Sandy's voices, commentaries to the action, are heard over the scene.

DEBBIE'S VOICE   Oh, remember how you got into that fight? It was awful.

SANDY'S VOICE   You know, I-I always resented Abraham being, you know, he was so willing to kill, uh, his son. It used to bother me.

DEBBIE'S VOICE   Yeah? I think it was jealousy. You wanted the part of God.

The music stops; the screen is washed clean by a black wipe, which turns into Debbie's bedroom. She and Sandy have just come in; Debbie has closed the door. Sandy stands against a dresser, his arms crossed, showing the elbow patches on his suit jacket. Debbie sits on the edge of her bed, eager to talk to her brother. One wall of the bedroom is covered in the same loud paper as the living room. Sam and his feet, pedaling away on the exercise bicycle, are seen in the corner; his exercise bell rings in rhythm with his feet.

DEBBIE *(Looking up at Sandy)*   Oh, she's a lovely girl.

SANDY *(Nodding)*   I know, she's wonderful.

DEBBIE   You gonna get married?

SANDY *(Sighing)*   I guess. You know, that's the thing—

DEBBIE *(Interrupting)*   Oh, what do you mean you guess? Yes or no?

SANDY   I mean, I mean—you know, it looks like the direction we're heading in.

DEBBIE   Well, are you in love with each other?

SANDY *(Sighing)*   Yeah, I suppose so. I—you know, I don't know what to say. You—because, i-uh-uh-it's a package deal. I get-I get a wife, I get a French wife and I get two kids overnight.

DEBBIE   Yeah?

SANDY   The question is, Do I want that? I like the idea that she's French. That I find romantic. But do I want to have two kids suddenly? And-and what? You know, I—

DEBBIE *(Interrupting)*   Oh, kids are nice, Sandy.

SANDY *(Coughing)*   I know, but you have to—you have to . . . get used to them, you know . . .

DEBBIE *(Overlapping, shaking her head)*   Of course, I never hear from my two older ones. Oh, Sandy, it's such a terrible situa—

SANDY *(Interrupting)*   You still haven't heard anything at all?

DEBBIE *(Still shaking her head)*   Oh, the-they're thirteen and fourteen, they hitchhiked to Texas. I had the police. I don't know their whereabouts.

SANDY   I know . . . I know . . . so they-they can't find any trace?

DEBBIE   The youngest one is selling stolen cameras. I'm worried.

SANDY   Really?

DEBBIE *(Nodding)*   I'm worried.

SANDY   Yeah—well, take it easy.

DEBBIE *(Looking over her shoulder at Sam on his bicycle)*   Yeah? Take it— Well, Sam doesn't want to know about it. You know, he keeps having heart attacks. He's . . . never gets off the bike.

SANDY *(Nodding)*   Uh-huh. Do you hear from our parents at all? I mean, do they—

DEBBIE *(Interrupting)*   Oh, yeah. You know, they sit in Miami.

SANDY   Mm-hmmm.
The exercise bell continues ringing in the background.

DEBBIE   Dad's gonna be eighty.

SANDY   That's amazing.

DEBBIE   Yeah.

SANDY   Amazing.

DEBBIE   In good shape. Mom's blind in one eye . . . deaf in one ear.

SANDY   Oh. I hope the same side of the head, right? Because that's important, so she's even—

DEBBIE *(Interrupting)*   Don't make jokes.

SANDY   She should be, even at that age . . . it's very—

DEBBIE *(Interrupting)*   Don't . . . I miss you.
Sandy mutters; the exercise bell continues to ring.

DEBBIE *(Getting up from the bed)*   I never *(To Sam, furiously)* S-Sam! That's enough with that bell! I bought him a bell for Christmas and I never hear the end of it!
She storms out of the room; Sandy follows her. Their voices are still heard as Sam's hands leave the exercise bicycle handles; the hands are seen opening up a pack of cigarettes, removing one and lighting it.

SANDY'S VOICE-OVER   So I send money to Miami all the time, but I don't know what else I can do, uh, for our parents.

DEBBIE *(Offscreen)*   Yeah . . . well, you're good like that, you're good like that. You keep up.

SANDY *(Offscreen)*   You know?

CUT TO:
INTERIOR. ROLLS-ROYCE—DAY.

Isobel and Sandy sit in the back seat of the Rolls-Royce, talking.

ISOBEL   You know, I like your sister. She's very nice.

SANDY *(Sighing, kissing Isobel's hand)*   Yeah, she's great. She's a little screwed up, but she's . . . but-but—

ISOBEL *(Interrupting, looking at her hands)*   She's, um, she's very funny.

SANDY   She's-she is. She's—   well, w-w-when-when you told her that you—that you had been a, uh, leftist, you know, and-and that, uh, that you'd been in jail and all, I—she—I thought she'd—you know, her mouth was hanging open. 'Cause she's intensely middle-class, you know? I find that extremely difficult to swallow even now, you know? 'Cause y—

ISOBEL *(Interrupting, reacting)*   But I told you. It was—things were very different in this time in sixty-eight.
A police car is seen suddenly through the back window of the Rolls-Royce. Sandy and Isobel, oblivious to the police car's proximity, continue their conversation.

SANDY   I know they were different, but, but I can't see you standing in the streets throwing rocks and bottles.

ISOBEL *(Touching her mouth, smiling)*   At the barricades.

SANDY *(Overlapping)*   I ju—   I-I don't have that image of you. You're too sweet to ever think of . . . of—

ISOBEL *(Interrupting)*   I had to—   because we had to . . . It-it was the only way to change the spirit of-of relationships between people, you know?

SANDY *(Overlapping)*   —you know? *(The lights on the police car's roof begin to flash; its siren starts to blare. Sandy turns and looks through the back window. He sees the police car pull away from behind the Rolls-Royce, passing it, and moving up ahead. Sandy, reacting, speaks to his chauffeur).* G-G-George, you're going too slow, they're gonna get you. *(Sighing, to Isobel)* I-I know, but, you know, it's just such an odd thing. *(Scratching his eye)* I-I-I-I can never picture you just-just hanging in there with the workers, you know, and-and storming the—

ISOBEL *(Interrupting)*   You know, the workers were not with us. They were fighting for their own salaries and own . . . own conditions of life.

SANDY   Yes, and so what were you doing?
The chauffeur pulls the Rolls-Royce to the side of the road and stops. A police sergeant, getting out of his car, is seen through the dashboard window of the Rolls-Royce. The sergeant gestures to George, the chauffeur. George's arms and shoulders are seen getting out of the Rolls-Royce. The camera shifts to the

unfolding scene, filmed through the dashboard window; George is seen hand-
ing a paper to the police sergeant. Isobel and Sandy, totally absorbed in their
conversation, are heard over the action.)

ISOBEL *(Overlapping)*   And we were fighting for . . . for . . . for the spirit
of things and for—   maybe we were romantic, you know. But they
thought we were romantic and—

SANDY *(Interrupting, offscreen, as oblivious as Isobel to the unfolding scene)*
Yes?

ISOBEL *(Offscreen)*   I remember when I was in jail I thought it was so
romantic and so exciting.

SANDY *(Offscreen)*   Oh, terrific. Right? And-and-and you met a lot of
interesting men in jail? It's . . . uh . . .
Sandy laughs. The camera moves back to him and Isobel in the back seat of
the Rolls-Royce.

ISOBEL *(Laughing)*   You know, men and women are separated in jail.

SANDY *(Laughing)*   I find-I-I find it very, very difficult to have a-a-a
commitment like that. I feel . . . *(Once again, the camera is focused on*
the scene outside. A second police officer has gotten out of the car. He takes
George by the arm and leads him away. Sandy's voice is heard over the action)
. . . in, to survive in life you want to stay loose, you want to keep
flexible . . . *(Noticing, finally, the scene outside)* What the hell is going
on out there? What are they—
Sandy gets out of the Rolls-Royce. He walks over to the police sergeant as the
second police officer puts George in the back seat of the police car. The camera
stays far away from the scene so that it is difficult to see the group actually
speaking, even though all the action is seen and heard.

SANDY *(To the police sergeant)*   Hey, what's going on? What-wh—   Can
I . . . ?

POLICE SERGEANT *(Overlapping)*   Oh, Mr. Bates, how are you?

SANDY   Fine.

POLICE SERGEANT   Geez, you know, I've always enjoyed your films.

SANDY   Thanks very much. *(Gesturing)* Wh-wh-wh-wh-wh-what's he
done? What's the problem?

POLICE SERGEANT   Well, I've got a warrant for his arrest.
The second police officer moves around the police car and climbs into the driver's side; a dispatcher is heard on the police radio as the sergeant continues to talk to Sandy.

SANDY   You're kidding. For what?

POLICE SERGEANT   I'm sorry. Out of Pennsylvania. It's for mail fraud.

SANDY   For what? Mail fraud? My-my chauffeur? You're—

POLICE SERGEANT *(Interrupting)*   That's right.

SANDY   Oh, I . . . it's . . .

POLICE SERGEANT *(Overlapping)*   Listen, do you have a license? I mean, can you-can you drive this car?

SANDY   I can drive it if I have to. What are you—   Why are you gonna take him down?

POLICE SERGEANT   I have to. I'm sorry.

SANDY   What—   Are you sure you got the right guy?

POLICE SERGEANT   Yes, I do.

SANDY   I . . . oh . . .

POLICE SERGEANT *(Overlapping)*   Oh, hey, by the way, Mr. Bates. The next time you do a film, how about doing one about a police sergeant, huh?
The sergeant laughs as Sandy gets back into the Rolls-Royce, this time in the driver's seat. The sergeant gets into his car.

SANDY *(Reacting)*   I can't believe this . . . Oh, Jesus . . .

POLICE SERGEANT *(To Sandy, loudly from his car)*   Hey, I got a great story that I'll tell you, okay?

ISOBEL *(Overlapping, to Sandy)*   What happened?

SANDY   What happened? He—   They're booking my driver for mail fraud, if you can believe that.

CUT TO:
INTERIOR. SANDY'S OFFICE—DAY.

A thin, cadaverish-looking delivery man, holding a paper bag, stands forlornly near Sandy's secretary's desk. He looks down at the sales slip in his hand while Sandy's secretary is heard talking on the phone with Sandy.

SECRETARY *(Offscreen, into the phone)* Really? You're kidding . . . Oh, that doesn't make sense. I checked every reference. They're impeccable.
The secretary's hand is seen on the screen, throwing a coin on to the desk in front of the delivery man as she talks, fumbling for the correct change.
The film cuts to the pay phones in the Stardust Hotel lobby; Sandy's voice is heard; he is obscured by a wall, talking into the telephone. An old woman walks by, seen through some doors leading outside; she stumbles by with a crutch walker.

SANDY *(Into the telephone)* How can they be impeccable? I-I-I-I had six chauffeurs in two years. Yo-you get me drunks, you get guys who can't understand English. One guy ran over an old lady, with me in the car. And now this guy's wanted for mail fraud. It's humiliating.
Several guests pass by; Ed Rich, a robotlike man in a white suit and thick black glasses, stops walking when he sees Sandy talking on the phone. He stands directly behind Sandy, watching him; a girl in a striped bandeau ignores the fact that Sandy is talking on the phone and hands him a pen.

GIRL IN BANDEAU *(Overlapping Sandy's speech)* Would you sign my left breast?
And the film cuts back to the cadaverish-looking delivery man in Sandy's office. While Sandy's secretary continues to talk to him on the phone offscreen, more coins are dropped on the desk in front of the delivery man.

SECRETARY Oh, by the way, Dr. Melnikoff called. He said you should stop using that, uh, shampoo solution he gave you to rub in your hair. He says they just found out it causes skin cancer.
Sandy is totally hidden by the pay-phone wall now; the girl in the striped bandeau walks away, Sandy's signature on her chest.

SANDY *(Offscreen, into the phone)* He's had me on it for nine months, now he tells me it causes skin cancer?
Ed Rich, still seen standing behind Sandy, can no longer contain himself. He walks over to the offscreen Sandy and shakes his hand. Daisy and Jack pass by, giving Sandy a quick look.

ED RICH Ed Rich. I'm with the New York City Landmarks Committee.

SANDY *(Offscreen, into the phone)* Jesus oh, . . . *(To Ed Rich, seen shaking Sandy's offscreen hand)* Oh, hi, happy to know you.

ED RICH *(Still shaking Sandy's hand)* We're having a fund raiser next month.

SANDY *(Offscreen, muttering)* Oh . . . oh, I'll be glad to come. Just—uh, call me when I get to town.

ED RICH *(Still shaking Sandy's offscreen hand)* It-it's a wonderful cause, to preserve old buildings.
Sandy, still on the telephone, is partially seen still shaking hands with Ed Rich.

SANDY *(To Ed Rich)* Oh, I'm sure, I'm sure, I'm sure. Just call when I get back to town. I'll be happy to make it. Really.
Sandy laughs; he reaches up with his arm and slaps Ed Rich on the cheek.

ED RICH *(Nodding)* Oh—oh, okay, fine. Thank you.

SANDY *(Laughing)* Cheer up.
The film cuts to heaven, complete with clouds, enveloping fog—and a fully instrumented jazz band. The worn, tired passengers from the first train in the beginning of the movie come wandering onto the screen, walking through the clouds and fog. Sandy's voice is heard over the scene.

SANDY'S VOICE-OVER What is that? Wh-wh-what the hell is that? That-that's the silliest thing I've ever seen. What is that? Uh, those people that are marching in the background, they-th-those-those are all the people from the-the train. I mean, th-they wind up in the—in the garbage dump. What the hell are they doing here?
The jazz music stops and the movie cuts to the beachfront of the Stardust Hotel. The film executives seen earlier in the film, Walsh and Smith, and newcomer Jones, all wearing sunglasses, are gathered around Sandy and Isobel, who are seated at a round umbrella-topped table. Isobel sips some coffee, nodding; mostly empty tables make up the background.

JONES They wind up in jazz heaven. It's commercial. It's upbeat.

SMITH *(Overlapping)* They wind up in jazz heaven. It's upbeat. It's commercial.

SANDY It's stupid.
Bill, the writer responsible for "Jazz Heaven" rewrite, sits at another table, looking concerned.

BILL I thought you'd like it, Sandy. You-you love jazz.

SANDY *(Gesturing at Bill)* Who is this guy, anyhow, to rewrite the end of my movie? *(Sandy gestures at Jones, sipping a drink, wearing a cowboy hat, and Smith, also wearing a hat, standing a few paces behind Jones; both lean against a railing)* And-and since when are all these guys involved? What the hell is going on?

Sandy looks at Walsh, the thin female executive, seated at a table smoking a cigarette; her sunglasses rest on the top of her head.

WALSH These are the new heads of the studio.

SANDY *(Reacting)* What do you mean the, uh, every six months I meet a new group of studio heads.

WALSH It's very disconcerting to me too, but you know the mortality rate in this business is unbelievable.

SANDY Yeah, I'll say it is, it's like the black plague. Jesus. And-and . . .
He is interrupted by a forties-looking female fan who approaches him, carrying a pencil and a matchbook.

FEMALE FAN I think you're wonderful. Can I have your autograph?

SANDY *(Overlapping, signing the matchbook, but talking to the executives)* Yeah. I don't want anybody going to-to Jazz Heaven.
A little boy in a T-shirt comes over to Sandy; he stands behind the forties-looking woman. He holds a book and a pencil in his hand.

LITTLE BOY *(Overlapping)* Me, too. Me, too.

SANDY *(Overlapping, talking to the executives)* That's a—that's a-a nitwit idea.

FEMALE FAN *(Overlapping)* Thank you.
She walks away. Sandy takes the book from the little boy. He opens it up to the inside front cover, not reacting to the book's title: Mark Twain's The Adventures of Tom Sawyer. *He continues to talk to the film executives, signing his name automatically.*

SANDY And, you know the whole point of the movie is that nobody is saved.

WALSH Sandy, this is an Easter film. We don't need a movie by an atheist.

SANDY To you—to you I'm an atheist.
Another fan, a severe-looking young man, walks over to Sandy; he holds a paper and pen.

YOUNG MAN One more, sir.
Sandy takes the paper, not looking up at the young man's intense expression; he continues his conversation with the executives.

SANDY To God I'm the loyal opposition.
Bill laughs.

YOUNG MAN *(Watching Sandy sign the paper)* Oh, you know, I'm your biggest fan. I think you're terrific.

SANDY *(To the young man)* Oh, thank you.

WALSH *(Reacting)* His public adores him.

SANDY Yeah. Today they adore you, and tomorrow it's one of these. *As the young man walks away, Sandy makes a gunlike gesture with his hand, a foreshadowing, perhaps, of things to come.*

BILL You're paranoid.

WALSH I think you're being a little paranoid.
Sandy stands up, pulling Isobel from her seat by her arm.

SANDY No. You know what I'm being? I'm being realistic. You know, and that's why you don't like the movie. *(To Isobel)* Come on . . .

WALSH It's not a matter of what I like. Listen, I've been on this side of the business for four years now. Too much reality is not what the people want.
Isobel and Sandy walk away, past empty tables with their umbrellas opened in their centers, lined up on the hotel's boardwalk. Sandy moves quickly, gesturing.

SANDY Jazz Heaven. That is the stupidest thing I've ever heard. You can't control life. It doesn't wind up perfectly. Only-only art you can control. Art and masturbation. Two areas in which I am an absolute expert.

CUT TO:
INTERIOR. SANDY'S HOTEL ROOM—DAY.

Isobel's face fills the screen. She is brushing her hair, reflected in the dresser mirror.

ISOBEL I feel very tired.

SANDY *(Offscreen)* Yeah? Isobel, I want you to come and live with me. *Isobel walks away from the mirror; the camera follows her as she sits down on the edge of the bed, still vigorously brushing her hair. Sandy continues to talk to her offscreen; he is never seen.*

ISOBEL   Can we not talk about it tonight?

SANDY *(Offscreen)*   N-n-no, I want to talk about it. I've been thinking about it all day. Y-you know, it-it-it—I was just very, very surprised before, that's all. But I—you know, when I think it over, it's a very, very important thing to me.

ISOBEL   You know you don't have to say that.
Isobel, still seen very close up, stops brushing her hair and starts making bizarre stretching movements with her facial muscles. Sandy continues to talk to her offscreen.

SANDY *(Offscreen)*   I know I don't have to say it, but I—you know I feel that way. I've very, very complicated feelings toward you. You know, I-I—you know, I like to be with you, and I-I-I-I don't want to screw up this relationship. I—you know that I love you, I trust you, you know? You're one of the few people that I really have fun with and-and, you know, gee, if it wasn't for you this past year, I-I'd have been absolutely, y-you know . . . *(Reacting finally to Isobel's bizarre facial gestures)* Isobel, what are you doing? I'm pouring my heart out here and you're-you're behaving like a crazy person. Iso-Isobel, will you stop that for a minute?

ISOBEL *(Still grimacing)*   Yes, but I'm just doing my exercise.

SANDY *(Offscreen)*   I—yes, uh, but this is important, what I'm saying. Can you—is—

ISOBEL *(Interrupting, grimacing)*   Yes, but my exercise too.

SANDY *(Offscreen)*   . . . uh, yes, I know, but you—uh, you—

ISOBEL *(Interrupting, still grinning bizarrely)*   I need it for my muscle.

SANDY *(Offscreen)*   . . . you-you-you look like you're having a fit. Will you . . . Isobel?

ISOBEL   I'm not.

SANDY *(Offscreen)*   Isobel, I'm serious. I want you to move in with me. I'm-I'm-I'm serious. I-I-I think that-that-that you should live with me and that, and that—I think we would have a lot of fun together.
Isobel finally stops her exercises, listening seriously to Sandy's words. Her eyes are wide; her face still fills the screen.

ISOBEL   You, I'm not, I'm not sure about anything, you know? I'm just . . . I'm just thinking of it.

SANDY *(Offscreen)* What do you mean you're not su— Yeah . . .

ISOBEL *(Interrupting)* It-it's such a big decision for me, too.

SANDY *(Offscreen)* I-I'm—I know it's a big decision for you, but—

ISOBEL *(Interrupting, looking down for a moment)* You know, it wasn't so easy to-to leave my husband. And now to think of the children, and—

SANDY *(Offscreen, interrupting)* It's good that you left your husband. I think it's a good thing.

ISOBEL *(Nodding, looking down)* Yes . . . I'm sure . . . of-of it too.

SANDY *(Offscreen)* And-and I think—I think you're—

ISOBEL *(Interrupting)* But I'm not sure about the rest, you know? It frightens me too. I think we'll have to think about it.

SANDY *(Offscreen)* I see. So now-now that I feel that you should live with me . . . now you, all of the sudden, you feel differently, right?

ISOBEL *(Looking directly at the camera, at the offscreen Sandy)* Oh, but it is not so—it is not so clear.

SANDY *(Offscreen)* But don't you see? To me, you may be the perfect woman.

CUT TO:
INTERIOR. STARDUST HOTEL AUDITORIUM—DAY.

The camera is focused on the movie screen, where an x-ray of a skull is illuminated against an operating-room panel. Old science-fiction genre music plays in the background. Tony Roberts' voice is heard over the x-ray.

TONY ROBERTS *(Offscreen)* You're mad.
The film cuts to Tony, dressed as a doctor, complete with an illuminating disc on his forehead, standing against the operating-room doors.

TONY You're a respected, well-known, established New York doctor. How could you get involved in something like this?
The camera moves past rows of test-tube bottles to Sandy, also dressed as a doctor, standing between Dorrie (known here as "Rita"), her hair splayed on her pillow, and Doris, wearing glasses and braids; they both lie unconscious on operating tables.

SANDY But you know I've never been able to fall in love. I've never been able to find the perfect woman. There's always something wrong. And then I met Doris. *(He turns and touches Doris on the head)* A wonderful woman. Great personality. But for some reason, I'm just not turned on sexually by her. Don't ask me why. And then I met Rita. *(Touching Rita/Dorrie on the forehead)* An animal. Nasty, mean, trouble. And I love going to bed with her. Though afterward I always wished that I was back with Doris. And then, I thought to myself, if only I could put Doris' brain in Rita's body. Wouldn't that be wonderful? And I thought, Why not? What the hell, I'm a surgeon.

TONY *(Reacting)* Surgeon? Where'd you study medicine, in Transylvania?
The audience in the auditorium laughs; the busy, melodramatic music continues in the background.

SANDY *(Gesturing)* So, I performed the operation and everything went perfectly. I-I-I switched their personalities and I took all the badness and put it over there. And I made Rita into a warm, wonderful, charming, sexy, sweet, giving, mature woman. And then I fell in love with Doris.
The audience continues to laugh; the music stops and the film cuts to the packed auditorium. A bland-looking man stands up and addresses Sandy, who is sitting in a straight-backed chair, a microphone in his hand. Sitting next to him is Tony and, next to Tony, Vivian, dressed in a new print dress, still nodding and hanging on to every word.

BLAND MAN *(Standing up)* Do you really feel there's such a thing as a perfect mate? I mean, don't you think the basis of any mature relationship is really compromise?

SANDY *(Holding his microphone)* I think any-any relationship, uh, is not based on either compromise or maturity or perfection or any of that. It's really based on luck.*(Pausing while the audience laughs)* You, uh, you know that's-that's the key thing. People don't like to acknowledge that because it means a loss of control, but you really have to be lucky.
There is a quick cut to the intense young man who'd asked Sandy for his autograph while he'd been talking to the movie executives. Then the camera moves to another man in the audience, who asks Sandy a question.

ANOTHER MAN   I have a question for Mr. Roberts. Was the scene between you and Sandy Bates in the wax museum an homage to
Vincent Price's horror movie *The House of Wax*?
*As Sandy hands the microphone to Tony, the man who'd asked the question
turns and winks at a fellow sitting behind him.*

TONY *(Answering the question)*   An homage? Not exactly. We just stole
the idea outright.
*The audience laughs and the film cuts to an outside gazebo at the hotel. Several
people are sitting at scattered tables; mood music plays in the background
while couples dance; waiters bring drinks to the tables. The hotel and its
twinkling lights are seen in the distance. Tony and Sandy sit at one of these
tables, drinks in front of them, deep in conversation.*

TONY *(Looking down, fingering his glass)*   You set things up so you can
play a little golf, get a little poon, you smoke some good grass, and
that's what life's about, you know? Oh, he doesn't want to listen.

SANDY *(Nodding)*   Mm-hmm . . . right, right . . . yeah, keep going
. . . mm-hmm. It's shallow. It's shallow. You don't see that it's
shallow?
*The film cuts for a moment to three young men, wearing almost identical
white dinner jackets, staring at Tony and Sandy.*

TONY *(Offscreen)*   Shallow?

SANDY *(Offscreen)*   Yes.

TONY *(Offscreen)*   Did you see the shallow girl that I'm with?
The camera is back at Sandy and Tony's table.

SANDY   No, I haven't, uh—

TONY *(Interrupting)*   *Playboy* centerfold.

SANDY   Oh, perfect, perfect. You met her in a hot tub, right?

TONY   She's a lovely girl. She's very healthy.

SANDY   Right? Yeah, I'm sure.

TONY   Won't eat meat.

SANDY   Into m-massage, right?

TONY   Sweets. Just amphetamines.

SANDY *(Nodding)* Mm-hmmm . . . Mm-hmm, yeah, exactly.
The camera cuts to a middle-aged couple sitting at another table, looking into each other's eyes.

TONY *(Offscreen)* Well, y-y-you don't make such good picks, you know. A lot of your picks have left a lot to be desired.
The middle-aged couple stop looking at each other and turn to stare at Sandy and Tony.

SANDY *(Offscreen)* Li-like what? Like Dorrie? Dorrie was fabulous.
The camera goes back to Sandy and Tony.

TONY Dorrie was a loonie.

SANDY *(Gesturing)* Dorrie was great. She was bright, she was quick, she was wonderful—

TONY *(Interrupting)* She was bright, there's no question.

SANDY Yeah. She-she had a perfect personality. She was-she was completely self-conscious, um, out of bed, and when you got her in bed, she was completely unselfconscious. I mean, it's a perfect balance.

TONY *(Nodding)* Yeah, yeah, she could be very fine and funny and bright and wonderful two days a month.

SANDY Yeah . . . exactly. Oh, well—

TONY *(Interrupting)* The other twenty-eight, she was lost.

SANDY *(Looking away, sighing)* Mmmm . . . but what a two days, let me tell you.

TONY When she was on, she was a ten. She was dynamite.
The film cuts to a huge concrete pipe storage lot. As Tony and Sandy talk over the action, Dorrie, Tony and Sandy are seen walking through the maze of steel and concrete pipes; Dorrie keeps taking pictures with a camera.

TONY'S VOICE-OVER Do you remember when we went to that place with the pipes?

SANDY'S VOICE-OVER Th-th-that was her photography period. That was hilarious.

TONY'S VOICE-OVER Oh, yeah, I remember you bought her a camera.

SANDY'S VOICE-OVER Well, she kept hinting. That's all she hinted, was-was-was for a camera.

The screen shows Dorrie taking a picture of Sandy; Tony jumps out of a nearby pipe.

TONY'S VOICE-OVER   And graphics . . . all she talked about was-was graphics.

SANDY'S VOICE-OVER   Yeah, she was obsessed. She was obsessed. Well, you like to pose for pictures, though. You were . . . you were in all your hammy glory.
The screen shows Dorrie clicking away at Tony with her camera; he is standing in front of some huge pipes.

TONY'S VOICE-OVER *(Laughing)*   I wanted to go hear jazz . . . *(The flashback cuts to a shower stall where Dorrie and Sandy silently wash each other, smiling. Dorrie starts scrubbing Sandy's hair)* . . . and you guys went someplace else. You wanted to go home and rehearse or something.

SANDY'S VOICE-OVER   No, we . . . we had to rehearse . . . We-we-we-we're artists. You know, we had work to do that night.

TONY'S VOICE-OVER   Oh . . . yeah . . . I can imagine.
The mood music stops. The silent shower scene fades into the Stardust Hotel lobby. It is later that night. Sandy is walking quietly through the lobby doors, heading for the passageway to his suite, when Jerry Abraham, in a loud paisley shirt, jumps up from a couch, drink in hand.

JERRY *(Running up to Sandy)*   Hey, Sandy. Jerry Abraham, remember me? We grew up together.

SANDY   Jer— Of course I— You asked this the other day. Of course I remember you. Why should I forget you?

JERRY   Well, you know, people grow up, they-they become big hot shots, they forget.

SANDY   We played stickball together, right?

JERRY   Yeah. We went to Hebrew school, too.

SANDY   So . . . ? Yeah . . . So what are you doing? What are you up to?

JERRY   You know what I do? I drive a cab.

SANDY   You— Well, you look good. You— There's nothing wrong with that.

JERRY   Yeah. But look at me compared to you. I mean, all these beautiful broads, you know?

SANDY Oh, Jesus. Listen, I got a headache.

JERRY Hey, you know that's great.

SANDY I think I'm a little drunk. What do you want me to say? I wa-I was the kid in the neighborhood who told the jokes, right?

JERRY Yeah.

SANDY So, so—we, you know, we live in a—in a society that puts a big value on jokes, you know? If you think of it this way—*(Clearing his throat)* if I had been an Apache Indian, those guys didn't need comedians at all, right? So I'd be out of work.

JERRY So? Oh, come on, that doesn't help me feel any better, you know?

SANDY *(Touching Jerry's shoulder, gesturing and laughing)* I don't know what to say, I got such a headache. You know it's luck. It's all luck. I was just lucky. I'm the first to admit, I was a lucky bum. If I—if I was not born in Brooklyn, if I had been born in Poland, or Berlin, I'd be a lampshade today, right?

JERRY Right.

SANDY I mean, it just—it could happen just like that. So, you know, be thankful that you're not Nat Bernstein.

JERRY Nat Bernstein?

SANDY Remember? Yeah. Wasted away.

JERRY Yeah, he was a guy from the neighborhood, right?

SANDY Incurable disease, it was absolutely terrible.

JERRY Oh, wow.

CUT TO:
INTERIOR. SANDY'S HOTEL BEDROOM—NIGHT.

The door opens and Sandy comes into the room, closing the door behind him. It is very quiet. He walks to the bed where Isobel lies peacefully asleep. He looks down at her, touching her shoulder, then he sits down next to her head, still looking at her, as the film cuts to:

INTERIOR. PHONE BOOTH—DAY.

Sandy is in the booth, talking on the telephone and leaning against a wall covered with election-campaign photographs; sea gulls are heard in the background.

SANDY *(Into the telephone)* Y-yes, of course, Harvey . . . No, I understand that. O-of course, it's-it— The point is it's immoral for them to touch the end of my film . . . *(Sighing)* Jesus. Well, I-I don't know what to say . . . So then we'll sue them . . . Well, can you . . . I . . . can you call me back later this afternoon at the hotel and find out? . . . Well, yes, I'll be . . . Later this afternoon . . . Okay, okay. *Sandy hangs up the phone and rubs his eyes. He overhears Daisy in the adjoining phone booth. He stops rubbing his eyes and leans over to the wall, listening.*

DAISY *(Offscreen, into the telephone)* God, the thing is, though— God, I'm crazy right now. I just . . . just— I don't seem to be able to sleep, you know? I-I-I have to do-do some practicing on the violin, 'cause I gotta go back to the Philharmonic in a couple of weeks. But, uh, you know, I-I— Last night I had a migraine, and I-so I took some, some Darvon and-and-and that made me so nervous that I-took, I took, uh, forty milligrams of Valium . . . *(The camera moves from Sandy to Daisy, no longer wearing her sunglasses, in her phone booth. She is talking into the receiver, almost cradling it as she smokes a cigarette. She touches her mouth)* . . . you know, and then I—and I still couldn't sleep. I was up all night . . . Yeah . . . Well, well, I got a message on my service that Sarah called . . . Yeah, I know, I haven't talked to her in about a year, you know, and uh, I-I-I-I got upset. I started eating. I ate a pound of cookies last night . . . Yeah, I'm really fat. Really fat. And, uh, J-Jack, um, Jack was so sweet about it . . . No, he-he, no, he doesn't know about my relationship with her. I mean, he knows that we lived together in Israel, but he doesn't—he doesn't know that— He-he was so affectionate last night, in-in bed, you know, he wanted— I-I told him I had herpes . . . *(Pausing)* Yeah . . . Well, no, uh, take the-the call, I'll hold on—I'll hold on a second. *Upbeat jazz starts playing as the film cuts to the long Stardust Hotel boardwalk. A soldier and his girl friend stand in the background, staring into each other's eyes; Sandy's and Isobel's voices are heard.*

SANDY *(Offscreen)* Geez, I don't like the idea of your kids riding on the train alone.

ISOBEL *(Offscreen)*   They will be okay, I'm sure.
   Isobel and Sandy are now seen, their backs to the camera, walking from the
   hotel to the large, old-fashioned railroad station at the end of the boardwalk.
   As they talk, walking closer to the station, their forms get smaller and
   smaller. Though they are seen, the effect is like a voice-over situation because
   the camera is so far away.

SANDY   Who knows what goes on on those things, you know? There's
   a lot of weird people out there. A lot of perverts and-and crazies.
   They're liable to get molested or robbed . . .

ISOBEL *(Laughing)*   Oh, not my children. Maybe the other way around.

SANDY   If-if I knew exactly when they were coming, my chauffeur
   could've picked them up, you know? He-he could have broken out
   of jail and gotten them.
   People pass by them, a sailor, a woman, couples; some of them glance at
   Sandy. One man actually starts walking with Sandy and Isobel.

WALKING MAN *(Overlapping Sandy's speech)*   Are you Sandy Bates?

SANDY *(To the man, trying to get rid of him)*   Uh, no. *(To Isobel)* The kids
   will probably be starved.

WALKING MAN   Yes, you are.

SANDY *(Shaking his head, trying to get rid of the man)* Uh, no, no, no, no, no, no, I'm not.

WALKING MAN My mother buys meat in the same butcher shop your mother does.

SANDY *(Laughing)* Oh, great.

WALKING MAN *(Handing Sandy a piece of paper)* Can I have your autograph?

SANDY *(Reacting)* Oh, Jesus.

WALKING MAN Could you just write "To Phyllis Weinstein, you unfaithful, lying bitch"?

CUT TO:
INTERIOR. OLD-FASHIONED ICE CREAM PARLOR—DAY.

Sandy and Isobel, with Isobel's small son and daughter, come through the door, chatting; they walk past several people sitting at small round tables and go to a large table near a window with an ocean view. Sandy carries Isobel's daughter in one arm; the other arm holds a suitcase. The parlor has a forties feel to it, with its white walls, old linoleum and hanging lamps.

ISOBEL *(To her children)* Oooh la la. Que *c'est joli . . . Oui, ma chérie.*

SANDY *(Looking around)* Okay.

DAUGHTER *J'ai soif.*

SANDY Okay, look, okay, we can sit by the window. It'll be nice.

DAUGHTER *Je suis fatiguée.*

SANDY *(Overlapping)* *Oui, oui.*

DAUGHTER *Je veux de la glace.*

SANDY *Oui, oui, oui,* hey.
Isobel laughs.

SANDY We're gonna go sit by the window, have a nice time . . . don't —I wouldn't attract attention. I don't want to attract too much attention.

ISOBEL *Regarde la mer. Eh. Regarde.*

SANDY *(To the daughter)* Okay, okay. Uncle Sandy. Can I put you down first?

ISOBEL *(Laughing)* Quickly.

SANDY Heavy kid. Geez, she's really heavy.
Isobel continues to laugh happily.

SANDY Unc-Uncle Sandy. Oh . . .

ISOBEL *(Bending her head to her children's level)* *Tu t'assis là. Alors, qui est-ce qui va manger de la glace?*

DAUGHTER *Moi!*
The group sits down, Isobel at the head of the table, her children on one side and Sandy opposite them.

SON *Je veux du chocolat.*

ISOBEL *Tu veux du chocolat? Moi, je crois que je vais manger du chocolat.*

SANDY *(Coughing)* Okay, okay, not too much . . . We don't want to attract too much attention.

DAUGHTER *T'es fou, t'es fou, t'es fou, t'es fou. T'es—*
A woman sits in the background eating French fries; she looks at the group for a moment. Sandy mutters to himself and the camera cuts briefly to a man and a woman, sitting at another table. They look at the group as well, whispering to each other as they gaze.

MAN AT THE OTHER TABLE *(Nodding to his companion)* Blond kids.

DAUGHTER *(Overlapping man's speech)* *—une araignée. T'es fou.*

ISOBEL *Mais tu as fini?*

DAUGHTER *(Shrilly)* *Je veux aller là-bas.*

ISOBEL *Où veux-tu aller?*

DAUGHTER *T'es fou. T'es une araignée.*

ISOBEL Shh. Shh.

DAUGHTER *J'ai faim. Je veux un* ice cream.

ISOBEL *Oui, on va partir.*

SANDY *(Putting his finger to his lips, reacting)* Shhh. Shhh. Shhh.

DAUGHTER *(Loudly)* *J'ai faim. J'ai soif. J'ai faim.*

SANDY *(Reacting)* Shhh.

DAUGHTER *T'es fou. T'es un imbécile. Non, te-te . . .*
Isobel tries unsuccessfully to quiet her children. Sandy, frustrated, stares out the window at the beach. The jazz that's playing softly in the background stops and the film cuts to the beach, the waves rolling in the background. An elephant stands in the sand. Dorrie, sitting in a beach chair, elegantly attired in a print dress and sunglasses, smiles as a young Sandy, in his caped Superman costume, runs over to her. She hands him a gift-wrapped box.

YOUNG SANDY Thank you.

DORRIE *(Kissing Sandy on the forehead)* All right. Happy Birthday.

YOUNG SANDY You don't have to do that. Wow.
Sandy runs away. Dorrie stands up from her chair, looking offscreen; the wind blows her hair.

DORRIE What are you thinking about?

SANDY *(Offscreen)* I'm knocked out by this. I—you know . . . *(The adult Sandy walks over to her, holding the gift box with a flute inside)* y-y-you really didn't have to do this.

DORRIE *(Smiling)* I never forget a birthday.

SANDY *(Looking at the flute)* This is so great. But how did you know? It's exactly what I wanted.

DORRIE You always wanted to learn.

SANDY Yeah, I want— Will this play the Mozart Flute Concerto?

DORRIE *You* have to do that.
Dorrie holds out another wrapped gift, a book she's been concealing behind her back.

SANDY Oh, *I* have to do it! You mean it doesn't— *(Noticing the new wrapped gift)* Oh, Dorrie, what are you— This is a big day for me here.
Dorrie laughs as Sandy reads the title of his gift book.

SANDY *The Way of Zen.* What are you trying to tell me? That-that I'm not at peace, right? I-I-I think I need more than a Zen book. I need either a good rabbi, analyst or interplanetary genius to, uh . . . what is that? *(Dorrie pulls her other hand from behind her back and puts her hands together. She holds them up to Sandy and opens them)* Oh, Dorrie, what . . . *(He takes the pocket watch she's been holding in her hands)* Unbelievable. How did you get that?

DORRIE *(Laughing)* It wasn't easy.

SANDY I thought the museum was gonna buy it.

DORRIE Yeah, well, I knew you loved it.

SANDY This must have cost you a fortune. How could you do that? It's so extravagant. *(He leans over and kisses her)* That's . . . that's . . . gee, I-I—you got nothing else for me? I mean ju-just three? When I was a kid, the thing that I always wanted was an elephant, you know? *They put their arms around each other and walk away offscreen, leaving the beach empty except for the sand and the ocean. Sandy's voice, offscreen, is heard)* And I could never convince my mother to get one for me.

DORRIE *(Offscreen)* I would have got you an elephant.

SANDY *(Offscreen)* Yeah, but where were you?
The camera moves from the quiet ocean, the waves hitting the shore, back to the present, to the Stardust Hotel's boardwalk. Sandy, Isobel and her two children have left the ice cream parlor; they are walking to the hotel. A single trumpet is played by a musician in an open-walled bar in the background as Jack and Daisy walk by, spotting Sandy.

JACK Hey, look who it is.

DAISY *(Turning to see Sandy)* Hey. Hey. Hi.

JACK Say hello.

DAISY Hi, you guys.

JACK Hi, Sandy.

DAISY *(Gesturing to the children)* Hey, those are cute.

SANDY This is-is Isobel and this is—this is Daisy and Jack. Well, this is . . . we just—we just had . . . we were—we were just at the train station.

ISOBEL *(Nodding)* Hi. Hi.

JACK Hello.

DAISY Hello.

SANDY Her kids just came in. They—we picked them up.

ISOBEL Uh, yeah . . . yeah.

DAISY Hi, hi. Oh, what great-looking kids.
The entire group walks down the boardwalk together.

SANDY *(Gesturing)* And we ... uh, you—yeah, they-they're wonderful.
We got 'em—we got 'em some ice cream. *(Isobel laughs while the
children run up ahead)* at the—uh, you know ... What are you—what
have you guys been doing?

JACK I could go for a little lunch myself.
Isobel laughs.

DAISY We were walking around town ... we, um—

SANDY *(Interrupting)* Yeah, it's dead, isn't it?

DAISY You know *The Bicycle Thief* is-is playing in town.

SANDY Really?

DAISY Yeah.

SANDY That would be ... that would be a great way to—

DAISY *(Interrupting)* I've never seen it.

SANDY You've never seen *The Bicycle Thief*? It's fabulous.

JACK It's a movie I've seen five times.
Isobel laughs.

DAISY *(Motioning to Jack with her head)* No ... I ... He won't take me.

SANDY Oh, we should see it. *(To Isobel)* We should— You want to see
The Bicycle Thief?

DAISY *(Nodding)* Yeah ... yeah.

ISOBEL No, no, thank you. I have to get the children to the room.

SANDY *(To Jack)* Oh, she's never seen it?

JACK We—well, uh, why don't you guys go see *The Bicycle Thief*, I go
home and, uh, read, my Agatha Christie.

SANDY Oh, you should take her. I could see that—I would love to see
it. I've seen it, but I would love to.

JACK *(Talking as the group walks offscreen)* ... take you back in the car
if you want to go ...

The film focuses on the single musician playing the trumpet for a brief moment, then cuts to a darkened movie theater; a light beam from the overhead movie projector flickers on Sandy and Daisy. He is eating popcorn; Daisy smokes a cigarette; they are both slouched comfortably in their seats. They are practically the only people in the theater. The sounds of an Italian actor in The Bicycle Thief *is heard over the scene.*

The film then cuts to a boardwalk; on one side is a large, many-windowed pavilion. On the other side is the boardwalk's railing and the beach and ocean beyond. Sandy and Daisy's voices are heard at first, then the couple is seen strolling down the boardwalk.

DAISY *(Offscreen)*   What a great film.

SANDY *(Offscreen)*   Mm-hmm.

DAISY *(Offscreen)*   I mean, it's great.

SANDY *(Offscreen)*   Mm-hmm.

DAISY *(Walking onto the screen)*   You know, but you've got to look at it in context. I mean, it's—it's about survival in postwar Italy.

SANDY *(Walking onto the screen)*   Mm-hmmm. Mm-hmm. I was looking at it in context. I know.

DAISY   But-but-but you can't divorce it from the social roots, you know?

SANDY *(Stuttering)*   It's much deeper than a social problem. I mean, you know, there's so many wonderful ambiguities in it. It's much more profound than that—

DAISY *(Interrupting)*   Yeah, yeah. Yeah, but the conflict is clear. Right, huh? He's gotta have the bicycle or he's gonna starve to death. I mean, it's a . . . you know?

SANDY   Yes, of course, but forget about—forget about a social problem for a minute, will you?

DAISY   Yeah.

SANDY   I mean—I mean, you know, obviously . . . *(Peering into the pavilion's open doorway)* ob—   W-what is this place? *(Daisy murmurs. She, too, stops in the doorway of the large pavilion and peers in. They both walk into the unlit room and begin wandering around its huge interior, consisting only of scattered floor-to-ceiling columns. Sandy and Daisy's forms look dark in contrast to the bright sunlight outside the windows)* Ob-obviously if you don't have enough to eat, or something, that becomes a major problem.

DAISY *(Wandering around the pavilion interior)* Yeah . . . yeah, right, of course.

SANDY You know, I mean, the issues become very clear-cut.

DAISY Uh-huh.

SANDY But what happens if you're living in a more, you know, uh, a more affluent society. And you're lucky enough to-to not have to worry about that. Let's say you're surviving.

DAISY Okay . . . all right.

SANDY So, then you're problems become, how can I fall in love, or why can't I fall in love, more accurately, and, um, why do I age and die, and what meaning can my life possibly have? You know, the issues become very complex for you—

DAISY *(Interrupting)* Geez . . . *(Laughing)* You know, for a guy who makes a lot of funny movies, you're-you're kind of a depressive, you know?
Sandy and Daisy stop walking, and standing in one place, look around the empty pavilion and at each other.

SANDY I'm not a depressive. I—why? I-I-I have a good time. I have laughs.

DAISY Yeah?

SANDY Yeah.

DAISY Do you?

SANDY *(Defensively)* Why, do you not think so?

DAISY Well, I don't know. Like-like what do you do, for example, for laughs?

SANDY Oh, sure. What do I do? The usual. You know. Read, walk, communicate. All that stuff.

DAISY Mm-hmm.

SANDY Get undressed and perform the Heimlich maneuver on a loved one.
Daisy, laughing, walks over to the far side of the dark room.

SANDY   I—you know. I was—I was having a good time this afternoon. Why, has it—has this been dreary for you? Have I been boring?

DAISY   No.

SANDY   Tell me the truth.

DAISY   No, no. I've been having a really good time. Really.
A knocking sound is heard. Both Sandy and Daisy turn around to see where it's coming from.

CHARLOTTE *(Offscreen)*   Sandy.
The camera cuts to Charlotte, in a wide headband, standing at one of the windows, knocking on its glass. She walks inside the pavilion.

CHARLOTTE *(Looking offscreen at Sandy)*   Charlotte. Charlotte Ames. Your mother. How are you doing? I just knew that was you back there. Oh, you don't recognize me, right?

SANDY *(Offscreen)*   Sure I do.

CHARLOTTE *(Looking offscreen at Sandy)*   It's okay. I had some face work done.

SANDY *(Offscreen)*   You're kidding . . . you're kidding . . . you look . . . you look astounding.
The camera shows both of them now; they are practically in silhouette from the bright sun outside and the darkness in the pavilion.

CHARLOTTE   Would you believe it? Would you believe I played your mother in a movie?

SANDY *(Laughing)*   I'm-I'm-I'm amazed.

CHARLOTTE *(Laughing)*   Thank you.

SANDY   What a coincidence.

CHARLOTTE   I had my face done, I had my breasts done, I had my ass done, I got some procaine and silicone, some nipping and tucking.

SANDY   That-that-that's more than they do on the West Side Highway.

CHARLOTTE   Well—

SANDY *(Interrupting)*   But why? I don't understand you. You-you were always a-a-a wonderful-looking—

CHARLOTTE *(Interrupting)*   You know.

SANDY   What?

CHARLOTTE   I'm an actress. You gotta keep young.

SANDY   So what . . . but . . . what . . . what?

CHARLOTTE   Otherwise the public loses interest.

SANDY   Yeah, but I mean . . . you always looked great to me, let me tell you.

CHARLOTTE   That's sweet. Listen, tell me, what the hell are you doing up here?

SANDY   Well, I—well, we were just driving through. We were at the movies, you know. I'm-I'm still stunned to see you, I must say.

CHARLOTTE   You gotta tell me whatever happened to what's-her-name . . . that actress . . . uh, Dorrie?
The camera cuts to Daisy, looking out the windows in the far corner of the pavilion; Sandy and Charlotte continue to talk over the scene.

SANDY *(Offscreen)*   Dorrie? Dorrie's . . . okay. Dorrie's—uh, Dorrie's living in Hawaii, and she's married and she's—you know, she's fine.

CHARLOTTE *(Offscreen)*   I liked her.

SANDY *(Offscreen)*   Oh, yeah, she's great.

CHARLOTTE *(Offscreen)*   She was special. I re— Yeah, I dug her.
Sandy laughs offscreen as the film cuts to:

INTERIOR. SOUND STAGE—DAY.

The sound stage is busy; a man offscreen shouts out some instructions. Lights and wires are scattered all over. In the bright background, a group of extras dressed like nuns practice a tap-dancing routine. In the dark foreground, Dorrie's voice is heard.

DORRIE *(Offscreen)*   I can't play this. I don't have that kind of flair.
Dorrie's silhouette is now seen; Sandy's voice is heard over her dark form.

SANDY *(Offscreen)*   Will you stop it? You're fine. *(Sandy walks onscreen, also in silhouette, and continues)* You just refuse to trust yourself. That's all.
A stage light goes on, illuminating Sandy and Dorrie. Sandy is in a monk's costume complete with a wide-brimmed hat. Dorrie stands to Sandy's left, her arms crossed, not looking at Sandy as he tries to placate her.

DORRIE I'm not good. I don't know what you see in me.
The light goes off; Dorrie and Sandy are once again in silhouette; two crew members walk by.

SANDY Will-will you relax? Will you— You-you're a bundle of nerves. You're great.
Another light goes on, dramatically lighting Sandy and Dorrie again.

DORRIE I can't help it. I should be playing Cynthia's role, she should be playing mine.

SANDY I should-for- *(Stuttering)* It's not—

DORRIE *(Interrupting)* She's much funnier and a lot more beautiful.
Dorrie walks offscreen.

SANDY *(Looking offscreen at Dorrie, gesturing)* Don't get hysterical, will you? She's-she's fine, but you're great too.

DORRIE *(Offscreen)* The crew laughs at her. They can't take their eyes off her.
A stage light goes back on, dramatically illuminating Sandy. Throughout the remaining scene, the stage lights go on and off, showing Sandy and Dorrie in darkness, then dramatically lit, then in darkness again.

SANDY Oh, stop it. W-w-what are you—what are you taking?

DORRIE *(Offscreen)* My diet pill.

SANDY That's speed.

DORRIE *(Offscreen, sighing)* I don't want to be fat.

SANDY Fat? How can you be fat? There's no chance you could ever be fat.
The nuns in the bright background go through their tap-dancing routine; Dorrie walks back onscreen. She and Sandy continue their discussion, going back and forth from darkness to light.

DORRIE I am. I'm overweight. You just refuse to see my bad points.

SANDY What's— You're killing yourself with those diets. First it's no pills, then it's all pills, then it's . . . then it's . . . then it's no steak, and then s-six steaks a day, and-and-and twelve glasses of water.

DORRIE I'm tired of feeling gross.

SANDY You could be— You're not gross, obviously you're gonna kill your appetite if you take speed. But then you can't sleep nights. You gotta take those terrible sleeping pills. And-and you mix that garbage with your antidepressants.
A group of monks walks by, seen by the illuminating light that continues to go on and off.

DORRIE The doctor said it was fine. I did.

SANDY You never asked the doctor. Stop telling me . . . *(Looking offscreen at Charlotte and gesturing)* Is she fat? Is she fat? Talk-talk to her. Talk to her. I can't believe it.
Sandy walks offscreen; Charlotte takes his place next to the upset Dorrie.

CHARLOTTE Listen, Dorrie, listen to me. You are such a sweet, young . . . you're beautiful.

SANDY *(Offscreen)* You're fine.

CHARLOTTE *(Rubbing Dorrie's head)* Anything you do looks great, honestly. You're at the age where you can't do anything wrong.

SANDY *(Offscreen)* You're terrific.

CHARLOTTE Hey, come on. If you had scar tissue, it would be beautiful.

SANDY *(Offscreen)* She-she-she refuses to believe anything.

CHARLOTTE *(Kissing Dorrie's ear and patting her)* Listen, I'm the one with crow's feet on her crow's feet, huh?
Charlotte leaves; Sandy's voice is heard over Dorrie's form, lit now by the stage light. She is hugging herself, still looking distraught.

SANDY *(Offscreen)* You're wonderful. The-the pic— The picture's almost over. I— Wh-why don't we go away for a while? We-we could drop out. We could have a kid or something. W-would you like to do that? We-we always talked about that.

DORRIE You know I'd like that.
Sandy walks back onscreen as the stage light goes off, silhouetting the couple once again.

SANDY All right, so . . . of course we'd have to fool around a little bit, but I—you know, you could swing that if you put your mind to it. I mean—

DORRIE *(Interrupting Sandy, fidgeting with her hair)*   Oh, shit! Now my skin hurts. That's a sure sign I'm getting depressed.
The bright light goes back on for a moment before the film cuts to the inside of Sandy's Rolls-Royce. Daisy is seen sitting in the passenger seat. They are returning to the hotel after their afternoon away.

DAISY *(Smiling)*   So do I really remind you of an old girl friend? *(The camera is on Daisy; Sandy, who is driving the car, is heard laughing)* That's not bad for a little violinist from Winnetka, you know.

SANDY *(Offscreen)*   Yeah, I gotta give my one classical-music joke which I put in every single picture and I invariably cut it out.

DAISY *(Looking at the offscreen Sandy)*   Yeah?

SANDY *(Offscreen)*   Um—the, eh, uh . . . *(Clearing his throat)* "I don't know much about classical music. For years I thought the Goldberg Variations were something Mr. and Mrs. Goldberg tried on their wedding night."

DAISY *(Laughing)*   Great gag. Yes.

SANDY *(Offscreen)*   Yeah, it's true, it goes right out of the picture, right? Yeah.

DAISY *(Laughing)*   So how do I remind you of Dorrie?

SANDY *(Offscreen)*   How?

DAISY   Yeah.
The camera moves over to Sandy sitting behind the wheel. Daisy's voice is now heard offscreen.

SANDY   Well, you guys are both, you know, uh, sort of seductive and attractive. Stop me if this gets nauseating. *(Daisy laughs offscreen)* And-and—uh, you know, beautiful, and-and there's a—not a tragic sense, I wouldn't say, but-but this kind of a—you know, a lost feeling.

DAISY *(Offscreen)*   Really?

SANDY   A little bit, yeah. Yeah. I sort of—you know, I don't know what you—you know, I don't know you well enough to say that, but-but, uh . . . you know, I would guess. It's just kind of a lost quality. Mm-hmm. Yeah, I mean— *(The car makes a strange noise and rattle)* Oh, Jesus.
Daisy laughs offscreen, not yet noticing the car's trouble.

SANDY *(Reacting)*   Uh-oh.

DAISY *(Offscreen)*   What's the matter?

SANDY *(Struggling with the steering wheel)*   Oh . . . nah . . . the goddamn chauffeur never takes care of the car. Hang on. Oh, brother. I gotta get . . . the—Jesus . . . really annoying.
The film cuts to the front of the car, parked on a country road; smoke seeps out of the open hood. The camera then moves to Daisy and Sandy walking down on a dirt road. It is dusk. They are surrounded by trees; birds are heard in the background. Daisy is still wearing her sunglasses; her arms are crossed.

DAISY *(Nodding)*   Oh, I know. No.

SANDY *(Gesturing)*   This is absurd.

DAISY *(Nodding again)*   I know.

SANDY *(Gesturing, reacting)*   You know, it's starting to get dark, I mean, there's no people, there's no—there's . . . you know?

DAISY *(Looking at the surroundings)*   Yeah, well . . . you-you know I'm sure we're gonna find something very soon. You know, there's gotta be something around here.

SANDY   I don't know. They're gonna find us wandering in the woods six months from now living on locusts and wild honey.
Daisy laughs as Eastern-like, haunting jazz music is heard faintly in the background. Sandy and Daisy stop talking and look it its direction.

SANDY   It's . . . *(Reacting to the music)* What the hell is that?
The camera cuts to a field in the background, strung with lights, then moves inside the lighted area as an astrologer in a white suit pops up, his face filling the screen.

ASTROLOGER   In the Earth's trinity, there are three signs. The Taurus, the Virgo and the Capricorn. The Taurians are determined, the Virgos analytical, and the Capricornians persevering. And all these—
A bald man, standing near by, interrupts him.

BALD MAN   We're not discussing—

ASTROLOGER   —three—

BALD MAN *(Interrupting again)* —astrology, this is science.
A young man walks in front of the bald man; the strung-up lights are seen in the background. The lights give the scene a peculiar look. It is not yet night, but the lights bring everything into sharper focus. People walk to and fro, on and off screen, the lights always seen in the background. The field people talk, looking straight ahead at the offscreen camera, addressing an offscreen Sandy or other field people. They are all vaguely familiar, many of them fans from the hotel, people who are in the movie in different roles.

YOUNG MAN *(Overlapping the bald man)* Oh, come on, science has failed.
Two twin boys walk by.

TWIN #1 How can you say it's failed?

TWIN # 2 Yes, you're just saying that because it hasn't solved every problem.

TWIN # 1 *(Nodding)* Yeah, look at penicillin . . .

TWIN # 2 *(Overlapping)* And look at space satellites.

TWIN # 1 Open heart surgery, heart transplants.
A woman with a veil floating over her head fills the screen.

WOMAN WITH VEIL My husband's alive six months now using a different person's heart. It's a Japanese heart, but he seems happy.
The camera moves over to a woman walking with her husband. She smokes a cigarette.

WOMAN WITH CIGARETTE Can we get back to the subject of UFOs? I mean, that's what this party's for, anyway, isn't it?
Three young men now walk in front of the camera, the same three men who'd stared at Sandy and Tony when they sat talking in the Stardust Hotel's outside bar.

IST YOUNG MAN Is it—is it true that you're a UFO freak?

SANDY *(Offscreen)* No, no, no, we—our car broke down.

2ND YOUNG MAN I really admire your work, sir.

SANDY *(Offscreen)* Well, thanks very much.

2ND YOUNG MAN You have such a degenerate mind.

SANDY *(Offscreen)* Oh, thank you. I take that as a compliment.
Another woman walks by; she is grinning and wears bright-red lipstick.

GRINNING WOMAN   Listen, they're in all different sizes and they're all different shapes—

1ST YOUNG MAN *(Interrupting)*   They're all over.
Sandy is finally seen, walking through the groups of people; Daisy, in her sunglasses, her arms crossed, follows him.

SANDY   You mean you actually see them?

FAT WOMAN   Every night. Every single, solitary night.

1ST YOUNG MAN *(Nodding his head at Daisy)*   She's just-just a friend.

1ST YOUNG MAN   Are you both into Martians?
A woman pushes through the milling people.

PUSHING WOMAN   Oh, I know you don't like to do this, but can I kiss you?
She kisses him, not waiting for an answer.

SANDY *(Overlapping)*   . . . a friend . . . no . . . yeah, yeah . . .
A blond middle-aged woman speaks up next.

BLOND WOMAN   You know, you should make a film about flying saucers.
As she walks offscreen a man with a beard, wearing beads, appears. He starts talking to an offscreen Sandy, staring straight into the camera.

MAN WITH BEARD   Yeah, you only make films about people with personality disorders.
A wild-haired man, also looking straight into the camera, starts to talk to the offscreen Sandy.

WILD-HAIRED MAN   Sandy—

SANDY *(Offscreen, overlapping)*   Yeah?

WILD-HAIRED MAN   I can prove that if there's life anywhere else in the universe, they will have a Marxist economy.
A woman, wearing a forties-style dress, approaches Sandy next. She, too, looks straight ahead at the offscreen Sandy.

FORTIES WOMAN   Mr. Bates?

SANDY *(Offscreen, overlapping)*   Yes?

FORTIES WOMAN   Excuse me?

SANDY *(Offscreen)*   Yes, uh—

FORTIES WOMAN   I'm an occult nutritionist. I was wondering if—

SANDY *(Offscreen, reacting and interrupting)*   Oh, Jesus.
Another woman walks by; she has short black hair and wears big glasses on both her forehead and on her eyes; she munches potato chips from a bag as she talks, looking at an offscreen Sandy. The camera follows her as she walks; she is always looking straight ahead at the offscreen Sandy.

POTATO-CHIP WOMAN *(Walking and talking)*   Uh, Mr. Bates, uh, excuse me, what have you got against intellectuals?

SANDY *(Offscreen, reacting)*   What? What? Against intellectuals? Nothing. Why?

POTATO-CHIP WOMAN   Mr. Bates, I've seen all your films. You really feel threatened by them.

SANDY *(Offscreen)*   Threatened? You're kidding. I've always said they're like the Mafia. They only kill their own.

POTATO-CHIP WOMAN   That's exactly the attitude I was talking about.

SANDY *(Offscreen, reacting)*   Oh, geez.
She leaves the screen, still eating her potato chips. Daisy and Sandy are seen walking through the field as another man comes up to them and starts talking.

MAN   Do you believe in magic? I know, I've read all your interviews.

SANDY   No. No, no, I do not. I used to do magic tricks when I was a kid, but, but no more. So—so what are you guys here for? To see flying saucers land? Is that gonna happen tonight?

MAN   Yes. When they arrive it's gonna be the dawn of a whole new civilization.
A different man, corpulent in his suit and carrying a wine bottle, takes the other man's place; others follow him in the background. Sandy is once again offscreen and the corpulent man addresses him, looking straight ahead offscreen.

CORPULENT MAN *(Gesturing with his wine bottle)*   Space creatures conspiring with the Soviet government already control our thoughts by sending out electrical currents from the top of the Empire State Building. *(Pausing)* And I'm the only one that knows.
The camera moves past a young girl, wearing a print dress, talking to an older man. It stops at a pickup truck, revealing the beautiful blonde with the dark lipstick who'd blown a kiss to Sandy from the party train in the

beginning of the movie. She is sitting in the front seat of the truck; she once again blows a kiss to Sandy. As she kisses the front window of the pickup truck, the camera moves back to the girl in the conservative print dress who is talking to the older man.

GYPSY GIRL   If you're alienated, can you still have children?

OLDER MAN   Oh, sure. Alienation only affects the mind. It has nothing to do with the rest of your body.
A skinny man approaches Sandy.

SKINNY MAN   Sandy, Sandy, you know this is exactly like one of your satires. It's like we're all characters in some film being watched in God's private screening room.
The hostility monster, seen in a previous scene, roars and walks over to the skinny man. He pulls him away.

DAISY *(Walking next to an offscreen Sandy)*   So I thought I saw a UFO once.

SANDY *(Offscreen)*   Really? You're kidding.

DAISY   Yeah, but I-I had taken a lot of mescaline at the time, so I don't know.
Sandy is back on the screen. He stands next to Daisy, drinking from a plastic cup; Daisy sips soda from a can.

SANDY *(Sipping his drink)*   Um . . . well, that will do it to you. That, uh—

DAISY *(Interrupting, sipping her drink)*   Yeah, I was down in Mexico. I was with my English professor. We were having an affair and-and he was married. It was—it-it was really a terrible situation.

SANDY   Yeah? You thought you saw a UFO?

DAISY   Yeah, we both—we really thought we did. I mean—

SANDY *(Interrupting)*   Yeah, well . . . that's-that's—uh . . . uh, an illusion.

DAISY   So—I didn't know you did, um, magic tricks?

SANDY   Yeah. When I was a kid.

DAISY *(Sipping her drink)*   Yeah?

SANDY   I would always practice to be popular. So I used to do these real . . . getting drunk.

DAISY So can you show me one?

SANDY Yeah. You want to see one?

DAISY Sure.

The Eastern-like music that was heard during the young Sandy's magic act plays in the background. Daisy's body is seen several feet above the ground, levitated, as Sandy moves his hands over her body. The field people are all gathered around Sandy performing his magic trick with Daisy. They gasp and applaud; the strung-up lights twinkle in the background. A Persian man, in a turban and suit, murmurs his approval in Parsi, a young girl with flowers in her hair watches, her eyes wide, as Sandy is seen passing a large hoop around Daisy's levitated body.

The camera then cuts to Sandy's mother and father, standing among the admiring field people. She wears a frilly hat; he wears an old banded visor cap. They talk to each other as an offscreen Sandy continues to perform his magic tricks. The field people continue to applaud and murmur their approval.

SANDY'S MOTHER Our son's a genius.

SANDY'S FATHER Well, he doesn't take after you, that's for damn sure.

SANDY'S MOTHER Well, he certainly doesn't take after your side of the family.

SANDY'S FATHER *(Yelling)*   Aw, go to hell!

SANDY'S MOTHER *(Yelling)*   Aw, shut up!
And the camera cuts to Walsh, the female movie executive, standing with Sandy's lawyer, his accountant and his manager. They stand among the field people, talking to one another and to an offscreen Sandy, looking straight ahead into the camera.

WALSH   If he's such a genius, how come he can't make funny movies?

LAWYER   Sandy, we'll sue them if they touch one frame of your film.

WALSH *(Smoking a cigarette)*   I promise you, you won't win.

ACCOUNTANT   By the way, Sandy . . . we got killed by the IRS.

MANAGER   They started looking at the back taxes.
Debbie, Sandy's sister, walks over to them. She, too, talks to an offscreen Sandy.

DEBBIE *(Crying)*   Sandy, you're my brother. You gotta help me change my life. I'm a mess.
Sandy's press agent, still in her neck brace, walks on to the screen; she, too, addresses the offscreen Sandy.

PRESS AGENT   And Sandy, don't forget lunch with the editors of those high school newspapers.
And Jones and Smith, the two studio executives who are always seen together, Smith always yessing Jones, repeating what he says, appear on the screen next. They, too, join the crowd addressing an offscreen Sandy; they stare straight ahead, staring into the camera.

JONES   And what about the cancer foundation . . .

SMITH   And what about the cancer foundation . . .

JONES   . . . and the leukemia victims . . .

SMITH   . . . and those leukemia victims . . .

JONES   . . . and the political prisoners all over the world?

SMITH   . . . and the political prisoners . . .

JONES   What about the Jews?

SMITH   The Jews!

JONES . . . the persecution in Europe, in Russia and . . .
Their voices fade away as a hospital bed, complete with transfusion bottles, is wheeled in by a cluster of doctors and nurses. They stand and talk to the offscreen Sandy.

NURSE That's right. All those silly magic tricks you do couldn't help your friend Nat Bernstein.
The camera moves over to Tony, wearing a white shirt, who stands near the hospital crew. He, too, looks at the offscreen Sandy.

TONY And what about Dorrie? You know what that was like. Do you remember the last time you saw her?
The entire field with its strung-up lights is seen for a moment. Daisy, in the background, is still floating in the air, as Sandy runs past her, holding the hoop. The haunting music stops and the film cuts to:

INTERIOR. SANITARIUM—DAY.

Dorrie's face fills the creen. She is wearing a white hospital gown. Her face is without make-up, stark. She looks directly at the camera, presumably at an offscreen Sandy, and runs her fingers through her hair.

DORRIE There's a doctor here that thinks I'm beautiful and interesting.
The film cuts to a slightly different angle of Dorrie's face, almost exactly in the same pose as the previous shot. This is done every time Dorrie utters a new phrase, so that the end result is like the jerky motion of quick flash cards, creating an unsettling feeling in its unnatural abruptness. One after another, shot after shot, Dorrie's face changes as she talks.

DORRIE There's a doctor here that thinks I'm beautiful and interesting.

Are you seeing anyone?

You look thin.

There's a doctor here that's crazy about me.

Are you seeing any—

You—this—

(*Laughing*) People—

Oh—

. . . be too close—

(Laughing) I—

. . . swim a lot.

I can't feel anything.

Yeah, they don't—

. . . can't concentrate—

There's no point to—

. . . too much—

. . . some fresh air—

. . . feel better—
The camera abruptly stops its quick cuts. It settles on Dorrie's face, still staring into the camera, still stark, as she runs her fingers through her hair. She cries.
And then, after this brief respite, the camera continues its quick cuts, faster and faster, until the end of the scene.

DORRIE You were always searching for the perfect woman. You wound up falling in love with me.

I can't be alone. B-but I can't be too close.

It's not you. I-I just can't feel anything.

Are you going with anyone?

(Crying) Are you seeing anyone? Are you in love with anyone?

(Rubbing her face with her hands) How do I look?
Dorrie laughs in the final quick cut before the camera leaves the hospital and moves back to the present, to a forest on the outskirts of the light-strung field. The magic show music plays as Sandy is seen running, running; some of the field people follow him in the distance. He calls after someone, as if trying to delay him from leaving. He stands by a clearing, talking to an offscreen strange-looking creature named Og. Science-fiction–like sounds buzz in the background.

SANDY *(Gesturing, calling offscreen)* Wait a minute! Don't go! I've got some questions.

OG *(Offscreen, speaking in a vibrating spacelike voice)* We can't breathe your air.

SANDY Yeah, at the rate we're going, we're not gonna be able to either. Do you-you guys gotta tell me, why is there so much human suffering?

The camera cuts to Og, the creature Sandy was addressing. Og is a Martian, wearing a robotlike suit and concealing helmet. Behind him are other space creatures; a large white light, the spaceship, sits near the trees in the wood's clearing.

OG *(In a vibrating voice)* This is unanswerable.

SANDY Is there a God?

OG *(In a vibrating voice)* These are the wrong questions.

SANDY Look, here's my point. If nothing lasts, why am I bothering to-to make films, or do anything, for that matter?

OG *(In a vibrating voice)* We enjoy your films. Particularly the early funny ones.

SANDY But the human condition is so discouraging.

OG *(In a vibrating voice)* There are some nice moments, too.

SANDY Yeah, with Dorrie.

OG *(In a vibrating voice)* That's right. And Isobel. Be honest.

SANDY You prefer Isobel?

OG *(In a vibrating voice)* There's no comparison. She's a mature woman.

SANDY Mature woman? What are you—what are you, my rabbi?

OG *(In a vibrating voice)* Hey, look, I'm a superintelligent being. By Earth standards I have an IQ of sixteen hundred and I can't even understand what you expected from that relationship with Dorrie.

SANDY I loved her.

OG *(In a vibrating voice)* Yeah, I know, and two days a month she was the most exciting woman in the world, but the rest of the time she was a basket case. On the other hand, Isobel is someone that you can count on.

SANDY *(Gesturing)* But shouldn't I stop making movies and do something that counts, like-like helping blind people or becoming a missionary or something?

OG *(In a vibrating voice)*   Let me tell you, you're not the missionary type. You'd never last. And-and, incidentally, you're also not Superman, you're a comedian. You want to do mankind a real service? Tell funnier jokes.

SANDY   Yeah, but I-I-I've gotta find meaning.
The weird buzzing music stops. The spaceship light vanishes; a wind blows back Sandy's hair as the ship leaves Earth.
And an old Big Band, Tommy Dorsey–like music begins in the background as the film cuts to three hot-air balloons floating down from the sky over the UFO followers on their light-strung field. The balloons are large; lights twinkle on the rim of the passenger baskets. The shadow of a man sitting inside one of the baskets is seen briefly as first one, then another, then the third balloon floats down to the Earth to the accompaniment of the Tommy Dorsey–like music.
The field people run over to the balloons as they sink noiselessly down to Earth; the canvases of the balloons billow over the field. There is much excitement; field people wave, holding sparklers and gathering around the balloons, hoping to greet the passengers who'd just come to Earth.
Sandy and Daisy are the only ones who do not rush to the balloons. Sandy leans against the back of a pickup truck; Daisy sits on the hood. They drink and talk.

SANDY *(Sipping from his plastic cup)*   Wouldn't you know it, that they'd be hot-air balloons?

DAISY *(Sipping soda from her can)*   Well, what, you didn't really expect saucers, did you?

SANDY *(Sighing)*   I did. Yeah. I was hoping . . . yeah . . . I had some very, very profound questions that I wanted to ask.

DAISY   Yeah? Oooooh. Uh-huh.

SANDY *(Staring at Daisy)*   You know, you look incredibly beautiful to me.

DAISY   Oh, thanks. We should go back to the hotel, don't you think?

SANDY   No. I-I-I don't want to.

DAISY   Oh, come on, we've been gone for hours. They're gonna wonder about us.
Daisy hops off the pickup truck; she and Sandy begin walking through the field.

SANDY *(Hugging Daisy)*   No, no . . . I never want to go back to the hotel. Never. I want—what I want to do is run away with you. *(Daisy murmurs as Sandy hugs her closer. They continue walking)* I'm serious. I want to get in the car and just give up everything, you know?

DAISY   Oh, come on. You're just a little drunk.

SANDY   You know, you know? I just want to give up everything and just . . . we'll move in together and I'll just—

DAISY   No, it's a . . . I would be no fun to live with.

SANDY *(Overlapping)*   —I'll . . . You would be nothing but fun. You'd be great.

DAISY *(Shaking her head)*   Really. No.

SANDY   No. You'd be—

DAISY *(Interrupting)*   No. I would be very bad trouble. Believe me. You don't know me.

SANDY   No. Mmmmmmmmmmmm. Why? What are your problems?

DAISY   Oh, I just, uh . . . *(They both laugh)* Um, men. I have terrible trouble with men.

SANDY   Why? Why?

DAISY   Oh, it's just that . . . whenever a man gets close, I get crazy and then—then it's over.
Sandy and Daisy stop walking; they look at each other. The hot-air balloons are sprawled on the earth in the background; some field people mill around the balloons, talking and walking among themselves, while Daisy and Sandy continue their conversation.

SANDY   Well, you go with Jack.

DAISY   Well, that's something else. He's very sweet and he really cares about me and it's . . . solid, you know. I need that.

SANDY   Uh, as soon as I saw you in the lobby, I thought that you would be absolutely fun for me.

DAISY   This is . . . you've got an incredible sixth sense to pick me out of that whole crowd of people. I'm nothing but trouble.

SANDY   Nothing but tr— Ah . . . I think I can handle it. I—
He stops in midsentence. They kiss as Vivian's voice suddenly shrieks over the scene spoiling the mood.

VIVIAN *(Offscreen)*   There they are! Oh . . . *(The camera cuts to Vivian, Jack, Isobel and two policemen running around the hot-air balloons toward Sandy and Daisy. They are all wearing pajamas and robes; they look concerned, half put together. They all talk at once. Vivian, onscreen, continues)* Oh, I . . . what is going on here, Sandy?

ISOBEL *(Overlapping)*   We sent the police . . .

VIVIAN *(Overlapping)*   This is disgraceful. You're out here carousing . . .
The group surrounds Sandy and Daisy; Jack looks at Daisy. Sandy, reacting, walks away from everyone. Isobel follows after him.

SANDY *(To Isobel, gesturing)*   Leave me alone. I don't wanna go back. I'm tired of everything. I-I'm tired of my lawyer and my accountant and I'm-I'm—I-I can't help anybody. I can't help the Cancer Society and I can't help the-the blind people and the-the kidney victims. I can't help my sister and I don't wanna get married, Isobel. That's the last thing I need now, is a—is a family and a commitment and a-a-a . . . Isobel . . . Isobel . . .
As she hears Sandy's words, Isobel reacts. She turns and starts walking away from him. He continues to call after her as a young man approaches; he is a fan who'd asked Sandy for his autograph back at the hotel, when Sandy was sitting with his studio executives talking about "Jazz Heaven." The fan interrupts Sandy with a raised eyebrow and a gun.

FAN   Sandy? You know you're my hero.
The fan shoots Sandy; some field people gawk in the background. The hot-air balloons are still sprawled over the grass, and the film cuts to a street where a police car, complete with lights and blaring siren, rushes past the screen in the darkened night.

CUT TO:
INTERIOR. HOSPITAL EMERGENCY ROOM—NIGHT.

Sandy, lying on a hospital gurney, is pushed through the swinging doors by a young doctor. Isobel and Sandy's doctor follow close behind.

ISOBEL   Oh, my God!

SANDY'S DOCTOR   He-he's dead!
The camera moves over to a nurse, munching on a big apple, her face almost in close-up. Sandy's unconscious body lies on its gurney in the background.

NURSE *(Looking straight ahead, eating her apple)*   It's a shame. Poor fool, he's dead and he never really found out the meaning of life.

CUT TO:
INTERIOR. STARDUST HOTEL AUDITORIUM—NIGHT.

The screen is filled with a scene from the film The Creation of the Universe. *Pools of boiling lava are erupting; the sounds of earth explosions are heard on the soundtrack. Sandy's analyst's voice is heard over the Earth sounds and the erupting lava pools.*

SANDY'S ANALYST *(Offscreen)*   I treated him. He was a complicated patient. *(The camera moves slightly, revealing Sandy's analyst standing in front of the movie screen, still talking)* He saw reality too clearly. Faulty denial mechanism. Failed to block out the terrible truths of existence. In the end his inability to push away the awful facts of being in the world rendered his life meaningless. Or as one great Hollywood producer said . . . "too much reality is not what the people want." Sandy Bates suffered a depression common to many artists in middle age. In my latest paper for the *Psychoanalytic Journal*, I have named it Ozymandias Melancholia.
The audience applauds. Sandy's analyst walks off the stage, the lava still erupting and exploding in the background. Vivian, wearing beads and a dress, walks onto the stage, slightly standing to the left of the erupting screen.

VIVIAN *(Smiling)*   Thank you, Doctor. Thank you very much. Thank you. Oh, well . . . Sandy Bates's works will live on after him.
As she talks, Sandy's silhouette walks in front of the screen, standing to the right. He speaks, though his silhouette appears to be silently standing in the midst of the lava and its boiling pools. While he stands in front of the screen, the lava turns to swirling clouds of haze and fog.

SANDY   Yeah, but what good is it if I can't pinch any women or hear any music?

VIVIAN *(Ignoring Sandy's remarks, speaking as if she can't hear him)*   And now in this classic scene from his Academy Award–winning motion picture—

SANDY *(Interrupting)*   I would trade that Oscar for one more second of life.

VIVIAN   —he deals with the subject of immortality . . . a subject that plagued him. In this film, he played the part of God.

SANDY *(His silhouette gesturing)*   This was not easy, folks, because, uh, you know, I-I-I didn't know what the hell I was doing, and I don't have a good voice for God.

VIVIAN   And he received an Academy Award nomination for his convincing portrayal of God . . . although they had to use another actor's voice. *(The fog and haze scene turns into a dark, starry sky. Chuckling, Vivian continues)* And though this plaque is not an Academy Award, and its presentation is posthumous, I want to present it to that great comedian, the late Sandy Bates. *(Sandy's silhouette leaves the screen; the human Sandy walks on stage to the thunderous applause of the packed audience. Vivian, handing Sandy the plaque)* Here you go, Sandy.

SANDY *(Taking the plaque)*   Thank you very much.
The audience is seen enraptured and applauding wildly in a quick cut; Vivian's and Sandy's voices are heard as she gives him the podium offscreen.

VIVIAN *(Offscreen)*   Here you are, Sandy.

SANDY *(Offscreen)*   Thank you. Thank you so much. *(The camera cuts back to Sandy on the stage, alone now, holding the plaque. Shooting stars are seen on the screen behind him. Sandy continues)* I'm very honored to get this, you can imagine. I—um, you know—uh, some time ago I had a love affair that-that ended, uh, sort of, uh, unhappily. And—um, just-just a little while back, just-just before I died, in fact, I was—uh, I was on the operating table, and I was searching to-to try and find something to hang on to, you know? *(As Sandy talks, the shooting stars turn into a large blow-up of Sandy's face, then into bolts of lightning cutting through billowing clouds; wind and thunder is heard over some jazz music. The lightning and tumultous weather becomes a bucolic forest clearing which, in turn, becomes hellish as the trees catch fire and begin to burn, more and more fiercely. Sandy continues his speech in front of the screen)* Uh—'cause, uh, when you're—when you're dying, uh, life suddenly really does become very authentic. And-and—uh, something . . . I was reaching for something to give my life meaning and-and a memory flashed through my mind. *(The camera cuts briefly to the audience, looking up at Sandy onstage, then moves to Sandy's penthouse. The sun is shining through the windows; Sandy sits in front of them eating ice cream out of its container. The jazz music, a Louis Armstrong record, is quite loud now. Sandy's voice is heard over this scene, describing the action as it unfolds)* It

was one of those great spring days. It was Sunday, and you-you knew summer would be coming soon. I remember, that morning Dorrie and I had gone for a walk in the park. We came back to the apartment. We were just sort of sitting around. And . . . I put on a record of Louis Armstrong, which is music that I grew up loving. It was very, very pretty, and . . . I happened to glance over, and I-I saw Dorrie sitting there. And I remember thinking to myself . . . *(Dorrie is seen now, lying sprawled on the floor, browsing through the Sunday* New York Times. *She is dressed casually in slacks and shirt; she appears to be very unselfconscious, enjoying her reading)* . . . how terrific she was, and how much I loved her. And, I don't know . . . I guess it was the combination of everything . . . the sound of that music, and the-the breeze and, and how beautiful Dorrie looked to me. And for one brief moment, everything just seemed to come together perfectly, and I-I felt happy. Al-al-almost indestructible, in a way. *(Dorrie looks up at Sandy, who is sitting offscreen. She smiles into the camera and goes back to her reading. Sandy is then seen again, briefly, eating his ice cream and looking intensely at Dorrie)* It's funny that that simple little moment of contact moved me in a very, very profound way.
Louis Armstrong's voice singing "Stardust" is heard. As he belts out his song, Dorrie's form stays on the screen. She looks up, smiling at the offscreen Sandy; she fingers her hair; she browses through the paper; she looks up at Sandy again, smiling, gazing back at him.
The song ends. The camera leaves Dorrie and returns to the audience in the auditorium. People turn and look at each other, restless, reacting.

MAN Cop-out artist!

WOMAN That was so beautiful.

ANOTHER MAN Why do all comedians turn out to be sentimental bores?

CUT TO:
INTERIOR. HOSPITAL EMERGENCY ROOM—NIGHT.

Isobel is gazing down at the unconscious Sandy, still lying on his hospital gurney. The doctor talks to her offscreen; Isobel's face fills the screen.

DOCTOR *(Offscreen)* Uh—he-he's all right. He just fainted. I'm sure it's just nervous tension.

SANDY *(Offscreen)* Dorrie . . .
Isobel's face reacts to Sandy's words.

DOCTOR *(Offscreen)* He had some hallucination about being shot with a thirty-two pistol by a fan.

SANDY *(Offscreen)* Dorrie—*(Isobel, reacting, runs out of the hospital room; Sandy sits up on his gurney, fully conscious now)* Isobel. Isobel!
The film cuts to the exterior of the hospital. It is morning. Isobel, still in her nightgown, is running down the steps of the hotel, staring straight ahead. Sandy follows her, gesturing. An Armenian fan in a print shirt and hat follows Sandy, talking to him, oblivious to the drama being played in front of him.)

SANDY *(To Isobel, gesturing)* Come here. I want to talk to you.

ISOBEL *(Walking briskly)* I don't want to talk to you. I don't want to be involved with you.
She walks away offscreen.

SANDY *(Calling after Isobel)* Isobel, don't be silly.

ARMENIAN FAN *(Overlapping, to Sandy)* I want to invite you to my brother's restaurant.

SANDY *(Overlapping, to Isobel)* Isobel . . . No-no, no, no.

ARMENIAN FAN My brother Ozzie's got a terrific restaurant.

SANDY *(Finally reacting to the Armenian)* I . . . No, no, I don't, I don't—

ARMENIAN FAN *(Interrupting)* Armenian food. My mother's the cook.

SANDY I don't eat—I don't eat Armenian food. I . . . uh—

COP *(Interrupting, offscreen)* Mr. Bates!
Sandy turns around, looking offscreen at the policeman.

ARMENIAN FAN We need a picture of you. You know, maybe sitting at a table.

COP *(Offscreen, overlapping the determined Armenian fan)* Could you come over here a moment, please?

SANDY *(Gesturing, to the fan)* No, no, no, no, no. It's, uh . . .

ARMENIAN FAN It'd really be terrific.
Sandy walks over to his Rolls-Royce where two policeman stand waiting for him; he leaves the Armenian fan standing by the hotel steps. The policemen stand in front of the car; the camera shows them through the windshield, gesturing and talking to Sandy.

SANDY *(To the cop)* Wh-wh-wh-wh-why? What's the matter?

COP Uh, the Rolls-Royce—

SANDY *(Interrupting)* Yeah, it's mine. This is mine. I already went through that.

COP Yeah, well, we found a thirty-two-caliber pistol in the glove compartment.

SANDY *(Gesturing)* Yeah, that's mine, too. I-I-I carry a pistol. I-I-I—it's . . . uh, it's, uh . . . I've a . . . thing about Nazis. It's a little—it's a little paranoid weakness that I have.

COP Uh, you have a permit, I'm sure.

SANDY I-I don't need a permit. I never shoot the gun or anything. But-but, you know, I-I've had family that's had problems and that kind of thing, so I . . . so I—you know, I-I-I keep it.

COP I-I-I'm sorry, but . . .

SANDY *(Overlapping)* It's strictly a Nazi thing.

COP Sorry, but we'll have to have you come down and answer a few questions.

SANDY Oh! That won't be necessary. Really, you . . . I-I-I-I . . . You can make an exception in my case. I'm a celebrity.

CUT TO:
INTERIOR. JAIL—DAY.

Sandy sits on the floor of a barren cell, leaning against the bars. He stares at a fat man in a suit on the other side of the cell. It's George, his chauffeur. George smiles at Sandy; jazz music plays in the background and the film cuts to:

EXTERIOR. RAILROAD STATION—DAY.

Isobel, holding her son's hand on one side, her daughter's on the other, is marching toward the Stardust Hotel's old-fashioned railroad station. Sandy runs down the boardwalk toward them. He catches up with them and walks alongside the threesome, his hands in his pockets.

SANDY Isobel, I want you to come and live with me.

ISOBEL *(Looking straight ahead)* No, thank you.

SANDY *(Coughing)*   Don't be ridiculous.

ISOBEL *(Turning to look at Sandy)*   You make me feel ridiculous.
They all enter the station.

SANDY   I've been under stress lately, you know what I mean? Th-the,
uh . . . A broken romance and the death of a friend, and, you
know—

ISOBEL *(Interrupting)*   Go find Dorrie. She's much better for you.

SANDY   No, no, no. That's over. Th-that, that's over, believe me.
Uh . . .
He sighs.

ISOBEL   I don't want to hear anymore!
*Isobel, reacting, continues her conversation in French. Still holding her chil-
dren's hands, she marches to the railroad tracks.*

SANDY *(Overlapping Isobel's French)*   I love you. I mean . . .
*Sandy's voice trails off as the film cuts to the outside of a railroad car.
Through the window pane, Isobel can be seen walking down the aisle. Her
two children take a seat; Isobel sits down in the seat behind them. Sandy, still
running after them, takes a seat behind Isobel. Though he can't be heard, his
mouth is still moving; he's still trying to convince her to stay with him.
The camera cuts to the train's interior. Sandy, sitting behind Isobel, his arms
on the back of her seat, is talking. Isobel stares straight head, trying to ignore
him.*

SANDY   I tell you, this has been a very, very interesting weekend for
me. A lot of—a lot of very strange thoughts went through my mind,
and I-I feel very differently about a lot of things.

ISOBEL *(Staring straight ahead)*   I am not your type.

SANDY   Yes! No, but you—

ISOBEL *(Interrupting)*   You like that—those dark woman with all their
problems.

SANDY   Those dark woman? No!

ISOBEL   They give you a hard time and you like it.

SANDY   You think I like that, right?

ISOBEL *(Fighting back tears)*   Yes.

SANDY *(Gesturing, touching Isobel's shoulder)*   No, you're wrong! I'm tell-ing you, I was—I was—I was thinking about a lot of unusual things over the weekend, and I feel much . . . I feel lighter. Do you know what I mean? And-and, um . . . I had a very, very remarkable idea for a new ending for my movie, you know? We're—we're on a train and there are—there are many sad people on it, you know? And-and I have no idea where it's headin' . . . could be anywhere . . . could be the same junkyard. And, uh—   But it's not as terrible as I origi-nally thought it was because-because, you know, we like each other, and-and . . . uh, you know, we have some laughs, and there's a lot of closeness, and the whole thing is a lot easier to take.

ISOBEL *(Shaking her head, reacting)*   I don't like it.

SANDY   Uh! You don't like it?

ISOBEL   It's too sentimental.

SANDY   So? But so what? It's the good sentimental. That's what you —you know . . . I—i-it's . . . A-a-a-and, and you know, it's—   But there's this character that's based on you that's—that's very warm and very giving and you're absolutely, um, nuts over me. You're just crazy about me. You just think I'm the most wonderful thing in the world, and-and you're in love with me, and you're . . .*(Isobel tries not to smile, but she can't control herself; she chuckles)* And-and despite the fact that I do a lot of foolish things, 'cause-'cause you realize that-that-that down deep I'm-I'm . . . not evil or anything, you know? Just sort of floundering around. Just-just . . . ridiculous, maybe. You know, j-just searching, okay?

ISOBEL *(Giggling, shaking her head)*   I don't think it's realistic.

SANDY *(Touching his mouth, gesturing)*   Wha—? Now? This is . . . *Now* you're gonna bring up realism, after . . . after . . . ? This is a hell of a time to—   Now, I know one thing: that a—that a huge big wet kiss would go a long way to selling this idea. I'm-I'm very serious. I-I think, I think this is a big, big finish. Do you know what I mean? *The music swells. Isobel smiles and turns around in her seat to face Sandy. He leans over the back of her seat and kisses her.*
The train engine is heard. The camera is outside the train again, showing Sandy and Isobel still kissing through the window. The train begins to move; Isobel's two children, looking up over their seats, watch Sandy and Isobel, big smiles on their faces. Sandy and Isobel continue to kiss as the film cuts to:

INTERIOR. STARDUST HOTEL AUDITORIUM—NIGHT.

The audience looks up at the movie screen, clapping and talking enthusiastically. The projector light goes off and the house lights go on. People get out of their seats, talking and gesturing among themselves.
In the midst of the milling people is the actor who'd accosted Sandy in the lobby of the hotel; he's talking to Sandy's sister Debbie, who is offscreen.

ACTOR   He just killed me. I mean, d-did you feel that?

DEBBIE *(Offscreen)*   I know. I think it was great. Just great.

ACTOR   I just can't believe the stuff he gets into.

DEBBIE *(Offscreen)*   He's always so funny.

ACTOR   It's so deep. I mean, it's—
He is interrupted briefly by two male fans, walking past them and talking.

MALE FAN # 1   In my—in my eyes . . .

ACTOR *(Overlapping the fan's speech)*   All that stuff about life and . . . how we should, everybody should love each other. I mean, you know, he's telling us heavy, original things.

DEBBIE *(Offscreen)*   He's wonderful. He's very heavy. He's always been heavy.
They walk off; Charlotte and Sandy's lawyer are seen now, moving through the crowds.

CHARLOTTE *(Still wearing her headband)*   What did you think the significance of the Rolls-Royce was?

LAWYER   I think that's . . . uh, uh, represents his car.

CHARLOTTE   Really?

LAWYER   Mm.
Next Dorrie and the young actress who was talking to the older man in the field are seen leaving the auditorium.

ACTRESS   You're not fat! I mean, fat?! Would you—   Come on! You're not fat!

DORRIE   I am.

LARGO *(Reacting)*   God, you're just so ridiculous!

DORRIE   I'm gonna have to go on another diet. I think it's horrible!
They walk away, revealing Vivian talking to a man in a suit.

VIVIAN   And I tried to play the role sympathetically, but the role was just too thin.
Tony and his Playboy bunny walk down the aisle as Vivian and her escort walk off.

TONY   He said to me, "Wear this mustache, it'll be funny." So I listened to him.
Daisy, wearing her sunglasses, and Isobel are among the last to leave the auditorium. They walk past the rows of chairs, deep in conversation.

DAISY   You looked so beautiful, I couldn't believe it. You really did.

ISOBEL *(Chuckling)*   Oh, thank you. But-but can you hear me?

DAISY   Yeah.

ISOBEL *(Chuckling)*   Can you hear my English?

DAISY   Oh, your English was fine. It was fine. It was fine.

ISOBEL   Oh!

DAISY *(Gesturing)*   Did you find— By the way, I want to ask you . . . Did you find, when you did, like, kissing scenes with him . . .

ISOBEL *(Chuckling)*   Oh . . .

DAISY *(Moving her hands near her mouth)*   Did you no- . . . Did he open his mouth with you, and-and wiggle his tongue around?

ISOBEL *(Laughing)*   Yes! Yes, he did! *(Laughing)* And he never lets you go!

DAISY   It's the most irritating thing, right?
They laugh as they leave through the doors of the auditorium.
An old Jewish man and Rash, his wife, are the very last ones to leave. The old man gestures at the movie screen with one arm; the other arm is around his wife.

OLD JEWISH MAN *(Shaking his head)*   It's amazing, Rash. From this he makes a living? I like a melodrama, a musical comedy with a plot.
He continues his speech in Yiddish; they walk out of the room. The auditorium is empty for a moment, holding only the stage, the silent movie screen, and the rows and rows of chairs. Piano music is heard as Sandy is seen walking down the aisle. He goes into one of the first rows of chairs; he bends down and picks up his sunglasses. He puts them on and walks back up the aisle.

Sandy pauses for a moment, turning to look back at the movie screen, then he walks out. The auditorium lights fade into black, revealing rows of archlike ceiling lights. They, too, darken. And the piano music stops . . .

Over a black background, while credits pop on and off the screen, accented by music from the movie:

Featured Cast

Helen Hanft	Daniel Stern
John Rothman	Amy Wright
Anne DeSalvo	Gabrielle Strasun
David Lipman	Bob Maroff
Joan Neuman	Leonardo Cimino
Eli Mintz	Robert Munk

Production Manager	MICHAEL PEYSER
Assistant Director	FREDRIC B. BLANKFEIN
Second Assistant Director	YUDI BENNETT
Location Managers	LOIS KRAMER HARTWICK
	RANDALL BADGER
Script Supervisor	KAY CHAPIN
Production Coordinator	SUSAN DANZIG
Assistant to Mr. Allen	GLORIA NORRIS
Unit Managers	CHARLES ZALBEN
	EZRA SWERDLOW
Still Photographer	BRIAN HAMILL
Camera Operator	DICK MINGALONE
Assistant Cameraman	DOUGLAS C. HART
Second Assistant Cameraman	THOMAS G. WESTON
Gaffer	DUSTY WALLACE
Key Grip	BOB WARD
Property Master	JIM MAZZOLA
Construction Coordinator	EDWARD SWANSON
Construction Grip	JOE WILLIAMS
Assistant Film Editor	MICHAEL R. MILLER
Sound Effects	HASTINGS SOUND EDITORIAL, INC.
Sound Editor	DAN SABLE
Assistant Sound Editor	LOWELL MATE

FOUR FILMS OF WOODY ALLEN

Apprentice Film Editor	BERIAU PICARD
Sound Mixer	JAMES SABAT
Re-recording Mixer	JACK HIGGINS / MAGNO SOUND
Boom Man	VITO ILARDI
Art Director	MICHAEL MOLLY
Set Decorator	STEVEN JORDAN
Set Dresser	JOSEPH BADALUCCO, JR.
Master Scenic Artist	JAMES SORICE
Scenic Artist	COSMO SORICE
Art Department Coordinator	CAROL JOFFE
Assistant Costume Designer	JEFFREY KURLAND
Men's Wardrobe Supervisor	LEE AUSTIN III
Women's Wardrobe Supervisor	ROSE ANELLO TRIMARCO
Hair Stylist	WERNER SCHERER
Makeup Artist	FERN BUCHNER
Production Auditor	PATRICK MCCORMICK
Production Accountants	BERNSTEIN AND FREEDMAN P.C.
Extras Casting	NAVARRO-BERTONI CASTING INC.
Casting Associate	GRETCHEN RENNELL
Insurance Broker	ALBERT G. RUBEN CO.
Transportation Captain	HARRY LEAVEY
Second Assistant Director	ED LEVY
DGA Trainee	THOMAS REILLY
Production Assistants	CHERYL HILL
	HELEN ROBIN
	JAMES BREENHUT
	ROGER PARADISO
	MARGARET ROIPHE
	PATTI PERRET
	STEVE ROSE

Camera and Lenses by Panavision®
Prints by Technicolor®

The story, all names, characters and incidents portrayed in this production are fictitious. No identification with actual persons is intended or should be inferred.

This motion picture is protected under the laws of the United States and other countries and its unauthorized distribution or exhibition may result in severe liability and criminal prosecution.

STARDUST MEMORIES

Approved No. 26157   (emblem)   (I.A.T.S.E. insignia)
MOTION PICTURE ASSOCIATION OF AMERICA

"Stardust Memories" copyright © United Artists Corporation
MCMLXXX

Woody Allen	SANDY BATES
Charlotte Rampling	DORRIE
Jessica Harper	DAISY
Marie-Christine Barrault	ISOBEL
Tony Roberts	TONY
Daniel Stern	ACTOR
Amy Wright	SHELLEY
Helen Hanft	VIVIAN ORKIN
John Rothman	JACK ABEL
Anne De Salvo	SANDY'S SISTER
Joan Neuman	SANDY'S MOTHER
Ken Chapin	SANDY'S FATHER
Leonardo Cimino	SANDY'S ANALYST
Eli Mintz	OLD MAN
Bob Maroff	JERRY ABRAHAM
Gabrielle Strasun	CHARLOTTE AMES
David Lipman	GEORGE, SANDY'S CHAUFFEUR
Robert Munk	BOY SANDY
Jaqui Safra	SAM
Sharon Stone	PRETTY GIRL ON TRAIN
Andy Albeck	STUDIO EXECUTIVES
Robert Friedman	
Douglas Ireland	
Jack Rollins	
Howard Kissel	SANDY'S MANAGER
Max Leavitt	SANDY'S DOCTOR
Renee Lippin	SANDY'S PRESS AGENT
Sol Lomita	SANDY'S ACCOUNTANT
Irving Metzman	SANDY'S LAWYER
Dorothy Leon	SANDY'S COOK
Roy Brocksmith	DICK LOBEL
Simon Newey	MR. PAYSON
Victoria Zussin	MRS. PAYSON
Frances Pole	LIBBY

FOUR FILMS OF WOODY ALLEN

Bill Anthony	FANS—HOTEL ARRIVAL
Filomena Spagnuolo	
Ruth Rugoff	
Martha Whitehead	
Judith Roberts	SINGER—"THREE LITTLE WORDS"
Barry Weiss	DANCER—"THREE LITTLE WORDS"
Robin Ruinsky	QUESTION ASKERS—SCREENING
Adrian Richards	
Dominick Petrolino	
Sharon Brous	
Michael Zannella	
Doris Dugan Slater	
Michael Goldstein	
Neil Napolitan	
Stanley Ackerman	REPORTER—SCREENING
Noel Behn	DOUG ORKIN
Candy Loving	TONY'S GIRL FRIEND
Denice Danon	FANS IN LOBBY
Sally Demay	
Tom Dennis	
Edward Kotkin	
Laura Delano	
Lisa Friedman	
Brent Spiner	
Gardenia Cole	
Maurice Shrog	
Larry Robert Carr	
Brian Zoldessy	
Melissa Slade	
Paula Raflo	
Jordan Derwin	
Tony Azito	
Marc Murray	
Helen Hale	
Carl Don	
Victoria Page	
Bert Michaels	
Deborah Johnson	
Benjamin Rayson	DR. PAUL PEARLSTEIN
Mary Mims	CLAIRE SCHAEFFER
Charles Lowe	VAUDEVILLE SINGER

STARDUST MEMORIES

Marie Lane	CABARET SINGER—"BRAZIL"
Gustave Tassell	CABARET PATRONS
Marina Schiano	
Dimitri Vassilopoulos	
Judith Crist	
Carmin Mastrin	
Sylvia Davis	HOSTILITY VICTIM
Joseph Summo	HOSTILITY
Victor Truro	HOSTILITY PSYCHOANALYST
Irwin Keyes	FANS OUTSIDE HOTEL
Bonnie Hellman	
Patrick Daly	
Joe Pagano	
Wayne Maxwell	
Ann Freeman	
Bob Miranti	
Cindy Gibb	YOUNG GIRL FANS
Manuella Machado	
Judith Cohen	FRIENDS OF SANDY'S SISTER
Madeline Moroff	
Maureen P. Levins	
E. Brian Dean	POLICE SERGEANT ARRESTING GEORGE
Marvin Peisner	ED RICH
Robert Tennenhouse	AUTOGRAPH SEEKERS ON BOARDWALK
Leslie Smith	
Samuel Chodorov	
Philip Lenkowsky	AUTOGRAPH SEEKER/ASSASSIN
Vanina Holasek	ISOBEL'S DAUGHTER
Michel Touchard	ISOBEL'S SON
Kenny Vance	NEW STUDIO EXECUTIVES
Iryn Steinfink	
Frank Modell	REWRITE MAN
Anne Korzen	WOMAN IN ICE CREAM PARLOR
Eric Van Valkenburg	MAN IN ICE CREAM PARLOR
Susan Ginsburg	USHERETTE
Ostaro	ASTROLOGER
Wade Barnes	UFO FOLLOWERS
Gabriel Barre	

Charles Riggs III
Geoffrey Riggs
Martha Sherill
Ann Risley
Jade Bari
Marc Geller
Daniel Friedman
James Otis
Judy Goldner
Rebecca Wright
Perry Gewertz
Larry Fishman
Liz Albrecht
Sloane Bosniak
James Harter
Henry House
Largo Woodruff
Jerry Tov Greenberg
Mohammid Nabi Kiani
Alice Spivak   NURSE AT HOSPITAL
Armin Shimerman   EULOGY AUDIENCE
Edith Grossman
Jacqueline French
John Doumanian   ARMENIAN FAN
Jack Hollander   COP ARRESTING SANDY

Animals Provided by Dawn Animal Agency
Balloons Furnished by Sky Promotions
Rolls-Royce Provided by Cross Highway Garage
Piano Music Arranged and Performed by Dick Hyman
"Hebrew School Rag"
"Just One of Those Things"
"Easy to Love"

Jazz Heaven Orchestra Featuring   JOE WILDER

HANK JONES

RICHIE PRATT

ARVELL SHAW

EARL SHENDELL

STARDUST MEMORIES

SONGS

"Tropical Mood Meringue"

SIDNEY BECHET
MUSIC BY SIDNEY BECHET
COURTESY OF CAPITOL RECORDS
INC., PATHE MARCONI, EMI

"I'll See You in My Dreams"

DJANGO REINHARDT
MUSIC BY ISHAM JONES AND GUS
JONES
COURTESY OF CAPITOL RECORDS
INC., PATHE MARCONI, EMI

"Tickletoe"

LESTER YOUNG WITH COUNT BASIE
AND HIS ORCHESTRA
MUSIC BY LESTER YOUNG
COURTESY OF CBS RECORDS

"Three Little Words"

PERFORMED BY JAZZ HEAVEN
ORCHESTRA
MUSIC BY BERT KALMER AND
HARRY RUBIN
ARRANGED BY KIRK NUROCK

"Brazil"

SUNG BY MARIE LANE
MUSIC BY ARY BARROSO
LYRICS BY S.K. RUSSELL

"Palesteena"

ORIGINAL DIXIELAND JAZZ BAND
MUSIC BY J. RUSELL ROBINSON
AND CON CONRAD
COURTESY OF RCA RECORDS

"Body and Soul"

DJANGO REINHARDT
MUSIC BY EDWARD HYMAN,
ROBERT SOUR, JOHN W. GREE, AND
FRANK EYTON
COURTESY OF CAPITOL RECORDS
INC., PATHE MARCONI, EMI

"Night on Bald Mountain"

VIENNA STATE OPERA ORCHESTRA
MUSIC BY MUSSORGSKY
COURTESY OF VANGUARD RECORDS

"If Dreams Come True"

CHICK WEBB
MUSIC BY I. MILLS, E. SAMPSON
AND B. GOODMAN
COURTESY OF COLUMBIA RECORDS

FOUR FILMS OF WOODY ALLEN

"Hebrew School Rag"	PERFORMED BY DICK HYMAN
	MUSIC BY DICK HYMAN
"Just One of Those Things"	PERFORMED BY DICK HYMAN
	MUSIC BY COLE PORTER
"Easy to Love"	PERFORMED BY DICK HYMAN
	MUSIC BY COLE PORTER
"One O'Clock Jump"	PERFORMED BY JAZZ HEAVEN
	ORCHESTRA
	MUSIC BY COUNT BASIE
"Sugar"	MUSIC BY MACEO PINKARD AND
	SIDNEY MILTON
"Sweet Georgia Brown"	MUSIC BY BEN BERNIE, KENNETH
	CASEY AND MACEO PINKARD
"Moonlight Serenade"	PERFORMED BY GLENN MILLER
	MUSIC BY GLENN MILLER
	COURTESY OF RCA RECORDS
"Stardust"	PERFORMED BY LOUIS ARMSTRONG
	MUSIC BY HOAGY CARMICHAEL
	LYRICS BY MITCHELL PARISH
	COURTESY OF COLUMBIA RECORDS

The producers extend their appreciation to the following galleries and artists:

Hal Bromm Gallery	"POSITION OF TWO ARCS OF 171.5°
	AND 188.5°"
	"POSITION OF TWO ANGLES OF 90°
	AND 35°" BY BERNAR VENET
Sidney Janis Gallery	"GIRL IN CHAIR DANGLING LEFT
	ARM" BY GEORGE SEGAL
	"MONTANA" AND "ANZA" BY MAX
	COLE
Robert Freidus Gallery	PHOTOGRAPHS BY LEE
	FRIEDLANDER
Magnum Photos	PHOTO MURAL/WARD 81
	BY MARY ELLEN MARK
Opus Films	SELECTIONS FROM "HOT SPOT"
	AND "COLTERS HELL"
	ROBIN LEHMAN

STARDUST MEMORIES

The producers gratefully acknowledge the cooperation of:

Ocean Grove Camp Meeting Association

New Jersey Motion Picture and Television Development Commission,
Joseph Friedman, Executive Director

Governor's Office for Motion Picture and Television Development,
Theodora K. Sklover, Executive Director

Mayor's Office of Motion Picture and Television,
Nancy Littlefield, Executive Director

The Upward Fund Inc.

Planting Fields Arboretum

Mr. Allen's wardrobe furnished by Ralph Lauren

THIS MOTION PICTURE HAS BEEN RATED

PG   PARENTAL GUIDANCE SUGGESTED
SOME MATERIAL MAY NOT BE SUITABLE FOR PRE-TEENAGERS

BY THE CODE AND RATING ADMINISTRATION

(Emblem)
MOTION PICTURE ASSOCIATION OF AMERICA

THE END

About the Author

After he was rejected from both New York University and City College, WOODY ALLEN turned to a professional writing career, at first for television and comedians. In 1964 he decided to become a comedian himself.

Woody Allen's first screenplay, written in 1964, was the enormously popular *What's New, Pussycat?* He has also written, directed and starred in nine films to date: *Take the Money and Run, Bananas, Everything You Always Wanted to Know About Sex, Sleeper, Love and Death, Annie Hall, Manhattan, Stardust Memories* and *A Midsummer Night's Sex Comedy.* Mr. Allen also wrote and directed *Interiors.* In addition, Mr. Allen has written three plays for Broadway: *Don't Drink the Water, Play It Again, Sam* (the latter starring himself in both the play and the subsequent film version) and *The Floating Light Bulb.*

Mr. Allen has written and appeared in his own television specials and is a frequent contributor to *The New Yorker,* among other periodicals.